Medicine-Crow, Chief and Visionary.

ROBERT H. LOWIE

THE

CROW

INDIANS

Introduction to the new Bison Books Edition by

Phenocia Bauerle

University of Nebraska Press
Lincoln and London

Frontispiece: Smithsonian Institution Photo No. 3414-A

First Nebraska paperback printing: April 1983

Library of Congress Cataloging-in-Publication Data
Lowie, Robert Harry, 1883–1957.
The Crow Indians / Robert H. Lowie; introduction to the new Bison Books edition
by Phenocia Bauerle.—Bison Books ed.
p.   cm.
Reprint. Originally published: New York: Farrar & Rinehart, 1935.
Includes index.
ISBN 0-8032-8027-0 (pbk.: alk. paper)
1. Crow Indians.   2. Indians of North America—Social life and customs.
I. Bauerle, Phenocia.   II. Title.
E99.C92L913   2004
305.897′5272—dc22
2003028181

Published by arrangement with CBS Educational & Professional Publishing.

PHENOCIA BAUERLE

Introduction to the new Bison Books Edition

I am a Crow Indian who was born on the reservation. But I was raised off the reservation in a household that recognized and practiced the traditions of my people. As a child I frequently returned to the reservation to take part in ceremonies and visit family, taking for granted the duality of living in both the Anglo and the Crow worlds. As I studied Native American literature and my own people, the problems caused by accepted anthropological approaches became glaringly apparent to me. Robert Lowie's *The Crow Indians* is one of the most popular and widely used ethnographies of the Crow people because he recorded the ways of the Plains when those ways had not yet been completely replaced by life on the reservations.

Lowie's work has shaped my life in ways that I might never have considered had I not majored in English literature as an undergraduate. His writings haunted me as I made my way through the literature about and studies of the Crow people. I found references to his books about the Crows in numerous other books; his body of work established him as an expert on my people. I have noticed that among the books in my family's household, *The Crow Indians* sits quietly on the bookshelf, undisturbed. It is there as a kind of presence but it is seldom used or referenced. I have owned numerous copies of the book and, though I frequently lose track of the copy I have been using, I always find it and return it to its place on my shelf, continuing its life as a presence.

When rereading *The Crow Indians* as a resource for a paper I was writing on Crow belief systems, I came across several statements by Lowie that I believed were either misinterpretations or simply misinformation. I mentioned Lowie's observations in my paper but amended his claims with information gathered from personal knowledge and through interviews with my grandfather and other tribal members. In the interest of brevity I will mention only a few of the discrepancies.

To Crow people perhaps the most troublesome thing in Lowie's text is the treatment given to the Crow religious belief system. Lowie's interpretation that the Crow religion was centered on sun worship is skewed because the Crow people do not worship the sun as a god. We hold only First Maker, the Creator, in a position deserving of worship. The Crows do believe that certain entities have power and are worthy of respect and certain rituals may be designed to show these entities respect, but prayers and worship are only extended to First Maker. While many stories that Lowie listened to and many things in his research led him to believe that the Crow worshipped entities other than First Maker—such as the sun or Old Man Coyote—the confusion is a result of translation problems and assumptions that were already being made about American Indian cultures at first contact.

The Tobacco Society as discussed in *The Crow Indians* is also sorely misunderstood. The ceremony itself is the first, and oldest, ceremony of the Crows because it provided the motivation for the separation of the Crow people from the Hidatsa. The ceremony that takes place—planting sacred tobacco seeds linked to the origin of the Crow—recalls the birth of the Crow people through their break from the Hidatsa, their search for the sacred plant, and the eventual discovery and planting of the Tobacco. The Tobacco ceremony and Tobacco dances are held at different times during the year as means of giving thanks and remembering what makes the Crow people and culture special and important. Membership in the society is exclusive, and Lowie's explanation of the society's adoption process is similar to how it took place. But he left out much detail about the process and often is unsure of exactly what he was witnessing. Again the conflict likely stemmed from a lack of understanding of language and the role that it plays in culture. Without proper translation there is much misinterpretation.

As we translate languages we translate cultures. It is now obvious that simple translation is not as easy a task as it was perceived to be a century ago, when it was assumed that language was used in the same way among all cultures. An interpretation of worship, meaning respect or reverence in a spiritual way, might have plausibly led Lowie to assume that the Crow worship numerous things that are used in ceremonies. Likewise, since he came from a predominantly Christian world it was probably difficult for him to understand why such complex and involved ceremonies would exist if the people did not in fact worship the sun or the Tobacco. What Lowie missed was the recognition and respect that the Crow people have for all things and the belief that while all things are important, in certain contexts some may be more important than others.

While Lowie's work is the benchmark for ethnographies on the Crow people, a great deal of misinformation within his text has been replicated in other articles and in the minds of people who have read the book, producing a variety of misconceptions about the Crow worldview. As a result, many Crow people find the book of little use. Some want nothing to do with it, others (like me) keep it only as a presence, and a very few actually read through it to find where it is accurate and where it is inaccurate.

Lowie's work continues to trouble me and others who know where the misrepresentations lie, yet we continue to simply acknowledge the work's presence rather than revising the foundation laid by Lowie. To understand both the importance of and the problems with Lowie's book, the complex relationship between ethnography and American Indian people needs to be illuminated and understood.

The motivation behind traditional ethnography was to understand foreign and exotic cultures before they disappeared completely. It was a laborious process, and although great care was taken to record details and describe what seemed to be the mundane facts of everyday life, these ethnographies often contained gaps. Ethnography, then, became a combination of nostalgia and science and a very powerful mainstream culture tool to represent the worlds of people who often did not venture to represent themselves.

The feelings that many American Indians have toward traditional ethnographies range from caution and skepticism to disregard and distaste. These feelings are not unfounded. Just as it is difficult to know and understand a history and world created generations earlier, it is even more difficult to accept that these false impressions cannot be easily changed. It is hard to come up against misrepresentations and misguided assumptions daily while knowing that this is the result of a well-meaning ethnographer who visited your people decades before you were born. This is the kind of emotion that accompanies ethnography for many American Indians.

Lowie's work created a twofold result. While helping to preserve cultural beliefs and practices through the written word, his work caused part of Crow history to cross over into Euro-American history as a written record that acts as a formal collective memory. This crossover incorporated the Crow people into a body of work through which others began looking critically at the differences that exist among different cultures. This record eventually proved to be very helpful in studying and recording the details of Crow actions and beliefs. Yet Lowie's descriptions of Crow people and the Crow way of life also created a delayed suspicion among Crows of those who came to "study" the tribe after him. As English was spoken and written with increased frequency and fluency among the Crow, many tribal members recognized the misrepresentation and misunderstanding that existed in the writings of anthropologists and ethnographers on the Crow. This awareness of inaccurate representations caused the Crow to be wary of anthropologists and ethnographers who came to study them.

These long-held misrepresentations, inaccurate portrayals, and (sometimes) flat-out exploitation, when combined with U.S. history and past and current Indian policy, make conducting an accurate ethnography of American Indian people—something that has not been widely done in the recent past—a complicated and delicate matter.

Reading and using a book that established many of the inaccuracies about a people is something of a conflict of interest. *The Crow Indians* is no exception. But before dismissing the book, perhaps one needs to take a look at the text more closely. It is important to remember that blessings often come in disguise.

Robert Lowie came among the Crow during a time of great change. The reservation had been established and tribal members were adjusting to the new way of life. A great amount of negotiation was still going on between cultures as Crow people took on Euro-American ways yet found the places where new values and practices intersected with tradition. But for most Crows the core Crow beliefs were still the primary guide to life. Though many look at the end of the Plains era as the end to a set way of life, the reality is that lifeways began to transform rather than die out or be replaced by the Euro-American ways spreading over the country. In his years of studying the Crow people, Lowie witnessed the adaptation of a culture rather than a dying out of particular ways. *The Crow Indians* records that culture as "the Crow way of life," and no doubt these ways were all components of how the Crows lived. But it is important to understand that culture is not static and a constant blending occurs between cultures that exist near one another. This cross-influence was prevalent among tribes in North America; the way that people lived constantly fluctuated and changed. When Europeans arrived on the continent some dramatic changes took place. But American Indian cultures are resilient and adaptive, as can be seen in the continued presence of tribes all over the country today. When Lowie came to the Crow he no doubt believed the Crow culture would slowly die out. His carefully devised studies allowed him to construct a Crow world that he saw disappearing. He was recording part of the Crows' adaptation process to fit with the way that the world around them changed.

This book was clearly no small accomplishment, as can be seen from the range of material about the Crow that is covered to the extent to which Lowie tried to explain Crow practices and beliefs in a way that people unaccustomed to this culture would understand. I have no doubt that the difficulties that Lowie admits in not knowing the Crow language and not being able to express himself in a way that was natural to his culture were the same difficulties that some of his informants had in explaining the Crow way of life. As a result, portions of the text are not good explanations of how the Crow peoples' belief systems operate.

The information and details that Lowie recorded are valuable in their own right. It is important for the reader to know that discrepancies and inconsistencies exist between the way things are represented in *The Crow Indians* and in the way that these ceremonies and beliefs actually operate.

Though problems do exist within the book, should it still be read and used? The care and time that went into preparing *The Crow Indians* was great, and Lowie did write the book to help people understand and appreciate Crow lifeways and beliefs. Do not turn away from the text simply because it is not entirely accurate. The information that Lowie recorded is valuable and much of it can be very helpful. As American Indian people continue to adapt, more opportunities will arise to amend the history that was written without the input and understanding of these same people. Today, as American Indian people speak both the languages of their tribes and the language of their country, it is of utmost importance that books such as this be read and reread in order to gain an understanding of the changes that need to be made to recorded history. For those of us who have grown up knowing and living the ways that are inaccurately described in this book, it is sometimes hard to understand what part of Crow culture outsiders do not understand. This book offers a chance for the Crow people to see themselves from a different perspective and to work at improving cross-cultural understanding. For Crow people this book stands as a valuable resource both for cultural preservation and for change.

What has haunted me as simply a presence has been transformed into a force for change and renewal. Lowie's work is a starting place for understanding. I see this book as an opportunity for Crow people to discuss and articulate our culture, to provide our own explanations so that those who understand our culture to be different than what is presently written in books may help to write a culturally accurate interpretation of history and beliefs that we will leave our children.

Preface to Reissue, 1956

SINCE the theme of this book is the aboriginal Crow culture, which has inevitably disintegrated with the dying off of the older generation and the spread of education, there is little to add to the former edition beyond a few up-to-date statistical facts and a brief reference to two alien religious movements.

To Mr. W. H. Farmer, writing on behalf of Mr. Walter U. Fuhriman, Director of the Missouri River Basin Investigations Project (Billings, Montana) I am indebted for the following data (letter of October 26, 1953): The resident population of Crow Indians at the time in question was 2,309, to which might be added 926 nonresidents registered as eligible for enrollment in the tribe. The residents are predominantly full-blood, 77.8 per cent of the family members being at least three-quarters Indian, while the corresponding figure for nonresidents is only 17.7 per cent. The cash income of 400 resident families totaled $1,712,308; the average family income was $3,643; the median, $2,706.

As for the new cults, they are a Sun Dance religion that is *not* a revival of the ceremony described in this book, but a form introduced by the Shoshone (Wind River, Wyoming) in 1941; and the Peyote faith, borrowed from the neighboring Cheyenne Indians in 1912, but of limited appeal even in 1931, when I last visited the Reservation. The use of narcotic but harmless cactus "buttons" conforms to that among other tribes and has been often described. The cult involves a quaint blending of native and Christian ideas.

More indicative of modern trends is the career of Robert Yellowtail (page xxii). Since his resignation as superintendent of the Reservation he has taken an active part in Montana politics, even running for the U.S. Congress and announcing his candidacy for the Senate.

ROBERT H. LOWIE

Berkeley, California
1956

Preface to 1935 Edition

IN 1907 Dr. Clark Wissler of the American Museum of Natural History commissioned me to make an initial survey of the Crow Indians. From this reconnaissance it appeared desirable to make systematic investigations, to which a number of subsequent expeditions were devoted. The specimens collected are exhibited or stored in the Museum, which published the scientific results in its series of Anthropological Papers (see Appendix I). There they have hitherto remained buried so far as the public at large is concerned, though I have naturally drawn upon them in more general treatises.

It was Dr. W. I. Thomas, the well-known sociologist, who first urged me to render the material more accessible to those primarily interested in human behavior. Indeed, the highly encouraging comment on my description of Crow religion by the late Dr. Nathaniel Söderblom, Archbishop of Sweden, in the last edition of *Das Werden des Gottesglaubens* proved that my data had a potentially wide appeal to the non-specialist. Later my friend Professor William Lloyd Warner insisted that even anthropological students would profit from a summary that would disentangle essentials from the envelope of detail inevitable in a monographic record.

A grant by the Committee on American Native Languages (under the auspices of the American Council of Learned Societies) enabled me to revisit the Crow in 1931 for the purpose of further linguistic studies. This renewal of contacts definitely impelled me to write this book.

The audience I have in mind, then, embraces anthropologists not primarily specializing in the Plains area; sociologists, historians, and other social scientists eager to grasp the varied patterns of human societies when not deterred by overabundance of technicalities; and, last but not least, the laymen who are interested in aborigines as human beings.

Phonetic refinement would be out of place in this volume, hence in rendering native words I have dispensed with virtually

xiii

all diacritical marks. Vowels are approximately as in Spanish; "x" stands for the German "ch" in "ach"; "c" for the English "sh" in "shall"; "ky" is a palatalized sound something like "t" in "nature" but pronounced farther back; single quotation marks after t, k, p indicate strong aspiration.

I wish to express my gratitude to Dr. Clark Wissler for granting permission to reproduce illustrations originally made for my technical publications in the Anthropological Papers of the American Museum; and to Miss Bella Weitzner, of the same institution, for providing the relevant blocks. To Mr. Matthew D. Stirling of the Bureau of American Ethnology I am indebted for the use of several photographs, including the fine picture of Medicine-Crow.

Contents

Introduction

IN June, 1833, Prince Maximilian of Wied-Neuwied, a scientifically trained German explorer, arrived at Ft. Clarke, a trading-post on the Upper Missouri in what is now North Dakota. Back of it lay the Mandan Indian village of "Mih-Tutta-Hang-kusch," with the friendly Hidatsa in close proximity; and both tribes were playing host to a Crow band of seventy lodges under the chief Rotten-belly. Fine figures of men, picturesquely long-haired, the Indian guests, spurless but cracking their elk-horn quirts, rode to and fro on mounts gaily bedecked with red cloths and mountain-lion skins. Their camp was crammed with horses, kept close at hand for fear of hostile marauders. The conical tents were set up in no special order, and instead of scalps dangling from the tips of their poles the Prince saw only pennantlike streamers of red cloth waving in the wind.

Threading their way through the settlement, Maximilian and his party were attacked by packs of wolflike curs, whose onset they could check only with difficulty by a fusillade of rocks. In Rotten-belly's lodge a small fire was burning, surrounded by men of consequence, all of them stripped to their breechclouts. Himself in mourning, the chief was wearing his ugliest clothes, and his close-cropped pate was plastered with clay. He sat opposite the entrance—in the place of honor—and the Prince was made to sit beside him on buffalo skins. Lighting a long, flat-stemmed pipe of Dakota pattern, Rotten-belly held it for each of the guests while they took a few whiffs. Then the pipe was passed about the tent from right to left.

The haughty bearing of the Crow impressed Maximilian, as did their craftsmanship. He admired the women's porcupine-quill embroidery and the men's bows of elk or mountain-sheep horn, some of them covered with the skin of a rattlesnake; and the draftsman of the expedition sketched a quiver decorated with a quill rosette.

From Charbonneau, a white man settled for thirty-seven years among the Hidatsa, the traveller gleaned some facts about the sister tribe, which he eked out with information otherwise obtainable. The Crow, he learned, were very closely related to the Hidatsa, with whom they had once formed a single people. But in contrast to these Upper Missouri villagers, they never planted anything except a little tobacco. As hunters of buffalo and other game they roamed over the Yellowstone and Bighorn country, extending toward the sources of the Cheyenne River and the Rocky Mountains. Altogether their number was set at between 1000 and 1200 warriors, corresponding to a population of 3250 to 3560, housed in 400 lodges. Of horses they owned more than any other tribe of the Upper Missouri region, possibly 9000 to 10,000. Dogs were overabundant,—poor Maximilian estimated the number in the single band he saw at 500 to 600; but unlike some other tribes, the Crow never ate them.

Morally, Maximilian's informants gave the Crow an indifferent character: though they never killed whites, they did not scruple to rob them; their women were rivaled in debauchery only by the Arikara; and perverts were common.

There were no fewer than eight men's societies, such as the Bulls, Kit-foxes, Ravens, and Big Dogs. Novices, Maximilian learnt, had to buy membership, partly by surrendering their wives to the old-stagers. He also gleaned some hints as to religious practices. Smoking was strictly ritualized: no one ever took more than three puffs at a time; each man always handed the pipe with a ceremonious sweep to his left-hand neighbor; and a pipe was never smoked if a pair of shoes (*sic*) were hung up in the lodge. Tobacco was one of the three holiest objects of worship, hence all children wore a small package of it as an amulet necklace. The two other great supernaturals were Sun and Moon. To the Sun a man always offered an albino buffalo cow if he had succeeded in killing one. The dead were placed on scaffolds set up in the prairie.

As to political relations, the Cheyenne, Blackfoot, and Dakota were hostile; the Hidatsa and Mandan, allies, from whom the Crow had long secured European goods, bartering in exchange their superfluity of horses. But a short time before Maximilian's visit a special post, Ft. Cass, had been erected on the Yellowstone to minister to Crow trade.

This is the gist of Maximilian's report. It exaggerates the importance of the Moon; his guide saw the men's societies through Hidatsa eyes; and Indian morals are judged by European standards. But apart from these details the record stands unscotched by later evidence.

Trustworthy native tradition carries us back farther. It pictures a people roving afoot with pack-dogs, pursuing game with bows and arrows. The tales mention chipped stone knives, stone mauls, drills of elk antler. Survivals lingered on into the historic period. A tiny bone awl formed part of the Sun Dance bundle (p. 300), and in the same ceremony an antler wedge was driven with a stone hammer. I myself have seen women mashing fruit with stone pounders. In short, the Crow lived originally as Stone Age hunters. Still, when seen by Maximilian, they had come to lean on an Iron Age technology. At least a quarter of a century earlier white traders had come, and their stock had preceded them. The Shoshone had brought horses, as well as Spanish bridle-bits and blankets; and these the Crow could trade on their annual visits to the Mandan and Hidatsa against guns, ammunition, axes, kettles, awls, and other goods. The tribe was thus flooded with iron tools, glass beads, and cloth. Aboriginal arts were not yet seriously impaired in 1833 and some features of civilization were slow in coming.

Wagons did not appear before 1874, and the first farming implements were provided about the same time. But the old life was bound to recede, and what turned the scale was the extinction of the buffalo. No longer able to live by the chase, the Crow inevitably became either farmers or beggars. This change not merely touched the food-supply but went deeper. Hides had been dressed for clothing and tipi covers; they were now perforce supplanted by calico and canvas. Then there was the irresistible appeal of cheap labor-saving devices. Matches—and even the earlier strike-a-lights—were vast improvements over the hand-twirled fire-drill; it was easier to cook in metal kettles than by dropping hot rocks into a rawhide filled with water; colored glass beads could be bought too easily to warrant the labor of getting and dyeing porcupine quills for decorative embroidery; and ultimately it was far less troublesome to have a frame house put up than to chop down trees in the mountains, drag the logs to camp, trim them into poles, and sew the ever-diminishing hides of larger game animals into a tipi cover.

By 1907, when I first visited the Crow Reservation, southeast of Billings, Montana, the process had become essentially completed. The Indians had turned tillers of the soil, farming as best they could with such aid as the Government gave them. Many still wore moccasins and some clung to the traditional *style* of dress, but the materials—except for festive occasions—came from the white man's stores; tipis were still abundant in the summer, but the covering was of canvas; and it required no ethnologist to determine the origin of the stoves, tables, and chairs. What remained to the outer view were only meagre survivals of the buffalo-hunting days.

But that did *not* hold for speech, belief, or social custom. Some of the younger people, of course, had attended the schools at Carlisle, Riverside, or Hampton, and spoke English as well as any frontiersman, but men and women of mature years knew practically none at all; in fact, even today many of the old folks have made no further progress. What was more, notwithstanding such fair-sized towns in the vicinity as Billings, Montana, and Sheridan, Wyoming, and the railroad that traversed the Reservation, its inhabitants preserved a large part of ancient belief and practice. Christianity, propagated by several missions of varying denomination, had not taken firm root, and even among the school-bred generation faith in the visionary experiences of the pagan period remained unshaken. "When you listen to the old men tell their experiences," a man in his thirties told me, "you've just *got* to believe them."

In the spring the Tobacco society of each district sowed its crop of the sacred weed; and a Government farmer uttered the wish that the Indians would take as much trouble with more useful plants. Vapor baths were commonly taken as a devotional act. Everyone knew his clan, and very few broke the rule against marrying fellow-members. No man dreamt of speaking to his mother-in-law. As late as 1931 my chief interpreter would not so much as pronounce an Indian word that entered into the name of his wife's mother; and a man of largely white blood told me he had been married seventeen years but had never been on speaking terms with his mother-in-law. His young daughter alleges that he once forgot himself and from time to time she still pokes fun at him for his heedlessness.

By 1907, of course, wars had long ceased, but not the war psychology. Men were still rated according to their valor. They

proudly displayed their scars to a sympathetic inquirer and publicly told about their exploits at any large gathering. All old and
middle-aged men had belonged to the military clubs. There were
some who had served as scouts under Custer or Terry; and at the
Agency tribesmen pointed with scorn at the Indian policeman
who in 1887 had killed the prophet Wraps-up-his-tail.

In short, the culture I studied in the field seasons of 1907
and 1910-1916 was spiritually very much alive; and even in 1931,
when I returned after a long absence, the rise of a literate generation and the advent of the automobile had not been able to kill
it utterly. It is a living culture, then, that is described in the following pages.

Anthropologists whom fortune has taken to the interior of
the Congo or New Guinea turn up their noses at work on "primitive" tribes surviving in a civilized country. Naturally, such lack
the glamour that envelopes exotic peoples who have remained
virginally uncontaminated by an industrial age. But the explorer-
ethnologist labors under handicaps that counterbalance his advantages. Traveling in uncharted territory, he cannot prepare
beforehand like the worker, say, in our Plains region, who stands
on the shoulders of all his predecessors and can define his problems with a nicety beyond his rival's reach. From the experience
of earlier students he knows what details are significant in setting off his tribe from its neighbors. If he inquires whether it is
customary to raise a tipi on a three or four-pole foundation, if he
notes the precise arrangement of painted lozenges and triangles
on a rawhide bag, it is because these apparent trivialities have
proved important in defining tribal individuality. The advantage
the trained observer enjoys over the untutored literate native,
missionary, or Government official is precisely that he knows
which of the thousands of available facts to be recorded are at
the present stage of science significant.

Another point is not always understood. As there is no
Simon-pure race nowadays, so there is no Simon-pure culture.
Quite apart from the spread of Caucasian civilization, Congolese
Pygmies have been influenced by Bantu neighbors, one Australian
group makes distant trips to others, Papuan sailors carry their
earthenware hundreds of miles from the place of manufacture.
Smoking was an inveterate Crow custom, but the tobacco they
smoked was not the tobacco they grew; their pipes seem to have

been imported from the Dakota or Hidatsa, and this certainly held for the redstone ones of Dakota pattern noted by Maximilian. In short, white influence, however devastating in its ultimate effect, is not a thing *sui generis;* aboriginal peoples have borrowed from one another for thousands of years, and the attempt to isolate one culture that shall be wholly indigenous in origin is decidedly simple-minded.

Again, there is a widespread and most naïve misunderstanding as to what the best investigator *can* directly observe in the most primitive tribes. Of course, he is able to note that these people bake food in earth-ovens and propel canoes by crutch-paddles. But he cannot directly experience a "mother-in-law taboo": all he *sees* is a certain old woman who will not talk to a certain man; he cannot divine their relationship, he cannot see with his own eyes whether this rule embraces others, such as the woman's sisters or the man's brothers. Still less can he observe the sentiments associated with a ritual, the feelings of a husband toward his wife, the motives that animate a war leader. For all such data he is dependent on what informants tell him whether by spontaneous self-revelation or in answer to more or less skilful inquiries. In short, he must frame questions, elicit answers, listen to the unprompted outpourings of his natives precisely as does the ethnologist among a Plains Indian people or the sociologist in a settlement of Southern Negroes. This brings us to the all-important matter of communication.

A missionary who settles with remote aborigines for a decade can doubtless acquire an intimate knowledge of their language. Not so the ethnologist with a year or two at his disposal. Native languages are incredibly copious in vocabulary and abound in grammatical subtleties and idiomatic phrases, so that adequate comprehension requires years of study. To do without interpreters, as the explorer of literally virgin soil must do, is accordingly a far more serious source of error than the rational use of interpreters, coupled with the possibility of grasping the—often highly significant—*obiter dicta* of chance interlocutors able to speak the investigator's tongue. Of course the ethnologist ought to learn what he can of the language,—not with the chimerical hope of being able fruitfully to dispense with translators after a few months, but in order to check their accuracy.

From the beginning of my work I have tried to pick up

Crow and have phonetically recorded prayers, songs, and tales, which my native friends understand as read to them and jubilantly beg me to reread *ad infinitum*. (My chief interpreter—an austerely fair judge—declares that I "have a fine Crow pronunciation but speak with a foreign accent.") I know several thousand words, have made some progress with the study of the grammar, am able to bandy routine phrases with a passer-by, can put simple ethnographic queries unaided. Yet I can follow a Crow conversation only when I am conversant with the subject-matter, and I absolutely disclaim any ability to deliver a speech or tell a story of my own in half-way idiomatic Crow; I can avoid error only by slavishly clinging to the forms learnt. Some years ago I attempted to translate a simple story from a schoolbook into Crow: my interpreter would not let a single sentence stand as I had written it. I should not dream of investigating the more elusive subjects of ethnography without the help of a good interpreter.

Even if the ethnologist had mastered the general vocabulary and the intricacies of grammar, he might yet utterly miss the implications of a sentence of which he grasped every part. Take the following, for example: "Come [imperative], holding your rope." What does it mean? Well, it was a young man's stereotyped way of promising an older man a horse in return for a prayer on the donor's behalf. Very easily understood when you know, but how are you to guess? Again, in 1931, while I was phonetically writing down a text from dictation, a young man who had never seen me approached to see what we were doing. He began by laying down the axiom that Crow speech could *not* be written, but lingered long enough to become convinced of the contrary. He finally tore himself away with the following remark: "A white man—it is unbelievable—is talking our language. *I arrived where they seized my arms*. I was in a hurry and I have stayed till now. I have come to my senses. If I keep on staying, I'll be here till night. I am going." Unless the hearer knows that "seizing one's arms" was used in the contests of medicine-men to denote the overpowering of a rival, the phrase is utterly unintelligible. In the context above it means as much as, "I was bewitched, charmed, spellbound."

In other words, each aspect of native life has a highly specialized vocabulary, all of which would be involved in a perfect knowledge of the tongue. Every technological process—say, the scraping, wringing, smoking of hides—has a distinct designation; often a particular type of motion employed will have a special term lacking in English. The terms for relatives introduce unfamiliar classifications and discriminations: a woman uses one word for "father," a man another; some cousins are regarded as brothers and sisters, others as parents and children (see p. 19). Social institutions, such as the taboos and license between certain relatives, introduce further vocables for concepts we lack; and there is a full terminology of religious experience, with terms for visions, mysterious beings, sorcery, and often with highly figurative phrases for some of the implied activities. A Mezzofanti, devoting himself unremittingly for a year to a study of the language and nothing else, might in daily intercourse with the Indians acquire a tolerable knowledge of the language. The idea that any one could do so in a few months is, in my opinion, preposterous. I do not wish to cast aspersions on the good faith of such claimants; my experience has merely convinced me that they are not sufficiently critical of their linguistic achievements.

The ethnographer in the United States thus enjoys one extraordinary advantage over his colleague who investigates Congolese Pygmies or Papuans. He can usually converse directly with a fair number of Indians who know English and whose chance remarks furnish valuable clues for further questioning of old informants. He can often train one of these literate natives to translate with accuracy, and can check him by the renderings of other interpreters. Naturally learning as much of the vernacular as is humanly possible and, *with a full realization of his limitations,* he will use this knowledge as a further control.

My own field methods, then, have been those customary in this country. In my Crow work I would engage the best available interpreter,—one conversant with both his own language and English. With him I would ride on horseback or drive to the best informants for the aspects of culture I happened to be investigating at the time. Several of these, such as Gray-bull, proved such mines of knowledge that I tapped them again and again, thus also establishing a certain personal bond. On a subject of any difficulty, such as the Sun Dance, the Tobacco organization, and the military clubs, I obtained the individual reminiscences or judgments of all the old men and women accessible. Important myths were taken down from the lips of several narrators, prayers were sometimes dictated by the same witness in different years.

Of my several interpreters one stands out as my greatest aid,—James Carpenter. The son of a white man and a Piegan Indian woman but raised among the Crow from infancy he has always been passionately interested in the old ways of his adopted tribe, and as meticulous as any scientist in his ideals of accuracy. After an eight- or ten-hour working day spent with me in taking down texts, he would spontaneously scour the countryside to secure renderings of doubtful words or supplementary information from competent authorities. I was even able to teach him a simplified phonetic system of writing, and in consequence have been able to get valuable corrections and additions by means of correspondence.

I am only too well aware that all the techniques ethnologists have devised are still no equivalent for viewing the life of the Indian as it *might* have been experienced by an intelligent squaw-man or trader in a continued intimacy of twenty years. It is, after all, one thing to have been on a war party and another to have the warriors' tales; one thing to have wooed native women, another to observe them and get their accounts of Crow wedlock. Though no full and high-grade sources are extant for the early Crow, I have therefore gratefully used what there is of old and recent material. I am not ashamed to confess that Beckwourth, a braggart mulatto, Leforge, a squaw-man, Linderman, a one-time trapper turned author, have noted things I failed to get; and I have always been glad that in essentials my data are corroborated by Mr. Curtis's book, published before some of my technical papers, though not easily accessible. The present account, avowedly incomplete, is as authentic as conditions permit, and is so recognized by those literate middle-aged Indians who have seen the monographs on which it is based.

The Crow Indians have had their share of the tribulations usually created by aboriginal contacts with white civilization. Buffalo hunters find it hard to turn to the plough, especially in regions of uncertain rainfall and crops. Then there has been the inevitable suffering from introduced diseases, from the rapacity of white men encroaching on their old domain or cheating them in transactions they were unable to understand. Within the last generation, however, a new spirit has arisen among them. The Crow leaders of today have been educated in local or boarding-schools, are conscious of their ancient wrongs, know and assert their legal rights. They present their grievances to Congress and serve as tribal delegates in Washington.

With the appointment of Mr. John Collier as Commissioner of Indian Affairs the history of the Crow has entered a new phase. A severe and sometimes savage critic of earlier administrators, he was expectantly hailed as a deliverer by the educated residents of the Reservation. This does not mean that his plans have been uniformly approved: conditions on Indian reservations differ to a degree few outsiders would believe possible, and some of Mr. Collier's ideas the Crow regard as inapplicable to their own situation. But, to quote one who has valiantly fought for his tribe, "he is the most human Commissioner of Indian Affairs I have known."

It is obviously premature to pass judgment on Mr. Collier's practical achievement either on behalf of the Crow or the Indians as a whole. But one of his moves has created a profound psychological effect. It had long been the Bureau's policy to give employment to Indians when possible,—as policemen, clerks, or teachers. But Mr. Collier put Robert Yellowtail, a Crow educated at Riverside, in charge as Superintendent of his reservation. Knowing the background of his people, he has been able to explain to them in their own language and in a manner adapted to their ability to assimilate, what are the Bureau's policies and why certain grievances cannot be redressed forthwith. Whatever may be the ultimate outcome of Mr. Collier's experiments, now that the Crow are recognized as full-fledged citizens of the United States, there can be no doubt as to his wisdom in sharing responsibility with one of their own number. Every well-wisher of the Indian will eagerly watch the results of his bold innovation.

THE CROW INDIANS

THE CROW INDIANS

I. Tribal Organization

SOUTHEAST of Billings, Montana, and northwest of Sheridan, Wyoming, about 1,800 Crow Indians are now living on a reservation rather near the core of their old tribal territory. The Reservation is locally subdivided, the Lodge Grass, Bighorn and Pryor districts being the most important. However, there has been free intercourse back and forth, and such local differences as evolved were due to the influence of individual personalities, say, Medicine-crow at Lodge Grass. The Crow name for themselves is "Apsāruke," which early interpreters mistranslated as "gens de corbeaux," "Crow (or Kite) Indians." To me the word was explained as the name of a bird no longer to be seen in the country. The squaw-man Leforge defines it as "a peculiar kind of forked-tail bird resembling the blue jay or magpie" which tradition assigns to the fauna of eastern Nebraska and Kansas at the time the Crow lived there. Apart from this fanciful localization, his and my data thus agree well enough.

In speech the Crow are "Siouan," i.e. related to the Sioux (Dakota) in the sense that English and Russian are both "Indo-European," for in either case only a philologist could prove any connection. On the other hand, the veriest layman can hear that English bears some relationship to Dutch or German, and that Crow and Hidatsa are still closer to each other,—the affinity being probably something like that of, say, Danish with Swedish. A Crow visitor does not at once follow the conversation of Hidatsa hosts, but he can recognize dozens of words that are quite or almost identical in the sister tongues, and he soon gets his bearings. Compared with Crow and Dakota, Hidatsa, though much nearer to the former, proves intermediate; that is, Crow has deviated farther from the common parental language. Hidatsa and Crow are so similar that the tribes now speaking them cannot have separated in dim antiquity. According to my

3

guess, the split occurred about five hundred years ago: the Crow then moved westward and developed changes in speech and custom before reëstablishing intercourse with their old relatives. However that be, the sense of kinship between the two tribes is very real, and they sometimes refer to each other as basically a single people.

There was only one Crow language, but not one Crow nation. The Indians themselves speak of three local divisions. Once, along the lower Yellowstone as far as the Missouri confluence, roamed the River Crow, less appetizingly named in the vernacular as the Dung-on-the-river-banks (minésepēre). The two others are conveniently lumped together as Mountain Crow, the native terms being the Main Body (acarahō'; literally, Where the many lodges are) and the Kicked-in-their-bellies (ērarapī'o). The latter, I learnt, joined the Main Body in the spring, but spent the winter in the country of the Wyoming Shoshone, that is, in the Wind River region, where Maximilian makes the entire tribe seek pasture for their horses during the cold season. This agrees with the account of one of my informants, who describes the Main Body moving to the Basin in the winter and ranging from the site of Buffalo, Wyoming, to the Pryor district in the spring. Others bound the territory by the Tongue River on the east and the site of Livingston on the west. The Kicked-in-their-bellies are plausibly conceived as a recent offshoot from the Main Body that never fully established independence. Mountain and River Crow thus figure as two major subdivisions of the tribe. For obvious reasons the former had more frequent contacts with the Shoshone, and the latter with the Village tribes and the Assiniboine; and thus minor differences would arise. The Horse dance, for instance, was peculiar to the River band, who learnt it from the Assiniboine. But essentially the Crow remained one people, referring to themselves as bī'ruke, "we," much as a Frenchman might say "nous autres." Legend tells of tragic clan feuds, but the two main groups as such were never hostile. The worst remembered blow to solidarity occurred when the Main Body once vainly asked the River Crow for help in fighting the Dakota. Not long after this rebuff the Mountain people defeated their enemies, killing twelve men without more than a minor injury to one of their own. Triumphantly they now returned to strut before their pusillanimous tribesmen, and the women whose mourning ended with the victory made up ribald songs poking fun at the two River Crow chiefs. But the misunderstanding was a temporary one.

The bands, then, were politically distinct. But how shall we conceive the ancient "chief"? The native term, batse' tse (probably from batse', "man," and i' tse, "good, valiant") denotes the standing that goes with military achievement, but need not imply any governmental functions. There were four normal types of creditable exploit: leadership of a successful raid; capturing a horse picketed within a hostile camp; being first to touch an enemy (the "coup" in the narrower sense); and snatching a foeman's bow or gun. A man who had scored at least once on each of these counts ranked as a batse' tse. Such men formed a body of social leaders; on the other hand, to lack all these standardized points was to be a nobody. Possibly at one time, only men attaining or approaching a chief's record made up the band council. At all events, one member of this military aristocracy, without acquiring a special title, became head of the camp. He was neither a ruler nor a judge and in general had no power over life and death. He decided when and where his followers were to pitch and to move their lodges. Further, every spring he appointed one of the military clubs (p. 172) to act as police (ak'i'sate), sometimes reappointing the same society several times since there was no fixed rule of rotation.

The foremost duty of the police was to regulate the communal buffalo hunt. They severely whipped any one who prematurely attacked the herd, broke his weapons, and confiscated the game he had illegally killed. They also stopped a war party setting out at an inauspicious moment, directed the movements of the camp, tried to settle amicably any disputes within the band, and in general maintained order. Leforge once joined two Indian scalawags in mischievously chasing some buffalo into a camp, where they tore up several tipis. The police ordered them to remain outside the camp for a month. "It was a distressing penalty; but we stayed out. We should have received much worse treatment had we violated the order." The offenders were hard put to it at times, both for lack of company and of food,—though their sweethearts furtively smuggled provisions out to them. Aside from this, the owners of the damaged lodges had to be indemnified.

Appointed by the camp chief, the police were considered subordinate to him; and he could thus, according to Leonard, a fur trader of the thirties, veto every one of their acts. However, the statement must be taken with a grain of salt. The chief himself was not an autocrat, and the constabulary normally acted only on special occasions, such as those mentioned above. Apart from these the people hardly felt the weight of authority.

According to one informant a head chief remained in office until he voluntarily resigned, but Lone-tree more convincingly explained that a camp chief served as long as the tribe enjoyed good luck under him, failing which there was a change.

At large gatherings another functionary appeared as the camp-chief's aid, to wit, the herald or crier (acipē'rira'u). Riding through the circle of lodges, he reported aloud any matters of public interest, summoning the aged to a feast at some hospitable lodge, announcing the disappearance of some tribesman or the approach of a battle. Sometimes he explicitly appeared as the chief's mouthpiece, prefacing his proclamation with the statement that he was not voicing merely his own judgment. Before an engagement he encouraged the Crow, proclaimed the chief's orders, exhibited picked young warriors where all could see them, and eulogized them before the assembled throng (see p. 231). A crier was a man of distinction, being chosen most probably as the leader of a lucky war party. The office survived intertribal wars, of necessity sometimes devolving on men deemed ineligible fifty years ago. Thus, during the Fourth of July celebration at Lodge Grass in 1911 White-man-runs-him held the position. Though he had gained some celebrity as a surviving Custer scout, he did not escape malevolent comments: "In the old days," I heard, "we should not have picked out a man like him to serve as herald."

Notwithstanding the emphasis on social position, the Crow were democratically organized, since eminence rested on individual merit. Moreover, except on such special occasions as the communal hunt or great ceremonial festivals, every one was allowed to act much as he pleased.

This unquestionably was the ideal, but reality sometimes departed from it: a man who had somehow acquired power might selfishly make the most of it. In theory unusual success of any kind had a religious basis, coming through the favor of supernatural beings. But there was also a social factor,—a large body of kindred. No worse insult could be hurled at a Crow than to say, "You are without relatives"; it meant that he was a person of no account. On the other hand, a man of vigorous character, surrounded by twoscore young daredevils related to him, might easily dominate a band of a few hundred souls.

In the semi-historical traditions that reflect aboriginal custom two motifs recur, singly or in combination: the lonely orphan outcast who becomes eminent by supernatural revelation; and the camp bully who, secure because of his supernatural guardian and his numerous followers, rides roughshod over the feelings of his fellows. The legends explicitly contrast the ignominious status of the orphan with the good fortune of a youth who has parents. For this difference has implications: a boy with parents also has on both sides uncles, aunts, and cousins, all morally obliged to aid and shield him. Bereft of such support, a kinless boy becomes the butt of mockery. When he ventures to woo a mythical beauty, she spurns him with venomous abuse: "Many have wished to marry me, and I would not take them. You are worse-looking than all the rest. . . . Your feet are like a bear's." Another story begins as follows: "There was a young man who had parents and was well off. He had for his comrade a young man who was poor and lived with him." The poor man marries a good-looking young woman, whom the wealthy friend promptly abducts. Again, the hero Twined-tail and his two brothers are introduced as miserably poor. One of them, Eats-like-a-wolf, plays at the hoop-game against Earth-bull. "This one named Earth-bull had many relatives; his relatives were bullies. In the game this Earth-bull's spectators [supporters] were many, Eats-like-a-wolf had no spectators." Accordingly, when the friendless player scores, his opponent challenges the count and is backed by his henchmen. "Eats-like-a-wolf was looking around for supporters, there was no one he could appeal to." Twined-tail, dirty and ill-clad, speaks up on his brother's behalf, but the opponent taunts him with his poverty and wretched appearance. Cut to the quick, he betakes himself to the mountains, is blessed by a supernatural, and thus gains distinction on a war party. Returning, he and his companions deride his old enemy; and when Earth-bull furiously advances, he is characteristically routed by the speech of one of Twined-tail's followers, "whose kin were many and vigorous."

The story of One-eye is instructive in several ways. As the bullet-proof chief of the Piegan clan, he hectors his fellows, taking away their wives and horses at will. His ascendancy rests on the blessing granted by a benevolent being, who is outraged by his protégé's wickedness and transfers power to one of his victims, an inoffensive lad "who had no parents." In consequence, One-eye is worsted and put to death.

One-eye's browbeating of his band at first blush suggests the behavior of a Negro potentate. But there is a basic difference. Spoliation and maltreatment of subjects is the constitutional prerogative of a West African despot; but though exceptional circumstances may make a Crow an autocrat *de facto,* he is never one *de jure.* The first thing One-eye's conqueror does is to reassure the people: *he* will not be like One-eye, and to prove it he at once restores wives and horses to their rightful owners. Even One-eye is not a full-fledged autocrat. When his brother-in-law proposes peace with the Whistling Water clan, the chief does not issue an arbitrary decree, but appeals to his followers: "Well, boys, seek a decision. If you approve of your brother-in-law's speech, decide accordingly. If on the other hand you think that now, their chief being dead, we ought to go there and afflict them, then decide accordingly. Think it over now." To be sure, after pondering, they reply, "Now we shall decide; you are our chief and we'll do precisely what you say." But the very fact of One-eye's calling his men into consultation shows how repugnant despotism is to Crow notions of "constitutionality"; and this is again borne out by the chief's response. "Well, boys, you have bidden me do as I please. I first asked you to do as *you* pleased, but you declined. If I now do as I wish, do not talk in criticism about it."

The One-eye tradition envisages a social group that differs from the linguistic unit we call the Crow and from its political subdivisions, the River and Mountain bands. The latter were each constituted by members of the same thirteen *clans,* while our story pictures the males of one clan—the Piegan—as the core of a local group, with occasional but rare additions of men from other clans who throw in their lot with the kin of their Piegan wives. However this be, the Crow clan of historic times can be defined with precision. It was matrilineal since the children of a family all took their mother's clan name; and it included not only individuals related by blood through their mothers, but also unrelated folk reckoned as kin by a legal fiction. Considering only the blood-relatives, a person was always in the same clan as his mother and her sisters and brothers, his mother's mother, mother's mother's brother, and mother's mother's sisters; his sister's children; and various other kinsfolk, such as the children of his mother's mother's sisters. On the other hand, a man could never properly belong to the clan of his children, who were born into their mother's group; and even if he adopted a child it automatically fell into the clan of his real offspring, to wit, their mother's. With the Crow rule of descent, a child could belong to the father's clan only if its mother married a man of her own clan, a practice forbidden by the customary law of "exogamy."

The thirteen exogamous maternal clans were grouped together in very loose nameless bodies according to the following scheme:

I	Newly-made Lodges	(acirārī'o)
	Thick Lodge	(acitsi'te)
II	Sore lip Lodge	(acī'oce)
	Greasy-inside-the-mouth	(ū'wutace')
III	Without-shooting-they-bring-game	(ū'sawatsi'a)
	Tied-in-a-knot	(xu'xkaraxtse)
	Filth-eating Lodge	(acpe'nucc)
IV	Kicked-in-their-bellies	(ē'rarapī'o)
	Bad War Honors	(ackya'pkawi'a)
V	Whistling Water	(birikyō'oce)
	Streaked Lodge	(acxatse')
VI	Piegan Lodge	(ackyā'mne)
	Treacherous Lodge	(acbatcu'a)

There is some doubt whether the last two pairs of names represent each two distinct clans or merely synonyms for the same clans, in which case the total number of these groups would fall to eleven.

Fellow-clansfolk recognized mutual obligations, which characteristically overrode their sense of duty to any larger group. Thus, a murder would readily precipitate a blood-feud. On the principle of "one for all, and all for one," the victim's clansmen sought to kill either the murderer or one of *his* clansmen.

Certain occurrences probably assignable to the first half of the nineteenth century illustrate the native point of view. Arrow-head, a young man of the Piegan clan, was ambushed and killed by the Whistling Waters. As soon as the news reached his elder brother, Raven-face, he set forth against the hostile clan but was severely wounded. Subsequently he went for a vision and gained power, while his comrade, Dangling-foot, who belonged to neither of the two contending clans, took care of his family. On Raven-face's return, he and his friend chanced upon a party of Whistling Waters, who at once decided to kill their enemy. But Dangling-foot, a sharpshooter, put them to flight, killing Honest, according to one version Arrow-head's slayer, who characteristically adjures Dangling-foot to keep out of the fray since he belongs to neither clan. In one account Honest is even scalped and the two victors blacken their faces in token of victory, precisely as if they had killed a Cheyenne or Dakota, and stage a victory parade. "Then the Piegan clan people were happy; they had their revenge." Honest's death was explicitly accepted as atonement for the kill-ing of Arrow-head.

Thus solidarity seems to rest solely on maternal kinship. Each clan is like an independent modern state in its relations with other units of like order; and in a feud two such groups act as they would toward hostile tribes. But this view must be seriously modified. The story itself proves a distinct form of bond: a neutral from personal friendship takes up cudgels on behalf of one of the contending parties, and it is he that wipes out the blot on the grieving clan's 'scutcheon. Now this phenomenon is far from unique, and is even better illustrated in another version of the same happenings. When Raven-face's arm is shattered by the Whistling Waters, one of his adversaries turns out to be a boyhood friend. This man, a good marksman, pretends to shoot Raven-face but purposely misses him. When his fellows upbraid him, he angrily admits having done so on purpose and bids them go hang ("Whatever you want to do, do!"). In short, clan loy-alty *may* yield to the tie of comradeship.

But still another sentiment counted for something,—a faint anticipation of nationalism. Extremely tenuous as it certainly must have been, it was not wholly lacking. Under normal condi-tions the clans were *not* warring against each other, but expected to form a united front against hostile aliens. It is on behalf of such union that the police society pacified aggrieved tribesmen and that neutral clans repeatedly strove for reconciliation. In the earlier feud of the Whistling Water and Piegan clans, outsiders figure as vainly pleading with the combatants: "It is bad, don't do it, *we are one people;* all over our children are related to one another, don't do it." Similarly, after the Dangling-foot episode there was danger of further strife, but the neutrals continually urged the two factions to cease fighting. However, there was so much gossiping against Dangling-foot that he wearied of it and separated from the main camp with thirty or forty lodges. Now the folly of separation was demonstrated; for the seceders chanced upon a large body of Cheyenne and were virtually destroyed.

This last instance suggests how we are to picture the situation indicated in the One-eye story. With Crow clans maternal and exogamous, the condition of a local group as described in that tale is unthinkable as a permanent one. Obviously One-eye and the men of his council,—all of them conceived as brothers-in-law of the stranger in their midst,—are of the Piegan clan, while their wives must belong to other clans. Since, however, children take their mother's name, the new generation would cease to be Piegan. On the other hand, the clans had headmen, who became such because of their valor, and sometimes under their guidance occurred a *temporary* separation, acdū'sau, from the main part of a band for purposes of buffalo-hunting. Onion and later Gray-bull were mentioned as Filthy-eater headmen; Plenty-coups for the Sore-lips; Pretty-eagle for the Piegan clan.

The native word for "clan" is ac-ambare'axi'a, "lodge where there is driftwood," the idea apparently being that clansfolk cling together like the driftwood lodged at a particular spot. Certainly the sense of cohesion illustrated by the above semi-legendary accounts of feuds is corroborated by historical evidence. When Fire-bear, the Indian policeman, killed Wraps-up-his-tail in 1887 (p. xi), the victim's clansmen planned to avenge his death; and, some say, it was to prevent this that the U. S. Government continued to keep Fire-bear in its employ.

The following exemplifies how similar difficulties were adjusted by customary law. The Sioux once stole the fastest horse in camp, but a Whistling Water recaptured it. He was fleeing with a Sore-lip named Birds-all-over-the-ground, who coveted the horse so much that he killed his companion while he was taking a drink. The pursuing Sioux heard the report and arrived on the scene, but the murderer, mounting the fast horse, made his escape and was credited with its recovery. However, subsequently through some Sioux visitors the Crow learned the truth. The victim's father at once began to wail, and his clan prepared for vengeance. Then the Sore-lips loaded horses with gifts, brought them to the old man, and begged him to desist. Their chief likewise offered a peace-pipe to the head of the Whistling Waters, who held a council. They decided to forgo hostilities in deference to the pipe and because the affair had taken place long ago. "Today," I wrote in 1912, "the murderer's deed is forgiven." Leforge, however, who knew the offender, declares that though people tolerated him they would not associate with him.

According to Leforge, the members of a clan set up their lodges next to one another and adhered to the same relative position whenever camp was pitched. My informants flatly contradicted this: the circle, they aver, was not the regular form of encampment but reserved for special occasions, and the clan did not occupy any definite place in it.

Clan-fellows often feasted together, and when I first knew the tribe, helped one another in various ways. When one of their members, for example, entered the Tobacco order, the rest contributed toward the expenses of initiation. A somewhat earlier incident is typical. The Piegan Indians stole Spotted-fish's favorite mount, but four Crow recaptured it. He offered them four horses and other property for it, but they demanded an elk-tooth dress to boot, which he refused to add. However, his clansmen accumulated a large amount of property and bought the horse back for him.

Since a clansman was called a brother, his wife was treated with the same license as a blood-brother's wife, even to the extent of ribald jesting with her (cf. p. 28). Further, an otherwise jealous husband would not resist his wife's dancing with a member of his clan. When Big Horn Indians visited at Lodge Grass, a Sore-lip visitor's wife would receive meat from a Sore-lip woman of the district which acted as host. If the woman was alone, she would return moccasins and the like; if her husband was present, he would send back horses and other valuable gifts for his clans-

woman's husband. The exchange follows the pattern that holds
for a blood-brother and sister.

Anciently the territory occupied by a band was communally
owned, hence the question of its inheritance never arose. With
the allotment of land to individuals by the Government, the tendency was to regard a man's brothers and sisters as his heirs,
i.e., relatives of his own clan rather than his sons. In 1907 officials
were still concerned with adjusting the discrepancies between
Federal and native conceptions. The Crow had naturally applied
their pattern for the inheritance of horses and other possessions
to the new form of property. However, before dying, a man might
call out that he wished to give one or two horses to his wife or
son, and such a wish was respected, though the bulk of a herd
would fall to the brother's share.

Sacred objects and ceremonial privileges were often bequeathed to the eldest son, but succession was irregular, not necessarily following either the paternal or the maternal line. Thus,
Old-woman got the Tobacco mixing prerogative (p. 287) from
her father, but also felt affiliation with a certain Tobacco chapter
because her brother was a member. Sometimes the very same set
of ritualistic objects were transmitted according to both prin-
ciples. Humped-wolf is credited with simultaneously transferring
power to three sons and one uterine nephew. One of the famous
Sun Dance dolls was revealed to a woman, inherited by her son,
and passed on to his brother. So far, then, transmission was
matrilineal. But the next heir was Bear-from-above, his predecessor's son, who kept the doll until his wife's death, when he
buried it with her. Sharp-horn inherited *his* Sun Dance doll from
a brother; on the other hand, Flat-head-woman bequeathed his
Arrow bundle to his eldest daughter. Another medicine used in
the Tobacco ceremony had been passed on from mother to daughter, while the founder of the Blackbird chapter received his
blackbird medicine from his father. Medicine-crow also had a
vision of the crane, like his father before him. As to shields, I
learnt that an owner might will his to a son *or* to a younger
brother. Failing any such disposition, a ceremonial "son" of his
might ostentatiously mourn over the owner's death and thus
establish a moral claim to it which the bereaved family would
recognize.

In short, sacred possessions, including privileges, were preferentially kept within the close family circle, but without hard-and-fast bias in either direction. Some, it should be noted, were not automatically passed on even within the group of immediate kin: for a minor privilege, such as using a special form of facial decoration, a man might pay a horse to his own parent.

One notion that militated against one-sided prevalence of either maternal or paternal succession to religious forms of property was the deep-rooted belief that husband and wife were intimately associated in ceremonial activity, certain feminine disabilities to the contrary notwithstanding. Thus, though Flat-head-woman left his bundle to a daughter, her husband fully shares the responsibility of custodianship; husband and wife were as a rule jointly initiated into the Tobacco organization; and so forth. For instance, Medicine-crow might be said to have inherited a certain sacred rock from his father. But actually it was his mother that had had a vision of the stone and through it made her husband prominent.

Bundles and other sacred prerogatives were property in the most literal sense of the term, for men were always eager to pay extravagant prices for even a share in the good fortune their possessions implied. They were, indeed, by far the most valuable type of property. Apart from them, there could not have been a great deal left for disposal, especially before horses came into the country, for mourners distributed much of what they owned among the people, and when a great chief died, even his lodge might be abandoned.

The clan division offered a natural line of cleavage for a competitive entertainment. Gray-bull remembered a contest as to war scores between the Thick Lodges and Without-shooting-they-have-game; and Shot-in-the-arm described one between Whistling Water and Greasy Mouth people of the River band. These groups seated themselves on opposite sides of a tipi. A spokesman for the Whistling Waters first proclaimed the number of picketed horses cut by each of his fellows, who assisted him in the count. In this connection he also recited the deeds of clansmen for the Mountain band. When both sides had finished their reckoning, the representative of the winning side planted a stick in the ground. There followed the enumeration of guns snatched from the enemy; of the coups struck; and of the successful war captains (not of successful parties they had led).

The married women kidnapped by each clan (see p. 186) were also counted. Shot-in-the-arm, himself a Greasy Mouth, described his clan as triumphantly victorious on every point in this contest, which was called matdacpī'o. The winners, he added, generally made their children give away presents, but this was not obligatory. On the other hand, Gray-bull declared that the losers had to bring pemmican to feast their opponents.

There are no elaborate traditions of clan origins, but clan names, including some not yet cited, are often accounted for. Thus, according to one report, men anciently dubbed They-eat-their-own-nasal-mucus once abandoned a wounded comrade and were hence nicknamed "Piegan" because they had acted like enemies. A more frequent explanation debits the Piegan clan with the damning act and thence derives the name "Treacherous Lodge." "Earless Lodge" is ascribed to the Piegan clan because one member is said to have cut off his wife's ear as a punishment for adultery. The ū'sawatsi'a were called "Not-Mixed" from being composed largely of war captains, i.e., these leaders were "not mixed" with common folk. The acpe'nuce derived their name from one of their members whose wife eloped but was recaptured and made to eat dung. The Bad Leggings, I was told, were renamed Greasy-inside-their-Mouths because they had once left the main body of the Crow in search of food, had killed fat buffalo, and when they spat into the fire, the spittle burnt like tallow. A variant of this tale is at least equally plausible: a poor orphan once obtained some grease and expectorated into a big fire. His saliva, mixed with the fat, started up the flames and the onlookers laughingly said, "Your spittle must be greasy." After he had got married, people nicknamed his children "Greasy-inside-their-mouths." This version seems to fly in the face of maternal descent but is wholly in consonance with the established custom of twitting people with the absurd behavior of their *paternal* kindred (see p. 21).

As to the associations of clans, there is no convincing statement as to how they came about. According to some Indians, the old clans increased in population and were then subdivided, while others—e.g. acpe'nuce and xu'xkaraxtse—were reduced until their members joined forces in order to form a larger whole. As to the nature of the relationship itself, on the other hand, the Indians are in fair agreement: there was mutual helpfulness.

Ever since Old-dog could remember, the Greasy-inside-their-mouths and the Sore-lips were on intimate terms, inviting each other to feasts, and camping together on a buffalo hunt. When the son of a Greasy-inside-the-mouth scored in battle, his praises were sung not only by his father's clan but also by the Sore-lips. Similarly, with the sons of Thick-Lodge and Newly-made-Lodge men. When an irregular marriage occurred within the clan, Arm-round-the-neck explained, the social difficulties were in a measure overcome by transferring to members of the clan linked with one's father's the respect normally due to the paternal clan (see p. 20).

The relation to exogamy is not so clear. Mr. Curtis believes that the rule formerly held not only within a clan but also extended to the linked clan. My information, however, contradicts this, at least as a general principle. Big-ox, a renowned medicine-man, was an ū'sawatsia, and had one wife of the Tied-in-a-knot and another from the Filth-eating clan; Blackbird-running, who belonged to the Kicked-in-their-bellies, married a Bad War Honors woman; and so forth. One man emphatically declared of the Newly-made and the Thick Lodges: "They are two, separate, they intermarried continually." He held the same view for all the clan associations except the last two of my list.

It seems a fair guess that practice varied in different major groups. In some, we may conjecture, the intimacy had grown to a point where members of the linked clans felt a sense of kinship barring marriage, while in other associations that stage was never reached.

Though the clans loomed large in the tribal life, they did not greatly impress themselves on tradition except for the narratives of the above-mentioned feuds. The trivial episodes accounting for clan names have already been related. On the other hand, various drolls are current to illustrate the stupidity of the Bad War Honors. People say of them, "The Bad War Honors are crazy. Once a Crow party camped together were attacked by the Piegan Indians. All fled except one young man, who climbed a tree. At first he remained unobserved. Then the enemy cut up a tipi and began pilfering its contents. When one of them opened a bag and took out some buckskin, the ackya'pkawi'a said, "Don't take that!" The enemy thus discovered his whereabouts and killed him. On another occasion an ackya'pkawi'a saw another Crow wearing beaded buckskin leggings with red fringes. He asked how they were made. The owner told him to get his wife to cut leggings after the same pattern, boil buffalo bones till the grease floated on top, cool the grease, plunge the leggings into it, and then place them on the ground. "The next morning, when you get up, they will be just like mine." The Bad War Honors man followed these directions, but when he got up his leggings were so greasy that he did not know what to do with them.

Magpie, whom I knew personally, figured as the "incarnation of an ackya'pkawi'a" (ackya'pkawi'a-kā'ce), and quaint anecdotes were told about his behavior. He once tried to strike mice with a pitchfork and struck his own foot. His wife told other Indians how he had once put on his moccasins on the wrong side and never noticed the error until his attention was directed to it. Again, he wanted to call Lewis Moccasin and instead uttered his own name. Once he even mistook a Crow for an alien visitor to the Reservation, invited him to his home by means of signs, offered him food, and only detected his mistake when the supposed foreigner spoke Crow.

It was principally a man's wife, his brothers' and clansmen's wives, and his joking-relatives (see p. 22) who poked fun at a man for being a typical ackya'pkawi'a. Gray-bull refrained from chaffing Magpie because Magpie's son, Yellow-brow, had become his son-in-law.

But, true to the custom of blaming a person for what his *father's* kin had done (see p. 21), the Crow twit a man with having a father who is a Bad Honors. If the son of an ackya'-pkawi'a is guilty of some foolish act, those privileged to throw it into his teeth will say, "He is one of those who told the enemy not to take the buckskin," or "He is one of those who boiled their leggings." Medicine-crow's father was an ackya'pkawi'a, and whenever Medicine-crow had done anything wrong, his wife would scoff at him, saying, "It's because his fathers are Bad Honors." The import is that of our "He's a chip of the old block" or "That's the Irish of it."

[Note. In an Appendix are given some technical details on the clans and clan associations.]

II. Kinship and Affinity

THE maternal clan system notwithstanding, there is an intensely close bond with the father and all his kin. Medicinecrow was one of the most distinguished men I knew. In his childhood his father—actually the paternal uncle who had inherited the boy's mother—quarreled with his wife and separated from her. In Plenty-hawk's account of these happenings the lad is pictured wistfully running to his "father"—even contrary to his mother's wishes. " 'Father,' he cried, 'I have been terribly lonesome.' With him he ate, with him he stayed. 'Father, do not send me home this time,' he said." Such attachment might persist into manhood. Spotted-rabbit was the handsomest of all Crow ever known, he owned the best of horses, and was living amicably with his parents. But there was fighting, and his father was killed. Then he began giving away his horses in exchange for Crazy Dog regalia (p. 331): he wanted to die. "Because my father died I'll be a Crazy Dog. . . . When anybody calls for his father I am scared because I have none. I am very eager to die and catch up with my father."

On the other hand, a father is full of loving-kindness for his children. When a person adjures another to grant a special favor, the phrase used is often, "You love your children," i.e. "By the love you bear your children, I beg you." In one variant of the Old Woman's Grandchild myth, the hero's mother wants all the sinews in a buffalo's carcass. Instead of asking her husband directly, she instructs their little boy to beg for them: "When your father comes home and you ask him to do something, he always does it. I'll make you say something to him."

A son does not use the same term as a daughter in speaking to or of his father. The masculine vocative is axe'; the feminine, masā'ka. In reference, "my father" is biru'pxe for men, masā'ke for women. I once evoked a burst of merriment by asking a girl, "dĭ'rupxe cō?" ("Where is your father?") The word chosen implied that I took her for a boy; I should have said, "di'sāke cō?" Incidentally, though biru'pxe never occurs in direct address, its diminutive form biru'pxekyāta, "my little father," may be so used, though with a quaint change of meaning. Men so called each other who shared the favors of the same woman, whether wife or mistress. Thus, when Spotted-rabbit as a privileged character had a love affair with the wife of Two-faces, the husband did not resent it but regarded the hero as his iru'pxekyāta. In another tale two men who have stolen each other's wives become reconciled, establishing the same relationship. Sometimes a young man who craved an older man's sacred power temporarily yielded marital rights to him. Gray-bull, for instance, once offered a medicine owner the possession of his mistress and later of his wife. The owner was reckoned Gray-bull's maternal uncle, but thereafter the two men called each other biru'pxekyāta.

The term "father," as used in Crow, has a far wider denotation than in English, and this applies to most of the kinship designations. As Leforge, too, has noted, the number of physiological offspring of a particular person in a lodge was neither easily discoverable nor too closely investigated. Adults loved children generally, and the feeling was naturally intensified by close association irrespective of blood-kinship. However this may be, the several "father" terms noted above certainly embraced the following relatives besides one's own father: the paternal uncle, the father's maternal uncle, the paternal aunt's son. Of connections by marriage, the husband of any aunt, paternal or maternal, falls into the same category. In addition, adoptive and ceremonial fathers are designated by the identical words.

It may seem odd that the paternal aunt's son—a cousin, a member of one's own generation—should be classed with the father. But this is merely of a piece with the idea that clansmen are in a sense equivalent. By matrilineal descent this particular cousin must belong to the clan of the speaker's father and is thus put into the same category. I have heard Gray-bull when about sixty-five years old address as father an interpreter in his twenties.

Similarly can be explained the idea of including the father's maternal uncle. Crow and Hidatsa are among the few primitive languages that lack any uncle term; a maternal uncle is simply an "elder brother." But we have seen that a *father's* brother is the same as a father. Hence, the matter stands thus:

father's elder brother   = father
maternal uncle   = elder brother
∴ father's maternal uncle = father's elder brother = father

Both sexes use the same two words for the father's sister, the terms varying merely according to whether she is addressed or simply referred to. Furthermore, the principle of the two terms is wholly distinct. The paternal aunt is addressed like one's mother or mother's sister, viz., i'gya'. But "my paternal aunt has gone" would be basbāxi'a kandē'ky; while "my mother has gone" is masa'ke' kandē'ky." In other words, in address the Indians ignore the difference of clan between mother and paternal aunt; in reference, the distinction is expressed. Indeed, the paternal aunt term includes *all* women of the father's clan from his own generation downward. Given female descent, this means that the daughter of an isbāxi'a (this term is always used with some possessive prefix) is also an isbāxi'a; or, that the same word is applied in reference to a paternal aunt, a paternal aunt's daughter, a paternal aunt's daughter's daughter, and so on *ad infinitum.*

Comparison with related Siouan tribes shows that addressing the father's sister as if she were a mother is a recent development; anciently the paternal aunt was distinguished from the mother and her sisters,—as she is in Hidatsa, and even in modern Crow when she is merely mentioned.

There is a general word for any paternal clansman, viz., ā'sa'ke (plural: ā'sa'kua). It is not used in address, where each sex substitutes the appropriate father term. But there is one notable exception. When a Crow prays to the Sun, he may address this god as "mā'sa'ka."

The mutual behavior of a given individual and his paternal clansfolk was of practical importance. They were treated with great respect. A person would not walk in front of one unless he had given him a present: to quote Old-dog, they were regarded "like medicines." Sometimes a man would invite a group or all of his ā'sa'kua to a feast. When they were through eating, the guest nearest the door would be asked, "What will you give to your son?" His answer was likely to be phrased like a prayer for an extension of life; he might reply, "I dreamt of the plums and chokecherries ripening, and I give this to the boy," i.e., "May he live until the plums and chokecherries are ripening once more!" The next ā'sa'ke possibly prophesied that the host would strike a coup or kill an enemy. Another might have dreamt of a very old man and uttered a corresponding wish for the entertainer's longevity. When all had spoken, the host would rise and say, "If I strike a coup in the next battle, I'll give a horse to So-and-so; if I see the chokecherry blossom, I'll give a blanket to So-and so," etc.

It was eminently proper to feast members of the paternal clan or to present them with gifts. There is a popular story about four friends (or brothers) who decided what each of them should do to distinguish himself. The first was to fast and torture himself in order to get a revelation; the second, to pray constantly to the Sun; the third, to make a practice of erecting sweat-lodges; the fourth, to feed and make donations to his ā'sa'kua. The vision-seeker very soon became prominent and was killed at the height of his glory. The Sun-worshipper next gained fame, then he, too, was killed. The sweater lived to a proper age, rose to the position of a chief, then died. The fourth man lived to be very old and a great chief; he had the strongest power of all. "Since then we have given food to our clan-fathers."

The obligations, however, were reciprocal. As the clan son revered, entertained, and enriched his ā'sa'kua, they in turn prayed on his behalf, rejoiced over his deeds, and served as his publicity agents. When a boy had acquitted himself creditably on a raid, his ā'sa'kua came toward his lodge, performed a short dance, and sang his praises. When Yellow-tail had shot his first deer a similar celebration was planned, but owing to the breakdown of old custom the idea was not carried out.

Often, though not necessarily, an ā'sa'ke conferred a name upon an infant. Quite generally, honorific appellations were derived from some father's clansman, and nicknames frequently expressed not a peculiarity of the bearer's but rather some idiosyncrasy or absurd behavior of his father's clansfolk. As already explained, this held generically for sons of Bad War Honors men (p. 17); and I know of two instances of a woman's antics suggesting sobriquets for the children of her brother.

These well-established customs prove beyond cavil that the Crow by no means ignore the father and his relatives. The maternal clan relationship is simply *one* legal, ethical, and sentimental tie among others.

But this is not all. Though contests about war exploits were arranged along clan lines (p. 14), the opponents might also be the *sons*, respectively, of two clans. Sometimes the sons of men of a certain clan were pitted against those of the linked clans, e.g., the sons of Tied-in-a-knot men opposed the sons of Those-who-without-shooting-bring-game.

The importance of the father's clan appears conclusively in the singular institution of the joking-relationship, said to have been originated by Old Man Coyote. For only those are ī'watkusū'a, one another's jokers (singular: ī'watkuce'), who would be of the same clan *if* descent were paternal. In other words, they are the sons and daughters of fellowclansmen.

There were two aspects to this relationship, a comic and a serious. On the one hand, ī'watkusū'a were allowed to play practical jokes with impunity. For instance, if a man recognized a wagon outside a house as his joking-relative's, the fancy might seize him to reverse front and rear wheels. Under ordinary circumstances the owner would show resentment, but not as soon as he discovers the identity of the joker: then he must not get angry, he merely bides his chance for getting even.

One ī'watkuce' might mock another who had made himself ridiculous. A certain good-looking young man married an old maid. Fire-weasel's wife, a joking-relative, then berated him: "You had better marry a frog or mouse or some other animal than an old maid. What is an old maid good for?" The man did not reply but sat there laughing. A man was derided for clinging to one wife, for always wearing old clothes, for returning from a raid without booty. His abusers might say, "You are a bad person; whatever you do, you are a bad person." Even without due cause, ī'watkusū'a might reproach one another. A man would tell a woman, "You are crazy, you are lecherous," and she might reply in kind. To a woman one said such things as: "You are not good enough to attract any man"; "You have never put up a tent"; "You have never beaded any blankets"; "You have been kidnapped again and again"; "You are exceedingly lazy, you never do beadwork or make moccasins for your husband."

Most significantly, the joking-relatives are a person's privileged mentors and censors when he has performed some veritably objectionable deed. In contrast to his own clan, whose function it is to shield him from social obloquy, the joking-relatives deliberately try to make a man ashamed by publicly jeering him and twitting him with his improper conduct. From others such mockery or rebuke would be an impertinence. At least in some measure the prerogative extends to sons of the *linked* clan; this, however, may lead to a conflict. For instance, Bull-tongue was a Newly-made Lodge, and his father a Thick Lodge. Since these are linked clans, all of Bull-tongue's clan and his own daughter would, by the extension, be on joking terms, which is contrary to the respect due to the paternal clan. The native view seems to be that in such a case only a little joking was proper.

A quaint usage permitted a man to cut off some of an i'wat-kuce''s hair. The parallel was drawn with a man's discarding a woman (p. 57), and here, too, a good horse was given away. Indeed, a person who lost a whole braid might receive four horses by way of indemnification. According to One-horn, the hair was given to a chief, who put it on a shield or a war shirt. Once two i'watkusū'a, Smoke and Hairy, after the fashion of jokers, were disputing about their coups. Suddenly Hairy got angry, cut off a long braid of hair from Smoke's head, and gave him his best horse. The son of a Whistling Water once met a female i'wat-kuce', cut off a lock of her hair, tied it to a long stick, and carried it about the camp, singing. The woman's two sons urged her to retaliate, so she once sneaked up behind him while he was seated, cut off some of *his* hair, and went through the same performance. She had received many presents from the man, and now gave him three horses. After the hair-cutting the persons involved ceased to joke with each other.

It was something of a disgrace to have one's hair cut in this way, and some, I heard, would have rather died than suffer this indignity. Women jokers never cut off each other's hair. A Crow who had rescued a fellow-tribesman in battle might save a man from thus having a lock clipped. If he walked up to the victim and said, "On such and such an occasion I saved a Crow, and now I will save you too," the prospective hair-cutter desisted.

Turning from a person's paternal clan to his own, the mother is addressed as i'gya' and spoken of as masa'kc', by both sexes. As noted, the former term includes the maternal *and* the paternal aunt, while as a reference term a distinct word marks off the father's sister. The two "mother" words embrace certain connections by marriage: since a father's brother is a "father," his wife naturally becomes a "mother"; and a woman addresses her husband's mother as though she were her own.

A Crow mother as a matter of course lavishes upon her children all her loving-kindness, intercedes on their behalf, and grieves over them with extravagant manifestations of sorrow. Traditionally, Spotted-rabbit's mother ranks as the supreme mourner. When her son was killed she did not have him buried for a very long time, but carried his corpse about when the Indians moved, leaving it a little ways from the camp. Then she would once more gash her arms and head. "When she wailed throughout the camp, all the people cried."

Parents are known as ak'e' (or ak'se'). They do not speak of their children by a specific kinship term but by the generic word for "child," or rather "offspring" (dāk', -rāk'), which also designates the young of an animal. This word is specialized as to sex by adding the words for man and woman; thus barā'k' (e) is "my child"; barā'k'-batse', "my son"; and barā'k'-bī'a, "my daughter."

When either parent addresses the child, a different stem is employed, "my son" becoming irō'oce, "my daughter" xū'utse. Quite logically, these words for speaking *to* and *of* a child are used not only by the actual parents, but also by those classed with them. Thus, a man, being a "father" to his brother's children, calls them irō'oce and xū'utse, respectively; and a woman correspondingly uses these words to her sister's offspring. Since, furthermore, my father's sister's son is "my father," this cousin addresses me, his mother's brother's child, as "son" or "daughter." This odd way of putting a relative of one's own generation into the one above or below, respectively, is impressed at an early age. In my hearing a four-year-old boy, Sunrise, called a two-year old girl, Good-skunk, his daughter. I asked him: "darā'-k'bīa cō?" (Where is your daughter?) At once he puckered up and protruded his lips towards Good-skunk, as Indians often do instead of pointing with the index-finger. In reality she was a daughter of his mother's brother; he, her father's sister's son.

There are also curious examples of generation leveling. My mother's brother and my mother's mother's brother are necessarily in my clan and perhaps for that reason are classed with my elder brothers,—for the Crow sharply distinguish between elder and younger brothers and sisters. Moreover, the sexes have each its own way of designating these relatives: bīikya' is a man's way of addressing an elder brother, maternal uncle, or maternal grandmother's brother; while a woman substitutes basā'are. For younger brothers both sexes use matsū'ka; and since the maternal uncle is regarded as an elder brother, he in turn naturally considers his sister's sons as younger brothers.

Sisters are also distinguished as to seniority. Both sexes may use either of two forms—basa'kā'ata or maku'kāta—for "my elder sister." The former is certainly the diminutive form of "my mother"; the latter probably the diminutive of the Hidatsa maku', "my grandmother." An elder addresses a younger sister as xū'-utse, as a parent does his or her daughter; an elder brother uses basa'tsī'ita, the word the maternal uncle also applies to his niece. In talking *about* her younger sister, a girl says "basō'oka."

All these terms may be applied, according to sex, to kinsfolk within one's clan; and generically a person refers to his or her blood or clan siblings as bacbatse', my men, and bacbī'a, my women. Both sexes mark out those of closer relationship as baku'pe (first person form; third person: aku'pe). Just how near a bond this implies is not certain. According to some, the child of a mother's sister or of a father's brother might be so reckoned. But others say that aku'pua would be brothers and sisters sharing at least one parent; and Flat-back went so far as to limit it to a full brother or sister. However this be, blood-brotherhood *can* be expressed by appropriate additions, e.g., isbī'a t'a'tse, his "straight" sister; aku'ptā're, his genuine sister.

The mutual attitude of close siblings shows the spirit of helpfulness that prevails among all clansmen, only to a greater degree. Sisters help one another, sometimes as wives of one husband, and make moccasins or finery for their brothers. It is mainly a bride's brothers that appropriate the horses presented to her family. The attachment of two brothers to each other is touchingly brought out in the story of a disabled warrior reluctantly abandoned by his fellow-braves. He bade his younger brother go home with the rest and comfort their parents. "The boy set out but returned to his brother. Instead of going farther he began to cry. 'If I leave my brother while he is still alive, I'll never forget that. I will not go, I'll stay with him.' So his comrades gave him . . . ammunition . . . and he returned to aid the crippled man."

An elder brother is the symbol of protection, so that a herald encouraging the camp before a battle will present a warrior selected for special valor as standing to the people in the relationship of an elder brother (p. 232). Again, we learn, Holds-the-tail "always gave all kinds of gifts to his brother, for he loved him"; and when Size-of-iron was killed, Holds-the-tail performed one of the last of Crow Sun Dances in his honor. An elder brother was vitally interested in his junior's fame. At a meeting of his military club Young-jackrabbit once refused a pipe that would have pledged him to reckless bravery; but his own elder brother seized him by the hair and forced him to touch the stem. "He wished me to die," Young-jackrabbit told me, "that is why he desired me to smoke the pipe." This, of course, implied no hostility whatsoever, merely the overpowering wish to see his kinsman become a great man.

The bond between siblings is so strong that the blood-sister of the camp tyrant, One-eye, did not shrink from roundly abusing him for an insult to her husband (see p. 58). This is really a most extraordinary situation, since normally a brother and sister for all their mutual affection are no longer free in conversation after childhood. Beginning with puberty, they may speak to each other on important matters, but are neither supposed to chat nor to be together by themselves. If a man enters his brother-in-law's lodge and finds his sister there all alone, he withdraws at once after conveying any important information he has to give. Leforge, who notes this taboo, adds that even today when sister and brother ride in the same wagon, she will not sit beside him but contents herself with the wagon-bed behind. This seems to be a more general rule, for about twenty years ago when I once had occasion to drive an Indian's wagon in the company of his wife and children, the woman would not sit at my side but took the position described by Leforge.

Notwithstanding this taboo, a sister often exerted influence on a man in dissuading him from marrying a woman she disliked and sometimes could make him divorce a wife of whom she strongly disapproved.

Grandparents are not distinguished according to the father's or mother's side, either in direct address or reference. The grandfather is called axe'-isaʷke by boys and masā'k-isaʷka by girls; talking about him, they would say, miru'px-isaʷke and masā'kisaꞌke, respectively. These are all simply combinations of the words for "father" with the term for "old man." For grandmother, both sexes have a single word, whether in address or reference,—masaꞌkāꞌare. This, too, is easily analyzed, being composed of the words for "my mother" and "old woman." The above-mentioned terms include kin of the grandparents' generation, e.g., the grandfather's brother and the grandmother's sister or mother's paternal aunt, respectively. It seems to be optional whether the maternal grandmother's brother is to be reckoned a grandfather according to his generation, or an elder brother according to his clan.

Strangely enough, grandparents have no special term for addressing their grandchildren, but like the children's parents use irōꞌoce to boys and xūꞌutse to girls. On the other hand, in talking *about* their grandchildren they say bacbāpiꞌte, my grandchild. The hero of one of the most popular of tales is named Old Woman's Grandchild, but when his adoptive grandmother speaks to him, she always addresses him "Son."

A child may also be spoken of as bacbāpiꞌte by his paternal aunt. This is intelligible enough, since this woman's son is addressed as father (p. 19). The cousin being in the parent's generation, *his* mother naturally ascends to a still higher plane.

Grandparents sometimes adopt children; and Leforge even has it as a standing custom that a young couple give the firstborn child as a present to the *father's* parents as soon as it can be weaned.

The method of addressing or referring to a spouse depends in some measure on the stability of the marriage. In no case are the specific words for "my husband" (batsireꞌ) and "my wife" (buꞌa) used in address. If the union is a permanent one, the spouses call each other by name or address each other as hēꞌha. In a tale a young man rapes a buffalo-cow stuck in the mud, and goes off. She subsequently gives birth to a boy and when he is grown together the two go to seek his father. They reach camp, and the buffalo-woman bids her son address her one-time lover as his father. The man asks, "Why am I your father?" The boy takes him to his mother, who then upbraids her lover: "Why don't you recognize your child? Indians are wont to know all their children." "That is so, yet I am single, so I did not know him." She reminds him of their dalliance and adds: "You said

'hē′ha!'" He sits pondering for a while and recalls his amour
with the cow and how he had called her "hē′ha." He then takes
the buffalo-woman into his lodge, and they get married for good.

When a marriage is considered unstable, demonstratives are
employed in speaking to and about a spouse. But they do not
seem to be restricted to such unions. Thus, the wife of an informant always spoke of him as "that old man."

There is evidently a good deal of latitude in these cases;
moreover, extensions of meaning occur. A man calls not only
his wife but also her sister hē′ha, only so long, however as she
remains a possible wife, for when married to another she is addressed by name and may be spoken of as So-and-so's wife. A
woman may call her husband or sister's husband hira′, instead
of hē′ha, and also barū′aritse; she may likewise refer to her
husband as "the boy's father."

Several designations are clearly derivative. From u′a, his
wife (bu′a, my wife) we get bu′aka, my brother's wife or mother's
brother's wife, where the final a is changed to e for reference instead of address. For the latter it is allowable to use the sister-
in-law's name. A woman may also address her sister's husband
and her husband's brother by name, but other forms are optional:
if he is older, she might regard him as an elder brother; if
younger, he is sometimes spoken to as a younger brother or even
by the term for son. In reference, "my husband's brother" is
bactsite′. A man designates his wife's younger sister as bu′a-
karicta, my young wife; a wife's elder sister as bu′a-wā-ise′, my
wife's old one.

A man is on terms of the greatest familiarity with his own
brother's or clansman's wife. Similarly, he may treat his wife's
sister with the utmost license, e.g., raising her dress so as to expose her nakedness; and she may jest with him in corresponding
fashion. In 1916 I spent a good deal of time in the camp of one
informant, who was forever fondling and teasing his wife's
younger sister, while she returned his treatment in kind. They
were not in the least embarrassed by the wife's or my presence
nor by that of an adult son by a previous marriage of the man's.
It is only a man of outstanding chastity that would forgo such
prerogatives with a sister-in-law (see p. 319). On the other hand,
Gray-bull held it proper to put a stop to such behavior when his
wife's sister got married to another man; he remained on speak-

ing terms but no longer joked or played with her. According to
Linderman, a real taboo develops in such cases, even to the point
of barring conversation.

A man is extremely circumspect in the presence of his
brother-in-law, whom he addresses as bā'aci and refers to as
barā'ace. These terms embrace the wife's mother's brother as
well as the wife's brother and the sister's husband, since a maternal uncle always figures as an elder brother. Two brothers-in-
law are supposed to be extremely friendly and to exchange gifts.
They are permitted to speak lightly on impersonal matters, but
under no condition must they bandy personal remarks savoring
of obscenity. There is apparently no objection to telling an
obscene myth before a brother-in-law, but according to Leforge
even this was deemed gravely indecorous. The bond and the
taboos linked with it sometimes outlast the marriage on which
the relationship rests. On the other hand, adoption into a society
might transform a brother-in-law into a "son." A distinction is
drawn between the wife's own brother and her remote kinsmen
addressed by the same term. It is her closest "brothers" that enjoy the greatest respect, while some jesting is possible with the
others, especially on military matters. Thus, White-man-runs-
him married one of Old-dog's clan sisters, and the two men would
jocularly say to each other, "You have never been on a war
party." Similarly, Gray-bull was wont to chaff Scolds-the-bear,
who was at a disadvantage, being afraid to respond because of
Gray-bull's superior prestige as a warrior.

Even in such distant relationships of the brother-in-law
category personal allusions to sex are rigorously barred. I once
pretended to be Arm-round-the-neck's brother-in-law, but mis-
pronounced the proper term of address so that it was mistaken
for a reference to my informant's genitalia. Playing the assumed
part, he at once dealt me a light blow. Even outsiders respect
this taboo. A man at once breaks off a ribald remark if he sees
his victim's brother-in-law entering the scene. If the speaker
is unaware of the fact, a bystander warns him, otherwise the
person addressed will himself correct the jester, who forthwith
stops and feels severely rebuked. If a man wants to make another the butt of an obscene remark in the presence of his wife's
clansman, this "brother-in-law" may be requested to go away.
Otherwise the clansman strikes the joker for making the com-

ment in his presence. Failing that, the person jested with says to his brother-in-law, "Strike him, or I'll strike *you*."

There are no corresponding customs between two sisters-in-law. They do not joke with each other and may address each other by name; or the older calls the other "daughter," and is addressed as "elder sister" (maku'kata). If of about the same age, they are likely to apply to each other the term hī'ra, used with any female comrade. In reference, "my husband's sister" is baku'a; my brother's wife, basbī'akaricta, my young sister (really, woman). A woman is likely to give presents to her brother's wife. She resents infidelity on this sister-in-law's part and may, after a quarrel with her, prevail upon her brother to divorce his wife (see p. 26).

In a man's own generation there are connections he must definitely avoid,—the wives of his wife's brothers. For example, Bear-crane had a son named Old-crane and a daughter married to Bird; and there was never any conversation between Bird and Old-crane's wife. They were each other's uce' (plural usu'a),— a generic expression for all tabooed relatives. Leforge tells a characteristic anecdote. While out flirting one day, he unwittingly pulled aside the blanket of a woman and tapped her on the shoulder, only to discover that it was his brother-in-law's wife. Leforge's adoptive mother made him indemnify the affronted woman's husband by the gift of a beautiful shirt.

There are no restrictions on the social intercourse of a woman and her parents-in-law. She treats and addresses them as though they were her own parents. In speaking of them she has the option of using either the parent term or the expressions for "my old man" and "my old woman."

On the other hand, a definite taboo precludes any conversation or close contact with a wife's mother or her grandmothers; and, reciprocally, a woman neither speaks to her granddaughter's or daughter's husband nor looks at him. If there are several unrelated wives, the prohibition extends to their respective mothers and grandmothers; on the other hand, it includes not only the son-in-law but also his brothers, though apparently not his more remote kinsmen. Moreover, a man is not expected to pronounce a word that enters into his mother-in-law's name; and according to Leforge the woman never utters the son-in-law's. Theoretically a man's usu'a include his father-in-law, but this prohibition is clearly less stringent.

In 1907 I experienced a good sample of the relevant behavior. I was in the tent of David Stewart, my interpreter, and wished to draw out his mother-in-law concerning the games played in her youth. Though she was only a few feet away, Stewart did not ask her directly, but put each question to his wife, who repeated it to her mother and then repeated the answer to her husband. In 1910 James Carpenter did not speak to his wife's mother or grandmother and would not pronounce the Crow word for "to mark, to write" because his mother-in-law's name was Marks-plainly. In 1931 he still kept up these taboos. Even a man of preponderantly white blood may maintain the rule, presumably in deference to the old woman's feelings (p. x). On the other hand, whatever taboos once held between a man and his wife's father have lost ground. Carpenter, with all his reverential attitude towards old tribal custom, conversed with his father-in-law, Flat-head-woman, as far back as 1914. It was also permissible to utter his name, though to do so in his presence would not be polite. However, even nowadays Carpenter's sons-in-law do not speak to him more than is necessary.

The taboos described are never conceived as the expression of hostility, but rather of the utmost respect. A substantial gift can, however, sometimes abrogate the taboo. If a man gives two or three horses to either parent-in-law, the ban may be lifted; according to one informant, a donation of a hundred dollars might suffice. Further, abolition of the customary rule occurs particularly after a wife's death; then her mother may absolve her son-in-law from all prohibitions by addressing him as "son," whereupon his relationship to her is assumed to have become filial and is not dissolved even if he should remarry. It is also possible for the son-in-law to take the initial step.

There was some variation in this procedure. Sometimes gifts were offered, yet the taboo persisted. Thus, Gray-bull once gave a horse to his father-in-law, and another to his mother-in-law, but spoke only to the former thereafter. The same informant gave his son-in-law Yellow-brow one or two horses, pronouncing the formula of adoption: "You, too, I shall make my child." Since then he would speak to Yellow-brow and smoke with him as if he were his son, but Gray-bull's wife was not affected by this arrangement.

All the taboos holding for affinities were likely to be affected by widowerhood or divorce. Young-crane's daughter had been married to Gray-bull's son Grasshopper. When the young woman died, her mother told Gray-bull of her intentions so that he could prepare his son, then she gave the widower a colt, spoke to him, and ever after treated him as a son, living with him and taking care of his daughter. Oddly enough, though Grasshopper subsequently conversed at ease with the old woman, his own brothers, White-hip and Cuts, who had been included in the prohibitions, failed to do so. They no longer avoided her, yet they would not speak with her any more than was necessary. Gray-bull told me that since his last wife's death he no longer avoided the wives of *all* her "brothers"; "My wife was the reason for my not talking to them, so now that she is gone I talk to them." However, he was not consistent, for he admitted still shunning the wives of his wife's own brothers or of her close kinsmen in the same category. Here again, then, the proximity of a relationship determines behavior. The same informant had been married five times. After a divorce he would cease to avoid his former wife's mother.

Intense as is the aversion to any unseemly conduct towards a man's mother-in-law, Plains Indian fancy has played with the idea of converting avoidance into its antithesis. In a Crow story, shared with the Assiniboine and Pawnee, a hunter urinates and asks his member whether it sees buffalo. It answers affirmatively and incessantly repeats the reply, threatening to continue until it is touched by his mother-in-law, who agrees to extricate her son-in-law from his plight. Still more characteristic is a Crow tale, also told by the Arapaho, in which Old Man Coyote craftily induced his wife's mother to accompany him on a war party and got an accomplice to intimidate her into yielding to the trickster's embraces.

III. From Cradle to Grave

BIRTH AND INFANCY

For a woman in labor the Indians planted two sticks into the ground at the head of her pillow and piled up soft comforters beneath. She knelt, spreading her legs wide apart, with her elbows resting on the pillow, and seized the two sticks. According to Gray-bull, all obstetricians were once women, but in recent times some men ranked among the most skilful practitioners. The husband was not present during his wife's travail. Indeed, no males, not even boys, were ordinarily allowed in the lodge lest their presence delay the delivery. Otherwise the husband was not subject to any taboo.

Gray-bull's wife learnt how to treat confinement cases from a visionary, to whom she paid a horse, and she regarded this information as a secret. She used a combination of a root and a horned-toad, which she would rub down the patient's back. In order to hasten a delivery, another witness said, the attendants gave the expectant mother a drink from the juice of some weed and held her tight above the abdominal region. Muskrat claimed knowledge of two roots easing a delivery, both having been revealed to her while mourning her husband and a brother, respectively. On the first occasion, a supernatural came up to her in her sleep and said, "Chew that weed (batse'kice; literally, man-imitation), and you will give birth without suffering." She boiled the leaves and drank the infusion, but she was not supposed to pull up the plant except for doctoring. The second time she was granted a plant called bice'-waru'ci-se (literally, buffalo-do-not-eat-it) and was told that it was even more effective than the first. Whenever any one touched Muskrat's face or body with it, she went into a trance from which she recovered by chewing the weed (see p. 265).

Not the doctor, but one of the women present, cut off all but three fingers' breadth of the navel cord. The part of a girl's navel cord that dropped off was rolled up in a piece of cloth and put into a beaded sack, to be fastened to her cradleboard. When she was old enough to wear an elk-tooth dress, this bag was tied to its back.

Obstetricians received generous fees. During one of my visits the Gray-bull couple were offered a cow if they should consent to treat a woman in childbed. Once Gray-bull's wife successfully doctored a woman whom two practitioners previously called had failed to relieve. The patient's kin gave her one horse, a blanket, four comforters, some new calico, and some money. When she herself was confined, Gray-bull paid the obstetrician three horses.

After parturition the mother received a portion of pemmican with fat, which she ate just once. For several days she abstained from cooked meat and was not allowed to stoop.

There were no special beliefs about twins, and Gray-bull had never heard of Crow triplets.

About two days after the delivery the mother pierced the infant's ears with a heated awl and stuck a greased stick through the perforations. When the wounds had healed, earrings were inserted. There was no ceremonial ear-piercing. The Crow cradle was a tapering board covered with skin, the pocket being tied by three pairs of beaded flaps with strings. This feature gives it a certain individuality among Plains Indian papoose-boards. It also differs from its closest equivalents among the Blackfoot, Nez Perce, Shoshone and Ute in being decidedly more angular at the top (Fig. 1).

Fig. 1.—Model of Crow cradle, showing characteristically angular top and beaded flaps.

In rocking their babies to sleep women often sing lullabies originally revealed in a dream or overheard by an ancestor when chancing upon some female animal putting her offspring to sleep or in some similar situation. Pretty-shield recently told Mr. Linderman about a song of this type which she herself had heard an antelope sing when bereft of her young. Of lullabies I recorded, one was attributed to a bear, another to a dog, the third to a wolf, the last mentioned being the most popular. It was revealed to a mother mourning the death of her child at the season when animals were giving birth to their young. On top of a wolf den, she saw a whelp big enough to come out of the hole and heard the young ones singing a song. She returned to camp. After a while she gave birth to a boy and a girl and would sing this song to them so often that they learnt it by heart and sang it in play till all the children knew it. These are the words:

awē'raxkēta   bāwasā'acīwa,
On the hillside   I was running,

bacū'ca   daxē'tsixēre
My knee   was skinned.

tsēt'   ā'cu   tsi'cikyāta,[1]   tsēt' ā'cu tsi'cikyāta,
The wolf   mask   wearer,   the wolf mask wearer,

awaku'saat   ē'rusak'
On the other side cannot ease himself.

īs   ara'papēi;   awak' ō'wate   barappē'kyāta
His face   itches;   in all seasons   he kills,

ciwi-cī'kyatāwe.
He gets yellow with fat.

mi'cgy   iaxba'sūrake   ōpī'rake,   ha'ha, hu'hu, ha'ha, hu'hu.
The dogs when sated   smoke,   ha'ha, hu'hu.

(Free translation: I was running on the hillside and skinned my knee. The wolf-mask wearer [or, The red-headed wolf] cannot ease himself on the other side from here. His face is itching, he kills something in all seasons of the year and gets yellow with fat. The dogs, when sated, smoke.[2]

CHILDHOOD

The Crow are not in the habit of punishing children by beating them. When a child continues crying for a long time, the parents put it on its back and pour water down its nose. If on some later occasion the child begins to cry, they simply say, "Bring the water!" That is usually enough to make him desist.

In general children had a free and easy life. Among Graybull's earliest reminiscences were the hunting of birds and chas-

---

[1] Also given as hi'cikyāta, altering the sense to "the red-headed wolf."
[2] This was cryptically explained to refer to coyotes envying dogs, which smoked when they had had their fill.

ing of butterflies. In the winter the boys, possibly accompanied by girls, often went afoot, killing all the rabbits they could. When near camp, they roasted or boiled their game. The one who had shot a rabbit got the best parts, the others throwing it on the marksman's back. If a boy allowed a rabbit to get out of the brush, his mates shot a hole through his jacket by way of teaching him to be more careful in the future. Boys sometimes divided into sides which competed as to the number of birds shot. Whoever killed the first bird announced it with a shout. The losers had to crack the live birds' skulls with their teeth and to chew the feet, legs, and wings. Opposite sides also gathered birds' eggs and pelted each other with them.

Archery was the typical boys' game. When the old woman in the Grandchild myth wishes to determine the sex of a youthful intruder, she puts into her garden a twofold bait,—a bow with arrows as well as a shinny stick and ball; since it is the bow and arrows that disappear, she knows it must have been a boy. In the early spring the youngsters would say, "Let us shoot at a grass target." They then gathered up pŭ′pua grass, making a bundle about a foot long and thicker at one end, and tied it together with sinew or, if away from camp, with willow bark. This target was laid down on a hillside, possibly 40 feet away. The players divided into sides and wagered their arrows. Each side shot off four or five arrows, and whoever came closest to the target took all the opponents' arrows. As a sequel they threw the wisp into the air and tried to hit it. According to Simms, an archer who had hit the grass at a distance took it between the index and second finger of the left hand, crossing and resting on the arrow, which was ready to shoot but pointed downward. Raising bow and arrow with the grass bundle still resting on it, he released it and shot. If he hit it in the air, he won an arrow. According to one informant it was the less expert marksmen who threw the grass up rather than let it glide down. Some players stuck an arrow into the wrapping of the grass bundle, but they were regarded as cheating and barred from the game.

There were several variants; for instance, "throwing a buffalo chip." One boy rolled a chip pierced in the center, and his mates shot at it. They staked arrows, the winner being the one who shot through the center or closest to it. Usually there were three or four players on each side. In another form of archery contest, a boy swung over his head a buffalo lung fastened to a strip of rawhide. The other players shot at it, pretending that they were chasing wild buffalo.

Similar games were played by grown-ups. Sometimes ten adult players, five on each side, engaged in "arrow-throwing." That is, they shot at an arrow thrown by one of them, and in order to score it was necessary to hit it or come nearest to it. Tally-sticks (baraki'ce) served as counters, the winner being the one who got all of them. At the close of the game, one informant said, all the arrows were piled up and the marksman who shot into the sheaf took them all. Towards evening two arrows were likely to be set up in the form of a cross, with others leaning against them. Any arrow thrown against this target and failing to touch it was added to the bunch. Sometimes as many as a hundred men took part, whoever hit the target winning all the arrows. One or two watchers at the goal, including boys, received as their fee some of the shafts that lacked a point or feather or were otherwise damaged.

To return to juvenile amusements, boys might go to the side of a creek and throw stones into the air, making them come down with a splash. They tried to recite the words "icbirikyū' bābi-rikyū'p" so that the last syllable would coincide exactly with the splashing of the water. Another pastime was to throw a ring of willow bark into the middle of a creek, opposite sides facing each other on the banks. The players would get their clothes wet, for each leader tried to catch the ring with a hooked stick and to drag his opponent into the water. Again, while swimming, boys would throw stones or sticks far out into the stream and bid one of their number fetch them. If he failed, the others threw him into the water, saying, "I'll make him look for his beaver."

In the spring the boys would put mud at the end of sticks, throwing it at one another. At night, for a variant, they attached live coals to the mud, which caused a swelling in the parts struck.

A returning hunter sometimes brought a buffalo calf for his children, who would either pretend to hunt it or keep it as a pet with a rope round its neck, little ones riding it double. After a hunt, boys themselves rode around looking for calves without mothers, killed them with arrows, and brought home the meat, giving their girl playmates the skins as coverings for their toy tipis.

In some amusements boys and girls regularly joined. Particularly from about ten years of age on, they would mimic the life of their elders. For example, when the camp moved, the children traveled apart, and girls from prosperous families, who owned small tipis, transported them in imitation of their mothers. Boys approached, and their herald announced, "Boys, offer a horse to the girl you want to marry." Then they would ride double with their favorites. When the adults pitched camp, the mock caravan at some distance did likewise. They played at married life. The boys went to their parents to get food for their "wives." After picketing their horses they supped, and after dark each went to his real home in camp. This game, called calf-skin tipi (nā'xapāsu'a), was specifically ascribed to the Hammers (p. 202), a boys' club patterned on the men's organizations. Imitation of their elders went so far that the members divided into opposite sides to abduct each other's "wives"; and if any one took his kidnapped "wife" back, the rival party seized the blankets of all his associates and tied them to sticks (see p. 189). The boys would also stage a triumphant return from a war party. If some of them had killed a coyote or wolf, they carried back a lock of its hair, and the girls were to dance with this "scalp." They went through the same performance with the head and other parts of a rabbit, tying them to long poles for the purpose (for the real scalp-dance, see p. 225).

The girls had little shields to play with,—just as their mothers were custodians of the real ones. A girl would make a male doll, show it to a boy visitor, and tell him, "That's you." Then he would bring her some food. Or, she might take the doll to her friend's lodge, and throw it in, saying, "There's your son!" The boy's mother then gave her beads or other presents. Several girls might pay a joint visit to a boy, announcing, "We are coming to you." His family then invited them in and gave them something to eat, whereupon the visitors lay down with the little boy as though they were his wives. When food was plentiful in camp, such a bevy might enter a boy's lodge, one by one, dance and sing, and each receive some pemmican from his mother. Sometimes a group of boys paid a joint visit to the household of one of their own number, singing victory songs at the entrance. They, too, would then receive pemmican from the inmates.

Naturally, boys and girls were not always in perfect amity. When girls were moving their mock camps, Young-crane recalled, boys on horseback would swoop down on them, knocking down their tipi and absconding with it. The girls would give pursuit, possibly recovering their lodge and sleeping in it during the night. Again, the girls packed dogs and led them around; and when the boys approached, the dogs would bark and scare them away. The sexes often were pitted against each other in a game with a big dry hide, perforated along the border and with a rope run through the holes. A representative of each group stood on the hide and ran round on it while each side pulled in opposite directions. If either got dizzy and stepped off the hide, his side lost. In one form of this pastime, played at night, the players lowered the couple four times, then threw them up into the air; the one able to stand up would win. It happened that sometimes the girl would throw the boy off while they were in the air.

Shinny is associated with the female sex, but it was more definitely a game for adult women and will be described under another head (p. 101 f.). However, there were other strenuous amusements for girls, including "ball-kicking." The player kicked the ball about two feet from the ground and then kicked it up, continuing so long as she did not miss it. There were stakes on the result. Specimens of balls collected by Mr. Simms for the Field Museum in Chicago consisted of a bladder filled with antelope hair and enclosed in a sinew network; the diameter was from 6¾ to 8½ inches. In another game, "kicking each other's soles," all the girls except one were seated with outstretched legs. The player standing up had her eyes closed and kicked at the feet of one of the others. Then she took on her back the sitter she struck and carried her far away. Thus she carried off one after another. After kicking, she would open her eyes.

To return to the boys, there were several winter sports. For awō′xarua, eight or ten buffalo ribs—usually those of a cow— were fastened together and covered with rawhide, and on this toboggan a boy would coast downhill. This diversion was not restricted to children; a young man would get a woman to toboggan with him, put his legs around her, and say, "I am eloping with her," as they were sliding down. If she was known as a wanton, he rested his legs on her shoulders. In case she did not like her companion, she would seize him by the hair and try to throw him off. Sometimes children upset such coasting couples.

Boys liked to spin tops (binna′ce) on the snow when it was several inches in depth, and girls also played at this game. A top was usually of cylindrical shape merging into a cone at the bottom. With a buckskin lash attached to a stick the player cleared the ground of snow, and with this whip he set the top spinning. Boys tried to make it go all the way round, each wanting to outdo the others in keeping it going the longest time. If one top upset another, its owner won and cried out, "You are knocked out!" Some cheated by substituting stone for wooden tops. These toys themselves served as stakes. Well-to-do parents made the best kind of tops for their sons, but these had to watch lest they were stolen by playmates. Sometimes the children first spun the tops, then raced to a distant goal. Footraces in general were popular, though horse-racing probably became even more so in later times.

The game described by some authors on Indian tribes as "snow-snake" appeared in several forms. For one of them a boy peeled a young willow stick, twisted the bark round it, and held it over a fire. Thus he produced alternately blackened and white spaces, the latter being painted red with property marks. Each player had ten or fifteen of these sticks and hurled his darts so they would touch the earth and then fly up. Whoever threw his dart farthest was the winner and took his opponents' sticks. Dave Stewart once won as many as one hundred and fifty. In such a case the lucky player was considered stingy if he picked up all his winnings himself; it was proper to have poor boys collect them for him and to let these boys have all but the longest sticks as their fee.

The snow-snake pastime was considered a variant of "throwing the horn" (āc-xaru′ci-re′′kyua), in which the dart used was of cherry wood and somewhat longer than a man's arm. The end was of horn, taken from a four-year buffalo or from the middle prong of an elk, and had been boiled, scraped and greased to facilitate sliding. The game was played on tough baked ground where spear-grass grew, and a slight elevation was essential. A player swung his dart in the air, horn end forward, and let go so it flew as far as possible and slid after striking the ground. Either arrows or the darts themselves were the stakes. Boys who had wagered their best horn darts were sometimes loath to give them up and tried to abscond with them. In an Old Man Coyote story the Trickster offered his dart in payment for the power to produce food by magic.

Doubtless children played various other games in direct imitation of adults, but "magpie" (ī'pia-reksu'a, impersonating magpies) was distinctively a boys' amusement. When there was plenty of meat in camp, they would assemble and go where there was black mud. With this they would daub their hands, legs, bodies, and faces till they could not be recognized, roll up their hair, and blacken it to look like bears' ears. They would select the fastest runner, sing over him, paint him all over with mud, and twist his breechclout so it would not impede him. All would then line up and dash for the camp, where the meat was hanging up. The people knew what was coming and would hide their meat if they could, but the boys would snatch what they were able to reach and make their escape, with old women after them in hot pursuit. Later one of the party would go back for buffalo chips. Then seated in the shade by a river bank, a fire was built, their spoils roasted, and the cooked food piled on leaves, where two boys cut it up. Someone would ask, "Who got this meat?" If it was some prized delicacy, like a tongue, its thief got the first chance to eat it. The others would say, "He is the best one"; and he himself would vow, "The next time, even if I get a drubbing, I'll try to get a good piece again." Gray-bull says that they imitated the military clubs: the four who had stolen the best meat were picked out, and each held up his booty, whereupon these prizes were put in the center on fresh boughs for the captors to eat in a little circle of their own.

When everyone had eaten, a herald would announce that whoever might be the first one to get up the rest would wipe their greasy hands on him. Each one kept some fat from the feast, or fat was set boiling for that very purpose. For a while all sat still, at last some one, a small boy probably, would forget himself and rise. Then all would leap up, one of the larger boys rubbing his hands with fat and wiping it on the transgressor, the rest following suit. When the victim jumped into the creek, the water would glide off the grease. Then they might while away the time chasing butterflies, and if a boy caught one he rubbed it on his chest because that would make him a swift runner. In the meantime the women in camp would prepare chips of meat with which to pelt the returning thieves, who would throw them back at the women.

Another prank was stealing the two outside poles of a lodge in the night. The inmates would give chase and the thieves had to run fast for if overtaken they lost their blankets. This was done for sheer mischief.

Frequently two boys formed a peculiarly close tie of friendship, each becoming the other's ī'rapa'tse. Such intimacy continued into adult life and might even take precedence of other loyalties (see p. 10). Comrades exchanged valuable gifts, went to war together, and shared each other's sweethearts,—the relationship then becoming specifically that of "little fathers" (p. 19). The bond, in fact, might affect even the next generation. A comrade's children called Gray-bull "father" and gave presents to his wife. In modern parlance the term ī'rapa'tse is loosely used, corresponding to "partner" in Western slang. Men who married sisters used it to each other without considering themselves related.

The corresponding friendship between women was less significant, but a term, hī'ra, was applied to a woman by her female intimates.

NAMES

Personal names were not distinctive either of clan or sex. Four days, or thereabouts, after the birth of a child the father might name it, but more commonly he invited a person of distinction for the purpose,—usually a noted warrior. The name was to reflect some experience of the godfather's, hence women as well as men bore names reminiscent of some feat of arms. For example, one woman was named Cuts-the-picketed-mule; another, Captures-the-medicine-pipe; a third, Pretty-enemy. Visionary experiences likewise determined the name-giver's choice; thus, Medicine-crow called a daughter of James Carpenter's "Walks-with-her-dress" because he had once seen a supernatural being bearing that name. Girls were sometimes named by old women but this was by no means a predominant custom.

The following illustrates the procedure followed. Once a man asked Bull-chief to name a newborn girl, in memory of that warrior's hardest fight. Bull-chief smoked some wild-carrot root (see p. 63) for incense, raised the infant aloft to symbolize the wish that she should grow up, and finally called her "Captures-the-medicine-pipe." It was customary to lift the baby four times, a little higher each time. The incense was held towards the face, which was painted red. Bull-chief had once rushed towards the enemy and snatched away a medicine-pipe protruding from their fortifications, and this exploit he commemorated in the name conferred on the little girl. On another occasion he gave a boy a name suggested in a dream. He also named his own grandson "His-coups-are-dangerous" to represent a coup he had struck under such dangerous circumstances that no other Crow had struck after him.

A godfather either received compensation on the spot, or the parents would say, "If this boy ever walks, he will give you a horse." If the child proved sickly, the godfather gave him a new name; and if the infant's condition then failed to mend, another man was asked to rename him.

Women rarely changed their names except after a namesake's death. Cuts-the-picketed-mule had formerly borne the same name as Medicine-crow's mother; when the latter died, her son dubbed her after a deed of his, viz., the cutting loose of two picketed mules. A woman who had thrown away her husband at a dance (see p. 57) bought the name of Ara'xinetc, originally that of a distinguished man. Subsequently, Muskrat purchased this name, paying a horse for it.

Men, according to Gray-bull, did not change names because of a namesake's death, but frequently did so after some creditable deed. My informant himself was known as "Last-bull" from birth, but after his first coup his fellow-clansmen called him after a famous warrior in his father's clan, who received a horse as his fee. Bull-chief's birth name, Bull-weasel, was derived from a weasel vision experienced by a clansman of his father's. However, when adult he did not enjoy a good reputation, having come home empty-handed from a raid. Subsequently his own father had a buffalo vision, called in my informant, and said to him, "I will make a man of you." He told him to take a bath and smoke himself with incense on coming in again. Then he painted his son yellow all over, put a red eagle feather on his head, and drew two slanting lines across his arms, one to bring luck in coups, the other in the capture of guns. "These two things," said he, "are what we like among our people. If you perform these deeds, I shall rename you. The first time you strike an undisputed coup and also get a gun, either then or later, I'll give you a new name. 'Bull-weasel' is not a good name for you, so you had better have it changed." The young man went out with the first war party, took the enemy's gun and struck him. When he got back, his father called him "Bull-chief." He became a captain and ranked as a very brave man. Bear-gets-up, originally known as Many-foxes, also performed a creditable deed and was then named after one of his father's brothers who had been killed. Thereafter he never used his first name, though he might have done so if he chose.

In common parlance, nicknames might supersede the formally given names. They were sometimes conferred because of some peculiarity of behavior. Thus, Old-dog was so called for leading an old dog to carry his moccasins on the warpath; correspondingly, another man was labeled Tough-necked Dog; and a third became Small-whetstone for wearing such a one round his neck. Some sobriquets were of definitely obscene character.

Frequently a nickname was given not because of the prospective bearer's idiosyncrasies but after the behavior of his paternal clansfolk (p. 21). For example, a certain woman pretended to be lying with a man but had merely laid beside her an unfolded *parfleche,* which she addressed in whispered words. Discovering her deceit, the inmates of the lodge named not her but a clan niece of hers "Lying-with-a-dry-hide." Another woman in a fit of anger once hit herself over the head with a stone club. Accordingly, one of her brother's children was named Hits-herself-over-the-head.

SEX LIFE AND MARRIAGE

Though neither boys nor girls underwent any initiation ceremony at puberty, first and subsequent menstrual periods in girls involved certain disabilities. Women in this condition formerly rode inferior horses and evidently this loomed as a source of contamination, for they were not allowed to approach either a wounded man or men starting on a war party. A taboo still lingers against their coming near sacred objects at these times. In the summer of 1931 the owner of such a bundle kept it on his back porch. There, he felt, it was less likely to be defiled by female visitors, who nowadays no longer announce their condition so as to permit removal of the medicines. In the winter time the bundle was locked up in an inner chamber.

According to Bull-chief and others, girls were often married before puberty; some informants went so far as to say that a girl's playmates poked fun at her if she were still single at the time of her first menses. Young-crane assured me that she herself had been married when still immature to the husband of her elder sister.

Strangely enough, opinion differs as to whether women had to dwell apart during their indisposition. Child-in-his-mouth and his wife circumstantially described the procedure. Such women, they averred, stayed in a special tipi and abstained from meat for four days, their sustenance being wild roots. When they had recovered, they bathed, got new clothes, smoked them over a fire of evergreen leaves, put them on, and returned to their homes. Yet most of the natives flatly denied the use of menstrual huts. On the other hand, Leforge, who lived among the Crow for years, discreetly mentions willow shelters to which married women repaired "at certain times" for a few nights, after which they took a sweat-bath and purified themselves with incense before returning to their lodges.

As already explained, members of the same clan were not supposed to marry or to have sex relations. A person who broke the rule was derided: people spoke as though he had married his sister even if there was only a remote relationship by blood or none at all. They would say, "ara'xuic kyawī'ky," "The part of his body above the genitals is bad," which seems to mean, "He is a lecher,"—a phrase also applied to one who took liberties with other tabooed women. In such marriages, Gray-bull remarked, children would belong simultaneously to their father's and their mother's clan, which reflection greatly amused him. It well might lead to odd results, since an individual normally owed such different duties to the paternal and to his own kin, with correspondingly distinct attitudes on their part toward him. Merging the two would thus lead to confusion.

Gray-bull's own son, who was present during the interview at which the subject was broached, had married a clanswoman, and his father felt that he deserved being laughed at. In such a case, a man's brothers-in-law (see p. 29) would be his own clansmen, i.e., his "brothers," who would tease him by addressing him as "brother-in-law." Similarly, they would mock his wife by calling her "my sister-in-law." The point is clear: an adult sister must be treated respectfully and is only addressed when it is necessary, while a sister-in-law is pre-eminently the person with whom a man bandies obscenity. Joking-relatives (see p. 22) in their delicate way would tell the husband that he had *no* brother-in-law, that his own rump was his brother-in-law; "Turn around and speak to your brother-in-law."

In 1912 informants could recall very few transgressions of exogamy within their memory. Gray-bull knew of six cases,— three of them in the Greasy-inside-the-mouth clan, two among the Whistling Waters, one between Thick Lodge people. Another authority added Curly's father (Bad War Honors) and Bobtail-wolf (Spotted Lodge). The older Indians were apologetic about recent instances, which they blamed on the system of sending boys and girls to boarding-schools away from the Reservation, where they could marry each other without suspecting any clan bond between them.

But this was not the only tie held to bar sexual intercourse. A person ought not to marry any one who stood to him in the relationship of "parent" or "child." Since a father's clansmen were all "fathers," union with one of them was ruled out. Specifically, a woman could not marry her father's sister's son— the cousin she called "father" (p. 19). However, here there was a difference of opinion. Young-crane puritanically adhered to the principle, declined offers of Sore-lip men for that reason, and was shocked into leaving a husband who took a "daughter" for a supplementary wife—even though this girl was related to him only through his marrying Young-crane (see p. 55). Old-woman corroborated the view that marrying into a paternal clan was as bad as marrying into one's own: she herself had been made the butt of raillery by joking-relatives for transgressing the rule. But others held no such extreme opinions. One-blue-bead's father and his wife had both been xu'xkaraxtse; that is, he married a "paternal aunt," who prior to his marriage addressed him as a "son." Ralph Saco's maternal grandfather, father, and wife were all xu'xkaraxtse, so that father and son both took wives from the paternal clan. Again, Bull-chief had two wives of the Newly-made Lodge clan, to which his father belonged.

From all relevant statements heard I infer that it was not ideal to wed a paternal clanswoman, but that little was said about it *provided* there was no close blood-relationship.

Sexual behavior was largely dominated by a double standard, which, however, was rather different from that of the Victorian era. That is to say, women were admired for immaculate purity, but they did not become outcasts by departing from the ideal. During the Sun Dance the honorific office of tree-notcher was conferred only on a married woman of irreproachable fidelity, and in the same ceremony the leader of the firewood expedition was expected to be equally chaste (pp. 312, 315). Even minor positions of religious character were held inconsistent with looseness. When I quoted a certain old woman's claim that she had filled such a post, my informant scoffed at the idea: Why, the Crow would never dream of choosing someone who was always running around with men. However, even a wanton was never ostracized, she simply lost prestige. Human frailty was too great to permit every one to be perfect. In 1931 Yellow-brow volunteered some reflections on the difference between White and Indian ethics. Was Old Man Coyote, the culture hero and trickster of Crow mythology, the equivalent of God or of the Devil? God laid down the Ten Commandments, Old Man Coyote did the opposite. The only thing the Indians held sacred [in sex life] was a bāwuroke', a virtuous woman; for the rest, one followed one's natural bent for pleasure according to Old Man Coyote's example.

In 1907 when at Crow Agency I saw a visiting Sioux woman, who was pointed out to me as a virginal spinster and one who as such was highly esteemed by her people. I have never myself encountered the Crow equivalent of this phenomenon, but it is vouched for by Leforge. He describes "a medicine woman and a prophet," Two-moons, who persistently declined to marry, though highly proficient as a tanner and bead-worker. "The people all held her in high regard, looking upon her as a chaste maiden." One day Leforge asked her when she would marry him. She looked around and asked him whether he saw the leaves of an evergreen bush. "Now, keep watch of them every day. When they turn yellow, come and ask me to marry you." The last

sentence rings true, the reference to the turning yellow of ever-
greens being one of the proverbial phrases to symbolize im-
possibility.

Quite a different anomaly has been noted among the Crow
since a century ago. Maximilian speaks of their many "bard-
aches or men-women" and quaintly credits this tribe with the
championship in unnatural practices. There certainly seem to
have been some of these inverts in every generation, for the
task of chopping down the first tree for the Sun Dance lodge
(p. 312) specifically devolved on a berdache (bate'). The only
representative of this class I have ever seen lived in the Bighorn district. He was then possibly fifty years of age, stood fully
5 feet, 7 inches in his moccasins, and was of large build. Dressed
as a woman, he might have passed for one except for his affect-
edly piping voice. Agents, I learnt, had repeatedly tried to make
him put on masculine clothing, but the other Crow protested,
saying that it was against his nature. He enjoyed the reputation
of great skill in women's crafts, but I also heard that he had once
fought valiantly in an encounter with the Dakota. Berdaches
naturally associate with girls and pretend to have sweethearts
among the men. Anatomically a berdache is said to be indis-
tinguishable from male infants at birth, but as he grows up
his weak voice sets him off from other boys.

A normal man was expected to gratify his passion. In the
Sun Dance, it is true, the office of leading an expedition for clay
was reserved for a man true to his wife and innocent of lecherous
dallying with his sisters-in-law. But, an informant laughingly
remarked, such characters were so rare that in his experience
Indians always had to fall back upon the same performer for
this service. Indeed, excess of virtue marked out a man for
raillery. If he lived too long with one wife, his joking-relatives
might say, "You are as though next to a dead thing" (dī wace'
ro'ckyusa'kēetak). For, Gray-bull explained, women are like a
herd of buffalo, and a husband who cleaves to one wife is like a
hunter who has killed the last of the fugitive animals and stays
by the carcass because he lacks spirit to pursue others.

Exceptionally brave men enjoyed special prerogatives. When
Spotted-rabbit had declared his intention of dying as a Crazy
Dog (p. 331), two married women visited him in his lodge and
lay with him. Their husbands did not mind, one of them even

encouraging his wife to mutilate herself after the hero's death as though she had been married to him. "Every night two or three women came to sleep with him." To be sure, some jealous members of the Spotted-lodge clan plotted to kill him, but they lost heart when they saw him approaching.

As a matter of fact, many husbands were intensely jealous and by no means willing to accord their wives the freedom they themselves enjoyed. About twenty years ago a young man, recently married, was speaking lightly of possible amours with other women. But he turned grave in thinking of the reverse contingency. "Do you know what I should do then?" he asked me; "I should never look at her or have anything more to do with her."

Behavior after proof of infidelity varied a good deal individually. Thus, there was an odd usage called "naming of women," (biā arā′sasua), or—more pointedly—"naming of married women" (bīa tsi′mbic dā′sasua). When on the warpath and on hostile soil, men might prepare some buffalo sausage and pass it about. Each would break off a piece and say, "I shall bring a horse for So-and-so," naming his mistress. Then he would eat his share. These must not be empty boasts, for good luck depended on the members' truthfulness. Some, indeed, would declare, "I wish to perform such and such a deed as truly as this story is true." Men who happened to be of the company might thus learn with astonishment of their wives' conduct. Some did not seem to mind it and caused no trouble on their return, but others left their faithless spouses.

Admitting individual differences, women were as a rule not inclined to jealousy. "Sweethearts in every camp," the squaw-man LeForge tells us, "was the custom, either for single men or young married men." The wife rather piqued herself on her husband's charms. "If two scratches were heard upon the outside of my lodge, just through the wall from my regular location in it, Cherry was pleased at this sign of some girl wanting to talk with me." She would even prepare a feast for the rival and send her home laden with gifts.

Flirting publicly, mounted on horseback and dressed in all one's finery so as to attract the women's notice, was an established custom designated by a special term (bī′etxasi′a, and the outfit used on such occasions is called ī wī′akyuxasawe.

There were many occasions for showing attention to one's sweetheart. In the fall, young men chose partners for going to the mountains, where the girls cut down trees, which their escorts trimmed and dragged for them. When braves came back from a raid, they would dress up, mount their best horses, and ride double with their sweethearts. Thus they would go to some tipi and sing in front of it. Similarly, young men and their mistresses would set out together for berrying or for gathering wild rhubarb. A girl might also lead her lover's fast horse till he came within sight of a buffalo herd, when he would mount it and try to get her the kind of hide she wished. The hides were packed on the horses, and the lovers rode home, the woman usually astride the buffalo horse. There was similar cooperation in the Sun Dance preliminaries.

Courting assumed various ways. The suitor sometimes waited for a girl where she was accustomed to come for water and made a direct proposal, which might be followed by elopement. After nightfall the young men were wont to roam about camp, blowing flutes for the amusement of their mistresses. Some ventured to pull up the pegs outside the part of the tipi where a particular young woman slept and tried to touch her genitalia,—a custom known as bī'arusace. Any one caught at this wanton act suffered punishment: the inmates stretched out his arms, threw a blanket over them, tied each hand to one end of a long stick, and then released him.

Philandering was one thing, marriage another. A lover might approach a young woman directly, present her with a horse, and induce her to elope with him. Sometimes such love matches resulted in stable unions. Or, young people on a berrying picnic, without further ceremony might decide on living together for good. A man occasionally used a go-between, a practice known as bī'a-kus-įrau, "talking towards a woman." But the most honorable way—certainly from the prospective wife's angle—was for the suitor to offer horses to the young woman's family, particularly to her brothers, and meat to her mother. Normally, it was only a young, good-looking and virtuous woman who was bought, —whether she had been previously married or not. As Gray-bull explained, men would not buy a wanton. "The Lumpwoods never came to the door of my tipi to take away my last wife. That is the sort of wife we paid for." He was referring to the privilege

peculiar to members of the Lumpwood and Fox societies of ab-
ducting such wives of the rival organization as had once been
their mistresses (see p. 186).

According to Crow theory, a couple were more likely to stay
together on the basis of purchase, and the qualifications of a
bought bride actually made this more probable. A man who had
paid for the eldest of several sisters had the right to marry the
younger girls as they grew up, cousins being often reckoned as
sisters. Similarly, if a wife and husband parted because of incom-
patibility, the man generally took to wife her next oldest sister.
Leforge's wife, according to his story, had a cousin who offered
to marry him if she passed the chastity test at the Sun Dance
(see p. 312). "All went well with her. The next day she moved
into our lodge as my second wife. She and Cherry got along
peaceably together, acting toward each other as sisters, and
asserting themselves to be such." The wife's younger sister is
characteristically called "young wife" (u'a-kari'cta).

Notwithstanding these customs, women were emphatically
not chattels and as a rule were not coerced into marrying men
positively distasteful to them. The levirate, for example, denoted
as "keeping a sister-in-law," was orthodox, but a widow did not
have to marry her brother-in-law. As to marriage with two or
more sisters, a bride-purchaser was by that very fact a man of
responsibility, hence presumably a good provider, and parents
were naturally inclined to let him take care of a younger as well
as an elder daughter. "Purchase," in fact, is hardly the proper
term in any case. Leforge gave presents to his bride's full brother
and two adopted brothers, and they gave presents to him; while
the young woman received food, clothing, and the like from her
relatives and friends. In other words, a dowry sometimes offset
the compensation offered by the groom. In harmony with this
conception, Gray-bull explained that the relatives of a woman
who ran away from her husband were not required to return an
equivalent for the gifts originally presented to them. However,
Shell-necklace held the contrary view.

Considering the early age at which girls married, it is not
surprising that their elders could and would influence their choice.
A certain degree of independence, however, on the part of the
girls is clearly reflected in tradition. One heroine persistently
declines all offers; another sets a fantastic task as the price of

her hand; a third promises to wed only that suitor who should bring back part of her slain brother's body.

Equally instructive is a scene described in a quasi-historical tale. One poor boy, maltreated by chief One-eye, has risen to power by divine favor and is biding his chance for revenge. His impatient comrade, wanting to expedite matters, on his own responsibility but without the hero's knowledge, woos One-eye's most beautiful wife on his friend's behalf. He says to her: "Strikes-in-his-younger-brother's-company is about your age. If you marry each other, that will be well. If you refuse and he gets angry, it will be bad." The girl pleads for and is given a chance to obtain her family's counsel and goes home. Her kinsfolk are perplexed, for they wish to offend neither the bullying chief nor his young opponent, whose star is evidently in the ascendant. At last one of her brothers speaks up: "Whatever you may do will not be good. Do what your heart prompts you to do."

In another tale a woman haughtily spurned the lover's advances. Andicicō'pc noticed a pretty young woman one evening and thus courted her: "Well, young woman, I like you, I want you for a sweetheart, I want you for my mistress." In reply she mentioned his mother by name and asked whether he was her son. "Yes, I am he." "Though you are a young man," she answered, "when I look at you, I am greatly displeased. By no means will I consent; do not say anything to me a second time, I cannot possibly consent." In some cases the supercilious beauty might say, "You are a good-for-nothing young man," or "You are pitiable." Then the rejected suitor might set off at once to wail for a vision. A supernatural being would perhaps appear to him—most probably in the guise of an elk—and blow a flute, causing all female animals to scamper towards him. The visionary, returning to camp, would duplicate exactly the kind of flute revealed to him, and then irresistibly charm the coveted woman, who would come hastening to him at once. After lying with her, he would cast her out the following day so as to disgrace her in public. Indians made the above statements as descriptive of actual practices, but they are exactly duplicated in folk-tales.

A slighted lover had an easier means of revenge. He might compose a song making the jilter ridiculous. This usually happened on the warpath, and the song was preceded by the statement that the speaker was going to speak the truth (see p. 49).

A song of this type was considered a blot on a wife's honor, but a single woman did not mind it.

Once a former mistress of Gray-bull's was accompanying her husband on the warpath. Gray-bull was jealous, walked behind, and composed these words supposed to be put into the wife's mouth:

> "When you go on the warpath, I will go, too."

As the party passed a little gap, the woman got just in front of Gray-bull, who said,

> "Yellow-one-far-away, go ahead."

What covert thrust was implied here, I cannot divine.

In the early part of a winter, before Gray-bull had become famous, another mistress told a woman that she did not regard him as a man at all, that he had scarcely any hair on his head, that she would leave him and sever all relations. The following spring Gray-bull went on the warpath. He made up this song in mockery of the faithless mistress:

> "Medicine-doll-woman, you do not know how to dance,
> [sneeringly] Pretending to own a gun-scabbard. Your
>   testes are hanging down."

Gray-bull's matrimonial career is highly instructive. In his early twenties he came back from a war party and found a young woman at his lodge, so he married her without ceremony. She bore him a son, who died. They lived together for four years,—until she discovered that her husband had been out berrying with another woman and angrily told him to marry her rival. Nothing loath, Gray-bull threw her property out of the lodge, and she departed, whereupon he married his mistress without further ado. However, one spring this new wife was stolen by a Lumpwood (see pp. 50, 186). When the abductor came for her, she clung to her husband, but Gray-bull, mindful of Crow etiquette, told her to go away. "If you have ever been married, you know how this felt," Gray-bull said to me. He was disconsolate, he could not sleep for four nights, brooding over his loss. Then he came to and cast about for a Lumpwood woman he might kidnap in revenge. One member had two wives, one of whom had been hidden. The other readily followed Gray-bull, taking her daughter with her. Her Lumpwood husband was overcome with grief and became a Crazy-Dog-wishing-to-die (see p. 331), staying at home and singing the death chant. One night, however, he came to Gray-bull's tipi, shook his rattle and stuck his hand inside. Intimidated because of the recklessness of Crazy Dogs, Gray-bull offered to send the woman back. He kept his promise and returned her with one of his best horses and a dress with five-hundred elk teeth. But as soon as he had gained his end, the Lumpwood tore off his sashes and fled to the mountains. Ever after he was looked upon with contempt. As for his own lost wife, Gray-bull avoided her for a year; even then he did not seek her, but she came to him; however, he would not keep her for good.

A brother of Gray-bull's had been killed, and his mother urged him to marry the widow, a virtuous woman. At last he yielded. Then another brother of his took a horse and some property to the widow's mother,—the horse being intended for the prospective father-in-law, the rest of the presents for the brothers-in-law. Some time after this visit one of the latter came outside Gray-bull's tipi and called him. Accompanied by two of his own brothers, my friend went to his bride's lodge, where he found her seated on a fine bed with a backrest. Gray-bull's brothers sat down in the rear, and all received food. When the meal was over, the brothers left. Gray-bull remained and lay with his wife. He felt bashful because she had never been his mistress.

This narrative requires little comment. Here was a man far from prudish, but awed into a reverential shyness in the presence of a pure woman,—a sister-in-law at that, with whom freedom would normally be a matter of course. Equally striking is the conflict between love and duty at the kidnapping scene, where the determination to show sportsmanship and play the game according to its rules triumphs over sentiment, precipitating an intense, though ephemeral, sense of bereavement. And thoroughly human is the cowing of an unquestionably very brave warrior by the hypnotic glamour that invested a Crazy Dog. Gray-bull's boast on another occasion (p. 50) likewise become intelligible. He knew from sad experience what it meant to have a wife snatched away from under his eyes, and he appreciated his last wife for not having exposed him to that risk by her past conduct.

Young-crane's experience may be cited as a feminine counterpart. As a younger sister, she was wedded before puberty by a chief. Her husband had two other wives besides her elder sister,—one of them of the Treacherous Lodge, i.e. of Young-crane's own clan. The three kinswomen shared one tipi, while the fourth wife occupied another. This arrangement was not imperative, however, there being instances of unrelated wives living in the same lodge. The chief had previously divorced a wife who had borne four children. When he married Young-crane, he gave her elder brother two horses and other gifts. She bore him no children, but her sister had three by him. Packs-hat, the oldest, always called Young-crane "mother," and her consecutive husbands "father," even when divorced from her. The chief was killed, and after a while Young-crane had an affair with Hunts-the-enemy, who accordingly married her without purchase. However, he subsequently married a kinswoman of Young-crane's— a "grandchild" of hers who had been wont to call her husband "father." This angered Young-crane and scandalized the people at large, who thought a man crazy to marry a girl that addressed him as a "father" (p. 46). Accordingly, she separated from him. Later Crazy-head, a chief, wished to take her to wife, and because of his position her brothers advised her to accept him, which she did without being bought.

This failure to pay for her probably had a good reason; for from her own tale Young-crane was by this time several removes from virginal purity, hence not likely to be purchased.

Marriage being wholly secular, divorce was frequent and required no ceremony. A husband might divorce his wife for crankiness, from caprice, or for adultery. But, as already noted; men's attitude toward infidelity varied considerably. Some vindictively maltreated an erring wife or exposed her to the lust of possibly many of their fellow-clansmen. They sometimes killed several of the lover's horses, took down his lodge, broke up the poles, appropriated what they wished of the contents, and destroyed the remainder. Others seem merely to have broken off all connections with their wives. Still others condoned the offence, especially if the lover was a great warrior and *ipso facto* a privileged character (p. 48).

In theory, jealousy was distinctly below a man's dignity; particularly was licensed wife-abduction by a Fox or Lumpwood to be met with stoical decorum. But, at times the flesh was weak, so that the husband or a kinsman of his might offer resistance. However, that involved loss of standing and precipitated a song of derision,—possibly also forcible seizure of the woman and destruction of the husband's blankets or other goods by the kidnapper's club.

It was much worse, however, if the rightful husband subsequently took back his wife. Physically that was simple enough, for after a brief period of triumph kidnapped women were usually dismissed by their abductors. Shell-necklace, who had three times kidnapped women in this fashion, told me he had not retained any of them longer than twenty days. While living with one of them, he kept her in a lodge apart from his regular wife. Usually a man soon tired of such a paramour and sent her packing with such words as, "I married you, I am through, go away!" (k'an dī awa'xpe, barē'tk', kannā'). Any Crow was then free to take her to wife *except* the husband from whom she had been stolen, for "to keep a wanton woman" (bī'a warā'x k'urā'u) was ignominious. People would tell him, "Your face stinks," or "You smell a vulva." Arm-round-the-neck was a chief, yet his jokingrelatives thus twitted him; and men like Flat-dog, Old-dog, and Yellow-wolf were similarly taunted.

In a version of the Creation myth Old Man Coyote has a curiously sophisticated debate with his comrade Cirape' on this subject. He asks Cirape': "Have you ever experienced having your wife abducted?" His comrade answers: "Why, several times I have had one taken away; it is worse than sustaining a charge by the enemy." Old Man Coyote proceeds: "Well, have you ever taken back a divorced woman?" Cirape' is indignant: "Why, I am a man of honor, I have self-respect, how could I take back a divorced wife?" Old Man Coyote says: "If so, you verily know nothing. . . . Three times I have taken back a stolen wife." And he goes on to explain that in such a case a mere glance of the husband's will suffice to remind the disgraced woman of the favor shown her, hence she will readily yield to any conjugal demands she might at first be inclined to refuse.

Thus, true to one phase of his character, Old Man Coyote flouts all notions of decency.

With the Hot Dance, introduced by the Hidatsa in about 1875 (see p. 206), came a novel formality. While a special song was being sung, a man, incensed after a recent domestic quarrel, possibly because of infidelity, or smarting under a slight at the hands of his parents-in-law, might publicly announce that he was "throwing away" his wife together with a horse. This signified that he treated her as so much rubbish to be swept out of his house. It mattered not whether such wives had borne any children. In 1912 one man was known to have thus cast off three women, all of whom were mothers. Plenty-hawk likewise once threw away a wife who had given birth to two children. The woman's clansmen disapproved of such abandonment but took no action and apparently had no redress.

But the woman as well as the man could take the initiative. If she found her husband definitely disagreeable, she might abandon him, even against her kin's advice. The tales rather suggest sympathy with a young wife eloping from an elderly husband. There is even an authenticated instance of a wife's publicly throwing away her husband because he continued marital relations with a former spouse. During a Hot Dance she made a herald announce that she was casting off a horse and her husband.

In case of divorce young children went with the mother. When somewhat older, the girls were likely to remain with her while the boys would be taken by the father. During Medicine-crow's childhood his stepfather divorced his mother, but the boy is represented as constantly running back to his father (p. 18). "Father, I was lonesome, I wanted to come; my mother was displeased, still I came." The story goes on: "With him he ate, with him he went out, with him he roamed about."

The subsequent relations of a divorced couple varied. Medicine-crow's stepfather remarried his wife, apparently because of their common bond with the boy. One of my interpreters told me his father and mother hated each other and never had any social intercourse. Similarly, Young-crane at first refused to be adopted into the Tobacco society by her previous husband, Hunts-the-enemy, but her then husband, Crazy-dog, persuaded her to yield. On the other hand, some divorced mates conversed together on amicable terms. After one of the two children of Plenty-hawk's discarded wife was old enough to be married, he sent his daughter a good horse and met her freely thereafter. He also gave her husband five horses.

A young couple were not obliged to settle either with the bride's or the groom's parents, but at the beginning of wedlock patrilocal residence was usual. The husband's parents presented their daughter-in-law with an elk-tooth dress and other finery,— a practice extended to any wife kidnapped by their son. She treated and addressed them as if she were their own daughter and assisted her mother-in-law in such chores as cooking and fetching water. Subsequently, independent households were apparently the rule.

A realistic tradition strongly supports this view of the normal arrangements. A vigorous strong-willed man of the Whistling-water people married the true sister of One-eye, chief of the Piegan clan (p. 8), begot many children, remained with his wife's kindred, and at first took no part in the feuds that developed. This condition is clearly considered anomalous, and the husband was made to figure as a benefactor of the wife's family and clan by strengthening their unit.

The same tale illustrates a wife's attitude when placed in an unusual position. One-eye's brother-in-law was eager to bring about a reconciliation between his own and his host's clan. He repeatedly invited the chief, but One-eye, while promising to come, continued dawdling in his lodge. At length his sister went to One-eye's lodge and abused him for holding back. When he finally arrived, she once more sneered at her brother: "You, the inside of whose eyes are dried up, seeing that you longed to thrust your fingers into his [my husband's] eyes, why didn't you thrust them in? On the hottest days he has dragged down tipi poles for you. Perspiring, with his back burning from the heat, he has butchered for you. On the coldest days he goes hunting for you. Whether it is hot or cold, he herds your horses. His kin are numerous, yet he is not living with them, he follows *us*. It would be fine for you to stick your fingers in his eye, why don't you do it?"

This billingsgate is especially remarkable because of the normal reserve between a woman and her adult brothers (p. 26). When I questioned Yellow-brow on this point, he explained that the rule might be broken for some extraordinary cause. In the case presented the motive was the woman's fear of losing her husband, who might have divorced her because of the affront offered by her brother. Conjugal attachment here evidently took precedence over loyalty to blood kinship.

Phenomena of this sort must temper the view easily fostered

by some of the spectacular customs described above. Husband and wife were often united by a deep emotional bond, and a stable marital life unquestionably figured as the ideal. The very terms a man and woman applied to each other in address or reference hinged on the permanence of their union (p. 27). A wife did not venture to call a man by his name if she was doubtful on this point; similarly, he called her either by name or by the interjection hē'ha *only* if he had no intention of abandoning her. Further, a women hardly used the specific term for "husband" (tsire'), unless she felt safe on this point.

The sentiments obtaining in any concrete instance naturally depended on the individuals. Women who had enjoyed their fling in youth sometimes settled down in wedlock and, though liable to be captured in the annual kidnapping, would sometimes beg to be allowed to remain with their rightful husbands. If they feared abduction, they might hide until the turmoil was over. On the other hand, Gray-bull's second marriage illustrates the attachment springing up even when the relationship is inherently liable to dissolution. In fact, the concept of veritably romantic love repeatedly crops up in the folk-tales. There is the story of the young Hidatsa who breaks his shinbone on a raid and has to be left behind by his companions, but is sought out and rescued by his mistress, though she has to traverse a large tract of hostile territory in the dead of winter. On the other hand, deeds of chivalry were performed "all for the love of a lady." In one story, Comes-from-across has refused to marry Knife. She is captured by the enemy while berrying. Her admirer goes to the mountains to mourn, evidently gets a vision, rescues her, and takes her to wife. Comes-from-across was a chaste girl and she did not abuse her lover in rejecting him; this presumably accounts for the difference of her fate from that of the "haughty beauty" model (p. 52).

The Crow cherished a definite ideal of womanhood: a woman who was virtuous, expert at feminine tasks, and physically attractive, was a bī i'tsi, "a good woman," the equivalent of our perfect lady, with the addition of good looks. Such a one was held in honor and exerted considerable influence on her husband, who rarely deserted her.

Undoubtedly there were husbands who beat their wives, and an adulterous woman was sometimes brutally treated. The enraged husband might even gash her hand or face with a knife, though the Blackfoot practice of mutilating her nose was not followed. But public opinion emphatically did not sanction an unprovoked drubbing; people gossiped about a man who habitually beat his wife without due cause.

Altogether the position of woman was far from unfavorable. To her lot fell the menial duties about the household, such as bringing water or firewood and cooking, but these were likely to be shared by other female inmates. In virtually every lodge Leforge found an otherwise unattached old woman, possibly the wife's mother, who slept beside the entrance, made up the beds, warded off intruding dogs with a club, and relieved a child-bearing woman of the heavier labors. In any event, there would be sisters or clanswomen to help. The women dug up edible roots, gathered chokecherries, wild berries, and other fruits, and preserved them as well as the meat. They were the tailors, manufactured and painted the rawhide bags, made tipi covers, pitched and took down the tipi, and decorated clothing with porcupine quill embroidery, and in later times with beadwork. From the nature of the case men were less regularly employed, but theirs were the more strenuous tasks of hunting large game, raiding the enemy, and defending the camp.

A wife was interested in her husband's appearance and actively aided in his toilette. One of Leforge's wives not only made fine buckskin clothing for him, but kept his hair in order, and scented him with sweetgrass. On the other hand, a man could give public distinction to his wife. When the camp was moving, for example, the honor of transporting shields fell to the women, who fastened them to one side of the pommel. In a polygamous household the wives might quarrel over this office, for the bearer was thereby marked out as her husband's favorite. Trophies were also handed over to wives or kinswomen.

In general, women were likely to be custodians of holy objects (see p. 14). For instance, a certain shield was placed by the owner's wife toward the east as soon as the sun rose and she would shift its position with the movements of the sun, wrapping it up at sunset.

Indeed, apart from the menstrual taboos, there were very few feminine disabilities in religious matters. One Sun Dance Doll bundle was not supposed to be unwrapped by a woman, but throughout the ceremony itself its owner was assisted by his wife (p. 304 sq.). This conception is eminently characteristic of the Crow. In the Tobacco society husband and wife were regularly adopted together, each being taught two songs by their sponsor. Similarly, when Lone-tree secured the Horse Dance bundle, he was allowed to choose certain regalia and his wife chose some others.

Women, as explained, had highly honorific offices in the Sun Dance; they could become directors of the Tobacco ceremony and played, if anything, a more conspicuous part in it than the men; they sometimes played the hostess in the Cooked Meat Festival; they were not debarred from sweating or doctoring nor from seeking a vision. Though the men sought visions more frequently, that was largely due to the preponderant motive for such quests,—the desire to obtain sanction for a war party.

Socially, the women enjoyed a good deal of freedom. Even in the matter of sex relations failure to aspire to the ideal implied no ostracism. A wife had definite property rights. In buying specimens I repeatedly noted that no husband ever attempted to influence, let alone coerce, a wife in the disposal of her own belongings. To offset their domestic work, women could indulge in a variety of amusements, such as ball and dice games, sometimes among themselves, sometimes in the company of their husbands or lovers.

Altogether Crow women had a secure place in the tribal life and a fair share in its compensations.

SICKNESS

Native theory often ascribes physical ailments to supernatural causes, such as the breach of a taboo or the malevolence of a ghost. The former generally admitted of no extenuating circumstances, as shown in a semihistorical tradition. Because a woman, contrary to a rule imposed by the chief, killed a bird that annoyed her, harm was bound to befall her brother in the impending battle. Even complete innocence was no excuse. Under no circumstances, one of my informants had been instructed, was the young of any animal to be taken to his tipi. When I met him, he had suffered from rheumatism for eleven years, so he inferred that some one must have broken the rule without his knowledge. In 1931 I took Yellow-mule to a restaurant in Lodge Grass;

before eating a cake he inquired anxiously whether it contained any eggs, for the eagle medicine he had once obtained from Yellow-crane prohibited his ever partaking of them.

Sorcery was sometimes used to afflict a personal enemy, but did not play the overshadowing part it does in Negro Africa. In a tradition already quoted from, the abused hero bides his time in taking revenge on the hectoring chief One-eye. "He stripped sinews, he wetted a small one and laid it down. He took a live coal and touched the very middle of this sinew. It crumpled up and shriveled. One-eye was lying down. When this sinew crumpled up and shriveled, he crumpled and shriveled up the same way. He died." Sometimes the sorcerer drew a picture of his enemy near a river bank, with his head nearest the water. Then he would smoke towards it and burn incense. The water came and washed the image away; and the sooner it did, the sooner the enemy died. As a variation the magician might put ashes or charcoal on the eyes of the image in order to blind the victim; or by corresponding changes he would strike him dumb, deform, or paralyze him. In the historic feud betwen Big-ox (whom I knew) and White-thigh, Big-ox made a drawing of his enemy on the ground, pierced its heart, blew smoke on it, and wiped off the picture, saying, "You shall be the poorest creature on earth, at last you shall be blind and crawl on your hands and feet." This came true. In the last case the magic may have become more efficacious because Big-ox had been blessed by the Thunder.

Such procedure is called "smoking against some one" (k'us-ō'piu), while any form of evil magic, including the charming of a person of the opposite sex, is termed du'ckyuō. I do not know of any means of escaping the effects except through the good fortune of having a patron of superior power. In other cases treatment was given by medicine men, batse' waxpe', who had received appropriate revelations. But this was not the whole story. There were physicians (ak'bāri'a) who worked without higher sanctions; there were household remedies and techniques; and sometimes it is not easy to draw the line between the two kinds of doctoring, for an herb or mechanical process may be ultimately traced to a vision. Again, a medicine-man may combat a natural cause of illness by his revealed power of sucking out an intrusive object.

Massage was practised with the aid of a "stomach-kneader,"

a stick about 18 inches long and widening at the bottom into the shape of a hemisphere. I once saw Gray-bull pushing it up a young man's abdomen. He explained that the Indians were careful not to press hard against the navel. The origin of this device is ascribed to the Seven Stars, who before ascending to the sky taught it to a woman. Subsequently she treated people troubled with a stomach ache and acquired wealth from the fees paid her.

A doctor may lance swollen parts of the body. In some cases, sores are washed and a poultice is applied with a special mixture. For a disease of apparently venereal nature the doctor put hot rocks under the patient's genitalia, made him drink some powder (for ammunition) put into warm water, and also threw some of the mixture on him.

The root of a plant belonging to the Carrot family (*Leptotaenia multifida* Nutt.) is used extensively both for ceremonial incense and as a cure-all. Its native name is ise', and some interpreters spoke of it as "bear-root" because in the summer bears are supposed to fatten on it. For a cold, ise' is chewed and swallowed; for sores it is chewed and rubbed on as a liniment; it is placed on an aching tooth and kept in the mouth against a headache. Other ingredients may be added: a mixture with buffalo chips is rubbed over a swelling; and boiled with tallow, the root furnishes cough medicine. Once I observed Muskrat treating a little girl for a swelling; she first chewed part of the root, then she rubbed it on the patient's leg.

Therapeutic potions of several varieties were in vogue. Bull-all-the-time showed me a bunch of pine needles which served as medicine when boiled tea-fashion. Certain river weeds called cu'cua were similarly prepared. The Crow also pull out another unidentified plant, ā'tsixu'xe, in order to chew the juice, which is good for the teeth and for one's health generally. In Pryor I bought some "sweet-sticks" from a woman who used to chew and soak them into a remedy for diarrhoea, though the interpreter credited them with a cathartic virtue.

As in Muskrat's case (p. 33), doctors derived specific not general powers from their visions. A man surviving a snake bite regarded the snake as his patron and set himself up as a doctor for snake-poisoning. Wounds were treated by men having a relevant blessing, usually obtained from a buffalo. Again, disease was often caused by a tangible object inside the patient. This a properly qualified physician extracted, as a rule, by sucking out the cause through a pipestem. Bull-all-the-time, while sleeping in his tipi, had once beheld an old man painted red and holding a pipestem, through which he blew at a recumbent sick person. My informant saw the sickness come out of the blood, and the patient recovered. He showed me the pipestem which had been revealed to him; near one end it had a horse's track incised on it, possibly to represent horses promised him as fees in the same dream.

Once Gray-bull's son, White-hip, was ill, some food having got stuck in his throat. Bull-all-the-time was called and ordered every one out of the lodge except the patient and his father. First he rubbed a substance on White-hip's chest, neck, and abdomen; next he sang some songs, sucked at the sick man's throat with his mouth, making a popping sound; and finally he produced the morsel of meat lodged in White-hip's throat. On another occasion, when a man had swallowed a fish bone, a crowd was already assembled to mourn his death. However, they offered Bull-all-the-time a gun and other presents, and he extracted the bone. In a third case he sucked at a woman's swollen leg with his pipe and made the swelling go down. He could cure spider bites, but not wounds or snake-poisoning.

Goes-ahead's technique was similar. In one case of pneumonia he drew out some of the patient's blood with his pipestem and spat it out. Such suction left no mark in the place where the blood was extracted. A woman—the mother of Bull-does-not-fall-down—received this power when mourning the death of a son and thereby cured Gray-bull. Returning with a successful war party, my friend was walking behind the bearer of the staff to which the slain enemy's hand was tied. Suddenly this hand struck Gray-bull on the ear, and he became deaf. When he got home, the woman doctor took him into a sweat-lodge, stuck her pipestem into his ear, and sucked out a little red stone. This, Gray-bull believed, the enemy's ghost had put into his ear; naturally he recovered his hearing.

The sweat-lodge, it should be noted, was not used primarily for doctoring but as an offering, especially to the Sun (p. 257).

Rheumatism was treated by snake or mole visionaries, who either used suction with a pipe, or burnt incense and rubbed on some tallow.

As the foremost of wound doctors (ak'ū'wacdī'u) my informants mentioned one Dap'ï'c. Remembered by Young-crane but only known second-hand by Gray-bull, he must have had his heyday about or before 1850. Sitting on a little island near the site of Thermopolis, Wyoming, for three days, the story goes, Dap'ï'c observed the underground spirits—probably the water-bull (bi'muin tsï'rupe) and a dragon-like creature (mapu'xta ha'tsgye, literally, "long-otter")—treating wounded men. One supernatural took him into the hot spring, sang songs for him, and gave him his own name, the one borne by him ever since. After his fast, Dap'ï'c went on the warpath and was shot, the bullet being lodged in his body. He then gave an exhibition of his power, sang a song, and dived into a river with an otter skin in his hand. After four breaths he came out, and the bullet was in the otter's mouth. Then everybody knew he was a wound-healer.

In a battle one Crow had an arrow shot into him, the head sticking in his wound. Dap'ï'c was called, sang, painted himself and his patient, and dived into the river with him. When he came out, the otter had the arrowhead in its mouth. In another fight a Crow was shot below the navel. The Indians dammed up a water-course near-by and laid the sick man on the ground. Dap'ï'c sang and hopped over his patient, then rode to camp with him, singing on the way. The next morning they laid the patient so he could rest on a high pillow, and several men sang on his behalf. No person or dog was allowed to pass in front of him. Dap'ï'c made his wife and daughter wear robes and all three of them approached the lodge, where the people still were singing. The spectators ranged themselves in two rows. Dap'ï'c turned into a bull and snorted over his patient, who rolled over. Then he made the wounded man seize his tail, which at once enabled him to stand up as though well. The doctor led him to the water, transforming himself back into human shape on the way. He waded with the sick man until the water reached up to his chest, then dived down alone, first whistling upstream, then downstream. The patient's blood flowed downstream, and he kept standing for a long while awaiting the doctor's return. His wound healed. It was only the patient that saw the doctor as a buffalo.

Possibly describing the same incident, Gray-bull mentioned a Crow so weak that he could neither walk nor stand, wherefore Dap'ï'c had to use his power to make him rise. In going towards a creek with this patient, he acted like a buffalo cow followed by her calf. At the creek a fish came out and ate up the pus around the wound. Dap'ī'c showed the spectators the hole in the sick man's body, then dived with him twice, and the man was as well as before. Dap'ī'c alone was able to cure wounded men immediately; he hardly ever failed. However, in his later years he was smitten with blindness for breaking one of his spiritual patron's rules.

Somewhat more recent practitioners were One-eye and the woman who restored Gray-bull's hearing (see p. 64). Neither permitted dogs about during their treatment; if a dog crossed their path, it was said, the patient must die. Gray-bull acted as singer when One-eye [1] treated Crazy-head, who had been shot from side to side. The doctor wore a buffalo robe and his forehead was painted with white clay. He tied a plume to the back of the patient's head, painted white rings round his eyes and touched his body all over with the tip of his hand, which had white clay on it. Standing at the door, he sang his song, while Gray-bull and his fellow-singers were indoors. The wounded man's relatives had asked as many young men as possible to sing the physician's song. One-eye danced at the door with one foot; he had a buffalo tail with a plume tied to it, and rubbed it against the ground till the dust flew. Every one cheered him. He went to the sick man, blew on his abdominal wound, stood back, extended his arms, and bent his body. Crazy-head, the patient, imitated these movements. When all the pus and blood had come pouring out of his wound, the people stood up in two rows from the lodge to the river. Evidently a performance similar to Dap'ī'c's followed, but being one of the singers, Gray-bull could not watch it. Young-crane, Crazy-head's wife, told me her husband was not cured by the doctor, at least not immediately. But some time subsequently he went out to ease himself and in the morning there were masses of blood there; and from that time on his health improved.

DEATH

A corpse was never taken out of the regular entrance lest some other inmate die soon after. Painted and arrayed in the dead man's best clothes, it was wrapped up in the yellow part of the tipi cover known as acdē'cire, which was tied together with

[1] Not the bullying chief of that name.

buffalo sinew, and carried out from wherever the last breath happened to be drawn. Those who wrapped up the body spoke to the spirit as follows: "You are gone, do not turn back, we wish to fare well." There were two main forms of disposal,—either in the fork of a tree or on a scaffold of four forked poles. In 1910 I still saw the remains of a tree burial, and I also recall a number of burial stages on the Reservation. The feet, I heard, were placed towards the east. After decomposition the bones were sometimes taken down and deposited in rock crevices. According to Beckwourth, such double burial was once common, and occasionally the favorite horse of the deceased would be killed and buried at the foot of the tree. For a great chief, I learnt, a special method was used. His lodge was decorated with horizontal red stripes, and the corpse was placed indoors on a four-pole platform; then the tipi was left to be destroyed by the elements.

The whole camp mourned over a man killed by the enemy. His corpse was laid outside, with a feather fan in his hand and chest exposed. His kinsfolk stayed away for two months, lived in a miserable lodge thereafter and never indulged in merriment until a member of the offending tribe had been killed. Such retaliation, on the other hand, immediately stopped outward display of grief "though the relatives' hearts might still be sad." Especially impressive obsequies were held in a slain man's honor by his military club. Child-in-the-mouth thus describes the mourning over a Fox: "If either a Fox officer (ak'-ba.ē'-wicec, literally, regalia-owner) or a private (ak'-ba.ē'reta, one who lacked regalia) was killed, the people laid him down on the ground. We put on all his regalia and painted his face. Crying very much, we moved toward him. We sang, some of us cried all the way, half of us sang. There was beating of drums as they sang and walked. When his friends wanted to cry, they got together and distributed pointed arrows. Then they acted as their hearts prompted them. Some pierced their knees; others in the same way pierced their arms. Some jabbed their foreheads. Those of his friends who saw him killed grieved and tried to hurt themselves. This dead person's kindred also tried to hurt themselves Some cut up their faces with knives. These friends threw back the covering of the corpse's face, looked at it, and cried bitterly. Then they sat down. His friends hung a great deal of clothing on lodge-poles. They stepped back and sat down when the crying was over. They distributed the clothing and all his property. When this was over, they went home. That was all. His kin packed the corpse on his horse and went to bury him. Whether on a tree, or in the rocks or on top of a hill, they laid him down. Having buried him, his kin remained there and cried. If subsequently they killed a young man of the same hostile tribe,—they were even. They blackened their faces and tied the scalp to a pole. One man held it, and dancing they moved toward camp. They danced hard; they were happy. Having killed one of the slaying tribe, they stopped mourning."

When a person had died from natural causes, only members of his family cut their hair, chopped off finger joints, and gashed themselves. Sometimes they absented themselves from camp for two months and remained in mourning for a whole season,—indeed Leonard, a trapper of the eighteen-thirties, extends the period to a year or thirteen months. In 1907 many of the old and middle-aged Crow lacked a finger joint. Such practices have become obsolete, but there is still great ostentation of mourning. In 1931 I saw a bereaved father, possibly forty years old, sobbing violently as he was being led away from his child's coffin by a friend on each side, and then flinging himself on the floor in an ecstasy of grief.

According to Catlin, bereaved men cut only several locks of hair, while a woman bereft of a child or husband would have her hair cropped short and ceased to mourn only when the hair approached its former length. Leonard considers shaving of the hair an alternative to the more general sacrifice of a finger joint, but my informants regarded both as common practices. Old women seen by Leonard had lost the tip of each finger, and some even had cut off farther; the men were careful to spare the two first fingers on the right hand, which were used in bending the bow.

Mourners distributed their possessions among the people, retaining only some clothing and their medicines.

The taboo against mentioning the name of a dead person was probably less rigid than in some other Indian tribes; however, it was certainly not proper to speak it before the deceased person's kin except while those present were smoking. The relatives themselves spoke of their lost kinsman by some new name, e.g. Currant was referred to as "Thistles." I personally noted the euphemism of designating one dead as "the one who is not here" (k'ōre'sa); for instance, a man thus spoke to Gray-bull about his dead wife.

Crow ideas as to a life after death have little to do with religion and may as well be treated in the present context. The word for soul, irā'axe, is connected with that for shadow, irā'xaxe, and probably with the term for ghost, a'parā'axe. The soul stays near the corpse, whence the owl-like cry sometimes heard there. But this must be merely a temporary resting-place, since the dead live in a camp of their own. However, the hereafter seems to have interested the Crow very little. There were no standard beliefs beyond acceptance of survival in superior conditions of existence. Some informants went so far as to deny any knowledge of life after death. The notions generally held were derived from the experiences of tribesmen who, according to belief, died but returned to life.

A brother of his, Old-dog told me, was about to die. He killed himself with a knife and lay there for a while, but ultimately woke up and told the following tale. A younger brother owning a fine gray horse had died before him and took the newcomer on it, riding toward the camp of the dead. To quote the visitor to the spirit land: "I could hear the singing of praise songs over there, also loud talking. They were singing: 'Is that person coming already?' Then my brother got angry and struck me in the chest, saying, 'You are stingy and think too much of your horse. If so, go back.' He jumped off, and I came back to life." This man told Old-dog and others that the dead camped like the Crow and were faring well. He continued to live until fairly recent times.

Another Crow apparently died and reached two rivers, beyond which he found a large camp of buffalo-skin tipis. He was invited into one lodge, where everything was furnished in the old fashion, with buffalo robes on the floor to sit on. The owner looked at the new arrival and said, "I see something about you that I don't like. I don't like otters. Your people are down there." The visitor said, "Then I'll go back home." He came to and told his story. He was eager to return to the dead, and actually died soon after.

One man had been wounded and was believed to be dead, but got up again the next morning. He told everybody that the dead were camped together and were better off than the Crow.

"Don't be afraid to die," he said. He lived to old age. When my informant was seriously ill, he was eager to see his dead parents and remembered the old man's story. He told me: "If it is so, I thought, I might be happy with my relatives since the dead are all camped together."

In contrast to the spirits who live in a camp apart are the ghosts who haunt the grave, hoot like owls, and appear as whirlwinds. When a Crow sees an approaching whirlwind, he thus addresses it: "Where you are going, it is bad, go by yourself!" To say to a person that he is like a ghost is one of the worst insults; in a folk-tale a wife at once leaves her husband when he makes the odious comparison. In another story Old Man Coyote marries a whirlwind ghost. Every night she puts herself and her husband on top of her lodge and goes magically traveling through the woods; during the day she sleeps. This reversed order of life proves unbearable for the trickster; he finally escapes with the aid of mice, who transform him into their own shape.

A ghost may make people insane by putting a tooth or a lock of hair from his body into the victim's. Gray-bull's experience (p. 64) is of the same type.

However, ghosts are not uniformly evil. They sometimes blessed people in visions,—especially, it seems, with the power to find lost persons or property. Once, when two Indians were missing, their brother gave horses and property to a man with Ghost power so he should look for the lost men. That night the medicine-man sent every one out of his tipi, the relatives of the missing man coming there but remaining outdoors. Then the sorcerer put out his fire, sang, and shook his rattle. Hooting like an owl, he went out by the smoke-hole but returned, the whole lodge shaking as he came back. The on-lookers heard voices but could not understand their speech. The shaman called the outsiders and rekindled his fire. The two young men, he declared, had not been killed, but were in camp at that moment. That very night one of them came back.

Women befriended by ghosts used similar techniques. One of them, Gun, would invite people, darken her room, make everyone sing and then listen. Some supernatural would be heard speaking, and though the visitors could not make out the meaning, Gun would interpret the words and prophesy as to the future. Another woman, Stop's mother, was once asked to find a lost woman. She put out her fire, closed the smoke-hole, sang, and hooted, while the tent began to shake as though from a whirlwind. The audience could understand neither the being that came nor the medicine-woman. A child who was with Gray-bull began to cry, then the noise ceased. The hostess rekindled the fire and announced that if the child had not cried she would have discovered the whereabouts of the lost woman. The relatives offered the medicine woman more gifts, but she refused to try a second time.

IV. The Workaday World

HUNTING

A CROW was not happy without a diet of the flesh of ruminants. Boys went out shooting rabbits for fun, but that would be starvation fare for adults. I have never met a reference to eating of fish; berries, and roots dug up by the women formed a regular part of the ancient bill of fare but only as seasoning or dessert; and the corn traded in from the Hidatsa was eaten for the sake of variety rather than as a substitute for meat. Even nowadays an old-fashioned woman will disdain excellent maize and clamor for mediocre beef as the nearest approximation to buffalo. Mythical heroes easily insinuated themselves into the good graces of potential helpers by leaving at their doors the carcass of an elk, deer, antelope, or buffalo. And one of my informants once worked himself into a veritable orgy over a legendary buffalo hunt, dwelling with such relish on the details of the butchering that my interpreter and I were bored to tears. "It is like the description of scenery in a novel," the interpreter volunteered by way of explanation.

Hunting of big game was man's chief task, and it was basic for many other aspects of life. Without it there would have been no horn cups or spoons, no rawhide or leather, hence no robes or tipi covers or containers, not even for the boiling of food.

Men hunted individually and in small groups, sometimes disguised in horned buckskin masks to stalk deer at their watering-places. But the communal hunt was far more important. Mounted on horseback the Crow were able to surround a large herd and shoot the game with relative ease. The earlier method was far more arduous: they had to get behind a herd and drive it down a cliff. If this was high enough, the animals were killed outright; otherwise they were impounded in a corral at the foot of the bank, where they could then be slaughtered at will. Deer or antelope were also driven into such enclosures on level ground. In order to keep the startled animals running in the desired direction, two lines of rock piles were erected to lead to the bank or pound, and between them men and women were strung out to

wave robes at the beasts that tried to escape. A tribal hunt sometimes yielded enormous quantities of meat.

A myth represents several hundred elk as perishing in a leap
down the fatal precipice, and a hundred years ago a chief showed
Leonard a site at which a single recent drive had destroyed seven
hundred buffalo. This had doubtless been organized with the aid
of horses, for the method survived well into the equestrian era,
being in fact recalled by some of my own informants.

Such major operations were not left to chance individual enterprise. The construction of a corral, the stationing of sentinels,
the appointment of scouts, and the need of checking premature
attacks that might cause failure, all required careful planning
and cooperation. Accordingly, the tribal hunt was preeminently
a period of rigid control by the camp chief and the police (p. 5).
What is more, the drives were often, perhaps regularly, combined
with magical rituals to ensure success. One informant remembered such a performance in his boyhood days. Its site was in the
Basin, where rocks 200 to 300 feet high extended for about two
miles. The medicine-men sang at night and appointed a leader.
Starting from the edge of the cliff and at distances of fifty feet
from one another, men and women were stationed in two wings,
the intervals increasing considerably with the distance from the
declivity. Other tribesmen formed an arc back of the herd and
frightened the game through this sentried passageway and down
the precipice. This was repeated on the two following days. On
another occasion the available bank was only some eight feet
high, hence the buffalo were made to jump into a corral of about
equal height at its foot. A space was left in the pound so that
carcasses could be dragged out for butchering.

For surrounding or impounding deer on level ground, one of
my witnesses recalled the following ceremony. One night the
herald ordered every one to keep still while a headman and four
assistants sang; only at certain points in the song the listeners
were to knock against their lodges and wish for a buck or doe.
Two men on the best horses led the drive from opposite sides,
encircling an area much larger than in a buffalo drive, and the
Crow kept closing in on their victims. Sometimes two swift runners set out to startle the deer toward the pound, one holding an
arrow, the other a feather; they were supposed to cross each
other's path.

Irrespective of drives and surrounds, the menace of a famine evoked game-charming by men with appropriate supernatural blessings. Thus, Bear-crane's brother had once found some buffalo hair and fat, which he wrapped up and tied to his backrest. That night he saw in a dream a man singing and rattling so that a great many buffalo came to him. This visitant told the dreamer to use such a rattle as he was showing him and thus draw buffalo toward himself. "The fat you picked up was myself; I am a buffalo. Take a buffalo hide, paint it; take this rattle, wrap it up with the hide, and hang it up." As a consequence Bear-crane's brother marked buffalo tracks in his tipi, bellowed successively in imitation of a bull, a cow, a little calf, and an old bull, shook his rattle, singing his dream-song, and rolled in the mud like a wallowing buffalo. The next morning the whole plain was covered with buffalo. Big-ox was another charmer of the last century. Once when game was lacking he had a buffalo skull brought and put its nose toward the camp. At night they sang and in the morning they sighted and killed six heads of buffalo. The next morning they also found several buffalo. When they had plenty, Big-ox had the skull turned the other way, then no more game was seen.

Jackrabbit-head, who had been blessed by the Seven Stars, went on the warpath once, but Yellow-buffalo, who bore him a personal grudge, had the Wind for his medicine and prevented the party from seeing any game animals. When they had been involuntarily fasting for three days, Jackrabbit-head ordered a buffalo chip to be brought, marked a buffalo track inside his tent, and placed the chip on it. He was wearing round his neck a sacred rock shaped like a human face and normally covered with buckskin (see p. 261). Uncovering the rock he rubbed fat on its face and put it first on the chip, later over his head in the place where he slept. Before sunrise scouts went to sight buffalo and found from three to four hundred, so that the party enjoyed plenty of meat all the way home.

WOMAN'S WORK

After a successful hunt with its gormandizing on the spoils the complementary feminine labors set in. Since fresh meat was not always to be had, some of it was dried, prepared into pemmican, and stowed away in rawhide cases for future use. An equally obvious sequel was the preparation of the hides. A good tanner was well thought of and sometimes offered her services to a neighbor who needed a new tipi cover and might pay her a horse. The skin-dresser's most essential tools were a flesher (Fig.

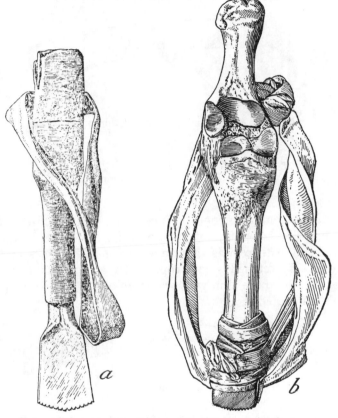

FIG. 2.—Fleshers; (a) all iron; (b) with handle of leg-bone.

2), an adze with an antler haft (Fig. 3), and—probably only for deer skins—the rib of a large beast as a beaming tool (Fig. 4). The fleshers I noted had a leg-bone handle with a toothed metal blade or were all iron, the rounded lower edge being toothed.

Hides were prepared differently according to whether they were to be worked into leather or made into rawhide bags. Further, some skins were tanned on only one side, others on both;

the process was not identical for buffalo and deer skins; and leather might or might not be smoked. White influence affected the implements and the technique, so that full details as to the prehistoric process can no longer be recovered. The essentials of leather-making, however, are clear enough. If both sides were to be dressed, the outer had to be cleared of hair; and in any event,

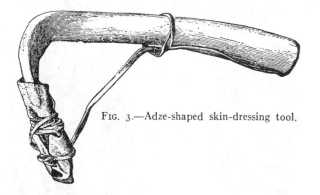

FIG. 3.—Adze-shaped skin-dressing tool.

the flesh was removed from the inner side, into which the tanner worked an oily compound of buffalo brains and liver. In order to soften the skin there was infinite scraping with stones and rubbing over a stretched sinew rope; also at various stages the worker saturated the skin with water, folded it up for temporary storage, and dried it.

FIG. 4.—Beaming tool.

Most of these processes are documented in ancient stories. In the Grandchild myth the Hidatsa beauty takes a buffalo hide, pours water on it, folds it up, and lays it aside for a while; later she puts it on the ground and begins to stake it. Another legend makes Worms-in-his-face demand that his wife should tan and embroider a buffalo hide within a single day. Disconsolate, she goes off crying, but animal helpers appear; four female beavers and as many badgers stake the hide; female rats, moles, mice, ants, bees, and flies remove the flesh, dry, scrape and smooth it;

a skunk, the beavers, and the badgers make it quite soft; a porcupine lends its quills and, assisted by the ants, completes the embroidery. When that is done, the beavers rub the hairy side, the porcupine scents the quillwork with "some yellow stuff from pines," and then they roll up the skin for the woman to take home. In a third tale the women tan buffalo hides with brain, liver, and fat. "First they took off the hair with scrapers. A woman boiled water and soaked the hide in it, made it very soft, and stowed it away. She took and twisted a stick around for wringing, laid on the stick, and fixed a rope for rubbing the hide."

These statements are eked out by Catlin's account of a hundred years ago, which seems to refer specifically to the Crow:

"The usual mode of dressing the buffalo, and other skins, is by immersing them for a few days under a lye from ashes and water, until the hair can be removed; when they are strained upon a frame or upon the ground, with stakes or pins driven through the edges into the earth; where they remain for several days, with the brains of the buffalo or elk spread upon and over them; and at last finished by 'graining,' . . . by the squaws; who use a sharpened bone, the shoulder-blade or other large bone of the animal, sharpened at the edge, somewhat like an adze; with the edge of which they scrape the fleshy side of the skin; bearing on it with the weight of their bodies, thereby drying and softening the skin. . . ."

Buffalo hides forming a tipi cover were naturally smoked by long exposure but the women made no special effort to color them. On the other hand, at least some deer and elk skins were deliberately smoked. Over a pit filled with rotten wood, to yield a smoldering fire, a small sweatlodge-like structure was erected. The skin was sewed up, laid over this frame, and staked down to prevent the escape of the smoke. If both sides were to be colored, the skin was turned inside out, and finally the stitches were removed. Such skins were used for shirts, leggings, and moccasins. According to Catlin, this process kept skins soft and flexible no matter how often they were exposed to wetness.

The women made various kinds of soft leather pouches, among them the long fringed ones for the men's smoking utensils (Fig. 5). These latter bags were decorated with elaborate designs in porcupine-quill embroidery, the predecessor of post-Columbian beadwork. But among the most characteristic containers about

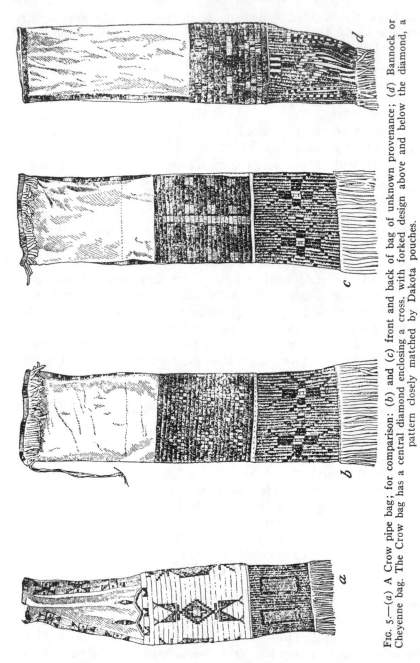

FIG. 5.—(a) A Crow pipe bag; for comparison: (b) and (c) front and back of bag of unknown provenance; (d) Bannock or Cheyenne bag. The Crow bag has a central diamond enclosing a cross, with forked design above and below the diamond, a pattern closely matched by Dakota pouches.

a lodge, even in recent times, were those of rawhide with *painted* designs. Some of these bags were rectangular, like the case of a Sun Dance doll bundle (see p. 300), and sometimes had a flap like the envelopes of our stationery. Another type, mainly for storing sacred objects, was roughly cylindrical, but tapering towards the bottom and possibly fringed at one side. However, of greatest practical utility was the "parfleche" (mickictce'), primarily a pemmican case. As Dr. Wissler has pointed out, its two flaps meeting in the center suggest the wrapper in which a druggist puts up his powders. However, parfleche flaps had little holes and strings for tying, and were symmetrically painted with distinctive patterns. In recent times, parfleches of cowhide have been used a good deal for storage; indeed, the native term for them is applied to our suitcases, satchels, or trunks.

On the rawhide bags which I bought, the designs are in black, red, dark blue, yellow, and green. Of these pigments, all are said to be aboriginal except dark blue, which partly replaced a virtual black. However, incising probably antedated painting for rawhide ornamentation. In some Crow parfleches at the Field Museum in Chicago the designs were made by scraping away portions of the layer underlying the hair of the buffalo, giving effects in light and shade. These specimens exhibit a diamond flanked by isosceles triangles,—figures commonly painted on rawhide.

Strangely enough, Crow parfleche painting differs widely from its equivalents among the Hidatsa, Blackfoot, Cheyenne, and Western Dakota,—all the tribes with whom they have had constant contacts. For instance, the Dakota and Hidatsa divide the decorative field into two panels enclosing the same design (Fig. 6k). Such bisection never occurs among the Crow, who prefer a central pattern flanked by two symmetrical designs. Thus, they favor a large hourglass in the middle, with an isosceles triangle on each side (Fig. 6e). Another typical arrangement has three horizontal layers; a stripe enclosing a triangle lies above as well as below a framed rectangle with a central diamond and flanked by isosceles triangles (Fig. 6g). Such configurations separate the Crow from past and present neighbors to the north and east, but they resemble so strongly the parfleche ornamentation of the Shoshone in Wyoming that the painting styles of the two tribes must be closely related in origin.

FIG. 6.—Painted decorations on parfleche flaps. Vertical shading indicates red; horizontal lines, blue; oblique lines, green; dots, yellow. The Hidatsa-Dakota style of (k) sharply contrasts with such typical Crow patterns as (e), (g), (h).

On the other hand, Crow beadwork suggests Dakota influence. Both tribes favor forked and stepped figures, diamonds and crosses, and the arrangement of these elements into large wholes is sometimes strikingly similar on tobacco bags (Fig. 5a). Moccasins also are often beaded after the Dakota fashion, for example, with a longitudinal stripe. However, one prevalent design, a U-figure—generally with small lozenges,—is shared by the Blackfoot rather than the Sioux. What the ancient style of *quill* embroidery was like, we cannot determine for lack of samples. In any case, the Crow women seem to have evolved an embroidery style under Dakota and Blackfoot influences, while their rawhide painting was affected by Shoshone models.

DRESS AND DECORATION

The Crow have very definite canons of personal beauty. The nose must be perfectly straight, and the face should be free of scars or pimples. A semihistorical masculine paragon is also credited with small feet and hands. Further, though the Crow are as tall as Nordics, anyone noticeably exceeding 6 feet in height is regarded as too tall to rate as good-looking; on the other hand, men of 5 ft. 7 in. are too short, and one nearly two inches taller spoke disparagingly of his own stature. The ideal limits are thus rather narrowly fixed.

However, judgments of beauty are largely affected by dress and decoration. Narrators enlarge on a hero's appearance in terms of his finery, and the difference it wrought is oddly brought out in the story of Twined-tail. Once a dirty, tousle-headed gawk, he suddenly reappears at the head of his company clad in the trappings of a conquered foeman. As his party dash into camp, people ask, "Who are these, who is their leader?" Unable to recognize him at first, they finally ejaculate, "Why, it is Twined-tail! How is it he is so handsome?" The story-teller quaintly intercalates: "Unknown to them, Twined-tail had been a fine-looking man all the time, but because he was poor he looked ugly; when he was dressed up he was handsome."

Clothing, then, was important apart from its protective value. On festive occasions old-fashioned costume would appear even during the last decades, but what it was like three hundred years ago we cannot determine with certainty. Thus, in recent times the men generally wore the gee-string, and even Maximilian notes the breechcloth; on the other hand, Mr. Curtis denies its aboriginal character. Conceivably the older covering was a skin kilt something like the garment worn by the main Sun Dancer (see p. 304).

Apart from this enigmatic garment, a man in the historic period unquestionably wore leggings reaching up to the hip, a shirt, moccasins, and a buffalo robe. The moccasins, I was told spontaneously, were anciently cut from a single piece of skin,—not provided with the separate stiff sole typical of modern footgear. Ordinarily there was no headdress, but on special occasions the men put on the usual Plains Indian feathered warbonnet, and ceremonially feathers and caps might appear. So far as I know, an eyeshade of rawhide has been noted only by W. F. Reynolds (writing in 1868), but since other Plains tribes had such visors there is nothing improbable in their occasional use by the Crow.

The chief part of a woman's costume was a long dress of deer or mountain-sheep skin that extended from chin to feet. It was richly decorated with elk teeth, subsequently imitated in bone, and trimmed with ermine skins. The calico substitutes were somewhat shorter and were worn with a modern leather belt. Women, too, wore moccasins and leggings, the latter, however, only extending to the knees.

Prehistoric practice as to personal adornment is not easily reconstructed. Necklaces of bear-claws, such as Maximilian's artist figures, were doubtless aboriginal. According to Mr. Curtis, the men also wore necklaces made of polished and clay-daubed discs cut from the bleached shoulder-blade of a buffalo, while the women decorated their ears with pendants of circular pieces of buffalo bone. Prominent men wore shell earrings, and in the recent period chains of bone discs for a neck and breast ornament have been popular. At festive gatherings I have seen men wield large eagle-feather fans, probably in part for show.

In 1910 I still saw one old Hidatsa with half his chest tattooed. Arm-round-the-neck did not consider this one-sided decoration the Crow style, but recollected tattooed men, some with the markings on their arms. Women's tattoo consisted in a circle on their foreheads, a dot on the middle of the nose, and a line from the lips to the chin. According to Curtis, only a small number of men had tattooing, which symbolized their medicine; four or five porcupine quills, held with almost touching points, were pricked into the skin of the chest, and then powdered charcoal of red willow and pine was rubbed in.

As for the hair, the only type of brush I have seen consists of a porcupine tail mounted on a stick, but the story of Spotted-rabbit credits him with also using a buffalo tongue. For some reason both sexes changed their style of hairdress some time in the nineteenth century. While the women I saw followed ancestral fashion in dividing their hair in the middle and reddening the parting, they wore a thick braid on each side, in contravention of ancient usage. Even Boller, observing as late as 1858 to 1866, still describes the women's hair as "falling free and unconfined over their shoulders." At night the hair was tied so as to prevent entanglement.

Recent masculine style, though otherwise varying, was also characterized by braids anciently lacking. Some twenty years ago an enterprising quarter-breed opened a pool room on the Reservation, where young men swarmed, pushing their cues, with braids dangling in front and back. Dandies affected a thin lock passed through a narrow brass tube between the center of the body and each of the major queues, which generally hung down over, in front of, or just behind the ears, while a long pigtail was worn in the back. A bang or "pompadour" was also popular in recent times. Bear-crane, who represented the older generation in 1910, had his hair parted in the middle and wore it unconfined in front except for a little braid on the right of the dividing line; in the back he had one long, thick queue. Above such a rear queue many young men fastened switches decorated with two elk teeth near the place of attachment. These switches are an old feature, the men being fond of lengthening their hair by splicing to it hair cut off from the heads of mourners. The basic style of old was probably to divide the hair roughly into two parts, then let it flow loosely down the back and the sides of the face. Sometimes this was combined with a lock falling down the center of the forehead, and one of Maximilian's subjects shows his hair coiled in a bulky foretop. In Shell-necklace's boyhood, men still wore their hair unbraided, and he ascribed the change to Nez Percé influence. To keep the free hair from blowing about their eyes, the Crow put little balls of pitch into their hair. A ruler-like quill-embroidered strip of rawhide was sometimes made to hang from the hair.

Travelers in the early 'thirties marveled not a little at the length of chief Long-hair's hair, which they set at from 9 ft. 11 in. to 10 ft. 7 inches. Ordinarily it was wound with a strap and folded into a container some ten inches long, which the chief carried under his arm or within the folds of his robe, only loosening it on festive occasions. Plausibly enough, Leonard describes it as the chief's medicine.

Both sexes perfumed the hair. According to Catlin, they oiled it every morning with bear's grease, and Curtis refers to the use of castoreum and sweet-smelling herbs, with cactus pith rubbed on for a glossy effect.

MAN'S WORK

To a transient visitor Crow men might easily convey the impression of laziness. If meat was abundant, a man neither concerned with joining a war party nor taking part in some cere-mony was quite likely to idle in his lodge. In the meantime his wife would occupy herself with domestic chores. If not making a dress, mending moccasins, or cooking meat, she was possibly spreading a handful of chokecherries on a flat stone slab outdoors, pounding them with a stone, pits and all, and drawing out this mass into elongated confections to be dried in the sun.

But this would be a one-sided picture. If a man labored less continuously than his wife, his were the more perilous occupa-tions of hunting and fighting. In the way of home industry there was indeed little for him to do. The Crow lacked such specifically masculine crafts of other primitive people as metallurgy and wood-carving; pottery, basketry and weaving were unknown; and everything connected with skins belonged to women's sphere. Nevertheless, men were not without tasks of their own,—above all, they manufactured their own implements of the chase and warfare.

Men, then, made arrowheads of stone or bone, though de-tails as to their technique are not available. The shafts and bows were made by experts; in recent times Hunts-to-die was distin-guished for his skill as a maker of both. A Crow would invite a number of these specialists to a big feast and distribute sticks so that each could fashion one shaft. Straighteners were made of the horn of the female mountain goat, four holes of successively greater diameter accommodating shafts of varying bore. Since this process left a mark on the wood, there was further rubbing between two grooved stones. The Indians set a high value on well-shaped arrows: if a married woman brought her brother a gift of food, he might reciprocate by a present of ten arrows for her husband, which rated as equivalent to a horse.

Only boys used simple wooden bows. The typical Crow weapon, so greatly admired by Maximilian (p. vii) and later travelers, was of horn or antler with a backing of sinew. Maximilian mentions the use of elk and mountain-sheep horn, Beckwourth refers to bows made of two buffalo horns; and Belden thus describes one of elk antler, telling us that its manufacture required three months.

"They take a large horn or prong, and saw a slice off each side of it; these slices are then filed or rubbed down until the flat sides fit nicely together, when they are glued and wrapped at the ends. Four slices make a bow, it being jointed. Another piece of horn is laid on the center of the bow at the grasp, where it is glued fast. The whole is then filed down until it is perfectly proportioned, when the white bone is ornamented, carved and painted."

The glue was made by boiling buffalo gristle or various other parts of a buffalo; and one layer of sinew was laid on top of another. The bowstring was also of sinew.

Arrows were carried in quivers of otter skin or buffalo skin which were sometimes embroidered in quillwork (p. vii).

While bows and arrows were common to hunting and warfare, fighting required some additional implements. There was, for instance, the "long bow" (icta'xia ha'tskite, or mara'xia ha'tskite),—actually nothing but a pair of sticks for striking coups. A good sample in the Field Museum consists of two slender wands tied together at intervals with quill-covered buckskin strings and wrapped specially with red and black cloth, a substitute for buckskin. Six feathers hanging down represent three Dakota and as many Cheyenne whom the owner had killed. According to Gray-bull, one of the sticks ended in a metal point so that at close quarters it could be wielded as a spear. The owner daubed his coup-stick with yellow or white clay according to his visions, which also determined the kind of wrapping. A man who eloped with another's wife would give her his coup-stick to hold. Genuine spears figured both in fighting and ceremonial; Maximilian's Atlas shows a mounted Crow holding a spear.

Still another weapon was the familiar egg-shaped stone club tightly hafted to a wooden handle (Fig. 7). Exceptionally heavy clubs occurred for ceremonial use, the stone being mostly cov-

ered with strips of quill-wrapped rawhide and further decorated with tin cones, feathers, and dyed hair.

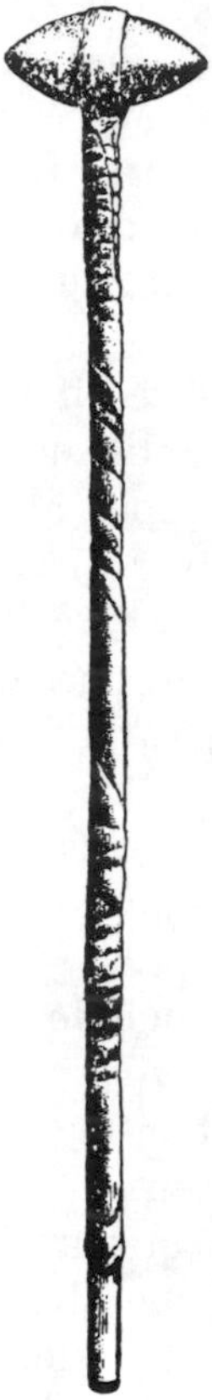

Circular shields of buffalo hide formed the only defensive weapons. Their value rested largely on their religious associations, for they were revealed in visions. A shield was not supposed directly to touch the ground; its owner unwrapped it with the circumspectness due to any sacred bundle; and like other medicines, each shield had its individual taboos. The decoration on the disc—or, more frequently on its buckskin cover—symbolized the visionary experience (Fig. 8). Like the war scenes on a man's robe, this painting was executed by men. Typical figures I have seen picture an eagle with a zigzag line—in other words, a thunderbird—, a buffalo, an elk. According to Grandmother's-knife the famous shield thrown by Rotten-belly before an impending battle (p. 234) bore the black figure of a man with disproportionately large ears; and another shield was said to represent the Seven Stars. Though the painting might be partly or wholly geometrical, some of these designs doubtless suggested natural phenomena. Besides the painted decoration there were appendages,—whole bird skins, feathers, plumes, buffalo tails.

FIG. 7. — War club with stone head attached to wooden handle.

DWELLINGS

While some phases of aboriginal life disappeared decades ago, the conical lodge, though with a canvas covering, has persisted until the most recent times, at least for summer use. Professor Walter Stanley Campbell of the University of Oklahoma has made a thorough study of Crow dwellings, based on scores of lodges. I have myself photographed the tipis in the process of erection as well as a complete camp circle arranged for a Fourth of July celebration some twenty years ago.

Catlin describes Crow tipis 25 feet in height, composed of twenty to thirty poles of pinewood, and capable of accommodating forty inmates. Professor Campbell sets the maximum number of poles at twenty-two but vouches for some 30 and 40 feet high, and since the tips tower far above the tipi proper, he aptly compares the total effect to that of an hour-glass. It is this almost

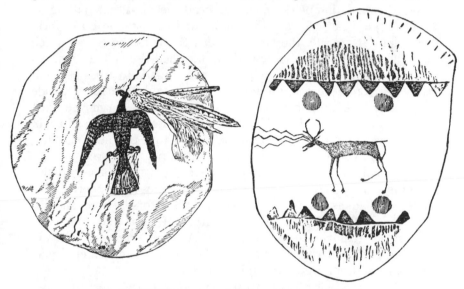

FIG. 8.—Shield covers symbolizing visionary experiences.

fantastic projection beyond the point of intersection that marks the Crow tipi off from others of the Plains region. Since the poles had to be brought down from the Bighorn mountains, the question arises how the Indians transported them in the days before horses, since human and dog traction hardly seem suited for the task. Mr. Curtis' answer is that poles were formerly of the lightest kind of fir, supporting a cover of only eight to ten skins; and one of my traditions presents cottonwoods as a makeshift in lieu of pines. All this suggests that the dwelling altered considerably with the white man's innovations. My witness estimated the average number of buffalo hides for a cover at fourteen, with a maximum of eighteen and even twenty.

Everything connected with the tipi belonged to the women's sphere of influence. Desiring extra long poles, they were bound not only to strip the bark but to pare down the logs to a suitable diameter, since a forty-foot pine would be far too thick at the base for a lodge pole. To prevent slipping on the ground they pointed the butts. Like the Blackfoot and Shoshone but in contrast to their Dakota and Cheyenne sisters, the Crow women invariably set up four—not three—poles as a foundation for the rest. It takes a pair to pitch the tipi, one woman raising the crossed foundation-poles above her head, her assistant pulling on a guy rope. The poles are then separated so that the butts form an oblong. Naturally the last pole set up carries the cover, which is brought around the framework and pinned in front. In making this adjustment a woman mounts on rungs made to cross between the two front poles or nowadays uses a regular ladder. Outside the framework are put two special poles, which when moved back and forth open or shut the smoke-hole. For greater safety in stormy weather an inside guy-rope is tied to a peg near the fireplace while outside guys are fastened to a peg on a tree.

It took an expert to design a cover, and the housewife employing her would pay her four different kinds of property. The designer had as many as twenty collaborators, whom she instructed in the requisite sewing together of skins and whom the tipi owner remunerated with a feast. A whole day was spent on making the sinew thread. Work on the cover was considered particularly appropriate to the fall of the year.

When the lodge was put up, the people burnt sagebrush and weeds inside and as the smoke appeared through the hides they said, "This will keep out the rain," and opened the smoke-vent. The housewife's husband invited old men to smoke with him; the guests recited coups and said, "In the spring this will be a very good tipi from which to make bags and moccasins."

The fireplace was approximately in the center of the lodge, and the rear (acō', acō'ria) was the place of honor. It was there that chief Rotten-belly received Maximilian, bidding the Prince seat himself at his left. On either side of the entrance was an arō''kape, and between it and the rear the icgyewatsu'a. In the latter were spread the robes for sleeping, and a husband and wife were likely to rest there when not receiving visitors. The bottom of the cover was pegged to the ground; according to

Bear-crane rocks formerly weighted it down, but another informant restricts this custom to the winter season. Against drafts the Crow used a hide screen (bitā'ricia), on which the owner often had his deeds depicted. Bedsteads were lacking; the Indians slept on several hides and covered themselves with skin robes. But they had backrests of willows strung with sinew, which were suspended from tripods and covered with buffalo skins.

For temporary use warriors, eloping couples, and visionaries sometimes put up a crude shelter (acta'tse') of sticks, bark, and foliage. More regularly, the Crow erected a shade beside their tipi during the hot season and spent the major part of the day there. Until recently a modern frame house, a summer shelter, and a canvas-lined tipi could all be seen next to one another. The Crow shade is of circular ground-plan and has a conical—not a flat—roof of boughs and foliage, thus suggesting the Sun Dance lodge of other Plains tribes.

DAILY ROUTINE

For lesser ablutions an old Crow filled his mouth with water, stretched out his palms so he could squirt the full stream on them, and then applied it to the parts to be washed. However, the daily routine—certainly in the summer time—included a bath in a near-by creek.

Water was credited with medicinal virtues. Early in the morning, winter or summer, the herald called out to the people to get out of bed, bathe, and drink all the water they could. "Make water come into contact with your body," the phrase ran, "water *is* your body" (bire' daxū'a hi'a, bire' daxū'a kōk). Or: "Get up, drink your fill, make your blood thin" (bire' da'satsi di ī're tā'tawi'a). This "thinning of one's blood" was simply a prescription to drink plenty of water. "This will keep your blood thin and you will not get sick. You will be active, your blood will not clog, it will flow through your veins. Water is our body. Whatever else there be, water is above all; without water you cannot live. If you use very little water, you will not live and enjoy life." On the warpath young men were also advised to drink all they could so they would be in a condition to fight the enemy more effectively. Also if they were wounded their blood would flow freely and there would be no danger of blood-poisoning.

Folk-tales refer to a young man's morning swim, to the joint bathing of a married couple, to a crowd of young people of both sexes disporting themselves in the water. I have seen a whole family bathing in unison, the husband wearing his gee-string, the wife her calico dress in the water. Is such prudery due to Caucasian influence? I have certainly never seen a Crow man without his gee-string, not even in the sweat-lodge. My interpreter and I once chanced upon a very old woman and her granddaughter bathing apparently quite naked in a creek, but they were greatly put out and hastily covered their bodies with their hands.

In the old days people ate when they were hungry, but then as now food was at once offered a visitor, no matter at what time of day he arrived. He did not have to consume everything, but was allowed to take the residue home and might even ask for a container. The hosts did not need to eat simultaneously; if they did, they ate apart from their guests. I have myself again and again witnessed this segregation; virtually always each family formed a distinct group, so that I have observed as many as four distinct companies at a meal. Sometimes my interpreter and I ate separately from the rest.

An arriving visitor is formally asked to enter, to sit down in a certain place, and to smoke. He may be welcomed by the exclamation "kahe'." Hospitality is still carried to extreme lengths. I know of one Crow who invited a kinsman and his wife to spend the Fourth of July week with him. The couple tarried for weeks, and since the visiting wife despised any food except beef, the host was hard put to it to purchase provisions. But it would have been quite contrary to the spirit of native etiquette to murmur any criticism of the inconsiderate visitors.

Guests from other tribes have long been common, and their appearance usually precipitates a lavish exchange of gifts. Ignorance of each other's tongue is no bar to animated intercourse in the Plains area because of the widespread gesture language (bāpā'tua). I remember a Cheyenne who thus carried on a lively conversation about ancient warfare with a group of Crow Indians without the exchange of a spoken word.

Notwithstanding the etiquette regulating social intercourse, some customs we might expect are lacking. There is no exact equivalent for our "Good morning!" in meeting outdoors, though a Crow is likely to ask, "Where do you come from?" "Where are you going to?" "What are you doing?" On my return one summer an Indian hailed me with the words, "I see you, I am feeling better" (di awa'kam mī itē'ky). An interpreter regarded this as a high compliment.

In the old days an approaching stranger was challenged by a pack of fierce dogs (see p. vii). Indeed, this was one of the main uses of these animals. Another was to carry moccasins for braves on a warparty; still another was to draw a travois (arā'k'ō). This was the familiar Plains Indian dray of two poles crossed and tied in front to the beast's back while the diverging butt ends dragged along the ground; in between there was a rectangular frame to which baggage could be fastened. In a popular Crow tale a little boy is strapped to such a travois while his parents are on the march and his mother is leading the dog. Suddenly some antelope appear on the scene, the dog breaks loose to give chase and spills the infant, who is thus lost but brought up by benevolent dwarfs. Unlike their neighbors, the Crow do not seem to have made much use of an enlarged travois for horses except to remove disabled tribesmen.

FIG. 9.—Firedrill.

In pre-equestrian days, I heard, a wealthy man was one who had a great many dogs; one Crow of old was said to have owned as many as a hundred. Long-limbed dogs were castrated and used as moccasin-carriers. Some dogs bore names; I once heard a Crow call two of his own "Yellow-dog" and "Wolf-dog" and saw them come to him in response. Except in the recent Hot Dance festival, dogs were not eaten, and even in that context some Crow made substitutions (p. 212).

Inconsiderable as the equipment of a tipi was, some of its features are noteworthy. The fire in the center was anciently made by a palm drill. The pitted board was of cottonwood or driftwood, the shaft of wild-grape or sagebrush; a model I bought shows a two-part construction, a short tip being lashed to a longer stick (Fig. 9). Drilling naturally passed out of use decades ago, being superseded by flint-and-steel strike-a-lights before the days of matches. Anciently buffalo dung or rotten sagebrush bark served as tinder, and burning buffalo chips were sometimes impaled on sticks to save oneself the labor of fire-making.

There were no earthenware vessels. Interpreters speak of "pots," "jugs," "kettles," and "buckets" in translating the native term "bira'xe"; but the utensils in question turn out to be of rawhide, stone, or soapstone. Stone-boiling in rawhide containers was called "potless boiling" (bira'xdeta waritsī'tua), but no informant knew the process first-hand. Other methods of cookery were roasting—especially applied to ribs; cooking in the ashes; and steaming. Wooden bowls served as plates; and while I never saw them so used, I bought one connected with a dice game (Fig. 10, o) and another with mixing of Tobacco.[1] In 1910 I noticed several men carrying such bowls fastened to their belts; according to my then interpreter, they were their "medicines." Formerly, I heard, men carried wooden bowls on warparties and at the enemy's approach mixed paint in them, with which they decorated themselves or their horses. Spoons, cups, and small dishes were of mountain sheep and buffalo horn. I bought a spoon of mountain-sheep horn used for mixing Tobacco. Buffalo paunches served as water-bags, and with stone mauls hafted to a wooden handle the Crow broke up bones in order to extract the marrow.

AMUSEMENTS

The daily routine was broken by an appreciable amount of amusement. There were pastimes for adults as well as for children, not only in the way of games but in the lighter activities of military clubs (p. 172) and the contests about war honors (p. 14 f.). Even the solemn festival of the Sun Dance (p. 297) offered diversion, being in part a dramatic spectacle.

---

[1] When this word is capitalized, the reference is to the sacred tobacco identified with the stars (p. 274).

In modern times several purely social dances have been derived from other tribes. Thus, the Owl Dance (pō'pate disu'a) comes either from the Missouri tribes of North Dakota or the Cree. When I witnessed it in 1907, the men and women sat on the ground, with several musicians in the center beating their small hand-drums. One woman went around, whipping first the women and then the men to make them rise and dance. At first the women formed a circle of their own, dancing by themselves. Then a man would select a partner or two by placing his hand round her (or their) waists, while they clasped him in similar fashion. The motion was a clockwise glide, but a few participants formed the arc of an inner concentric circle and moved contra-clockwise, facing the outer dancers.

The Goose Egg dance (bī'ra i'gye' disu'a) was primarily restricted to the River Crow, for Gray-bull had witnessed it only twice in his boyhood and said the Main Body were surprised when they first saw it. Men and women participants kissed each other publicly, while the boys jeered. The women held powder-bags and otterskin quivers in their hands. From a fuller report by Bull-weasel's mother, a River Crow, it appears that her people learnt the dance when visiting the Hidatsa. A procession led by two chaste girls, and made up of all the good-looking Hidatsa women, married and single, marching two abreast, came to the Crow encampment, six male singers and finally a herald bringing up the rear. The women formed a circle round the men and executed a step like the Owl Dance, but with only the women taking an active part. Each wore a blue flannel headband with two eagle tail-feathers and a blanket of red flannel held tightly below the neck; they were painted red round the eyes. When the herald got to the center, he cried out, "Young men, give presents to the young women you like and kiss them! If your heart is greater, so that you want to marry them, give them a horse and none will run away." At first the Crow men were bashful, being afraid of a rebuff. At last one of them arrayed himself in a fine breechcloth, got into the center, and inspected the Hidatsa women. He picked out the most beautiful one, put his arm around her and gave her a beaded blanket and a kiss. This was the beginning. All the other Crow hurried home to dress up. Then they, too, kissed the girls they wanted. One man picked out a pretty woman deserted by her husband and offered her a stick, saying it stood for a bay horse. Her mother accepted it in the presence of all her tribe. Another Crow, already married, gave a stick representing a white horse to a girl the Hidatsa men themselves had courted in vain. His wife burst out crying and went home. After the dance the singers thus addressed the River Crow: "We have given you this dance, take it home and try it. Because you have given us some horses you may have the chance." The visitors took their newly acquired wives home. When the snow was completely off the ground, the River Crow returned and at one stopping-place a herald ordered them to practice the dance so they could later give an exhibition to the Main Body.

"We called all the women into a large tipi, having picked out good male singers who had learnt the Hidatsa songs. The dress and paint of the Hidatsa were imitated exactly; the feathers had been previously arranged. Our five drummers were waiting for us. We had a trial dance first. We tried the step, but several did not know how to dance, some moving forward instead of sideways. The rest of us made fun of them. Finally we went through camp like the Hidatsa dancers, both single and married women. Two of us were big girls, I being one. They announced that we were virgins and should take the lead. We were to stand by ourselves. The herald, who followed the drummers . . . , then selected other pairs, making those of one height walk beside each other. I know the songs and sometimes I sing them and they bring back memories of the past that make me feel sad. We went through camp and formed a circle in the center, with the singers inside. Our dancing was not yet perfect. The herald stepped forth and said, 'What are you waiting for, young men? You saw what the Hidatsa did. Give presents to the girls you like and kiss them.' The young men brought in presents in compensation for the kisses. I was not kissed.

"Later the River Crow met the Main Body on the Bighorn, and they all camped together. There were plenty of lodges there. The herald cried, 'Get ready, let us show the Main Body our new dance and surprise them.' We were all eager to do it. We knew there were many good-looking men among the Main Body. We prepared our headbands with much more beadwork than the Hidatsa women and went to a preparatory lodge. Having no mirrors then, we painted one another's faces with a red stripe round the eyes. . . . We soaked white clay, put in sticks, and made white dots round the red paint, as the Hidatsa had also done. We were all dressed exactly alike. My former mate and I were again chosen for leaders. Afterwards we formed a circle. The herald cried: 'Come, young men, kiss the one you like best in return for presents, and if you want to marry her, give her a horse and take her away.' There was a big ring of spectators. We did the same thing as seen among the Hidatsa. I was standing there. In the main band Long-horse was famed for his beauty. He wanted to kiss a virgin and asked the young men whether there was any such there. My future husband pointed me out to him. Long-horse came toward me. He was wearing a fine blanket. I thought more of the blanket than the kiss. He took a long kiss, then walked off, leaving the blanket, which my mother took. . . . A Dakota who was present threw an ugly blanket over me, but I pushed it off. He did not seem to understand . . . , for he threw his arms round me. I pushed him off, and everybody laughed. He came in spite of that, but finally let me go. The herald rebuked me: 'He is not going to marry you, he only wants to kiss you.' I did not like him. We danced a little, then we stopped. My mate was not approached by any man, so at last her mother took her away. One man gave a girl a stick, another pointed one at me but I refused it. This time the people upheld me. The young men of the Main Body kissed all the women. Two of the River band women got married. After this we often performed the dance. I think after learning it from us the Main Body also danced it."

An older form of diversion came to my notice, though in bowdlerized fashion. As I was watching a Tobacco adoption ceremony at Lodge Grass on July 3d, 1910, a disturbance occurred outside. Two men were dashing through camp dressed as clowns (ak'bī'arusacari'ca = woman-impersonator?) and mounted on villainously bedecked horses. They were followed by younger men, but did not go through the customary performance because identified by the spectators. However, I obtained the following report of a standard performance.

The organizer meets his fellow-clowns in the brush, all bringing gunnysacks, mud and leaves. Of the gunnysack they make leggings and ponchos, while the mud serves as body-paint. They make cloth masks with eye- and mouth-slits and blacken them with charcoal. The nose is either marked with charcoal or molded of mud and stuck on. When quite unrecognizable, the clowns leave their hiding-place and approach camp.

As soon as the people catch sight of them, they cry, "The clowns are coming!" The performers walk as if lame and act as clumsily as possible, so that the onlookers crowding in upon them cannot help laughing. One clown, dressed as a woman, wears a fine elk-tooth dress padded to feign pregnancy; and he must walk, talk, and sit like a woman. Another, as musician, carries a torn drum,—the worst to be found. His songs refer jocularly to the rivalry of the Foxes and Lumpwoods. The clowns poke fun at every one, irrespective of his standing in the tribe, and whisper, telling one another to dance and amuse the people. They disguise their voices in speaking to their audience, who try to identify them. No sooner does the musician pick up his drum than his companions walk about, thinking up antics. But the singer at first merely rattles the drum and heaves a grunt. The spectators impatiently cry, "Dance, we want to see you dance!"

Before starting out, the clowns have prepared willow bows and arrows or worthless old firearms with which to frighten the people during the dance. They have also abducted the ugliest old horse, crooked-legged and swollen-kneed, and made it less attractive by tying down its ears, masking its face or plastering it with mud, and putting gunnysack leggings on its legs. The owner only discovers the theft at the performance, where it is ridden by one clown and the "woman" behind him. The horseman in front waves his arrow or gun, bidding the audience keep their distance, in which he is seconded by the "woman."

At last the singer beats his drum, and the clowns scatter, each dancing as ludicrously as he can. After a while the musician gets excited, throwing his drum to one side, his drumstick to another, and begins to dance without music. His associates follow suit. Finally all of them stop with one exception. The onlookers note him and cry, "There's one dancing still!" The other clowns turn around, and the rider bids his companion dismount to dance. "She" refuses, clinging to him till he gets angry and pushes her head, when she gets off and begins to perform. Her companion also prepares to dismount, but purposely tumbles down and pretends to be badly hurt. After a while he dances with his weapons, then proceeds to remount but overleaps so as to fall, when he again acts as if seriously injured. Some wags in the audience are likely to take part, asking questions and making such comments as, "These fellows must have come from far away." The clowns answer by gestures that they have come from a very great distance and are correspondingly fatigued, perhaps they indicate that they have come from the sky. Some one may ask, "How many days [literally, nights] did it take you to get here?" One clown begins to count up to hundreds and hundreds and would never stop but for the drummer, who seizes him by the back, saying, "You are crazy, you don't know where we have slept." Then he throws him down; the clown pretends to fall headlong, but stops after a while, and begins to laugh. Indeed, he seems to die laughing and kicks his feet up in the air.

When the clowns are tired, they decide to leave. The rider tries to clear a path for them, but the spectators shout, "Dance some more!" At first he refuses, then they cry, "For the love of your wife behind you, dance!" Then he tells the musician to sing again, and the dance recommences. After a while they try to escape, the horseman driving the audience back, but the crowd is so thick they only get a short way and have to repeat the performance. About every 50 yards they are obliged to dance again. They ultimately go through the entire camp to their hiding-place, but it takes them a long time. Little boys, as well as bigger ones, hem them in, trying to discover their identity, and pelt them with dung. While the rider holds off the outsiders, the clowns make a dash for the thickest part of the brush, doff their masquerade, put on their usual dress, and scatter in all directions, finally slinking back into camp.

This performance was anciently held in the spring, but in 1911 I again saw it in July. During a Hot Dance a group of youngsters dressed as clowns rode to the dance house, dismounted and, to the amusement of everybody, took part in the performance.

The above account omits a feature described by Bear-crane. The horseman wore a large phallus of mud and willow-bark and amidst the laughter of the audience pretended intercourse with his companion when they leapt from the horse.

GAMES

Children's games cannot always be separated from those of older people because all the young people imitate adult activities so frequently. The following games, however, are or were mainly played by grown-ups.

Probably the gambling game *par excellence* was "hiding" (bā'xua-hiru'a), known to ethnographers as the hand-game. Men and women played at it, but each sex by itself. Originally only four or five players participated on each side, but later the Lumpwoods and Foxes were sometimes pitted against each other, each club sitting in several rows on opposite sides of a large tipi, with robes, beadwork, and war-bonnets laid down as stakes. Two men in the rear kept the pipes going and worked magically on behalf of their respective organizations throughout the game. Drums were beaten and everybody sang songs. One player represented the Lumpwoods, the other the Foxes. Each appealed to his familiar spirit, pawing like a horse, snorting like a bear, hissing like a snake, or flapping his arms bird-fashion, according to the nature of his protector. At his opponent's second movement, the guesser, striking his chest hard with one hand while extending his other arm, indicated which hand concealed the elk tooth. A wrong guess was jeered and meant the loss of one of the tally-sticks, the game ending with the forfeiture of three. The winners beat their drums and sang victory songs to mock their opponents. They would give their tally-sticks to a famous chief, who held them up and recited a war honor for each counter.

Two differently marked bones, or bones with strings, could take the place of elk teeth; and one author mentions a shell as the object changed from one hand to the other under a buffalo robe. A set I myself bought consisted of two spindle-shaped bones, one with a string round the middle, and ten counters. The game went with all of the tally-sticks, one being given up for each erroneous guess. This suggests that the rule varied somewhat, the formal game by the two societies possibly having evolved along lines of its own.

The manner of guessing was conventional. A right-handed person struck his heart with his right hand, then pointed; a left-handed guesser used his left hand. If two persons were hiding the bones or teeth, and the guesser wished to indicate that the objects were, respectively, in the right hand of the opponent facing him on his left side and in the left of the one facing him on his right, he would flex all his fingers except the thumb and index, these being extended as far apart as possible to indicate the outside hands from the guesser's position, whence the designation "outside two" (asaʻka rū'pdakʻ). If the bones were supposed to be in the right-hand opponent's right hand and the left-hand opponent's left (from the guesser's position), he moved his hand down with the four fingers extended,—a guess known as "the middle" (ku'onak). If both concealers are believed to hold the bones in the hands nearer the door, thumb and index finger move in that direction, and the guess is termed "he went to the door" (biri'acdēky). Contrariwise, thumb and index move in the opposite direction, and the guess is called "he went to the lodge" (acu'c-dēky).

This popular game figures fairly often in native tradition. Old Man Coyote once assembled all creatures, winged and wingless, to make them play, helping each group alternately throughout the night. Finally the birds won, Magpie went up, raised his wing and got the first light on it, whence its white color. In another version the earth is represented as continually dark and the birds, backed by Old Man Coyote, play for daylight. Less mythological stories tell of men who lost all their belongings in this game, went for a vision, and as a result of the blessing they obtained recovered all their losses.

Dice are emphatically associated with women. When I tried to get an explanation from Gray-bull's wife, her husband grew very impatient. He said it was a woman's game, the women always went off by themselves in playing it, and he himself did not understand it though he had lived with Crow women all his life. There are two quite distinct types of dice,—"plum seed play" (buruʻpiru'a) and "four sticks" (bare' cō'pe).

Instead of plum pits, bones varying in shape—triangular, diamond-shaped, circular, etc.—are often substituted (Fig. 10). The marking likewise varies a good deal, and with it presumably the count. A set consists of six pits or bones, a wooden bowl, and ten or twelve tally-sticks. The player puts the dice into the bowl, with which he strikes a robe on which it rests, thus making the dice fly up. According to one explanation, if all dice turn up the same, i.e. either plain or marked, the score is 6; three marked discs and two marked triangles nets 1; two marked discs and one triangle, 3; and so forth. If a player was unlucky, she would turn to a friend, saying, "I am not lucky, wash them for me." Then her friend rubbed the dice between her palms and handed them back.

The stick dice were thrown on a flat stone in the middle of a circular piece of tanned hide marked with a white circle. I bought a number of sets,—some of four, others of eight sticks, which varied in length from, say, 7 to 12 inches. Only the widest were half an inch in width, a quarter of an inch approach-

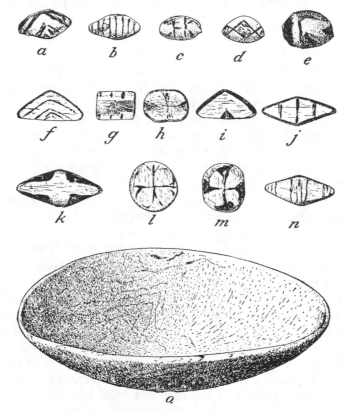

Fig. 10.—Set of bone dice, with wooden bowl from which they are thrown by striking it on ground.

ing the average. The sticks were grooved or ungrooved, the latter being quite flat on one side and very slightly convex on the other. Some of them exhibit a long line in the center, suggesting an incipient groove. Both types of dice bear burnt decorations, which vary greatly in pattern. When, as sometimes happens, both sides are marked, the designs on them differ. Transverse parallel lines are common. The figure of a gun or a man counts ten points, another form of mark scores 9. According to one informant women got famous warriors to paint their dice with pictures of men or horsetracks.

Dresses, elk teeth, and quilts were wagered on the outcome of dice casting.

Gambling also accompanied athletic games, foremost among them "mock-hunting" (batsī'kisu'a), i.e., hoop-throwing. I collected two types of hoop,—one a plain bark-wrapped ring not quite circular, with diameters of 9¼ and 10 inches (Fig. 11a); the other a netted wheel about a foot in diameter and with a circular opening in the center (Fig. 11b). A dart I bought was about 42 inches in length and terminated in two plumed prongs at one end (Fig. 11c).

The players took up positions on level ground, with two score-keepers holding small willow sticks as counters. Both contestants used the same ring, hurling their darts at it as it was rolling along. The one who came closest to the hoop scored. Others say the dart should pass through the hoop, and through the center hole of the netted hoop. Lacking stakes, the winner was privileged to chase his opponent and strike him on the back with the hoop.

The game was sometimes varied. One player rolled the hoop, the other threw a dart at it, which was stuck into the ground where the hoop fell, and the first player shot at it with bow and arrows, losing all the missing arrows. Several young men could join on each side.

This game, too, figures prominently in myth. Thus, it is when she peeps through the sky-hole and sees the hoop-players running to and fro in her native village that a woman married by the Sun is overcome with homesickness. Also there is the tale of a man who gambled away all he had at the "mock-hunt," not only his horses and tipi, but even his wife. Of course after a vision he recoups his fortune.

Shinny or "ball-striking" (bū'ptsaritu'a) was essentially a women's game, though sometimes the Night Hot Dancer Club and their wives were pitted against the Big Ear Holes and their wives, like the Foxes and Lumpwoods of earlier times. It was a spring game. The ball was tossed into the air and each group of players tried to drive it to the opposite goal, marked by blankets. Mr. Simms of the Field Museum in Chicago collected a ball of

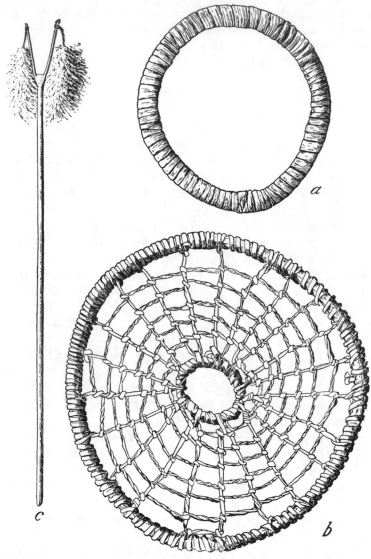

FIG. 11.—(*a*) Ring used in variant of the hoop-and-pole game; (*b*) netted wheel;
(*c*) dart for wheel.

flattened spheroid shape, with a seam in the middle; the stick
was a sapling 38 inches long and curved at one end. The Crow
seem to have allowed carrying the ball in their hands, a practice
barred by other tribes. For, the story goes, Long-ear's daughter,

once playing on horseback, dismounted when the ball was knocked toward her, picked it up, and remounted, her opponents seizing the horse's tail and clinging to its sides. Unable to get through them the rider threw the ball to the goal. At the same gathering another woman seized the ball and ran with it. Her opponents gave chase and grasped her belt, which she unbuckled and left in their hands. When they gained upon her, she growled like a bear, raising her hands, and frightened them off so that she was able to make her goal. This, my informant added, was great playing. Naturally all sorts of amusing incidents occurred. A woman once raised her dress in running away and managed to get the ball to a swift couple on her own side. The spectators said, "They saw her legs, but could not catch her."

When men and women played together, a particularly fast couple was chosen on each side, probably for the final drive to the goal. On such occasions the women dressed in their best clothes, wearing elk-tooth dresses that reached down to their ankles.

V. Literature

VERBAL cleverness is common among the Crow and they play with words as such. There are "tongue-twisters" like our "She sells sea-shells by the seashore,"—phrases to be rattled off at top-speed without confusion of the proper sounds. Perhaps the best-known is: basakapupe'cdec akapupapa'patdetk, "My people who went to the Nez Percé are not wearing Nez Percé belts." I once took the sentence down from my interpreter's dictation, carefully memorized it, and then fairly staggered an old Indian by quickly and correctly reciting it. True puns occur. I asked Yellow-brow what clan he belonged to. At once he answered in Crow: "As soon as you look at me, I am plainly revealed, you ought to know me. These lips of mine [pointing at them] are sore, I am a Sore-lip."

The attention to words as such attains incredible heights. One morning Yellow-brow prefaced his dictation with the remark that he wished to explain three words he often used in story-telling: One was "e"; sometimes it meant "yes"; sometimes an audience uttered it to encourage a narrator to proceed; finally, a speaker ejaculated it when he had forgotten something. The second word was "di'a": it could mean "Do it" as an imperative, but also—after a stop—"Go ahead." Finally, the expletive ha't'ak' could best be illustrated by a query and answer. One man might ask, "When did you make that sweat-lodge?" The other would reply, "Ha't'ak' (Why), I made it the day before yesterday."

That is to say, Yellow-brow considered speech not merely as a means of communication, but had begun to analyze its elements as to their meaning and use. No wonder my interpreter referred to him as "my dictionary." To be sure, not all men display the same interest in matters of diction; the extraordinary thing is that in one generation there are several people of this type,— illiterates like Yellow-brow and No-horse—recognized as masters of their mother tongue. About one of them I was told twenty-odd years ago that he would get up at a council and use words no one had ever before heard but which nevertheless every one at once understood.

With this power over their mother tongue some Indians unite unusual dramatic sense and great aptness at repartee. In 1931 I attended a council at which No-horse bitterly assailed Deer-nose, whose professions of piety as a member of the (Baptist) Church he contrasted with his inequitable distribution of meat at a fair. At one stage he said, "When white men tell you to jump, you jump, when they say, 'Walk,' he walks." In the course of the sentence No-horse suited his action to the words and executed a ludicrous jump, to the great amusement of the audience. Deer-nose, though less dramatic, was not backward in replying, and for several minutes vituperations flew back and forth in a steady stream.

A good many years ago I jestingly told an informant that I belonged to his wife's clan. After a while the conversation veered to military societies and discovering that my friend was a Lumpwood, I said, "I am a Fox; next spring I'll steal your wife." Instantly, connecting the threat with my previous statement, he shamed me by saying, "Go and marry your *sister!*" Chuckling over his victory, he added, "First *you* struck *me,* then *I* struck *you!*"

The Indians' extremely keen sense of incongruity has led to a distinct category of stories. Recent events of local interest that stimulate the risibilities of the people are worked up by gifted humorists into brief drolls, which are told and retold for popular entertainment. I remember a tale about a jealous husband who was about to shoot himself at sight of his wife's lover. However, the gun slipped down his throat and he began howling for help. The contrast between his timidity and his suicidal pretensions was considered extremely funny.

White-arm ranks especially high among narrators of this class. He dictated to me a story about a former Indian policeman I had known, one Scolds-the-bear. Once an aged Crow couple came to him with the request that he recover some stolen money for them; as inducement they offered him five dollars. Their idea was, of course, that he should exert himself in his official capacity. The policeman, however, was something of a wag and pretended to use whirlwind medicine for the purpose. Accordingly, he burnt incense and went through a lot of hocus-pocus, including a song in Hidatsa words, but of course failed to benefit his clients by these efforts. White-arm imitated the mock-performance and the song in a ludicrous way, which I could not duplicate if I tried. Nevertheless, even without these embellishments the Crow text, whenever read to Indians, immensely amused them, and I was obliged to repeat the reading again and again. I was equally successful with a somewhat more original performance. With the aid of my interpreter I concocted a grandiose account of how as a young man I had gone to the mountains for a vision. A huge bear had appeared and given me for my sacred song the lullaby on page 35; he had promised me great success on the warpath but imposed a taboo: henceforth I was never to eat the flesh of his kind. In consequence of this revelation I went against the enemy, cut an impossible number of picketed horses, and destroyed a vast host of Sioux. I could certainly not have wished for a more appreciative audience; one Indian auditor would fetch another to listen to these grotesqueries and would linger to hear the tale all over again. Though the ridiculousness of my going on a fast at all and my braggadocio about imaginary exploits were hugely enjoyed, it seemed to me that nothing struck my friends as more ludicrous than making the lullaby do the work of a sacred song.

Of course there are also serious narratives of actual occurrences, particularly of warfare. No-shinbone's report of a raid (p. 221) is a good sample. Its essence was sufficiently well known to be at once ascribed to him when I read the text to some Indians several years later. Compared with myths and tales of long ago, it has a very simple staccato style but, though bald, is not lacking in effectiveness. For some reason the sentence "We were so cold we almost died" always produced laughter. The repetitiousness, the listing seriatim of routine activities such as camping, fire-making, cooking, eating, smoking, sleeping is characteristic of Crow style.

Stories were properly told of a winter night when people were sitting by the fire or had stretched out before falling asleep. Some old person famed as a raconteur might have been invited to a feast and was then asked to entertain. He would begin by crying "ikye'!" ("Attention!") His auditors were expected to respond "e" (Yes) after every few sentences. As soon as this response failed him, the narrator knew that every one had fallen asleep and broke off his tale, possibly to resume it the next night. The etiquette followed is well brought out in the tale of Old Woman's Grandchild. Formerly people were afraid to tell stories in the summer. According to one Indian this was because the morning-star comes only in the winter time. The restriction to the night is similarly explained: the named stars all used to live on the earth and they appear only after dark.

Nowadays Yellow-brow, approximately 70 years of age, enjoys a well-merited reputation as a story-teller; young folks invite him to a collation of wild-cherry pudding and make him recount part of his repertory. He told me that his grandfathers, Good-buffalo-calf and Uses-scalp-for-a-necklace, were both eminent men and of distinguished families, both being thus well posted. Children liked to hear stories and would ask their elders to tell them, and in this way Yellow-brow acquired his stock,—mainly from his father's father.

A Crow audience, it should be noted, is likely to be critical even when listening to acknowledged masters. Thus, idiom requires a statement to end with the particle "tseruk" if the speaker is quoting what he has been told rather than reporting something personally witnessed. But in the story of Scolds-the-bear and the couple he duped, White-arm was said to use this particle too frequently: you were supposed to suffix it "only when it is right." Similarly, Yellow-brow was criticized for constantly interlarding his narratives with the expletive "ha't'ak'": this appeared as a reprehensible mannerism. Where such giants failed to escape, lesser men might naturally provoke derision, as happened in the case of one or two of Plenty-hawk's stories, which were bluntly branded as inferior, though of course not to his face.

It is difficult to determine precisely the standards applied in judging a literary performance. In general, the listener exacts a clear visual image, as definite a localization of the action as possible, and resents verbal inconsistencies. Thus, the suffix "kci" when added to verbs suggests sportiveness. Yellow-brow in one tale used it in connection with a victory celebration and was criticized for applying it to so serious an occasion. Presumably native sensibilities were shocked somewhat as ours might be by a reference to a "jolly funeral sermon." When characters are represented as speaking, the ideal is to define their identity beyond misunderstanding. My texts exhibit many sins against this canon, but I suspect that there are extenuating circumstances. On the one hand, stories are often so well known, or the implication so clear to a Crow, that a native auditor is not left in doubt; secondly, the unaccustomed use of dictation must somewhat distort the normal narrative style. By way of compensation I often find verbose reiteration of a person's identity. The narrator ushers in a quotation with "So-and-so it was that spoke" and concludes it with "It was So-and-so who spoke thus." When, as happens not infrequently, a character is anonymous, the storyteller does not shirk cumbersome phraseology, such as, "It was this man who had just entered who spoke." Apropos of this topic we must note that the Crow language is without any form of indirect discourse, hence the vivacity that appears in a literal English rendering does not accurately represent the aboriginal literary values, since the Indian has no choice in the matter. He cannot say, "They are telling me that I have not scored," but *must* express his meaning by, " 'You have not scored,' they are saying."

Clear pictures imply ample descriptive detail, and it is in the satisfaction of this demand that individual differences are clearly seen. In the Old Woman's Grandchild myth the hero and the snakes are trying to put each other to sleep by reciting phrases suggestive of dozing off. In half a dozen versions collected by me this "hypnosis" motif is identical, yet no two of them are quite the same. First of all, the variants are of two types: Grandchild either insists on telling stories first, or he allows the snakes to begin. The latter procedure evidently adds to the frame of the episode but obviously makes additional demands on the artist. In a text otherwise good but weak in this particular phase the hero merely says, "In the spring when there is a little wind in the daytime we sleep well"; and "In the summer, when the rain strikes the tipi and there is a rattling sound, we sleep well.'" Grandmother's-knife, though a story-teller of reputation, goes little beyond this. Grandchild is made to open the contest by saying, "In the fall, when it rains, we can hear the rain on the tipi and we shall sleep well." This he follows up with, "When we sleep among the pines with the wind blowing and hear the sound of the pines, we sleep well." There is no response, and he then kills all but one of his adversaries who wakes up in time to escape. Scratches-face chose the second alternative, which at once involves a complication: the hero must remain awake while the snakes are trying to hypnotize him, and this ability requires motivation. The traditional Crow device for this situation is to have the hero meet a jackrabbit before his visit and to exchange eyes with him: this enables him to *appear* awake while he is really asleep. In Scratches-face's tale, then, the snakes start: "In the spring when cherry and plum blossoms are in bloom, when we kill a deer we cook it on the sunny side of a cherry-tree thicket. In the fall when it is cool we are out a long time and when we come back to our tipi and find it warm, we go to sleep right away." At this juncture the boy wakes up and takes his turn: "When out hunting in the mountains, when we have killed a buffalo or deer toward evening and build a fire and cook, while we are cooking it grows dark. We are very tired. We take our cooked food and eat it. Rain comes and when we lie down to sleep, we sleep right away. All of you must be that way." Now all his opponents are asleep, and he cuts their heads off.

In approaching these incidents Yellow-brow at first inclined to the first type of version. He had already started with, " 'I am going to tell stories first,' said Old Woman's Grandchild." But he corrected himself, retraced his steps to the time before the hero's arrival, and like Scratches-face made him meet the jackrabbit en route so he could borrow his eyes. In other words, Yellow-brow knew both types of his myth and deliberately chose the harder one. And he elaborated it more efficiently than Scratches-face. For though the glassy stare of the jackrabbit eyes explains why the snakes believe their enemy to be awake, what really wakes him up so he can begin story-telling at the right moment? Yellow-brow supplies this deficiency: Grandchild bids his four magical arrows respond for him, and it is one of them that falls on his face to wake him up when his turn comes. Yellow-brow further creates something of a climax. The snakes suggest sleep with the words, "In the spring when we lie down under the young cherry-trees, with the grass green and the sun getting a bit warm, we feel like sleeping, don't we?" Grandchild begins with: "In the fall when there is a little breeze and we lie in some shelter, hearing the dry weeds rubbing against one another, we generally get drowsy, don't we?" At this point half of his auditors no longer respond. The hero continues: "In the daytime as the drizzle strikes the lodge pattering and we lie warming the soles of our feet, we fall asleep, don't we?" Again half of the snakes are asleep. The boy goes on: "At night when we lie down, listening to the wind rustling through the bleached trees, we know not *how* we get to sleep but we fall asleep, don't we?" Already all are asleep, but the hero wants to make sure—and the narrator presumably insists on *four* soporific utterances to conform to the sacred number: "Having looked for a hollow among the thickest pines, we make a fresh camp there. The wind blows on us, and we, rather tired, lie down and keep listening to the rustling pines until we fall asleep." Grandchild cries, "Attention!" There is no answer, and he proceeds to kill the snakes.

It is clear that Yellow-brow's actual *creation* is slight as compared with the bulk of the traditional material. His merit lies in his skillful manipulation of the transmitted stock-in-trade. He senses that the jackrabbit episode adds to the volume of his story and affords opportunities impossible in the simpler type. He has not invented the arrow motif but he uses it to supply the explanation of his hero's waking up which Scratches-face omits; his individual imagery is at least as rich as that of his competitors; and his feeling for climax is greater. All these are features the Crow fully appreciate. A good raconteur is one who tells the stories not in mere outline but with epic breadth, lingering on interesting details, and who conforms to the ideals of style.

From our point of view the longer Crow stories are generally lacking architectonically. The very attention to detail mars the effect because obvious implications have to be rendered explicit, because scenes like a buffalo hunt or the triumphant return from a raid are played up to the detriment of the story. No character simply goes from one place to another: he must start, proceed, come, and arrive! In the beautiful tale of a woman's devotion to her abandoned lover, the topography of the country she must traverse to reach him is first set forth by one of the members of the party and sketched again in the report of the actual journey. And when Yellow-brow told me the deeply moving story of his mother's brother Young-rabbit (p. 331), his expansiveness in describing his uncle's costume, rattle, gun, and the trappings of his horse almost obscured the essential human tragedy.

Again, inconsistencies occur. Even in the well-crystallized tale of Old Woman's Grandchild the adoptive grandmother is delineated with gross inconsistency. The dominant idea is without doubt that she is in league with the powers of evil and seeking her ward's destruction while feigning love for him; yet both the beginning and the close of the story convey a quite different impression.

It is not at all easy to classify Crow tales. There are true myths like the stories about Old Man Coyote and Old Woman's Grandchild,—stories that explicitly deal with a condition of life different from that of recent times and accounting for the origin of a natural phenomenon or of some established usage. But the line between these and more matter-of-fact tales cannot be sharply drawn, for marvelous happenings belonged to the routine of life until a few decades ago, as shown by reports of visions experienced by men I personally knew. Also the origin of certain institutions may crop up in relatively matter-of-fact settings. Nor do the Indians ascribe greater value either to the plainly mythical or the obviously non-mythical category. Asked which of all the stories known to him he preferred, Yellow-brow listed the Old Man Coyote and two realistic orphan tales, the Twined-tail tradition and the tale of the brothers Walks-toward-his-horses and Gun hammer.

Naturally, there are stories every one knows after a fashion. This applies particularly to the Old Man Coyote cycle, some very obscene parts of which might be told with evident gusto by almost any one, though of course with varying degrees of skill. Women of the old school were probably no more prudish than the men: Young-crane, at all events, quite spontaneously told me the story of how Old Man Coyote came to sleep with his mother-in-law. The adventures of Old Woman's Grandchild are likewise generally known, and even today a contrary child is compared with the legendary hero. Of course, between knowing the episodes and knowing them well enough to tell them there is a wide chasm. Merely to suggest the possibilities of a single narrator, I report that in the summer of 1914 Grandmother's-knife told me half a dozen Old Man Coyote stories and about twenty-five others, including the substantial historical tale of Raven-face. Gray-bull, in contrast to Grandmother's knife, made no pretensions to being a raconteur and only told me stories occasionally, sometimes for purely linguistic purposes, so that what I recorded from his lips is not at all a fair intimation of what he knew. However, I owe him a version of the twin boy heroes' tale not much under five thousand words in length; three Old Man Coyote tales; and four or five legends.

To turn to the stories themselves: The Old Man Coyote cycle comprises an indefinite number of episodes and was probably never told in its entirety by any one man, though several parts of it are often combined at a single sitting. Frequently the chief character plays a mean part: he gets food by deceit and is in turn robbed; he marries a ghost and has no end of trouble; he insists on flying with a flock of geese and tumbles to the ground; he feigns death so as to marry his own daughter, but is found out; he vainly imitates several friends who have magically fed him and only makes himself ridiculous by his failure. Yet this incorrigible buffoon and unscrupulous lecher created the earth and instituted many Crow customs. Some even identify him with the Sun, the greatest of deities (see p. 252).

Very different is Old Woman's Grandchild, son of the Sun by an Indian woman, destroyer of the monsters that once infested this earth. He ultimately ascends to the sky to become Morningstar, while his adoptive grandmother turns into the Moon. Strangely enough, the very same exploits told of this hero are also ascribed to twin boys, Thrown-behind-the-draft-screen and Thrown-inside-a-spring; and there is hopeless confusion between these two myths, which we know from other mythologies to be originally distinct, a view, indeed, held by the Crow themselves. Since interest in both centers in the destruction of monsters, we can easily understand how the same feats might be ascribed indifferently to the twin heroes or the child of the Sun.

Many stories known from other Plains tribes turn up in a Crow collection. There is the tale of a young man who marries a buffalo-woman and begets a child with her. He offends her and she leaves with her son to join her people. The repentant husband follows and must undergo a test,—that is, he must tell his wife and son—both now in buffalo guise—from the other cows and calves. With the aid of his son he succeeds and recovers his wife and child. The familiar feud between the Thunderbirds and a water-dragon is told, with a human hero aiding the birds by rolling hot rocks into the monster's mouth as it comes up to devour the young nestlings. In one version this idea is combined with another widespread motif: the slayer of the dragon is a boy raised by benevolent dwarfs after he has been spilled from a dog-travois. Inept giants are not wanting, though they play a minor rôle; and there is an indefinite number of stories about supernatural patrons. Indeed, a favorite theme is that of the poor orphan, the unlucky gambler, the destitute couple whom some powerful being pities and raises to prosperity and fame. Another recurrent human motive is the punishment of a haughty beauty who has spurned meritorious suitors. The total amount of this traditional material is not easily estimated. In 1918 I published a collection of about 300 sizable pages, but Mr. Simms and Mr. Linderman have recorded some stories I failed to get, and I have myself since then secured a fair supplementary collection.

Poetry is not so adequately represented, though several types of songs fairly fall into this category. Some are rather trivial, like those made up by a jilted lover to revenge himself upon a former sweetheart (p. 53). Other songs of mockery were leveled at each other by rival clubs, especially in connection with wife-abduction. Thus, Straight-arm, who had taken back a kidnapped wife, was derided as follows: "Straight-arm has taken back his wife. It is well for you to keep her, let your wife come." Again, a Fox once killed the fine buckskin horse belonging to a Lumpwood kidnapper. The Lumpwoods made up this song: "You Foxes, eat ye the dung of the buckskin!"

The military societies, however, naturally also had songs expressive of their higher aims. Thus, the Hammer boys would sing: "The men are afraid (of the enemy), *I* shall meet him." Again, a Fox might chant: "You Foxes, I want to die, thus say I." When the Big Dogs were mourning a member, they intoned such words as: "Comrade, I dismount, I shall go."

Warriors were addicted to more than one kind of bravado. Thus, Spotted-rabbit is credited with the following, each line representing a distinct traditional product not invented by him but learnt from his elders:

> "I am looking for fortifications. I am entering them, I am going."
> "I'll cause so many young men's wives to cry. I, I have to die, thus do I."
> "Young women are mad about me. Now I will not stay elsewhere, I do it (die)."

Such war chants were usually revealed. Indeed, a returning visionary might be asked, "Have you any songs?" (di'cūwici?) One of these was given as follows:

> "Whenever there is any trouble, I shall come through it. Though arrows be many, I shall arrive. My heart is manly."

The following was probably also regarded as originally inspired by a higher source:

> "Eternal are the heavens and the earth; old people are poorly off; do not be afraid."

The sentiment here expressed is one of the most characteristic of the Crow: mortals cannot expect to live forever like the great phenomena of nature; let them console themselves with the thought that old age is a thing of evil and court death while still young.

Of the religious songs many are connected with the Tobacco organization and the wording often explicitly refers to the sacred weed. Here are some samples:

> "I am trying to raise Tobacco. It is mine, there is plenty, it is said. It is growing well, it is said. It is mine, there is plenty, it is said."

> "As it grows, it makes them dance, when it has grown it makes them dance. Now it is glad, it makes them dance. Hē! It is down below, there it is down below, down below, already down below. Hē! Look here, hahē'i!"

> "I, the Tobacco, am a person, look at me. I, I am the Tobacco, I am the medicine-rock, look at it."

> "I am the Tobacco; my body is Tobacco all over."

Sometimes definite reference is made to a special chapter of the order, say the Weasels, as in Muskrat's words:

> "The weasels are coming out. I'll make the Tobacco come out."

In the Eagle chapter, too, some of the songs refer to the eponym:

> "When I come from the rear, I shall have my two songs. I shall carry my medicines on my back. All of you, you are poor. Look at *me!* Over the hills there I have stayed, over the hills, thence I have come. I am an eagle. I am coming. I shall walk towards the Wolf Mountains."

Naturally, songs heard in connection with a vision were sometimes of cryptic character. They are as enigmatic at times as those of hypnagogic experiences. Bull-all-the-time, for instance, fasting on a mountain, saw a visitant holding a pipe with human hair and heard him sing: "In any country as I climb and come up."

Prayers may be quite simple expressions of wishes, but sometimes they are fairly elaborate, possess a rhythmic quality, and take rank as at least poetic prose. A fair example is furnished by the address to the Sun when dedicating to him an albino buffalo skin:

"Greeting, Father's Clansman, I have just made a robe for you, now I give it to you, this is it. Give me a good way of living. May I and my people safely reach the next year. May my children increase; when my sons go to war, may they bring horses. When my son goes to war, may he return with black face [see p. 225]. When I move, may the wind come to my face [so game shall not scent me], may the buffalo gather toward me. This summer may the plants thrive, may the cherries be plentiful. May the winter be good, may illness not reach me. May I see the new grass of summer, may I see the full-sized leaves when they come. May I see the spring. May I with all my people safely reach it."

This may be compared with the supplication addressed to the Sun when offering him a sweat-lodge of various orders of magnitude:

"Hallo, Small Sweat-lodge, 'We are making it for you,' I said; now I have made it. Mountains of renown, Big Rivers and Small Rivers, smoke. You Beings Above, smoke. Beings in the Ground, smoke. Earth, smoke. Willows, smoke. When the leaves appear, when the leaves are full-grown, when the leaves are yellow, when the leaves fall,—year after year I want to keep on seeing [these seasons]. For this I offer smoke. Hallo, Fat, wherever I go, I want to chance upon something fat. Charcoal, wherever I go, may I blacken my face [in token of victory], safely I want to return. You, Winds of the Four Quarters, smoke! Wherever I go I want the wind towards me, wind do not send me there on my account (?)."

Finally must be mentioned the efforts at formal oratory, of which a herald's speech on the eve of battle is a fair illustration

(p. 231). The speech delivered by a certain actor in the Tobacco ceremony partakes of the nature of both oratory and prayer:

"There was a war party, I went along. They charged, they made a killing, I captured a gun. Then I returned. When I got to the Tobacco you had planted, there was great abundance, round about the chokecherries were very abundant. Then I came. When I reached the camp there were no sick people. In safety you were harvesting the Tobacco."

Reviewing the several kinds of poetry and prose produced by the Crow, we cannot fail to discern traditional literary patterns. No Crow poet or narrator begins anew; his choice of themes, of episodes in a tale, of the very imagery in a speech or song are in large measure predetermined. To take up the last point first, it is surely no accident that most prayers not only embody a wish for long life but embody it in the specific form of seeing or reaching such and such a part of the year, which, moreover, is designated not by the current words for the seasons but by such descriptive imagery as "the full-sized leaves", "when the leaves turn yellow", "when the cherries are ripe." Similarly, it is no mere chance when one story-teller after another describes an exceedingly old person in such terms as "He was so old that his skin cracked as he moved about the tipi." We are evidently dealing with a cliché. Another stereotype is to contrast men who should be straining at the leash to get at the enemy with women in labor painfully waiting for a delivery: "It is women who give birth to children and suffer; then and there we think the children will come forth, still they strain for a long time. Well! unlike them *we* go forthwith [into battle]."

A marked stylistic feature is the striving for antithesis. When a benevolent dwarf rescues an expectant father he couches his promise to name the infant in these words: "If your child is a little boy, I'll name it; if a girl, I will not." The dwarf's wife thus chides her husband for his tardiness in helping the hero: " 'Bring my son soon,' I said, you have done it late." And when the rescuer learns that the young man had suffered at the hands of the very man the dwarf had once blessed with power his moral indignation finds vent in these words: " 'Try to benefit your people,' I said to him. 'Take away and possess their desirable property,' I did not say. 'Kill them continually,' I did not say." In the stories we find such phrases as: "Of these warriors the

wounded were very numerous; those not wounded were few."
"He used to be wifeless, now he had a wife." "All were men,
women there were none." So, when Old Man Coyote directs a
duck's diving, he does not issue a simple command, but says,
"When you get to it, if you get to something hard, that is not it.
If you get to something soft, put it into your bill." A good illustration is found in the piqued buffalo-woman's message to her
husband: "Go, tell your father: The women will sit down, the
children will sit down. If going among the children he himself
picks out you; if going among the women he picks out me, we
shall go home with him."

Antithesis may of course merge into more generalized types
of balanced structure. A father admonishes a youth in these
words: "Whatever Plays-with-his-face may do, follow him
therein. If he dies, die with him. If he performs some good deed,
perform it with him. Whatever he may do, do it with him." This
sample illustrates also the tendency to list a number of features
and wind up with an all-comprehensive summary. For example,
we find: "Our horses, our goods, whatever we own we shall give
to him." Or, "When young men went to war afoot, when they
went hunting, when young men did anything at all, he was
handicapped."

Parallelism is of course conspicuous in the prayers already
cited and appears in various ways in the stories. For instance,
his comrade thus advises Old Man Coyote: "If you allowed the
people you made to eat wild cherries and any very good plants,
very good roots, it would be well. If they also ate buffalo and
deer and elk—these very good animals—, it would be well. . . .
If they built fires, cooked thereby and ate, it would be well."
In the building up of a plot parallel structure may be coupled
with parallelism of phrase. The episodes of the Grandchild saga
may be severally ushered in by the grandmother's mock-warning,
which is followed by the hero's questionings or feigned acquiescence, his deliberate flaunting of her counsel, his encounter with
the monster, his triumphant return to the old woman, who pretends to be weeping from sorrow over his supposed destruction.
Sometimes there is repetition of the same thought in different
phraseology. A boy affirms, "I'll remember, I'll not forget."
Cirape', in pleading for diversity of speech among Indians, says,
"If our speech were different, if we could not understand one

another, we could get angry at some one, we could get furious
at some one." Again, we find phrases like: "He divorced his wife,
he was wifeless." "His mother died, then he had no mother."
And a wife warns her husband, "Do not abuse me. Don't say,
'You are like a ghost.' "

Hyperbole sometimes figures rather amusingly. When Old
Man Coyote asks his comrade whether he has ever had a wife
abducted, the answer is: "Why, they have been kidnapped several
times; a charge by the enemy is less disagreeable." And in describing a swollen leg Yellow-brow said, "They noticed his leg;
his body was smaller than it."

In the tales soliloquy is fairly frequent. Old Woman's Grandchild says to himself, "Old Woman's Grandchild, I have reached
what your grandmother spoke about." His grandmother asks
herself, "What shall I do to get rid of this boy?" Old Man
Coyote also indulges in such monologues as, "Ancient Man,
every day you roam about, yet you have never chanced upon
anything like this."

There are also such refinements as rhetorical queries and
irony. Cirape' spurns the suggestion that *he* might have taken
back a kidnapped wife with, "What! I am a man of honor, I have
self-respect. How could I take back a divorced wife?" When
the boy hero meets an enraged snake, he mocks it with, "Well,
then, Pretty-one, what are you going to do, eh?" The more pre-
tentious attempt at corrosive sarcasm by One-eye's sister has
already been cited in another context (p. 58).

Naturally, symbolic expressions appear again and again that
are transparent to any Crow but presuppose knowledge of native
custom. Thus, "returning with blackened face" means triumph
(p. 225), "having one's moccasins made" indicates getting ready
for a raid, "carrying the pipe" is equivalent to being captain of
a party. Again, a man pledged to foolhardiness asks his wife,
"Why did you wish to marry me? Poor dear, do you not love
your forefinger that you married me?" This of course refers to
the widow's obligation to chop off a finger-joint in mourning.

Enough has been said to prove that Crow literature has a
definite formal tradition. The substance of songs, prayers, and
oratorical flights has been illustrated by the samples cited in this
and other chapters. There follow a number of representative
myths and tales.

VI. Selected Tales

THE following tales are among those dictated to me in Crow by Yellow-brow. I am confining my choice to stories recorded in the original, and the rendering is as accurate as seems consistent with intelligibility, my purpose being to afford some notion of the style as well as of the type of plot current among my Indians. In each case I have appended some explanatory comments.

OLD MAN COYOTE AND HIS DART

It was Old Man Coyote. He was going around, he was very hungry. He kept on going around. He got to a little coyote on slippery ice. He [the little coyote] had a little bell tied to the end of his tail. He would run on the ice: when he went trotting, this little bell punctured the ice when it struck it, and each hole would be filled with tallow. This coyote would turn back, retrace his steps, pick up the fat, and eat as he went along. Old Man Coyote watched him. "My younger brother, what you own [your power] is wonderful! Do it for me," he said. "Why, I get my food by it, I love it, I don't want to give it up. If I gave it away, I'd be hungry, I won't give it up," said this coyote. "Do it, my younger brother!" "This possession of mine is most valuable." "My dart is fine [said Old Man Coyote]; if I give it to you, give me your possession." He took it and gave it to him. "This is splendid!" This coyote liked it. "Well, all right," he said, and gave it him. He [Old Man Coyote] tied it [the bell] to the lower part of his blanket and went. He ran on the ice, he allowed it to strike it, he punctured the ice, and the holes were filled with fat. He turned around, took it and ate it. He liked it.

This coyote was holding his dart. It was Old Man Coyote that came to him. "My younger brother, I'd like to look again at that dart I owned. It's no longer part of me, but please give me my dart, I want to look at it again, then I'll go my way." Then he gave it to him. Old Man Coyote took it and examined it. Then he said, "Ha, ha!" [exclamation of ridicule] and ran away. "Long ago I used to do this for fun," he said and ran away. The little coyote said: "Old Man Coyote, don't do it four times!" Old Man Coyote said: "Just now I've told you that I used to do this long ago." "Nevertheless I have said it." Then he walked away.

He went on and reached a tipi. The ice was slippery. He went, he got there. "Well, Ancient Man," he said [to himself], "you are very hungry, for some time you have not done anything. If your hunger is satisfied, it will be well." He went and reached this ice. He went round a bend of the river, there was a second bend, and he still went around. He stopped. "Do this, keep on eating what is there, that's the way." He turned back, he picked up this tallow as he went. He retraced his steps, he ate up all the fat. "That's the way, keep on roaming about. Ancient Man, you always get hungry, what can make you hungry now?" He roamed about. After a while he had done it three times. Toward the end of his third trial he slipped forward and almost fell, but then he regained his balance and stood up. "Well! My anus moved, now we'll stop." He stopped, turned around, picked up the fat and ate it all. "Come on, your hunger is satisfied." He kept on roaming around. Then he got very hungry. "Come, Ancient Man, we have become very hungry again, we'll get to the river and feast." He went thither and reached the river. The ice was slippery. He tied this bell to the lower part of his blanket. He went running on the ice. As he started to go, he slipped, his anus struck the ground and got stuck to the ice. He remained there unable to help himself. He sat on the ice; he vainly tried to get free.

A prairie-chicken came. "My dear younger brother [said Old Man Coyote], come, I have an idea now." "Well, what is it, elder brother?" "Let us have a pleasant dance. You have big pouches, the space inside is pretty big, go ahead and fill them with roseberries, keep on pouring them out," he said. He kept pouring out plenty of roseberries, there was plenty.

A beaver came there. "My dear younger brother, come here, I want to invite that one, bring me an instrument to sing with!" "Yes, what shall I do?" "Bunch willows; your teeth are sharp, gnaw an armful and bring it!" "Here it is," said he and brought it. "Clip it for a grip for me!" "How long shall I make it?" "This size make it." He judged it, he made it the right size. "Here it is," he said and gave it to him, laying it down.

"Hallo, magpie, come, my younger brother." He came and got there. "What is it, my elder brother?" "Speak for me, please, you have a loud voice: 'That Old Man Coyote wants to feast you, he calls you, he is inviting you. Beavers, skunks, cottontails, jackrabbits, prairie-dogs, porcupine,—it is you animals whose feet touch the ground that he invites.' You, prairie-chickens, rose-berries are your food and it's not yet the season for you to dance, but if you do dance, you are the ones I most want to see. When you are through dancing, you'll eat plenty," he said.

He took this stick. "Hey there," he said, "I'll tell you some-thing." "Yes," they said. "When I sing, then all of you shut your eyes! At the height of my song, go under my anus." "Yes," said they. Then when he was at the height of his song, they went under his anus that stuck to the ice. It got loose. He cast about for the fattest animals and hit them severally on the top of their ears, knocking them down. He tried to get a very fat one-eyed prairie-dog to come closer. It never did. "One-eyed prairie-dog, what is the matter? It is you I want to show off, come close to me, I want to see you above all." "I am afraid of you, you are the one who caused me to lose an eye!" "No, indeed, come close, come to me and dance, I want to see you above all, come at least once!" he said. This prairie-dog went, first half shutting his eyes, he watched him. He went, he jumped back, he glanced. As soon as he opened his eyes, he saw his companions strewn about. "What! Old Man Coyote has been destroying us! Save yourselves!" he cried and went inside a crack in the ice. The rest separated and fled. Whenever he did thus he got a good meal. He got up, built a fire and cooked. He had a good meal.

* * * * *

Comment: I secured this tale from at least two other in-formants, and still another version has been printed by Mr. Simms. Yellow-brow shows the Trickster in his usual rôle of getting food by unscrupulous methods; overreaching himself, he gets stuck on the ice but succeeds in extricating himself and incidentally once more adds to his food supply by duping animals he pretends to befriend. Grandmother's-knife (p. 108) gives the main episodes in much the same way, even including the wording of the coyote's warning to the trickster and of the one-eyed prairie-dog's distrust. However, this narrator introduces an element of poetic justice: Old Man Coyote's hand gets stuck in the crack of a creaking tree, so that his counterpart Cīrape' makes off with his ill-gotten spoils. In my third variant, the tree incident is omitted, Cīrape' simply availing himself of the time while his companion is asleep.

THE CREATION

How the water and Old Man Coyote originated, I do not know. He spoke: "Why, that I am alone is bad. If I looked at some one now and then, if I talked with him, it would be well. That I am alone is bad," he said. It was Old Man Coyote [that spoke]. All over this earth was water. He was going about. He came, he reached two small red-eyed ducks. "Well, my younger brothers, in this going around of yours have you suspected that something exists?" "Why, elder brother, in this our moving about we have not suspected anything." It was the ducks that were talking. "Even though that is so, have you any suggestions to make?" It was the ducks: "Well, we do not know, yet something our heart believes." "That's it, that's what I am asking. What does your heart believe?" "Why, we are thinking how it may be far inside the water." "Go ahead, all right. You are able to dive long. Go diving. If you reach something inside the water, take some and bring it. Now here I'll await you, now go!" This duck's companion then dived. The other one went off. Then and there he waited. Old Man Coyote said: "Why, my younger brother must have died, he has not come back for a long time." It was his companion [that spoke]: "That is probably not so; our limit has not yet been passed, he will come. It is not possible that he is dead as yet, our limit has not been reached."

Time passed, after a long time this duck came out. He proceeded; he reached Old Man Coyote. "Well, my dear younger brother, is there something you are bringing?" "Yes," he said, it is said. "This time when I went, somewhere something struck me, I took it. Having taken it, I brought it, whatever it be." "Where?" said Old Man Coyote. "Here it is," he said and gave it to him. Some small root it was, they say, from a plant or a tree. Old Man Coyote took it and looked it over. "Well, some-where this earth is there, hence this comes from that place. Why, my younger brother, as for what you suspected, there is no doubt of it. Well then, now go [again]. This time if something hits you, do not look towards it. When you get to it: something hard, *not;* [1] when you get to something soft, put your bill into its hollow and bring it, take some and bring it." "Yes, that I will do, now I'll go." Right then he went diving. They remained waiting. Then after a long time Old Man Coyote asked this other duck, "How is it now? It is a long time, it seems." "He is dead now," he thought, that is why he said it. The duck it was that spoke, "No, he will come." He came back. After a while he came back. "Yes, how did you make out? Are you or are you not bringing anything?" "Yes, this soft thing, whatever it be, I have brought." He had put it into his bill. There was a little dirt, a little mud. Inside his feet he had it. He looked it over. Then: "Well, my younger brothers, this we'll make big, we shall make our abode." "As for us, we are powerless; *you* will do it." "Well, then, go, keep going around, go far away, stay away for a while." "All right."

This Old Man Coyote took the dirt and blew on it. He forthwith made the earth, though not large. Having done it, he was pleased. It was fine. Then the ducks came back. "What a surprise! My elder brother, why is this so fine?" "Are you pleased?" he asked. "Yes," they said. "All right, we'll make it big." "Do so, it is good." Then somehow he blew on this dirt. Now it became very big, as now. "Why, it is not well that there is nothing on it; if there were something, it would be well." "All right, where?" He took this little root, he made the grass, the trees, the trees on this earth, the different kinds of plants and food. He looked it over, then the duck spoke: "It is fine. But its being too level is bad. If there were rivers, if the earth were hollowed out into some little coulées and hills, it would be well." He traced rivers, he made water, he went around; the ducks went around, Old Man Coyote went around. "Why, these rivers are too far apart. If there were water here and there, between springs and coulées, it would be well. If we could drink water wherever we may go when we get thirsty, it would be well." "Thus I'll do," he said, and went.

Old Man Coyote pondered and looked around. "Why, my younger brothers, why, I have an idea. Why, if we had com-

[1] That is, "Ignore anything hard."

panions, if there were a number of us, it would be well. We are alone, we are bored. If we had companions, it would be well; where we live [the earth] is a big place." *"We,* we are powerless, do as you please." The ducks spoke thus. Then he took a little dirt, it is said. Old Man Coyote it was who spoke: "This I'll make into people." "Why, do as you please." How he did it, that we do not know: this dirt he took, he made persons; all were men, women there were none. With them he went around, he liked it. They continued going around. After a while this duck said: "Why, my elder brother, you made many companions for yourself, us you made alone." Old Man Coyote pondered. "Why, that is surely so. Your words are right. I'll make company for you, you shall not be alone." After a while he made different kinds of ducks. This duck was pleased. All these ducks were males. Then Old Man Coyote looked at all these people and was pleased. "Why are these people all men? Why, if there were women, men would be content and it would be well. There is no way for these people to grow. If there were women, by means of them they would grow, and it would be well." "Why, it is for you to decide." It was the duck that spoke. He took dirt, again with that he made women. The duck said: "Why did you make women for these persons and not make females for these ducks? Your not making females is bad; if you made some, it would be well." "I'll do it." After a while he made females.

That's the way it was. He went around, he went around. Wherever or however it happened, he saw a coyote, wherever he may have come from. "Why, come please, my younger brother! What a surprise! Where have you been keeping yourself? What place do you come from?" This coyote spoke: "Well then, my elder brother, where I come from I know not, I am on this earth, that is it." "Well, all right, what is your name?" "Why, Cīrape' they call me." This Cīrape' asked: *"You,* what is *your* name?" "They call me Old Man Coyote. You are my true younger brother, do you not know me?" Then after a while he answered: "I know you, I was looking for you, so I came." [2]

With him he went around. "Well, why the earth is fine, your residence is very big, everything could be made on it. All right, name different animals!" he said. "Yes." Buffalo, deer and elk and horses and bears,—these animals he named, made, and

[2] The rendering of this phrase is uncertain.

sent away. He made different small animals, then he made the
bear.

Then with the bear he sat down. Cīrape' and a buffalo bull
were there. Then the bear spoke: "I feel offended by Old Man
Coyote." "Don't say that," he said, "I am the one who made you,
I like you." "What! [3] By myself I have grown." Again [Old
Man Coyote spoke]: "What! I am the one who made you."
"Well, if that is so, make an animal so I'll see you forthwith."
"All right." Well, the bull was there, he took a muscle from him.
This coyote's claws he took, this bear's claws he took. A little
hairy worm was there. "Come here, my younger brother," he
said and took him. "I'll make a bird." He took the muscle and
the wolf's claws he took and made a beak out of it. The little
hairy worm he took and made the web of the feet. There was a
boxelder there, he took leaves, he made a tail from them. "Well,
of your claws give me one." This bear gave him that. "Yes," he
said. Out of it he made the wings. A prairie-chicken it was.

He said to this bird he had made: "Come, you are an incomplete creature. There is nothing you can do, I'll tell you what
you should do. Now and then, when any people roam around,
frighten them! That is your gift, that is what you will do." He
took dirt, he rubbed his body. Then it looked grayish and not
very well. He was looking at it. "Come, my younger brother,
I forgot something important." He came, he got there. "Now
by means of it I'll make you handsome. Something very good
I'll give you now. There are many very pretty birds, this way
there are none, you alone shall be thus." He took white clay,
this way he sprayed it. "Early in the morning, as soon as the
sun appears, just before it appears, dance, dance for your pleasure. Make your tails rattle, it is fun. When you dance, raise
your tails, rattle, loosen your wings, put your heads close to the
ground and dance. In the evening, too, do it for pleasure. Just
before sunset, at dusk, stop. Do you like it? How about what
I have given you?" he said. "What you have given me is good;
where is there anything like it?" "Well, if so, do it right away,
the rest of us shall watch you. Dance right there, spread your
wings." They raised their tails, they shook them, their heads
they put near the ground. "Hm, hm," he said and left.

This bear spoke: "When you made me, why did you not give

me that power? You have treated me unfairly. Come, give me some of that power. If you don't do it, I'll take back that claw of mine right away." "Why, 'I have grown by myself,' you said, some sort of dance you will make by yourself." [4] "Why, my elder brother, I didn't know, that is why. Some dance make for me." He envied this prairie-chicken's mode of dancing, that is why he acted thus. "Well, all right, you shall dance," he said. "How shall I act?" "Now I have given it to you, *you* shall dance." "All right, I shall dance." A tree was there; a little mountain-grouse was there. "Why, those chickens had no musicians. *I'll* have a musician." To the mountain-grouse he said, "Come hither and make music for me; stay on the other side of this tree. Now sing, I'll start to dance." Where he took it from, or how, we know not, he had a drum. Then this bear took sweet-smelling sagebrush and held it. Red paint he put across his forehead, with it he painted a line. He made the tear-line. This sweet-smelling sage he took, with it he shielded his face. This little mountain-grouse uttered its call. He beat the drum, he sang. This bear danced, he came. Towards the tree dancing he came. Then this prairie-chicken said: "*He* is no dancer, this one! I'll show you," he kept saying. Then this bear spoke thus [with a gesture]: "When you danced, did *we* dance? You want to dance." He was angry with this one. Would he harm him or not? Of a sudden he saw Old Man Coyote and stopped. The chickens did not dance, because they were displeased. The bear hugged this tree, he rubbed his face. He squirted out at the same time red paint and dust. That's how it was. "What are you trying to do? Why are you angry at him?" It was Old Man Coyote who asked the bear. "Well, why is that chicken dancing?" "Why, in the spring he is happy, the ground is visible, everything is growing, he likes it, that is why he feels like dancing. Why did *you* dance? You shall tell us that." "Why, when wild cherries or any plants are ripening I am pleased, that is why I danced. Still next year I shall do thus." "If so, it is well," he said, "do so! It is well."

"Now, go ye! [said Old Man Coyote]." The bear it was who asked: "All right, where shall I live?" "Why, you are bad, you are quick-tempered, you are bad, stay in a hiding-place. Stay among the woods, also in the mountains. Whatever you do,

---

[4] That is, "Why don't you then make a dance yourself?"

you'll be a failure." "What! [sneer]. We shall sometimes succeed." "Go, go and hide! Stay in the woods, among the mountains you shall stay. Whatever you do shall be a failure." Then
this bear said: "Ha! We shall sometimes succeed. What shall
I eat?" The bear it was who asked. "You shall keep on eating
anything that grows." "What else shall I eat?" "All right, Why
—as to something else,—roots." Old Man Coyote it was [who
spoke]: "Ha! Why, whatever decayed things you see you shall
eat." He was greatly displeased.

In the beginning the bear had bullied the different creatures
made by Old Man Coyote. He also had considered Old Man
Coyote in the same class and also tried to bully him. "Don't do
it, I am the one who made you." "Ha! [sneer], you did not
make me, there's no truth to that. I grew by myself." "All right,
if I took back your gifts, what would you do?" "Well, if *you*
made me, make an animal forthwith." This is how it was he
found out, then he stopped talking. This little chicken he was
about to maltreat, when he recalled [his argument with Old
Man Coyote] and stopped. This is what Old Man Coyote had
said: In anything he attempted he would be a failure. Thus it
was.

"Go ye!" With Cīrape', his so-called younger brother, he
went around. Cīrape' was roaming around. "By the way, Ancient
Man, there are many very fine things you did not make [though
you might have made them]." "What?" he asked. "Well, what
do these people eat?" "Why, here they are living in the best
way." "What!" It was Cīrape'. "What! If you let these people
made by you eat wild cherries, any very good plants, very good
roots, if you let them eat that, it would be well. If they also ate
buffalo, deer, elk, these very good animals, it would be well.
You might also make clothing and homes for them. It would be
well if they built a fire, cooked on it and ate. Do not allow the
other animals to throw missiles; let the people alone throw
missiles." Old Man Coyote asked, "Well! why do you say that?"
Cīrape' answered: "Why, these people do not run fast, and they
eat animals. If these animals threw missiles, that would be bad;
they are swift. If these animals threw missiles they would have
no use for them; if they killed something, they would not eat
it, they have no use for it. These Indians throw missiles, kill

and eat. The reason I say it is that they cannot run." "Yes, all right."

"Why, there are many good things you do not know," [Cīrape' continued]: "one of the very best things [conceivable] is that human beings should dislike one another. Why is there only one language when these people have increased so as to be very plentiful? It is bad. If some people were different, if their speech were different, and their language diverse, it would be well. Our language is one, for that reason we cannot feel anger [against one another], for that reason we cannot feel content, we cannot dislike any one, we cannot get furious, we cannot be happy.[5] If you made our speech different, if we could not understand each other's speech, we could get furious, we could be angry, we could be happy, that's the way it is. If one day we are happy, if one day we are unhappy, if the good and the bad mixed with each other, and we'll have something to do, and thus we'll like each other, thence we shall have chiefs. Why, only a while ago I told you you did not know many good things: flirting with women is a good thing that you don't know about."

Old Man Coyote it was that now talked for the first time; while Cīrape' was talking, *he* was silent. "Well, these are some very fine things. I like this, I was going to talk about it, I was putting it off, you are cunning, you knew about it and were the first to talk about it." Cīrape' said, "Now, how did you know?" Old Man Coyote said: "Why, from a long time ago I have known it." Cīrape' asked: "If so, how did you know?" "Why, when we go on the warpath, from somewhere we bring horses, we reach the camp, we flirt, we sing tsū'ra songs, towards a woman we make eyes, the women look at us. We go on the warpath, we kill somebody, I strike a coup, we take their bows, we reach camp, we sing tsū'ra songs, we make women dance, that's the way. It is good. One thing I'll tell you. Newly married women are wont to satisfy us; when we have been married for a long time, we get dissatisfied. When we marry others, in the beginning it is the same way, that's the way, once more we have a lively interest [in our partner]. Cīrape', I thought you were cunning, but one thing you did not know." Old Man Coyote was [still] speaking: "When we secretly have married women

---

[5] This expresses the idea that warfare is essential for human happiness. Without it there would be no war honors, no chiefs, no victory parades.

as our sweethearts and under difficulties, they generally give great pleasure." Cīrape′ said: "Why, if there is any one in that state, it is I." "If so, I'll ask you something." It was Old Man Coyote that spoke. "All right, as for this mutual wife-stealing of ours, have you ever experienced it? Has your wife ever been taken away?" he asked. "Why, several times they have been taken away; a hostile charge is less disagreeable, of all the different things it stands out." "All right, have you ever taken back a divorced woman?" Old Man Coyote it was [who asked this]. Cīrape′ said: "What! I am honorable, I have self-respect. How could I take back a divorced wife?" Old Man Coyote said: "If so, you truly know nothing. Cīrape′, the truth is my wife—she must have given pleasure—has been kidnapped, and three times I have taken back the divorced woman. If they abduct our wives and we take them back, if anything happens when we do like this [gesture], she recalls the time she was stolen, we don't have to remind them, they will do anything whatever that we desire.[6] Our having wives [like this] is incomparable, it is grand. You will think that *I* have been married, that you have never been really married. If some day you will do as I say, then you'll really be married."

Cīrape′ answered: "*You* might think it was grand. But though you do it, the other people will look at you and mock you. That is the reason why I don't take back a divorced woman. Any one knowing about it would mock you, that's why I have self-respect,[7] that's the reason."

So much for that. Old Man Coyote kept divorced women, hence from this time to the present the Crow have kept divorced women. What Old Man Coyote and Cīrape′ were wont to do before us we noted and since then we do the same.[8]

Old Man Coyote roamed about. "Where, I wonder, is my younger brother Cīrape′ now? My child has been killed, I am helpless. If I killed some of the killers, it would be well." Cīrape′ appeared from over there and came towards him. He caught sight of him. He [Old Man Coyote] had scratched his body, he made all his clothes very ugly. He painted tear lines, he made his hair look ugly. He came hither and met Cīrape′. "Well, well!

[6] The meaning of this is explained on p. 56.
[7] The interpreter first translated: "hold myself sacred."
[8] Now the two comrades are supposed to have gone each his own way and not to have met for a long time.

Why are you grieving?" he asked. "You do not look well, you seem to grieve over something." "Cīrape', that is it. Just before I came here my child went hunting, the enemy met him, they killed my child, they killed all my wives. They took all my horses, they made me most miserable. Now I seek something to supplicate, some one to whom to offer tobacco I seek, I am going about crying continually. I want to kill some of the ones who made me miserable, I want vengeance. Hence I roam around looking for something all the time."

Cīrape' said: "As for me, I am a scout. I am helpless. Scouting trips are the only things I do, I do not lead war parties. Over there lives a man who is a very holy war-captain. We'll make him smoke." "Go ahead, wherever he is, take me there!" To that holy man they went, they came. "How shall I act?" "Why, there is his sacred pipe, take it out, put [tobacco] into it, you cry, you make him smoke. If he is willing, our horses, our property, whatever we own, we'll give to him. Then he will go on the warpath with us. Then we shall kill one of those who made you miserable, then we shall be happy." "Yes, that is well, go ahead." They went thither, they came. "By the way, what is that man's name?" "They call him Crane-chief." This one to whom they came was a crane. They came, he put something into his pipe, crying he took the head of the pipe, the mouthpiece he pointed toward Crane, at the same time he cried. Thus he did and gave it to him. This Crane it was that spoke: "Well, how is it, Ancient Man, that you make me smoke?" "Well, the enemies came and killed all my children and my wives. They took all my horses, they have made me miserable, that's why I keep going around crying. I have no power I could implore, I am miserable, I am going around continually, I want revenge, that is why I am offering you smoke." "Why! It is something very easily done." Crane it was that spoke. "As soon as the sun sets, we shall go singing from door to door, we'll go right out. He [the enemy] is not the only man; we, too, are men. We shall kill some one."

Old Man Coyote spoke: "Yes, thanks! That is the very thing I wanted you to do. I thought you would do that for me, that's why I made you smoke. I'll go meanwhile to have my moccasins made. I'll complete my outfit. I'll be awaiting you." "Yes," said the Crane, "come as soon as the sun sets." He reached camp, whatever belonged to a war party he took, he completed his outfit. Then he remained waiting for others. Then when the sun went down, he came. "Well, it is done. Now then, let us go, everything is ready. It is women in childbirth that suffer and still exert themselves for a very long time after we think their child should come out then and there. Well, [unlike them] *we* go [forthwith] and it will be done. Yes, put young women behind you, singing from door to door we'll reach the edge of the camp. When the young women get off, we'll go immediately."

After they had put the young women behind them, they sang for pleasure from door to door. Then they reached the edge of the camp. The young women got off. Then they started on the war party.

They went on, somewhere they slept. Cīrape' said: "I have already said what I do: scouting is what I can do, that I have already said." He was this warparty's scout. Cīrape' sighted the camp. He signaled the sighting. They took their medicines and put them on themselves. Old Man Coyote came and reached the leader. "My younger brother, look out for me. They have made me miserable." This man made medicine. "Some one we'll kill, we'll take a scalp unharmed, without mishap we shall take revenge." "That is what I asked you to make medicine for." "All right," said this Crane. He sang and made medicine. They ran against the camp. They killed one of the horse herders. Then they ran off. They took a scalp. Somewhere they slept, then they went home.

They reached the camp. Early the next morning they signaled a killing. The coup-strikers, those who had other honors, all of them, the coup-strikers were in front, the other honor-men behind. Most of them were behind in a line abreast. They returned from a victorious raid. Then they reached the edge of camp. To the honor-men it was said: "Bring drums!" Towards camp they brought them. Old Man Coyote was very proud, recently he had cried and been miserable. He blackened his face, he was exceedingly proud (vain?). These Crow thereafter did the same. What Old Man Coyote did, whatever Old Man Coyote did, these Crow did the same. That I have seen. That is the way we have done since then.

*   *   *   *   *

Comment. The earth-diver part of the Creation story is probably known to every Crow. I have myself printed six shorter versions and collected a few additional ones. In all of them Old Man Coyote and the ducks play a prominent part, the birds figuring as beings independently in existence. Indeed, in one variant the ducks are the ones who first propose the diving for earth, and Old Man Coyote only enters later as their adviser. After the making of the earth, several informants represent the trickster shaping human beings out of mud; he then teaches them the arts of living,—how to make arrows, to dance over slain enemies, to wear clothing, to drill fire, to construct an antelope-pound. This aspect of Old Man Coyote's activities also figures divorced from cosmogony proper: in one tradition he gambles for daylight, wins, then fixes the habits of various animals and man's uses for them. Here his wife appears as a culture-heroine who originates moccasins, leggings, tanned robes, and methods of preparing pemmican. In a distinct story she looms prominently, debating with another woman, Hi'cictawia, how things shall be arranged on the earth and in Crow society, and significantly insists on the need for not making things too easy for the Indians. To return to the Creation story, there are narrators who draw into it a character called Cīrape', who is otherwise simply a companion of the Trickster's in his wanderings,—and one who not infrequently gets the better of him. On the other hand, Medicine-crow merged his major tale of the cosmogony into an account of how the Tobacco society started. Obviously, there is no one standard version: each narrator works into his cosmogony what seem to him suitable incidents.

Yellow-brow departs from the tendency to play up the sacred number four. Unlike Medicine-crow, who makes the fourth water-bird succeed, and another narrator, who substitutes *two* ducks but ascribes success to the fourth trial, Yellow-brow speaks of *two* ducks; at the first attempt one of them brings a bit of a root and at the second the desired dirt. He conforms to type as to the making of topographic features and the first shaping of human beings out of dirt, but strikes a somewhat different note in having the first human beings and ducks all male, which leads to special acts of creation and incidentally to extra dialogues with the ducks.

Yellow-brow played up the bear's cantankerousness with

expressive gestures and modulation of his voice, giving a comic effect. He expands the story by this episode and has a chance for developing amusing dialogues. The synthetic creation of the prairie-chicken (grouse) is worked in, while in Mr. Linderman's collection it figures as a separate Old Man Coyote tale. As explained, several versions introduce Cīrape' as the Trickster's traveling companion and interlocutor. Yellow-brow amplifies their conversation, thereby adding to the body of his narration and rendering possible some further comic details. He concludes in good Crow fashion with a successful war party and the ensuing victory parade. In all this he seems to me to display at once the strength and the weakness of a good native raconteur,—effective use of detail and failure to sustain a coherent structural unit.

VII. Old Woman's Grandchild

IN THE beginning we Hidatsa [and] Crow were one and the same people. It was the Sun who spoke. Who were his companions I do not know; he had companions, it is said. "Come, of what tribe are the best-looking women, do you think?" "Why, the Hidatsa are the ones that have the best-looking women, I think." "Now I'll marry, I think. I want to have a wife, that's why I ask you. If it is so, I shall marry a young Hidatsa woman. Then who, I wonder, is the most efficient suitor?" A porcupine spoke: "Why, my elder brother, my gift of speech is the best gift I have. If you hire me for courtship, I'll do it without trouble." "Well then, all right, now you shall go." "That will I," he said and set out.

These Hidatsa had a chief, his child was a young woman. This chief had a sister. This child of his, and his sister were about the same age. "Let us go, let us do quill-work; here it is hot, let us go away among the trees; in the shade there we'll do quill-work." They went. They entered the wood; a species of willow tree was leaning over, in its shade they did quill-work. They were passing the time embroidering without disturbance. Wherever he came from, the porcupine was by this leaning tree. "Comrade, look at that porcupine. Keep still, I'll catch it." This chief's daughter was the one who said it. She climbed the tree. Whenever this young woman got to the porcupine, he kept on going higher. Nevertheless she followed him. This paternal aunt of hers said: "Why, comrade, already you have gone exceedingly far. Turn back, come, stop." "No, I'll catch it." [1] When this young woman's paternal aunt looked at her comrade she was dim [unrecognizable]; at last she no longer saw her. Then the Sun took her and carried her off. As she was coming, one white tipi was there. There she went, she came, she got there. Outdoors she stood still. "Come inside here, daughter." She came in. It was an old woman. This one inside was staying without anything

[1] Yellow-brow pronounced the word for "I'll catch it" (burutsi'wiky) tripling the first "i" and raising the pitch.

happening; when the sun was not yet down, the Sun came back. "Here you are! Wherefore have you come?" "Why, peacefully we were living, *you* wanted to marry me, you were bent on it, now I have come, I want to marry you."

It was human beings that they ate. This old woman was boiling [flesh], she gave some to this young woman. "No, *I* do not eat this sort." This Sun spoke. "Well, if so, what do you eat?" "Buffalo and elk and deer—those I have been eating." The old woman spoke: "Listen, son, go; fetch the best buffalo for your wife. When you bring it, she will eat what she wants to eat." He brought a buffalo, the whole body. Time passed, one day their meat was gone, again he would bring some deer and buffalo. Without change they lived on. She had all but forgotten her home. After a time she was pregnant. After a while she gave birth. It was a boy.

Time passed.[2] Then now he [the boy] had grown older. This Sun made a bow for his son. He also made arrows. He hunted birds in the daytime. "You may kill any little birds, little rabbits." This Sun was speaking. "Son, you may shoot at all other birds, only meadowlarks do not shoot at," he said. [To his wife he said]: "Say! Woman!" The Sun said: "Do not dig up red turnips; do not turn over buffalo chips," he said. This boy was hunting. Now and then when he was about to shoot at some birds, and it [the aim] was just right, a meadowlark would intermittently shield this bird, allowing the bird to fly away, it is said. This meadowlark again and again did the same thing, he persisted at it. After a while this meadowlark did the same thing. "Ghostlike one,[3] what my father forbade me to shoot, I do not shoot at." He persisted. "I'll kill the ghostlike one." He took his arrows. When it [the bird] was sitting down, he [the boy] let fly. This meadowlark dodged. With his shot he ruffled the feathers along the back. The meadowlark went flying away, then near-by it sat down [and said]: "We were peacefully playing and flying around. Where does he [this boy] come from? He is bothering us. Wherever his home be, he has a home. Why does he not stay there?" said this meadowlark. This boy was standing, a thought came to him, he was sad. He cried.

He returned. He stopped hunting, he reached the lodge. His

---

[2] This is usually expressed by saying, "They lived on," which is here doubled.
[3] To compare a person with a ghost is a favorite form of vituperation.

mother said: "Here you! Why are you crying?" "My father told
me not to shoot a meadowlark. Whenever I wanted to shoot
at one of the birds, he was always shielding them. At last I
got angry and shot at it. It flew away and near-by it sat and
mocked me." "What did it say?" his mother asked. " 'I was playing around here. Whence does he come? Wherever it be, his
residence, he has a home, why does he not stay there where he
can do as he pleases?' it said. I thought we were people from
here, are we strangers? Where is our home, seeing that he could
say that?" This woman was silent. "Why, do tell me, mother,
mother of mine." This woman remained silent [at first]. "Well,
my son, it is so. We are alien people." This woman thought:
"That must be why, I believe, he said to me something: 'Don't
peel off buffalo-chips,' he said to me; there must be some reason,"
she thought. "Well now, I'll peel it, whatever it is I'll find out.
Go ahead, let us go around." To her son she said that. "Yes,"
he said, and they went. They walked around, a circular buffalo
chip they reached. This woman peeled it off. When she had
peeled it, there was a hole there. Her home was yonder, the tents
were white dots, she thought. She saw them. Away from it were
many hunters. A little beyond the tipis the hoop-players came
together, crossing one another's paths. On this side the ball-
strikers were constantly moving to and fro. This woman saw it.
She was sad.[4] "Son, come here, go, look down there!" This boy
went, he looked inside. "Our home is there, do you see it?"
"Yes," said this boy, "I see it." "Your grandfather is still there.
You have a grandmother, she is still there, all your kin are still
there. Listen, when your father comes back [at night], he does
anything you ask him to. I want you to ask him something."
"Yes, what shall I say?" " 'Father, kill an ā'cuci'se buffalo,[5]
wherever there are sinews in the body, take and bring all of them.'
If you say that and if he brings all, we'll be able to go home,"
she said. "Yes, I'll do it," he said. This woman said: "You might
forget it, son, be sure to say it." "I'll remember it, I'll not forget
it."

Then that night his father came back. This woman looked at
her son, she frowned at him. He had forgotten. She kept frown-
ing at this boy. "Mother, why do you continue to frown at me?"

---

[4] The sight of her long-forgotten people makes her homesick.
[5] A buffalo described as having one horn up and the other down.

She nudged him. Her son, the boy, said, "Ah!" He recalled it. "Father, tomorrow when you go hunting, kill an ā'cūci'se, take all the sinews from the body and bring them for me." "What are you going to use them for? There are so many." "I'll fasten my arrows with them and make my bowstring. Other kinds of sinews which I use wear out, ā'cūci'se sinews are tough, that's why I do it." This man: "Yes, I'll do it." This morning he went. This man at night brought all the sinews of some ā'cūci'se he had killed. In the morning this man right away went off.

"Mother, these sinews now are all brought; do as you wish." "Yes, it is well." She carried the sinews, the woman went out. She went along. It was a spider she reached. "Listen, twine these sinews, splice all of them truly, do it." "Yes, I'll be through quickly. Come ye after a little while." Then after a little while they came. "Well, how about your work?" "Already I am done, here it is." She took it. They came, they got to the tipi; she took her root-digger. "Something we'll dig up." They went out, they went. There they went. She got to where she had peeled off this buffalo-chip. Again she took it, she removed it. "Listen, come son, let us go to your people whom you wished to see." She removed this chip which she had peeled off. Spanning the hole, she replaced her digger. She tied the sinew to the end of the digger. She carried her son on her back, she went into this hole. She held on to these sinews. Then they went. Slowly they went. They went on and on. They did not reach the earth. There they remained hanging. "Well, why, son, do we not reach the earth?" "Why, he did not bring the sinews on the side of the [buffalo's] face, that is why, for that reason we cannot reach the earth."

Then, when this Sun came back, his wife and child were gone. "Why, where have my wife and child gone, I wonder?" he thought. Then, "Why, I forbade them to do something, they must have done it, that is why. I'll look for them." When he came, where they had gone there was a hole. Yonder far down they were dangling. "Why, if that is what they wished to do and had told me, I'd have let them go in peace. They have verily done wrong," he thought, he was angry. He took a ball-shaped stone. "Rock, follow that sinew, get down yonder. Strike not against the child, but the woman's head and kill her," he said. "Yes, I'll do it." He took this stone and threw it. There it went.

It proceeded, it struck this woman's head. It broke her support, this sinew. She struck the ground. There the boy roamed around, his mother remained there. Whenever he returned from hunting at night, he lay by her.

There was an old woman, she had a home, her garden was extensive. In the morning when this old woman came and got to her garden, her corn was pulled off, on the ground it lay scattered. When she got to her squashes, they lay punctured. There were holes in them. This old woman said: "What, I wonder, is this? All the time no creatures whatever ever reached me, what is this that has got to me? Now then, I'll find out." The tracks, she noticed, were small. "This is a child," she thought. "Well, now, is it a girl or a boy?" She made a bow and arrows. She put them in this garden. A ball she made; she put a shinny stick there. They were there. This old woman said: "If it's a boy, he will take the arrows and bow. If it is a girl, she will take this ball and shinny stick." This old woman lay down that night. The next day she was anxious; she came and arrived. She proceeded toward her garden, she reached it. When she looked this way, this ball was shot all over. The arrows and the bow were not there. "Why, it's a boy! Whence does he come from, I wonder? Wait, when he comes I'll catch him." Then she hid in the garden. She wanted to catch this boy. She waited in her garden. Then he came. The boy came; when he had come in, he stood there. This old woman called out: "Well, you there! little son, whence have you come?" "Why, I stay here." "Where is your home?" "I have no home." "All right, I am alone, I'll live with you." "Yes, I am willing." "Grandson,[6] do not shoot the squashes, do not tear apart plants, the corn is my food." He lived with the old woman. Then this night when she looked here, this boy was gone. "Where has this boy gone?" she thought. She looked for him. When she came, he was lying by his mother. "Grandson, I missed you, I was worried. Your mother has decomposed, it is bad. Do not go to her, she is dead, it is bad. What for? If you sleep at night at our home, it will be well. Tonight do not go around, there lie down at our home." "Yes, I will. I did not quite understand, that is why [I acted as I did]."

[6] The same term is used in *address* for son and grandson (see p. 27); the hero's name and his mode of addressing the old woman prove her to be his adoptive *grandmother*.

There he stayed. He roamed around, he hunted. Her corn
was plenty. "Grandson, when I am away, if you want to eat
corn, do not boil the red one, the rest that is not red [you may]
cook and eat that." Then when he looked around, his grandmother was not there. "Let me think, why did my grandmother
say what she said? Well, now, whatever it is, I'll find out." Then
he reached the garden. He took and brought the red corn. He
brought it and cooked it over the coals. When it was cooked it
popped, it crackled, the kernels were jumping. This thing which
popped turned into blackbirds. They flew off, at the same time
scattering. They went out at the smoke-hole, also at the door
they went out separating and escaped. "Well, they are amusing."[7]
The corn he took back, he laid it down in another place. He
went out, he closed the flaps. He also shut the door. "Thus I'll
do, I'll make it impossible for them to get out. Unknown to my
grandmother, I have discovered some extremely amusing things."
Having shut the door and closed all openings, he took the corn
and cooked it. Then it popped, it crackled. Everywhere indoors
the birds gave their bird calls, they were noisy, they flew about
in confusion crisscross. He took his arrows, different ones of these
blackbirds he killed one after the other, he truly destroyed them
all. He took cords, he kept tying these blackbirds against one
another, it was a very long string; he hung them up. Then his
grandmother came back. "Grandmother, why did you say I
should not roast red corn? I found out you forbade me to do
something amusing." "Yes, how is that?" "When I cooked them
they popped, what popped all around turned into blackbirds, I
killed all of them. I thought you'd eat them." "Well, I declare!
It is well." She came and got there; up above he had hung them.
"There they are." "Yes, it is well. Now then I'll go, I'll tend to
it." She carried them. "Go, go ye around; my child is ignorant,
that is it." She put them down and came back. She came. "Grandson, those blackbirds are the guardians of my garden. Don't do
it again." "Yes, I did not know, that's why [I did it]. I'll not do
that [again]."

Time passed. Sometimes she prepared food, she made a
great deal, she threw this food she had cooked behind the draft-
screen. Whenever this old woman took back the plate of this
cooked food which she threw behind the screen, it was gone, there

[7] It is very difficult to find the exact shade of meaning for the original word.

was nothing inside. Then once his grandmother was away, wherever she went to. Then he said, "This grandmother of mine puts away her food over there. None ever comes back. Why? Well, now, I'll see." When he looked that way [gesture], a dragon was behind this screen. It went clear around the edge of the tipi. When he looked at him, the lightning through his eyes was like the crack of a whip. "Here this ghostlike one is the one who always devours the food whenever my grandmother stores it." He took his arrows, he shot several times, he killed him forthwith. Then his grandmother came back. "My grandmother," he said, "I have killed the devourer of the food you used to store." "Well, I declare! Where?" "Here, come and see." She went and saw it. "It is a good thing you have killed the one who regularly devoured the food I was wont to store. Give me room, I'll go with it and throw it away." She took it, she put it over her shoulders, she dragged it, she took it, she wanted to reach the water with it. It was heavy. "Go, now go!" Now it turned out that this old woman had this dragon for her husband. Her grandson had killed him. This grandmother's husband, this dragon, spoke: "Old woman, you have often done various things, but now you have met your master. I thought I was powerful, but your grandson has killed me. Be on your guard!" This old woman was crying. She returned. This old woman thought: "I wonder, what could I do to get rid of this boy?"

Time passed. "Let me think, what can I do so he'll die?" she thought. "Grandson, you are ignorant, yonder dwells something evil. You might get to it [in your ignorance], be sure to avoid it." "What is it? [he thought to himself]. Well, I'll get there." "There is a hill on the side of yonder brush patch." "What is it, grandmother?" "A bear," she said; "whenever some one gets there, it eats him up, it is very dangerous." "Yes, it must be terribly dangerous." To himself he said: "Let me think. What my grandmother told about, I'll go and get to." "Well [also] yonder there is a little hill, a snake is there. It is also dangerous. Whenever people get there, it coils around them and kills them; it is extremely long." "Let me see, I'll go, for the fun of it, I'll get there," he said to himself, and went off. He proceeded, he reached this snake. This snake was furious. "Ah! [exclamation of challenge], that pretty one, what is he going to do, I wonder? Remain motionless," he [the boy] said. He killed him [the

snake] forthwith. "Let me see, I'll go to that aforementioned
bear, that also I'll reach." He went there, he came. He came,
he arrived. The bear's waist was very long. He was raging. He
came. "Ah, that pretty one, what is he coming for?" He [the
bear] let his ears droop, there he remained standing.[8] "Come
here." He came. He came and reached this bear. "Come," he
said, and with him he went. He got to this snake. He took it, he
put it round his [the bear's] neck, he rode him. Having made
this snake into a halter, he rode this bear. He went along, he
came to the lodge. "Grandmother," he kept saying. He reached
his grandmother. His grandmother came out. She saw him. "My
grandmother, here I bring a most pretty one, I give it you. Whenever you have been digging roots, carrying a pack, you have
come walking, henceforth ride this [beast]. When you dig, let it
carry [the roots] on its back, thus you will feel set up now that
you have a mount." "Yes, it is good beyond words. Grandson,
give it here, somewhere I'll put and tie it." This snake she used
as a rope, this bear she took with her, she led it. "Go ye, look
for safety! Something very powerful has reached us." Then
these ran away.[9]

The boy was going around. The old woman [said]: "What
shall I do to get rid of this boy?" Out from the river she stayed.
She was thinking it over. "Why, my dear grandchild, whenever
I bid you not to go somewhere, when I have told you in full
about something, you always want to go there. Now some most
dangerous things are over there! This time don't go there."
"What is it, my grandmother?" "Yonder below, under a rock,
the ground is narrow; there is a path, the path goes under a
many-limbed cherry-tree. Whenever any one goes there, this tree,
tumbling, falls on top of him and kills him forthwith. Now do
not go." "Yes, what you have spoken of I'll not get to," he said;
"yes, it is a good thing you told me." Well, he roamed about,
he was hunting continually. "Let me see, what my grandmother
spoke of, how is it? I'll go, for the fun of it I'll go." Now he went
along, he came. Whatever song it was,[10] he sang as he went along.
He came. The rock was narrow, the road was narrow, there was
no road anywhere else. "There is what my grandmother talked

[8] The boy, by his power, is represented as immediately cowing both the snake
and the bear.
[9] That is, the old woman proves she is in league with these evil beings.
[10] This sort of indefiniteness is evidently a mannerism of Yellow-brow's.

about." He pretended not to know, then when close to it he ran and came. When he came close to this tree he went fast. Then going under it, he went fast, and this tree thought, "He is going," [so] crashing it fell. He pretended to go, but jumped aside. In vain it [the tree] did it, it killed no one at all. It was lying on the ground; before it got up this boy jumped over it. It got up, this tree. This boy went far away. Turning back he returned. He came, he pretended to go under it, then he jumped aside. In vain this tree fell crashing. He turned back, he stepped over it, he went. The same way he continued. At last this tree was broken up, there it lay. It did not get up. He went back. He came, he got to his grandmother. "My grandmother what you spoke of is interesting. I fooled it greatly." "Yes, how did you act? [To herself]: This child of mine, it seems, reached what I spoke of. We were telling him not to reach it." "I pretended to want to go under that tree. Then when I jumped aside, it fell crashing. Over it I went jumping. Again I turned back. What I had done, that I did [again]. Thus I kept on, at last this tree lay broken up. Now it got up no longer. Now here I have come, that is how it was."

"Grandson," this old woman it was [who spoke], "it is so: what I am wont to warn you against, there you regularly go. There this way, then this way [pointing], a rock comes together there, when people go, there is a hollow there. Whenever people wish to jump over this hollow, this hollow spreads apart, they regularly fall in, it is exceedingly deep, then they are unable to get out. Do not go there this time!" "Yes, verily, it must be terribly dangerous, I shall not go to it." Then he took his arrows. He went around, he went. "Well, Old Woman's Grandchild [said he to himself], what your grandmother spoke of I'll see for the fun of it." Then he went there. He came to this hollow. He went to this rock that came together there, he looked for it, he came. "There is what your grandmother spoke about." He reached the hollow. He pretended not to know, he came up to this hollow. He pretended to be eager to jump over, it spread apart. Still he jumped aside. Now when it came together he stepped over it. Then when he had gone some distance, he turned back. He came to this hollow. He proceeded, he got there, he pretended to want to go, the hollow spread apart. Again he jumped aside. Then it came together. When it came together he stepped over it. He went past it. Again he did this same thing he had done. Then whenever it went together, he jumped over it. Thus he kept on the same way, at length it was destroyed. No longer it spread apart. He jumped over it, it could not spread any more. Then it remained stationary. He came back. His grandmother came out and saw him,—this old woman. He proceeded, he reached his grandmother. "My grandmother, when I reached what you spoke of, I fooled it thoroughly. I pretended to go over it, when it spread, I jumped aside, then when it came together, I went jumping over it. Thus I did repeatedly. At length it was helpless, it was destroyed. Unmoving it lay." "Well, well! A dangerous one you have met." Old Woman's Grandson said, "It is gone now."

Now he continued roaming about. His grandmother said: "Well, grandson, what I tell you, whenever I say you should not go [somewhere], you regularly wish to go. Now over there are some bad ones. This time do not go there, truly." "What, grandmother?" "Over there is one tent, don't get to it." Old Woman's Grandson took his arrows, he roamed continually. "Well, Old Woman's Grandson, whatever it be your grandmother talked about, we shall see," he said and came. He saw this one tent. "What your grandmother talked of is there." He went there, he came to it. He came, he stood outside. "Old Woman's Grandson, the one who used not to come to us has got to us. Come, enter." "Yes." He picked up a flat stone. He blocked his anus with the flat stone. Long poles went clear around on the floor inside. "Go ahead, go to the rear." He proceeded, he sat down. Then one snake went inside the earth. Through the earth opposite the [boy's] anus he wanted to go inside the anus. His forehead struck this rock which blocked the anus, and he fled. This Old Woman's Grandson was aware of it beforehand, he was smiling. Then others, entering the earth, would want to enter his anus and would strike this rock with their foreheads. They would flee. "Well, now, that Old Woman's Grandson who used not to get to us has come to us, prepare ye food on the fire for him, so he may eat." They cooked spleen for him. They took it out. This snake, the furthest on this side, said: "Give it here, I'll try it, I'll look at it right away." Taking it, he bit it in several places. His teeth he threw inside this cooked food. "Ha! Now I've made it good." This snake said that. This one next to him said: "Give it here, I too am going to test and look at it. Why, it might be bad and he might eat it." At last all of them did it. He came there. All had tested it for him. As a matter of fact, these snakes who had bitten the cooked meat, this spleen, put their teeth inside. They wanted to kill Old Woman's Grandchild thereby, that is why they did it. They gave him this spleen. "Well, feast on this spleen." Old Woman's Grandchild took it. Then he looked here and there. "These here are no good as cooks, is *this* cooking?" He threw this spleen into the fire. "*I*'ll cook it and then eat." This spleen he turned over repeatedly in the fire. These teeth they had put in were burnt. The snakes were suffering; they were holding their mouths with pain, their teeth were burnt and destroyed. He took the food and ate it, he ate it up.

It was one of these snakes spoke: "Old Woman's Grandchild, who would not come to us, has got to us, we'll pass the time telling stories with him." The snake spoke thus. On his way Old Woman's Grandson had met a jack-rabbit. [To him he had said:] "Give me your eyes." He took them, *those* eyes he used now. Of his four arrows he painted one red, one black, one yellow, one with white clay. His four arrows he stuck into the ground. He said to them: "Look out for me." "Attention!" they [the snakes] said. He laid down the arrows [saying to them], "Be sure to say 'yes' [i.e. to respond for me]." [11]

This snake said: "Come, I'll tell stories: In the spring the grass is green, in the shelter of young cherry trees the sun is a little warm, then when we lie down we feel like sleeping!" he said. Old Woman's Grandchild was asleep. However, when they looked, the rabbit's eyes, unchanged, were staring glassily. "He is not asleep," they thought. Whenever they said, "Attention!" these arrows kept saying, "Yes." After a while one of his arrows fell, it struck his face. He woke up at once. Now they stopped their story-telling. [He said]: "*I* am going to tell stories. "Yes, go ahead, you are doing the right thing. Your grandmother, though I have not seen her, must have been telling stories continually in your company. Tell a very good one for pastime, we'll listen." "That I will." These sticks which they put on the floor before them went clear around, they put their heads on them,

[11] The fragmentary character of this sentence is due to the narrator's at first forgetting the incidents and only subsequently and sketchily inserting them. He at first inclined to the version according to which the boy insists on telling stories first (p. 109).

facing the arā'co [space around fireplace]. "Attention!" he said. "In the fall, whenever there is a little wind, when we lie in some shelter, when dried weeds rub against each other and we listen, we generally get drowsy, is it not so?" Half of them no longer said "Yes"; already they were asleep. "In the daytime when it drizzles and the rain strikes the lodge pattering, we remain lying on the side, and warming our soles, then we fall asleep, is it not so?" Half already were asleep. "At night when we are about to lie down, listening to the wind rustling through the bleached trees, we do not know *how* we get to sleep, but we fall asleep, is it not so?" he said. Now all were asleep. "Having sought a hollow among the thickish pines, we make a fresh camp there. The wind blows on us, and we, rather tired, lie down and at the same time keep listening to the rustling pines, until we fall asleep." When he said, "Attention!" they remained silent: all truly were asleep. "These snakes are like ghosts. All the time they habitually do mischief." He took out his knife, the heads all were hanging over the poles. He took out his knife and chopped off the neck of the one furthest on this side. He went along in line, he chopped off their necks, he proceeded, he proceeded, he proceeded, only one was left. Then that one woke up. The snake said: "Ghostlike! [12] Old Woman's Grandchild now is destroying us," and went inside the ground. "Confound it!" Old Woman's Grandchild said. The snake said: "Old Woman's Grandchild, do not sleep in the daytime." Old Woman's Grandchild said: "If I do sleep in the daytime, what can he do? Too bad! I wanted to destroy them utterly, one has managed to escape."

Then he went. He went home. He came to his grandmother and reached her. She pretended to cry. This old woman saw her grandson. "Why, my grandmother, are you crying?" "I thought you were not coming back, that is why I cried, I was sad," she said. "No, I've returned, stop your crying." "Little grandson, what I warn you against, that you regularly want to do. Yonder are some very evil beings, very dangerous. Behind that hill is a lake, there dwells a huge bull. He sucks in anyone who goes in the direction of the wind. If there is a wind, the people are blown and go inside his mouth, and he devours them." "Yes," Old Woman's Grandchild said; "why, he must be really danger-

[12] Said to be a cry of alarm here, not a word of vituperation.

ous." He took his arrows, he kept going around. "What my grandmother spoke of, well now I am going to see it." Now there he went. He was coming. He saw this lake. "Yonder is what my grandmother spoke about." He went in the direction of the wind. Then it [the bull] was sucking. Then it was windy, he was blown to it, he came. He went into its mouth. This bull swallowed Old Woman's Grandchild. He came, he came to the stomach, he was looking around. The bones of the people swallowed long ago were bleached. There were also those just lately dead; still others were not quite dead yet, they were in a bad state, those recently swallowed were truly in good condition. Old Woman's Grandchild strolled around [inside]. He strolled around inside this bull's stomach. In this stomach were people. [The boy said to them]: "How is it you act thus? You must look out for your safety. Have you been all the time there without trying to save yourselves? You are men, how is it you act thus?" Those who had been there for a long time, the first ones, were already bleached. Those who came later but also had already been there a long while were no longer able to wrinkle [pinch] themselves. Their bodies were dead, [but] they were lying [half alive?]! [13] The newcomers were in good condition. "You here, why are you staying here?" "Why, this bull swallowed us, we are helpless, what shall we do for ourselves?" "Come on." Old Woman's Grandchild it was [that spoke]: "We'll have a Sun Dance. When I sing, all of you dance." Those who could not move [said]: "As for us, we cannot do it. We cannot move." "If so, just make your little heads alone dance. When I sing and all of those [others] dance, do *you* cause your little heads to dance even though only them [the heads]." Then he began to sing. Those in good condition danced. Those who could not move moved only their heads, they caused their heads alone to dance. Old Woman's Grandchild spoke. "That's the way for you to do it. We are having a Sun Dance, we want to get out, that's why we do it." [14] The [bull's] smooth kidneys were hanging down, he touched them. This Old Woman's Grand-

---

[13] Obscure sentence.
[14] This episode was an afterthought of Yellow-brow's and I have inserted it in the place he indicated. As in the case of other interpolations of his, the result does not make for wholly smooth reading. More particularly, there is obvious repetition of certain phrases (dealing with the several conditions of the persons swallowed).

child spoke: "Elder brother, what are these?" This bull said: "[Grunt], do not touch my slippery stone [whetstone]." He touched the aorta. "Elder brother, what is *this*?" "[Grunt], don't do it! It is my pipestem." His heart was hanging down. He touched it. "Elder brother, what is *this*?" "[Grunt], don't do it! that is what I plan with." He took out his knife. "Because he is so good he has the means of planning, look at it!" [15] This heart he cut to pieces. He also cut up the kidneys. The bull was about to die, he staggered around and died. He took out his knife and split the space between the ribs. [To the rescued people he said]: "Well! Stand up and go ye now! Wherever you may live, thither go!" Old Woman's Grandchild came back. His grandmother was thinking, "It is a good thing he is not returning." She was pleased. However, while she was thinking, her grandson came back. Then she pretended to cry. Old Woman's Grandchild [asked], "Why are you crying, grandmother?" "You did not return for a long time, I was sad, that is why I was crying." "Stop, I've come back now." "It is a good thing that the dear boy is back."

He roamed about. In the daytime he wanted to sleep, but he remembered [the warning]: "In the daytime don't sleep." So he would not sleep. Time passed. When he was exceedingly sleepy, he lay down, he stuck around him the four arrows he had marked. "Watch over me; if anything comes, shake me" [he said]. Then he slept. The snake came through the ground. One of the arrows fell, it struck against his shinbone. He woke up. "Ah! What is he coming for?" The snake fled. As soon as he fell asleep, it would come, the falling arrows would strike him and he would wake up. After a period of time he was sleepy [again], he could not help himself. When his arrows fell and struck him again and again, there was nothing [no response]. He slept very soundly. One of the arrows violently struck his nose. He woke up, [but] the snake already had entered his anus. At the waist he broke himself, [but] already it had passed beyond it. He broke himself off at the neck, [but] it had already entered the brain cavity.

This Sun would see his child, Old Woman's Grandchild, as he was roaming about. He would watch over him. Now he [the child] was lying on the ground. There were three distinct parts

---

[15] This sentence is, of course, ironical.

[of him]: his rump was lying separately, his body was lying separately; his head was also lying separately. The Sun saw his child. "What is the matter, I wonder, with this child of mine?" In the daytime he was wont to take a look at this child of his. He [the boy] did not get up, he was lying motionless. This snake had entered his brain cavity, there inside the head he stayed. His brain cavity was like this [gesture], his hand like this [gesture], he was waiting.[16] Whenever he should get out, he wanted to seize him by the neck. Whenever this snake wanted to get out, it would say, "Old Woman's Grandchild is powerful," and go inside. This father of his [Grandchild's] watched him from time to time. To a magpie [he said]: "Go, Magpie, go, see what is the matter yonder with my child. Find out the truth of the matter, why he is that way, and come and tell me!" "Yes, that will I." He went. This magpie proceeded and arrived. He pondered, he scrutinized it, inside the head was a snake, it had gone inside the head. This magpie found it out, then went. He went on his way, he arrived. Sun said: "Yes, how is it? Have you any information?" "Yes," he said. "What is it?" "A snake is inside his head." "Ah!" He pondered, he thought about it. Sun caused a wind, an exceedingly strong one. Motionless he had lain already one year. Then this Old Woman's Grandchild's head floated, rolling it entered a gully. The brain cavity was turned up. Then this Sun made it rain most violently. This whole country was covered with water, this gully was filled with water. Then he stopped the rain. Then he made it extremely hot. The Sun close to the ground filled this child's head with water, this water boiled. It was hot, hence this snake was uncomfortable. He was burnt. "Well, this Old Woman's Grandchild was powerful, nevertheless already it is a long time [since his death]," he thought. He [Grandchild] had his hand around his brain cavity, he was waiting. The snake said: "Even though he was powerful, he's been dead for a long time." He was suffering, he came out. As he came out, he seized him by the neck. He pulled him out. "*I* am powerful; we'll see whether you are powerful." The snake begged: "I have considered you an elder brother, I have considered you an elder brother," he said. He clutched this snake. Taking it, he looked for a rock. He went along, he took a jagged rock. "Ghost-

---

[16] As explained in the next sentence, the boy was waiting, with his hand ready to seize the snake as soon as its head should emerge from the brain cavity.

like one, you have made me furious, I am furious at you." He
took him. In the beginning snakes had long noses. By the neck
he clutched it, he rubbed it against this rock. The snake
[begged]: "I have considered you my elder brother, I've considered you my elder brother, I'll stop, put me down now, now
you are getting near my eyes." [17] "Ghostlike one," he said, and
nevertheless continued filing [the snake's nose]. "Henceforth
I will not enter any one's anus." Then Old Woman's Grandchild said: "All right, keep out of mischief always." As it entered
the ground, it said, "Well, as for that, occasionally nevertheless
I'll bite when I feel like it if there is a reason." "Confound it!"
he [Grandchild] said. Immediately he went off. Then he came
back; he came to his grandmother. He reached his grandmother.
She started to cry. "What are you doing, my grandmother?"
"Why, you did not return, hence I was crying." She had thought
that he was not coming back and was glad, then he came back.

Old Woman's Grandchild kept roaming around. "Grandson,
whenever I've been telling you of something and warned you not
to go there you want to go very much. Yonder live some beings,
they are bad. Don't go this time." "Yes; what are they?" "There
on the other side the Two Men live there. They are bad, don't
go," she said. "Yes, thus I'll do." He went roaming. Old Woman's
Grandchild [said to himself], "Old Woman's Grandchild, what
your grandmother speaks of, thither I'll go; what they are, what
they are like, I will see, I will know." Then he went there.
He came. When he got to the top of this hill, they were
butchering over yonder. "There are those my grandmother spoke
about." He went there. There were two of them. One of these
men was a wild sort of fellow; the other was not, *he* was
a sensible person. "Say, comrade, we have been getting along
well, now Old Woman's Grandchild has got to us, that is he
coming over there." "Yes, when he comes we'll treat him well."
He proceeded, he reached them. "Well, Old Woman's Grandchild, who used not to come to us, has now got to us. Come on,
stay right there, sit there and eat; the entrails are over there,"
he said. They laid them in front of him. "Eat the entrails! Take
this calf foetus to your grandmother; it is tender and good, she
will eat it." They brought it to him. The calf was old enough
to have a moustache. The end of the tail also already had hair.

[17] I.e., with the rock.

He saw it, they were bringing it toward him, he was afraid of it. This Serious One [said to his comrade]: "Don't do it, he is afraid of it." "How is it possible for him to be afraid of it?" Still he went on with it. Old Woman's Grandchild got up and ran away. Old Woman's Grandchild climbed a tree there, he ran up to the top. On one limb of this tree [the man] hung it, above it was Old Woman's Grandchild. "Elder brothers, remove this for me!" "Yes, we shall do it when we come back," he said. Forthwith they went off.

Old Woman's Grandchild stayed there. Now a year had passed. Then at some time these Two Men [were walking together]: "What did he do, do you remember [how] this Old Woman's Grandchild was afraid of the embryo calf and fled up a tree [while] below him we hung it [and] he stayed there? Finally how did he manage? Come on, let us look at it." "What! He could not be there, powerful as he is." "Let us go anyway, anyway we'll look at that." Here they came. They came, when they arrived he was still there. This foetus was already bleached. In a niche of this tree it remained hanging. "Come, elder brother, take this away for me," he said. This one who was not wild said: "Well, let us say something, let us demand his grandmother. He will consent." "He loves his grandmother, it is bad," he [the other] said. This Serious One [said]: "No, he is suffering, he will consent, you may do it [safely ask him]." "All right. . . . If you give us your grandmother, we'll take it off and remove it." "Yes," said Old Woman's Grandchild. "Well, but your grandmother may refuse." "No, she'll consent." Taking hold of it, they removed this foetus. He came down. "[Expression of fatigue:]" he said; "I am nearly tired out," he said; "now I'll go. I'll go and reach my grandmother, and I'll tell her. Come ye at dusk!" He went. Old Woman's Grandchild went there. He came and reached the lodge. Before he returned she kept thinking, "It is very good he is not coming back." Then he returned. When she said it [to herself], her grandson had come back. She now began to cry. He came and arrived. "Well, grandmother, why are you crying?" "Why, you were not coming back at all, that is why I cried. I am also sad, hence I cry." "Come, stop now I've come back." "What did you do to return so late?" she cried. "My grandmother, those Two Men had killed game. I came, I got there. My grandmother, to my amazement, though

I had thought that of all things on this earth I was afraid of none, I discovered there was something I am afraid of, now I know." "What is it, grandson?" "I discovered that a calf foetus is something I fear, now I know. Yes, the Two Men had killed game and were butchering, I came and met them. 'There come, eat,' they said. They gave me the entrails. 'Take the calf foetus and bring it for this grandmother of yours, it is tender, she may enjoy it,' they said, thus they spoke. Forthwith he brought it, I fled up a tree. This foetus they then hung on the limb of a tree. There I stayed. Then just now they came back. 'Come, elder brothers, remove this for me,' I said. 'All right, if you give us your grandmother, we will remove it,' they said. 'Yes,' I said; so they removed it. 'I'll go, in the meantime I'll tell her, come at dusk,' I said. I came [hither]. Now I have told you, this is it. What will you do, I wonder?" "I have always loved you, how could I refuse your request? I'll do it," she said.[18]

Time passed. Then it got dark. After Old Woman's Grandchild's coming these Two Men were met by Old Man Coyote, wherever he may have come from. To these Two Men [he said]: "Well, how goes it with you here?" "Old Woman's Grandchild is afraid of a calf foetus. We hung it up, he was above it, it was impossible for him to get down. Now we are about to go to him. We demanded his grandmother, he is going to give her to us, thither we are going." "Yes, all right, you are my true younger brothers, so I'll help you with it." It was dusk. [Old Woman's Grandchild said:] "Well, grandmother, now look out for yourself. It is time for their arrival." The old woman said: "Well, grandson, if they'll do what I say, I'll consent; if they refuse, then not." "Yes, grandmother, what is it?" "Those Two Men own something, a deer hide [from a tipi cover] is their most valuable possession. If they give it to you, I'll consent; if they don't give it you, then I will not." Then when it was dusk they came. "You can go, grandson, if they give you what I have bidden you ask for, I consent. Go, tell them." Thither he went. He came and got there. "Well, what news?" these Two Men said. "I'll tell you. 'Those men own a deer hide; if they give it you, I'll consent,' she says, thus she speaks. 'If they do not give it you, then not,' she says, that's what she said." These Two

---

[18] Why the old woman, eager to rid herself of the boy, consents to yield her body on his behalf, remains enigmatic.

Men remained motionless. "Why, if we give it away, that would be bad." They were sad. Old Man Coyote it was [who spoke]: "Why of those [hides] *I* own one. Even if you give that one away, I'll make one for you." "Your words are right," they said and gave theirs away. "Well, stay ye here, I'll go and I'll tell my grandmother." He came and got to her. His grandmother [said]: "Yes, what news, grandson? If what you were going to ask for is all right, where is it? I'll look at it, it might be a different one [hide]." [19] Here it is." This old woman took it, she scrutinized it. "Yes, this is it. Well, I am ready now, I'll consent. Go ahead, let them come. Why, now there are three of them! Who is the third?" "It is Old Man Coyote, he is that third man." "They have been trying to get the better of me, but could not do it; yet now I consent. Go ahead, I'll stay here. Let them come one at a time." She took a squash blossom and put it into her genitalia. She was waiting. One of these Two Men came. When intercourse was over, he left. Then this other one came. He, too, cohabited and left. Then Old Man Coyote came—cohabited and left. Old Man Coyote came back. He met the Two Men. "Well, dear friends, this one we cohabited with, what was it, do you think?" "Why, it was a woman we cohabited with." "No, indeed. When I got through, then I found out. What we cohabited with was a squash blossom, a long and grooved [hollowed] one, that kind is the one we cohabited with." "True enough."

This boy came. Old Woman's Grandchild went toward the Two Men and reached them. [20] Old Man Coyote [said]: "Now do not stay in this place, go somewhere now. Wherever you stay, look for a home." "Yes, that we shall do." To his home he [Old Woman's Grandchild] returned. To these Two Men Old Man Coyote spoke: "My younger brothers, Old Woman's Grandchild has not yet touched us. We have brought ourselves to him. Do not stop going! Wherever you go, go on! I myself shall seek a [new] residence. Myself I'll go away." "Yes," they said and went away. The Two Men together both walked away. One of them, this Serious One, spoke: "I kept telling you not to do it, nevertheless you would play your tricks. Now we have brought

[19] That is, she suspects they may be palming off a spurious hide.

[20] The context shows that this cannot be the narrator's intention since Old Man Coyote advises the Two Men to flee from Old Woman's Grandchild and avoid his vengeance. Probably the subject of the sentence ought to be "Old Man Coyote."

ourselves against something. Peaceably and well we were living, now that is over." Then wherever they went, they left. Old Man Coyote also went away.

Whatever evil beings there had been on the earth he [Old Woman's Grandchild] had destroyed. Old Woman's Grandchild continued to live with his grandmother. "Well now, my grandmother, now do not stay here." "All right, I'll stay above there," said she and went. This boy said: "As for me, I'll stay in some place there." Yonder he went. The North Star is he. This woman turned into the Moon. This is the end.

*　　*　　*　　*　　*

Comment. The theme of this myth is the extermination of the monsters once infesting the earth by the son of the Sun and a Hidatsa girl. A lengthy introduction explains how she was lured to the sky by a porcupine, how she and her offspring broke the taboos imposed upon them by the Sun, with the woman's consequent homesickness and unsuccessful flight; the rope by which she seeks escape with her boy proves too short, and her irate husband causes her death, dropping a rock as she hangs dangling in mid-air. There follows the discovery and adoption of the hero by an aged gardener, the only other main character. She is not consistently drawn. Undoubtedly the dominant conception of her is that of an evil old woman in league with the powers of darkness,—witness her revival of the snake used as a halter for the bear. To be sure, she warns her grandson against the several ogres in the neighborhood but always with the hope and knowledge that she is thereby tempting him to jeopardize his life; and Yellow-brow repeatedly contrasts her hypocritical weeping over the returning boy's prolonged absence with her pondering over ways to rid herself of this awe-inspiring conqueror. However, when she first meets the boy she gives no indication of any fell designs, though the boy's naughtiness—not to speak of his killing her husband—might well provoke resentment. We are evidently supposed to take her malevolence for granted. The curious episode of the Two Men complicates the problem. If she is really bent on Grandchild's destruction, why does she aid in extricating him from his plight? Yellow-brow noticed the inconsistency and very unconvincingly rationalized it away: had she really loved the boy, she would not have tricked her lovers with the squash blossom! As for her ultimate nature, Yellow-brow makes her turn into the Moon, but this view is not general. In fact, Plenty-hawk's variant would exclude it, since his preamble opens with a dialogue between Sun and Moon, both of whom are men. Again, Grandmother's-knife identifies the woman with a notorious witch, Hi'cictawia, who appears in several other folktales.

The hero's savior mission is explicitly stated both by Yellow-brow and other narrators. Other tribes have similar characters, though of different antecedents, to whom they ascribe the very same adventures. For instance, a Blackfoot story introduces a bully whose victim is rescued by a boy springing from a clot of blood, and this "Bloodclot" proceeds to kill an evil bear, a snake, and a sucking-monster. The Gros Ventre make the Bloodclot overcome a falling tree, a sucking wolf, and a witch who boils people by drawing them into her tilted caldron. This last adventure happens to be lacking in Yellow-brow's Grandchild saga, but it appears in the versions I got from Grandmother's-knife, Plenty-hawk, and Scratches-face, as well as in the story told to Mr. Linderman by Plainfeather. Again, the Hidatsa tell about twin brothers—Thrown-behind-the-draft-screen and Thrown-into-a-spring—who slay a sucking monster, a pot-tilter, and an ogre who burns up people by pointing his moccasins at them. This last episode, while again wanting in Yellow-brow's tale, appears in the Grandchild variants of Scratches-face and Grandmother's-knife. The Hidatsa, too, have a Grandchild myth, but the exploits they assign to him, apart from his conquest of the story-telling snakes, are meager.

Most remarkable of all, the Crow themselves are as likely to credit certain feats to Thrown-behind-the-draft-screen and Thrown-into-a-spring. Thus, Bull-goes-hunting, who gave Mr. Simms a very fragmentary Grandchild story, made his twin heroes conquer the pot-tilter, the sucking monster, falling trees and even the snakes with the fatal rectum complex! Grandmother's-knife told me both stories but reserved the sucking buffalo for the twins, explaining that all other evil beings had been destroyed by Grandchild.

What the Crow have done is evidently to weld into one unit two stories originally distinct. *Their* Grandchild is not merely the offspring of an interplanetary amour, but the savior of man-

kind par excellence, the counterpart of the Blackfoot Bloodclot
and the Hidatsa Twin Heroes. At the same time they have preserved or taken over the Hidatsa Twin story; hence though themselves aware of their distinctness and sometimes deprecating
confusion of the two plots, they find it easier to preach than to
practice keeping them apart. The reason is clear enough: given
the conqueror motif for a story, any adventure originally belonging to either cycle can be as logically associated with one as
with the other. Notwithstanding this complication, certain features can be definitely assigned to the original Crow Grandchild
myth by comparing all the available Crow versions and also
taking into account the Hidatsa equivalent. The latter may be
included not only because of the close relationship between the
two tribes, but for two more specific reasons. First, the Hidatsa
story shares with the Crow variants some features not found
elsewhere at all, or only among such immediate neighbors of
the Hidatsa as the Mandan and Arikara. For instance, while
many mythologies make the celestial husband forbid his wife to
dig up a certain root, the Hidatsa and Mandan, like the Crow,
add the taboo against shooting meadowlarks. Again, the extraordinary adventure with the calf foetus is told only by the Hidatsa,
Arikara, and Crow; and the old woman's test of the childish
poacher's sex is found clearly only in the Crow, Hidatsa, and
Arikara forms. Secondly, in all Crow versions the grandmother
is a gardener, her corn and squashes figuring rather conspicuously. But the historic Crow were pure hunters; hence their tale
is not only related to the Hidatsa one, but derived from it. This
seems especially plausible when two Crow variants credit the
Hidatsa with having the best-looking women; were the tale of
Crow origin, such disinterested objectivity seems unlikely.

Comparing the several Crow forms of the story with its
Hidatsa and Arikara equivalents, I suggest for the proto-Crow
form of Grandchild the digging and shooting taboos, the flight
by a rope just too short to land the woman on *terra firma,* the
dropping of the rock on her, the boy's adoption by an old gardener clandestinely married to a dragon, whom the boy kills, the
taming or slaying of a bear, the elaboration of the adventure
with the rectum-snakes, the episode with the calf foetus, and
the hero's translation to the skies. It seems to me that the
"prologue in heaven," attenuated in Yellow-brow's narrative and

wanting in most Crow versions but fully developed by Plenty-hawk and the Hidatsa, was likewise once part of the standard Crow form, but for some reason dropped out as a regular feature. The Crow standardized their Grandchild story by incorporating features of the rival Twin boys' cycle, thus making Grandchild the dominant hero of their folklore. Of course, suitable elements from other tribes could also readily find a place. Individual narrators were able to juggle freely the relevant parts of several mythologies, changing the sequence of events, dropping or ampli-fying episodes according to their memories and preferences or their skill in welding elements into a coherent whole. Consider-ing recent contacts with the Hidatsa, it may well be that on their visits to North Dakota some story-tellers refreshed their mem-ories by tapping the old fountain-head; and special details may have been borrowed from other mythologies. Since the tale has been constantly told and retold for decades, a particular narrator is likely to know several alternative methods of developing a certain episode and may deliberately choose one among them, as in the case of whether the snakes or Grandchild should begin the story-telling (see p. 144). It is remarkable that with all these opportunities for alteration certain details remain fixed to the very wording. For instance, Yellow-brow, dictating over fifteen years later than Grandmother's-knife, makes the sucking buffalo call his aorta his "pipestem," his kidneys his "whetstone"; and Plain-feather's (like Yellow-brow's) buffalo tells the boy. "That [my heart] is what I plan with." Again, in the Plain-feather variant we read: "Never does he show himself during certain moons; never until the buffalo-calves are born on the plains does the Morning-star shine in the sky." Grandmother's-knife con-cludes thus: "He became the morning-star and in the spring when animals are about to have little ones he does not come out, he does not come until all the animals have had their young ones." Similarly Scratches-face's hero announces: "You will not see me while buffalo are calving, but you'll see me after they have given birth to calves."

Notwithstanding certain omissions of potentially telling details, Yellow-brow's version strikes me as the best of the eight Crow variants I know,—both from the native and our own point of view. His is an ample canvas, yet unlike some other narrators he smoothly assimilates traits from the Twin cycle.

In the treatment of specific adventures we find a superior con-
creteness. Scratches-face gives much the same conversation between Grandchild and the buffalo, and similarly pictures the
different conditions of the men swallowed. Yellow-brow adds the
idea of making the victims perform a Sun Dance inside the monster's maw. He does not even forget the half-dead ones; when
they plead their inability to move, the hero says, "If so, just
make your little heads alone dance." So the visit to the snakes
is elaborated with the whole of the traditional stock-in-trade:
their attempts to crawl into Grandchild's rectum and the bumping of their noses against his stone, the mixing of their teeth
with the proffered spleen, the hero's thwarting of their ruse, and
the particulars of the story-telling contest are all there. A certain
rhythmic quality is obvious, and the dialogue—often quaint from
our point of view—is unmistakably vivacious.

VIII. Twined-Tail

IN THE early days the Crow were moving camp, they were roaming about, seeking food. Twined-tail [1] had two elder brothers—one named Large-inside, the other named Eats-like-a-wolf. He never rode a horse, he had no horse, he was poor. In moving they were afoot. In the summertime he wore hair [winter] blankets about the waist, he put on furry moccasins, the top of his leggings did not reach the bottom, on both sides it would not reach [there]. These elder brothers of his were also poor, that is why it was so.

Once his elder brother Eats-like-a-wolf was playing the hoop-game; he was gambling against a young man named Ground-bull. Eats-like-a-wolf had won plenty [of stakes]. This one named Ground-bull had many kinsmen, they were bullies. When the hoop-game was played, Ground-bull had many supporters; Eats-like-a-wolf had no supporters. Now Eats-like-a-wolf threw his hoop, he hurled his dart and shouted: "That one is a 'One-White' score," he said and turned around. Then Ground-bull came along and got there. "What! It has not touched it," he said. It was Ground-bull who spoke to his supporters. "Come, look at this, it has not touched," they said. Eats-like-a-wolf was looking around, he was seeking supporters, there was no one for him to appeal to. In watching this game, this younger brother of his, Twined-tail, was lying face down watching the gambling. His face was dirty, with the perspiration flowing; at his ankles there was jagged spear-grass. "Twined-tail, come! Look at this, even though you may be of no account. I have plainly scored. 'You have not scored,' they are saying." Twined-tail came and looked, he pondered. "You have plainly scored. How can they say it has not touched? You have scored," he said. It was Twined-tail who spoke thus. This one named Ground-bull said: "What is *he* coming for? He was staying among the crowd.[2] What is it to *him* if there was a score? If

---

[1] Yellow-brow said the hero's name was different prior to the events to be narrated, but he could not recall it.

[2] Obscure.

there was a score, would he thereby be riding a horse? Look at him! If I were like that, I should be too ashamed to approach camp. Over yonder in the mountains, in the high places, there I should now be staying, going around crying for a vision. Look at his ankles—the tangled grass. Look at yourself! You ought to be staying somewhere crying [for a vision]. There is nothing but water flowing from his face," said Ground-bull. This Twined-tail's tears were flowing. Eats-like-a-wolf [spoke]: "Why, you have done wrong in this gambling of ours. To my poor younger brother you have spoken evil words; I am poor, that is why. Let us stop," he said. They stopped playing.

Twined-tail stood up, he took his arrows and other implements, he took moccasins and a flint, he fitted himself out. Then he crossed the river and went toward the Wolf Mountains, he proceeded and reached the Wolf Mountains. Yonder on the hither side of Red Ground [a ridge] he lay down. This night at the furthest point north of the Wolf Mountains a man signaled and called him.[3] The next morning he woke up and left. He kept on along the foot of the Wolf Mountains and killed a calf. That evening he cured it and hung it up there in the shade. He slept at Amdṓ'ciat [foot of a particular hill]. The next morning he climbed the top; the sun had not yet appeared, from the back he climbed Red-Box [hill]. The top was level, an eagle was flying. Though it was far away, the Little Horn River was opposite. When he looked, [he saw] it was a girl with plenty of elk teeth, he [the eagle] was clutching her by her hair, she was dangling under him. "Well, well!" said Twined-tail. "I declare! It is one of our people that he has captured and is taking away," he thought. He went and climbed the hill; the sun had not yet appeared, he waited for it to appear. "When it appears, I'll cut my finger," he thought and stayed there. Then when the sun appeared, he put his forefinger on his gun and took his knife. He cut his forefinger. On a flat stone he laid his forefinger [joint], he held it out toward the sun and prayed for something. Whatever pertains to life he asked for. The blood from his forefinger came in sprays; when the sun was further up, he fainted, the blood oozed out of him. This day he lay unconscious till

---

[3] This is an established feature of certain visions. Bull-all-the-time in describing one of his experiences told me: "In my sleep I saw Pryor Gap and beheld a person holding out a blanket and making a sign for me to come over."

evening. When it got cool, he rose. That night he was so cold
he could not sleep. For all of three nights he failed to get a
vision.[4] On the fourth he was so cold he could not sleep; when
the middle of the night had passed then he slept. When asleep
he was standing outside a very large tipi. A girl with plenty of
elk teeth came out. "Come, enter." With her he entered. "Father,
here I am bringing someone." This man had a wife and was
sitting with her. Behind a pillow he had made a nest of various
kinds of eagle property. White men were staying in the rear.
"You have made a mistake," said the man, "we have been faring
well, now you have brought some one."[5] The woman said: "It
is well, it is a good thing that she is bringing him. Come, we'll
make incense for your child, ground-cedar incense." "However
it may have happened, I was an infant, they took me and smoked
me with incense, four times they lifted me up."[6] "I'll make the
child dance." Singing the Sun Dance song, they made him dance
thereby. However it may have happened, this lodge became a
Sun Dance lodge, inside were those who entered the Sun Dance
lodge. They made him see everything pertaining to the Sun
Dance, whatever they do. This man said: "Yonder is a man
[another supernatural]; *he* has a child and has invoked me [on
his child's behalf], now *I* will invoke *him*," he said and called
this man. What manner of being he was, that we do not know.
It was an old man; he had made his whole body and his hair
very red. He carried his pipe with him, came and entered. "Go
to the rear!" "Well, what is it?" "Why, I want you to look after
that distressed one, hence I called you, that is it," he said. He
took his pipe. "I'll take a smoke." He pointed his pipe toward
the sun and took a puff. It was kindled from the sun's rays. He
pointed it toward Small-River. There were lodges dotted all
over, there were plenty of horses, on this side of the creek the
horses were strung out, they came with a brown one in the lead;
with a deer-antler prong round its neck it came first. Then he
smoked again, he pointed toward Tongue River. A small caravan was coming there. He saw them. He smoked. Blowing the
smoke in the direction of the camp, the horses and the people,

[4] His strange experiences with the signaler and the eagle are merely anticipatory.

[5] That is, he is vexed at being disturbed by the Indian intruder.

[6] Obscure. The idea seems to be that the visionary himself is represented as
describing his experience, but inconsistently Yellow-brow shifts again to the third
person.

he smoked. This old man said: "Is it enough?" This woman
spoke: "May he own the camp!" [i.e., may he become chief!].
The old man said: "Where the winds are, may he hold the reins
and what pertains thereto! [7] Is this enough?" This woman said:
"May he own traveling in any direction!" [i.e., be a captain].
The old man said: "He himself holds the reins of the clouds.
Well, is it enough?" The woman said: "Now my child lacks red
paint." The old man said: "Why, the way the sun paints [sun-
dogs], all the red paint is there, I think. But this will do, with this
he can paint," he said. "Is it enough?" asked this old man. This
woman [said]: "Yes, it is enough." [8] Various other activities
they allowed him to see. This woman said: "The inside of this
lodge, what pertains to it, *I* own; my tipi is twenty-two [hides
in size]." "Well," this man said, "let us send your [plural]
child home." The Sun Dance Doll was attached to the feather-
fan hoop; they allowed this child, Twined-tail, to hold it. They
sang a ritualistic song; this woman's husband sang, the woman
accompanied the song; four times they sang. They spread the
door apart, they sang four times and went outside with him.
"Give that hoop to the sun, you wanted to own red paint." They
took this hoop back. How that happened, we do not know. It was
said: "Give the sun the hoop"; how they gave it we do not
know.

Whether it was before this vision of his or some other time,
a man in Mud-creek [i.e., Owl Creek] waved and called him.[9]
Also some time there were men coming home from a war party
to the west. They came home below where he was. He was lan-
guid, he was not himself, he would not have come to a death-
signaling. "Look! There, this way they went to war, with a
death signaling they return," they said. Whatever the source,
it was said. He woke up, the sun was very high when he got up.
"Yes, that's what I was seeking, it is well, I have had a vision,
I'll go home." Then he came down. His blood was evidently
exhausted, his paunch was empty, his legs were trembling, his
legs gave way and he would fall to the ground. He came, he got
to this [calf] meat of his. He got to water, he drank, he vomited,
it came out continually. He got to his meat and ate. "Well, they

---

[7] That is, May he control the winds!

[8] The invoked old man and the woman of the adopting tipi are the interlocutors.

[9] Cf. footnote 3.

have called me; whatever it be, I'll get to it and find out, I'll go," he thought. Having finished eating, he went. He went on; after a short walk he would stop, he was tired. He arrived. This night there was moonlight. "I think I'll die." His stomach was empty, his blood exhausted, his body was as though dead. When he fell asleep, two coyotes were going on a war party. Then not long after this they came, bringing horses. "Well, our nature is thus: When we travel and are at bay, we use the clouds for our safety," they said. Here a person came out suddenly, he came. He had the tail of a screech-owl on his head, he went singing, he decorated his forehead with yellow clay; his tear lines he had made black. "Battles are what I like best," he said.

The next morning he [Twined-tail] was almost well. He came along. Upstream from the site of his vision-quest was the [Crow] camp, he got there. Wherever they had roamed this summer, they now were camped there where that Agency now is. Soon after the pitching of the camp, this elder brother of Twined-tail, Eats-like-a-wolf, was herding horses; they were left on top. They came and sat on the edge of the top. It was fall, and now and then it snowed. Twined-tail said: "Well, elder brother, we are too poor, let us go to war and bring horses, then *we'll* ride." Eats-like-a-wolf asked: "When?" Twined-tail: "We'll go tonight." "Yes," he said, "let us go." They came back and ordered moccasins to be made. This Twined-tail had a friend; he, too, was poor. He looked for him, came, and got there. "Friend, tonight we'll go on a war party, look for moccasins!" he said. "Yes, I'll do so." "When the camp is asleep, come," he said. He came, he reached the lodge, they were ready. This one elder brother, Large-inside, called Eats-like-a-wolf. He came and entered. "Well, sit down." "When we go on raids we sometimes return empty-handed, sometimes we bring something. That boy who wants to go to war with us is poor. When did he say we should go?" "To-night," he said. "In that case he should have told us some time ago." [10] "He only had the idea just now, that is why." "I consent, it is settled, let us go," he said.

They went. That night they traveled, then they slept. The next morning they started and went on. There was a young man named Striped. He was brave, he was an exceedingly brave young man; however, he had been bewitched and when he went on

[10] Large-inside's captious criticism of his younger brother begins here.

war parties everything miscarried. Among the mishaps unfortunately he would even have to signal for the enemy's killing of one's own fellow-warriors. War captains did not like him. He came, he caught up with the party. On the next day, when evening came, Eats-like-a-wolf went aside with Twined-tail. "That young man," he said, "who has overtaken us is no good. He is bewitched. Whenever he goes out, everything miscarries," he said. "We are poor; on this raid of yours we should come along cautiously," he said. It was Eats-like-a-wolf who spoke thus. Twined-tail said: "Why, it does not matter. It is all right for him to come, though formerly it regularly happened that way, it is no concern of *ours*." "Your words are good."

He [Twined-tail] carried a white stick and whenever they stopped he would be whittling it. They traveled on and on, he would never cry [to a supernatural power]. These young men in his party would all wail by night and by day. All this time he did not wail at all. The snow was deep. Large-inside spoke: "Well, now, no matter how sacred you are, you ought to wail some nights or some other time, whether in the daytime or whatever time. For your followers you are not shedding any of your tears. All the time you eat, that is all you do. Your medicines you never put in the lead." He [Twined-tail] said nothing [in reply]. Twined-tail never told about his vision. "To yonder land we are going," he never said. He remained silent. Those on the war party traveled on and on. He carried this stick; whenever they made a stop he was busy with it. He would whittle it and straighten it. Then some day they began to suspect that enemies were close, they did this for a while, then it passed. Large-inside came and got to Twined-tail: "Well, whither are you taking us? You have not told us anything. Already [you are] dead, the insides of your eyes are big, looking at me that one would not recognize anything. What are you using that stick for? If they kill you, do you want them to tie your scalp to it, eh? Is it for that you are keeping it? Though I've already said it, [I'll say again]: do some wailing sometimes! All you do is to eat," said Large-inside. "Well," said Twined-tail, "why are you keeping on saying it? Is there a lack of wailing? Did we come because we wanted to cry? I thought we'd bring some horses, that's what we came for."

They went on, they came along, then some time in the

evening [he said]: "Boys, stop and prepare food, build a fire and we'll eat." The proper time for stopping had not yet been reached, nevertheless they stopped. Unknown to them he had an idea, that is why he stopped. These boys thought it was in order to eat that they were stopping. When they were through eating, he said: "Come, we'll travel." In the evening they stood up and went. They kept moving till dark, then late that night they reached a ridge. "There is a small clump of trees, there we'll sleep." There they slept. Then the next day Striped woke up and went on top of a hill. He came fleeing. "Why, dear men, we have reached a huge camp. We have passed the horses, the camp is just behind yonder [ridge], the odds are altogether against us," he said. "Look ye," he said. The rest of them got on top of the hill, they had already passed the horses, the camp was close. On the ground was deep snow. Their tracks were plain. The tracks of any one who should come for horses would be visible. They were worrying greatly. The camp was very large. They [the raiders] were at bay. "What shall we do?" they said. Twined-tail sat down, he did not move, he remained unperturbed, he said nothing, he did not even climb the hill. While they were saying "What shall we do?" he remained sitting undisturbed. Large-inside it was, he came and got to Twined-tail. "Long ago it was probable that you would do this to us, now you have done this. Look at me, look—our miserable children; [11] the odds are against us. If they find out about us and something serious happens, I'll settle with you first." He remained silent.

Striped said [to Twined-tail]: "My dear younger brother, I have come with you on your raid. Something has alarmed us. This gun of mine is most excellent, I give it to you. My flirting-outfit [12] at home I also give you. Go ahead, it is well that you have come on the raid [i.e., I have confidence in your success]." "Come," he said to this Striped. He owned a scout emblem. "Bring your scout emblem." "Yes," he said. He took and brought it. He brought it and quickly gave it to him. He laid it, sliding it among a clump of rose-bushes and micgyaxtsi' [unidentified shrub]. When he brought it and did thus, his pipe was inside the emblem. "Come, light it." He lit it and took a puff. "Puff

[11] Construction obscure. Perhaps the speaker is picturing the distress of the braves' children if the war party should be destroyed.
[12] I.e., a horse according to James Carpenter. See p. 49.

it towards my face, do it four times. Make it blow strongly."
He did it strongly that way. Then there was a terrible blizzard.
There was no place at all where they could look around. They
fled to the midst of this thicket. This day it did not stop at all,
it went on and on till sunset this way. Striped came and reached
Twined-tail. "Why, my dear younger brother, what I made
you do is most excellent, nevertheless if it thus goes on until
nightfall we shall not be able to do anything. If you could help
yourself, if you could stop it, if you could stop this blizzard, I
think we'll capture horses. If we reach our camp without any
mishap to us, I'll give you my lodge, buckets and plates,—all
of them. Put a stop to it for my sake." "Yes, that will I." "Go
ahead." He went out from the woods, he stood toward the wind.
He took his blanket, waved it [to the clouds] and made it come
down. This blizzard ceased at once; the sun was low.[13] "Well
now, everything inside a lodge I'll complete and give to you.
Look out for us, I have full confidence in you, we want to bring
plenty of horses to camp, look out for us." "All right," said he.
"Come, look for buffalo chips, take some and bring them. The
ridge is without snow," he said. They brought the buffalo chips
and laid them down. "There they are, go ahead." "Kindle some
of those bleached cherry-trees, they make no smoke." When
they had done it, he said, "Come, bend that small tree, make it
circular, make a hoop." "Now," said Striped, "inside this medicine there is a hoop, how about that?" "That is fine. Take and
bring it, it is well," he said. He brought it. He swept the snow,
this buffalo chip was burning slightly, he made incense for it.
He took his pipe and filled it. Twined-tail said: "Well, now I'll
do two difficult things. If I succeed, it will be all right, it will
be well; if I fail, it will not be well. Now I am going to smoke
this, that Old Man [i.e., the sun] is the one I want to light it
with. [Secondly,] what that Old Man paints with—his red paint
—I want to paint my face with." It was Large-inside [who
spoke]: "Why [the sun] is something strong! You fine fellow,
who on the earth lights his tobacco with that sun? Who paints
himself with it? You are surely not a person [i.e., a fool]," he
said. Twined-tail was silent, he held his pipe towards the sun and
puffed. He made the smoke come out in volumes thereby. It was
lit, he kept on smoking, he gave it to his companions. "Pray,

[13] Thus he shows the power over the winds granted to him.

let them smoke, pray for something." They did so. They smoked this tobacco, they prayed, he took the tail of a full-grown eagle and put it on the back of his head. He took this hoop and the wolf [emblem], he tied it on each side. He put it towards the sun. "When I get to the end of my song, I'll paint my face." He put his hoop towards it, he put it towards the sun, then he sang. The words of the song were: "I see the face of the one over there. I see him holding a scalp," he said. Large-inside [said]: "Ha——a! [sneer]. You fine fellow, you cannot possibly see that sun's face." "Still he persists, this one." Twined-tail thus spoke, to Large-inside he spoke.[14] "This Large-inside is my true brother [he prayed]. Tonight for my sake cause him to suffer [some trouble], yet I don't want to make him die, I'll take him back," he said. Eats-like-a-wolf said: "You have done wrong. He is always a fool, he always says something [foolish]," he said. Twined-tail said, "I have spoken, I can do nothing [about it], he will not possibly die." Again he sang. He made incense for his hand. He put his forefinger towards the sun. Then like this he rubbed [apparently] his finger around his face. He made it nice and blue around his face. As if [he had actually] rubbed it over and over, the color was very nice.[15]

"Now on this trip of ours we shall seek a brown horse wearing a deer-prong necklace.[16] Its herd is eighty head strong, I want to bring it, that I am coming for. Go, Striped, sneak towards the camp, find out where the horses may be." Then Striped did so. When it was dark, they went. They went thither, they proceeded. Before they got to camp, there was one horse staying by the side of a lake. Large-inside spoke: "I'll be the first one to sneak and take a horse," he said. He went to this one horse. He proceeded. When he got there, he saw the horse was very fat. There was ice on the lake. When he wanted to take it [the horse] to a cove, when he wanted it to be afraid of the ice, it was *not* afraid, it went on the ice. It slid and went far. When he got to it, it was very fat. "Well! I've got to an extremely fat one, I'll come out with it, even if it's the only one [I get], I'll reach the [home] camp [with it]," he thought. That night he labored over it [the horse], wanting to take it away from the

---

[14] He at last loses his patience and prays to have his brother punished.

[15] I.e., he does not actually rub anything over his face, but goes through the motions and magically effects his purpose.

[16] This refers to the vision and the expected fulfilment of its promise.

ice. They [the party] went on and got to the camp. He sent Striped and Eats-like-a-wolf, one on each side of the camp. "Go, bring ye horses," he said and sent off both, it is said. They went. After a little while three horses came out there. "I'll go and see the horses," said Twined-tail. He went, proceeded, and got to these horses. "This brown one I'll bring, the one with a deer-prong necklace," he had said, and so it was. He took, led, and brought it. "Well, boys, I named [mentioned] the brown one, this one I myself took and am bringing." He stood and when examining it [he saw] it was [so fat] its middle [of back] was hollow. It was unequaled. Then these who had gone to the camp both brought plenty of horses. They took them, all of them mounted horses and fled. That night they kept fleeing.

It was daylight, the sun had not yet risen when [they saw] behind a hill a man crying and at the same time running. "Well, what is that? Look!" said Striped. Then when he went on top, a man was running afoot and at the same time crying. He noted it was Large-inside. "Hi——! Stop!" he said. They stopped. He ran. Then he met Large-inside. He put him behind him, brought him and arrived with him. "Why what is the matter?" "Why along that lake I wanted to take one very fat, very good-looking horse. I took him to the ice, he went on the ice and fell down. Then I was helpless, I labored over him. At last I could do nothing, it was about daylight, I came thence," he said. Eats-like-a-wolf said: "Haha! He came on this raid with us. You persisted in saying various [impudent] things to him, now you have found out [it was wrong]." "Where are the horses you [should] give me, give them," said he.[17] When horses were given him, he sang praise songs and went along.

"Come, on," he [Twined-tail] said. They went on fleeing, this side they lay down. The next day Twined-tail woke up. "Well, boys, at the Tongue River there is one lodge, we'll get there and wipe them out," he said. "A young woman is riding a striped bay, she has many elk teeth, I'll capture her," he said. It was Large-inside who said: "Now that we are bringing these horses, it is enough, I think. You are taking it to nothing [you are going too far and imperiling everything]." Eats-like-a-wolf it was, he spoke to Large-inside: "Still he is doing it. We thought you had learnt a lesson." They kept on and reached Tongue River. "Come,

[17] This demand was felt to be a comical sample of his incorrigible effrontery.

Striped, scout towards it, look in the valley." "I'll do it," he said. He went dashing off. Not long after he came. "Why, one caravan is coming." Then they mounted their horses, Twined-tail rode his brown horse, in a coulée from the Tongue River he ran. They came. As they came out, the caravan was coming there; there was one man with two women. A young woman was riding a striped bay, she had many elk-teeth. This man, an enemy, dismounted. Twined-tail struck him and took his gun. He mounted and chased this young woman, he took hold of her bridle and brought her. Then he took all their horses, he took all the best of their belongings. Then they came. Twined-tail spoke: "Eats-like-a-wolf and Large-inside, this young woman I will not give you, I want to own her myself and marry her." He married her. The woman was very good-looking. They got to the top of the Wolf mountains. "Well, Striped, go, in the river valley seek our home!" He went. After a while he gave the coyote howl and came. "Well, have you any signs of it?" "Yes, a little ways up-stream from where your party started, in a river-bend, there is the camp." They were glad.

They came, they stopped in a coulée. Twined-tail with his wife carried their property. They went around where the trees were pointing [?]. His companions were lying at rest. He made his wife ride the bay. He dressed in all his enemy's belongings, he put on a bonnet with the tails, he rode the brown horse. Where the trees pointed there they came out. He came to his party and sang tsū'ra songs; he walked with his wife and pointed to her. He sang: "You have just died.[18] That is my sweetheart! Thanks." [19] he said. [These were] the words of his song. He painted his face yellow, he made it black around it. When his party were observing him, [they found] he had a good voice. Twined-tail unknown to them had been a fine-looking man before; because he was poor he looked ugly, when he dressed up he was handsome. His wife was an exceedingly fine-looking woman. Then the party came towards camp, they came, they stopped near the camp. "It is well. We'll sing the tsū'ra." They made a huge fire that night and sang tsū'ra.

Twined-tail said: "Now, as for the man who caused me

---

[18] According to my interpreter this is equivalent to saying "Damn you!" to his slain foeman.

[19] This is doubtless addressed to his supernatural friends.

distress, I'll make a song about him." "Go ahead," they said. He sang: "Ground-bull, leaning to one side, is a poor man. His mentula is on the side, there is plenty of semen in it." [20] Striped spoke: "Well, Ground-bull's wife is my sweetheart. Suppose I made a song about her?" he said. "Yet just recently I was suffering from having a spell cast upon me, hence I am hesitant," he said. Twined-tail spoke: "It would be well, they are no people,[21] do it, make the song about them, it will be amusing, do it." The wife's name was Coming-from-the-water. He sang: "Coming-from-the-water, come out, look at me, I'll go at once. There are no women who have not two husbands. Coming-from-the-water, you have big labia," he said. Thus he spoke. Where Curly's house is at the ford there they crossed; below at the cove was the camp. They ran through the camp, they came to the middle of the camp. The people said: "Who is the leader of these who are running through the camp?" They did not know. "What sort of person is this?" They did not know. After a while they found out: "Why it is Twined-tail! How is it he is so handsome?" Then they brought the drum and sang tsū'ra songs. Then after a long time when close to the end of it [they said], "Come we'll sing the Ground-bull song." They also sung the song about his wife. This woman fell to crying. Ground-bull dragged a club, he came for revenge. The aforesaid Striped formerly had been a person of spirit, he had plenty of kin. His people were brave. Striped said: "Don't come, go the other way! The person was poor, all that can be said to him, evil things, all manner of insults you said to him. But they were poor, they did not try to get even with you, now they have their revenge. They did not insult you, you are getting furious at them, don't come. If you get revenge on them, it is the same as if you were getting revenge on me. *I'll* take care of you. Go, go the other way." When they got to camp that's the way it was, Ground-bull turned about and went off.

This Striped said: "Come on, Twined-tail, I'll take you to your home." With him he took him to Striped's home. "Dismount!" With him he entered the tipi. Striped said to his wife: "This home of ours I give all to Twined-tail. Come on, we'll stay with some of our relatives," he said. Striped said: "From now

---

[20] Allusion to his many children.
[21] Presumably equivalent to "they are fiends."

on I make you my younger brother, I'll go on a raid with you and scout for you." This captive woman was of the Fox tribe [?], she remained married to him. Then this wife got pregnant and had a child. She was a handsome woman. This woman had a child, *she* was a handsome woman. Now Plays-with-himself's wife's mother, the one that's still alive [represents the next generation].

*   *   *   *   *

Comment. In contrast to the three preceding tales, which belong definitely to the mythical period in which animals talked as a matter of everyday routine, "Twined-tail" is wholly realistic. There are, of course, happenings that seem marvelous to us, but nothing my own informants would not have considered wholly within the range of possibility during their own lifetime. Take, for instance, the magical way in which the hero paints his face, thereby putting to shame his brother's skepticism: Gros Ventre told me he had *seen* Wraps-up-his-tail (p. 238) paint his face by pointing his finger at the sun, that is, without use of pigment produce a red stripe.

The story is typical in its theme: the lowly are exalted and the proud abased, all as a result of a revelation. Like a good Crow, Yellow-brow waxes expansive in describing the visions, the war raid, and the triumphant return to camp. In one respect, however, this story seems to me unique; there are faint beginnings of individualization. The two brothers are not defined merely in terms of their status, but are sharply contrasted in their characters. Eats-like-a-wolf is not merely the elder kinsman who resents the affront to his junior brother, but personifies the sympathetic and prudent counselor. He has misgivings as to Striped's companionship but gracefully waives his objections. Large-inside, on the other hand, is the typical nagging relative and doubting Thomas; his ungenerous carping and incorrigible impudence are brought out in relief and stressed as farcical. Striped represents still a different character motif. Here is a man not at all related to the hero, a man of valor upon whom without fault of his a shadow has fallen and who gratefully acknowledges the chance to retrieve his position in society. His part is in a sense that of a counterfoil to the villainous Ground-bull, whom he very properly rebukes and routs toward the close of the narrative. Twined-tail himself is, of course, the incarnation of the orphaned hero, handsome despite his mean appearance, loftily disdainful of Large-inside's thrusts in the sublime self-assurance of one who has seen the supernatural guides of his destiny.

IX. Club Life

I N the old days virtually every man belonged to some club (araxu'a'tse),—very likely joining that of his elder brothers and maternal uncles. Indeed, parents are known to have pledged an infant to take a dead brother's place when of age. But there was no obligation to do this, so that club and clan lines overlapped. Generally the society took the initiative: if a member died, they tried to fill the vacancy by offering gifts to one of his kinsmen. They were also likely to bait with presents any man of renown whose affiliation would shed luster on his club, giving it an advantage over rival groups. There was no exclusiveness: eager to add to its numbers, each club welcomed volunteers attracted by its dance or regalia. Formal initiation and entrance fees were lacking,—in striking contrast to the Tobacco societies (p. 274).

In about 1870 the Foxes and Lumpwoods had become the most conspicuous clubs and figured as rivals, but the Big Dogs and Muddy Hands were still active. None of them was in any sense a religious fraternity, their activities being social and military. Each spring the camp chief appointed one of them to serve as police (p. 5 f.), but rotation was irregular so that the same organization might act in this capacity year after year. Every club had its distinctive regalia, decoration, dance, and peculiarities of behavior, yet all shared essentially the same scheme of "officers," who were usually paired off in parades, and likewise the mode of electing them. These men were not at all the directors of their society—a duty informally assumed by influential older fellows. They were simply members pledged to be exceptionally brave and set off from the rank and file by honorific insignia or standards.

The system of these clubs was far from stationary, and in some measure we can get glimpses of its condition at different periods. The notion of foolhardly warriors existed as early as 1804, when Lewis and Clark discovered that a society of such braves among the Dakota was patterned on a Crow model. In

1833 Maximilian registered eight clubs,—the Bulls, Prairie-foxes, Ravens, Half-shaved Heads, Lumpwoods, Stone Hammers, Little Dogs and Big Dogs. From Beckwourth we learn that between 1825 and 1855 keen competition divided some of these companies; he specifically mentions the Foxes and Dogs. These earlier writers ignore the Muddy Hands, whom my informants describe as once prominent but fusing with the Foxes about 1865 or 1870. Lumpwoods and Foxes were then in the ascendant, with other clubs obviously dwindling or obsolete. Bell-rock set the number of Foxes at a hundred and estimated that of the rival company as considerably higher. In about 1875 the Hidatsa introduced the Hot and the Crazy Dog dance, which were linked with two corresponding organizations. The Crazy Dog dance naturally reached the River Crow first, but in spreading to the Main Body it assumed a new character (p. 213). The Hot Dance innovation led to the establishment of four societies, which took the place of the older clubs and were still in full swing in 1910.

Individual clubs have thus had their ups and downs, and altogether the system in its details has been in a state of flux. Owing to the element of rivalry a man normally belonged to a single club. But in the transitional period when the Hot and Crazy Dog dance were borrowed from the Hidatsa it was conceivable to belong simultaneously to one of the old and one of the new clubs. Thus, Bear-gets-up, like his deceased brothers, had joined the Lumpwoods and did not renounce his affiliation in becoming a Crazy Dog. However, when his Hidatsa comrade died, he dropped out of the organization.

Except for some special occurrence, a man would thus remain loyal to his first club. For instance, Lone-tree accepted a Crazy Dog invitation when this society offered him property on the death of his uncle; and he never joined any other club. On the other hand, there were often adequate reasons for shifting one's allegiance. Notwithstanding the tendency to affiliate oneself with a brother's club, by no means all "brothers" were fellow-members. A particular young man might thus be summoned first to succeed a kinsman in one club and later another in a different society. This is precisely what happened to Sharp-horn, who first lost a Fox brother, and later one who had been in the Lumpwood organization. Similarly, Child-in-the-mouth turned Muddy Hand. Subsequently one of his Fox brothers was killed, so he rejoined the Foxes. Bull-chief had one maternal uncle among the Big Dogs, another among the Foxes; first he joined the former society, but when the second uncle was killed, the Foxes lured him into their ranks by presents. Occasionally a man left his club in a huff. Sioux raiders once stole all of Fire-weasel's horses; his fellow-Foxes refused to help him, while the Big Dogs offered him horses and property, so he joined their numbers and never left them.

Since an overwhelming number of my informants had been either Lumpwoods or Foxes, my data on these two societies will give the clearest picture of the whole system when in full swing.

THE LUMPWOODS AND FOXES

I have followed Mr. Curtis in rendering the native name maraxi'ce for the former of these societies, but Knobbed Sticks would be more accurate.[1] Though there were no such emblems in recent times, tradition tells of a member striking a first coup with such a club, whereupon his entire society, hitherto known as Half-shaved Heads (see p. 182), changed its name in honor of his weapon. Bell-rock had heard his father speak of a former symbol of the organization consisting of a club carved at one end into a horse's head and with bells round the neck. Old-dog mentioned a similar stick but with a buffalo head; however, this was not, he thought, the badge of the rank and file but a single member's medicine, to which he individually prayed for food in times of scarcity. In the Hidatsa equivalent there was certainly such a stick, conspicuously associated with the capture of buffalo.

Whatever may have been the original functions of the organization, by 1870 its character had become wholly secular, and its officers' emblems were precisely like the Foxes', only the dance remaining distinct. The performers merely moved in their places, alternately raising the right arm as far backwards as possible and again bringing it to its normal position. A monitor holding a whip lashed reluctant members to make them get up and dance.

---

[1] Leforge's translation, "Red Stick" is preposterous (Marquis, 195); mara' means stick, but xi'ce is "swollen," "lumpy," "knobbed." He has confused this word with hi'ce, "red."

After the first snowfall the Lumpwoods frequently met of an evening in some suitable lodge, where they would remain for supper. The next evening they might similarly assemble in another tipi. They were like fellow-members of a friendly society. Irrespective of whether Lumpwoods were of the River Crow or the Main Body, they treated one another like brothers whenever they met. Four Lumpwoods of the Main Body, for example, once hunted buffalo for Bear-gets-up's benefit. If a man was adopted into the Tobacco or Medicine Pipe ritual, his fellow-Lumpwoods were ready to help him defray the expenses. Again, when a close relative had to be buried, a man naturally turned to his club associates for aid.

The club was subdivided, partly on the basis of age: there were the Lumpwoods without Sweethearts (maraxi'ce bī'a hirē'te); the Tall Lumpwoods (m. ha'tskite); and the Old Lumpwoods (m. mā.isā'te). Bell-rock, himself an outsider, mentioned the Lumpwoods proper, the Half-shaved Heads (itsū'sa tsiricū'tse), and the Wholly-shorn (daxō'xua). Hunts-to-die, a member, substituted the Little Rumps (isi's iatc) for Bell-rock's last subgroup. According to his report, it was because his brother belonged to it that he joined this division, and he always remained there. Two-foxes thought the younger Lumpwoods were called Ugly Faces (īs-xawi'ambice) owing to their excessive use of heavy paint. Bear-gets-up wavered between Liver-eaters (akapterū'uce) as the name of the whole club and of the older membership only.

The Lumpwoods reorganized early in the spring, officers being chosen for one year only. Old-coyote was about fifteen years old when he joined. His father was also a Lumpwood,— sufficient proof that membership was not a matter of clans. That spring a crier summoned all the Lumpwoods to a certain large tipi. They assembled there, Old-coyote sitting down in a corner. Four old men in charge of the proceedings were to select the officers. One of them offered a pipe to each man chosen for a particular position. The recognized officers included two leaders (base'); two bearers of straight staffs (mara-ta'tsc-ake', straight-stick owner) (Fig. 12d); two bearers of hooked staffs (mara-ckyu'pe-ake', crooked-stick owner) (Fig. 12e); and two rear men (hā'ke, the last). The front and rear pairs were without special emblems. When the electors had chosen the leaders, they

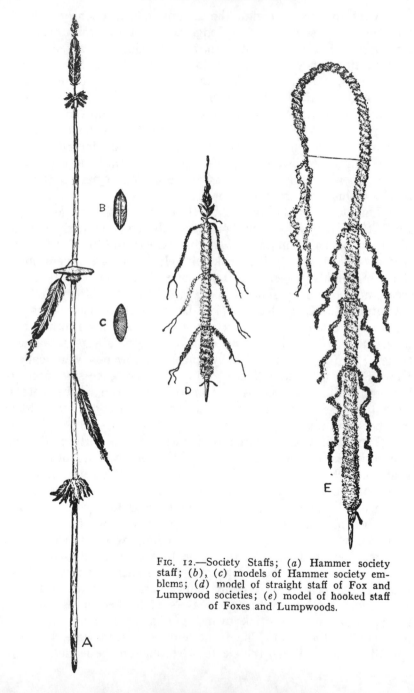

FIG. 12.—Society Staffs; (a) Hammer society staff; (b), (c) models of Hammer society emblems; (d) model of straight staff of Fox and Lumpwood societies; (e) model of hooked staff of Foxes and Lumpwoods.

came up to my informant. He begged to be excused because of his youth; he was not sure, so ran his plea, whether he could resist the temptation to flee. Three times he declined to smoke, still they insisted and pulled his head down by the hair so that his lips touched the pipe-stem. Thus they automatically broke his resistance and made him a straight-staff officer. He thought to himself he should not escape with his life if he encountered any enemies.

At the time of the assembly the four emblem-bearers received only dummies, i.e. a peeled willow stick apiece, with bark tied on to represent the genuine otter-skin wrapping. Old-coyote's father at once cried out for some of this material and got it in return for one of his best horses. When all the officers had been selected, the club paraded through the camp. Then they split into four groups, each going to the tipi of one of the standard-bearers. There the parents of the newly honored brave had prepared plenty of food to entertain their guests while a true emblem was being got ready instead of the dummy. A predecessor who had gained war honors in the same office wrapped the otter-skin round the stick and prayed on behalf of the young man: "I had such a stick in battle and had good luck. I hope this man will do the same." Then he handed the wand to the novice. For this service he was entitled to four kinds of property, but when Old-coyote subsequently struck a Sioux with his staff and captured his horse he gave the wrapper four extra gifts.

When Young Jackrabbit was elected, two old men went about offering filled pipes. After choosing the two handsomest men for leaders, they cast about for prospective standard-bearers. To quote my witness:

"All declined to smoke, then they came towards me. Some one asked them, 'Whom are you looking for?' They answered, 'Young Jackrabbit.' I was seated in the rear and tried to hide. They brought the pipe to me, but I refused to accept it. One of the pipe-carriers was my own older brother. He seized me by the hair, struck my chest, and said, 'You are brave, why don't you smoke the pipe?' He wished me to die, that is why he desired me to smoke the pipe. He said, 'You are of the right age to die, you are good-looking, and if you get killed your friends will cry. All your relatives will cut their hair, fast and mourn. Your bravery will be recognized; and your friends will feel gratified.' I took the pipe and began to smoke. They asked me whether I wished to have a straight or a hooked-staff. I chose the hooked-staff. My comrade also smoked the pipe.

"After the election we all went outside. A hooked willow stick was presented to me. I went home with my friends. My brother had an otter-skin there. A man who as bearer of the hooked-staff had once killed an enemy cut the skin into strips, wrapped them round the staff, and did the necessary sewing. I put on a blanket of beaded buffalo-calf skin fringed at the bottom and sides and tied round the neck with a string. We all went outside, the leaders in front. An old man slapped me on the chest and said, 'Now you are a brave man; when the enemy are in pursuit, you must get off and hold them back. If you are willing to do this, dance backwards when we have a dance.' I dressed up in my best clothes. That day I thought I looked handsome. The old men sang songs in my praise. Pretty-white took my hooked stick, smoked it with wild-carrot incense and said, 'One day when we fought the Cheyenne I had a hooked stick and went through the Cheyenne line without being shot. I wish my brother may do the same.' Then he returned the staff to me."

This narrative requires a comment or two. As already explained (p. 26), the informant's brother did not bear him a grudge, but merely wished to make him gain kudos. "He wished me to die" reflects the stock phrase used of club officers,—ce"kyuk, they are made to die. Actually, though they ran real risks, many of them survived. The elder brother's remark about Young Jackrabbit being of the right age to die expresses the proverbial saying that men ought to die in youth since old age is fraught with evil.

The freedom to choose either the straight or the hooked staff is borne out by independent testimony. Apparently one elector carried the willow dummies, another the pipe. When a candidate had been made to smoke, willy-nilly, they would simply ask: "Which stick will you have?" Then they gave him the kind asked for.

Finally, the promise of ample mourning in case of an honorable death was no empty boast and closely paralleled the corresponding ceremony of the Foxes (see p. 67). The old Lumpwoods who informally managed everything supplied each of their fellows with a butchering-knife and an arrow or two. The corpse, arrayed in the brave's finest clothing, was laid outdoors. Then everyone knelt down and cried. The dead man's closest friends cut off the last joint of one of their fingers. Others thrust arrows through their flesh after the manner of people torturing themselves at a Sun Dance (p. 321) and left them sticking there for a while during their wailing. Some ran arrows through their arms and legs, others drew blood from their foreheads. If some of the younger members shrank from gashing themselves, the officers cut them so as to draw blood. For some time the Lumpwoods would dance toward the corpse, at last they stopped and sat down. Then the slain man's parents distributed presents as a remuneration for the club's mourning; and whoever had outdone the rest in drawing blood from his head received a gift of special value.

A strange form of bantering called batbā'tua was in vogue among the Lumpwoods. This is translated "joking with each other," but the verbal stem is different from that of ī'watkuce, joking relative. Specifically, every Lumpwood had the privilege of jesting about a fellow-Lumpwood's recent bereavement to the mourner's face and without incurring his anger.

No jokes were cracked about such affinities as a wife's brother or a sister's husband, but the loss of a wife was a proper subject for this display of humor. Bear-gets-up tells of one instance. A Lumpwood had lost his wife and several of his fellows helped him bury her. They sat down with him for a while, then one of them said to the mourner, "You will not have a wife today, shall you?" Thus they jested about it at that very place, yet the widower did not resent it.

Bear-gets-up himself once rode to the Agency for rations, not knowing that an uncle of his had died in the vicinity. He approached a group of old men including several Lumpwoods, one of whom said, "Uncle-dead, get off here and take a smoke."

At one time, the same informant said, Two-whistles and White-buffalo were the only Lumpwoods whose mothers were still alive, so they generally gibed at their fellow-members for being motherless. When the people had moved to a new camp site, White-buffalo would ask any man he met whether he knew of any Lumpwood living with his mother. The person asked repeated the question to the first Lumpwood he saw, and *he* would tell his fellow about White-buffalo's query. They all bided a chance to get even. At last his mother died one night, and he came to the Lumpwood lodge, looking for two men to assist in the disposal of the corpse. Bear-gets-up said, "It is very good for you not to have a mother. You will never again say 'i"gya" (mother). I am very glad your mother is dead; you will be like myself, motherless." Thus he got even.

Once, when the Indians were going to the Agency for a Fourth of July celebration, Yellow-face heard of his half-witted brother Eating-fish's death and turned back because, he said, he was having bad luck. Thereupon one Lumpwood asked another in the mourner's presence, "Why is Yellow-face turning back?" The answer was: "He is going back *to eat fish.*" Such puns, incidentally, are not uncommon in daily life.

Bear-wolf, a noted warrior, had died, and his brother Charges-strong was driving the corpse to the burial place. A fellow-Lumpwood who had heard of the death met the mourner and said, "Stop, I wish to talk with you. How much will you take for your apples in this box?" Charges-strong laughed but said nothing. "Why don't you answer? What have you in this box?" "A man." "Who is this man?" "Bear-wolf." "Oh, I thought it was a box of apples." Such jesting may be kept up indefinitely. On another occasion a Lumpwood was going to bury his mother on a hill, packed the corpse on a horse's back, and went behind, crying. A fellow-member met him and called out to the leader of the horse, "Hē! Why don't you stop? That young one is after his mother, he wishes to talk with his mother."

According to Sitting-elk, one of these jokers might say, "Your sister (or mother, etc.) is dead." The mourner would reply, "I eat the flesh" (irū'cec bū'ciky), meaning "The flesh of the dead person is still fresh." The mourner did not get angry at such comments by a fellow-Lumpwood; on the contrary, he liked to hear them.

Certain members ranked as chief jokers in this sort of pleasantry, and in 1910 four such were still living in Pryor,— Hunts-to-die, Fox, Sharp-horn, and Red-eye. The custom had not always been associated with the Lumpwoods, being at one time characteristic of the Big Dogs. A Big Dog once instructed two old Lumpwoods in the practice, renouncing it on behalf of his own club; and when these men died, two other old members were chosen as their successors. Such chief jokers were expected to gash themselves with special vim at a mourning ceremony. Fire-weasel thought the Big Dogs did not absolutely give up the batbā'tua prerogative, but no longer used it regularly after passing it on to the other club. According to him, what happened was that a Big Dog chief once initiated a Lumpwood into the Medicine Pipe dance (see p. 269) and took this occasion to transfer the privilege to his "son." A somewhat different version was offered by Sitting-elk. A Big Dog was adopting a Lumpwood into the Tobacco society. Then all the Lumpwoods brought property for the adopted, addressed him as "father" and asked him to transfer the batbā'tua practice to them. Both accounts characteristically treat a type of behavior as a copyrighted form of property that may be sold and bought. They also illustrate how the irrelevant event of adoption into a religious body could affect the features of a secular club through the personal relations of the ceremonial "father" and "son." Why any society should attach value to such a custom as the batbā'tua remains an enigma.

*　　*　　*　　*　　*

The Foxes (i'axuxke; to be precise, Kit-foxes) were in most respects the counterpart of the Lumpwoods. When the latter discarded the knobbed emblem and adopted the straight and hooked staffs of the rival club, the similarity was naturally intensified. However, the Foxes danced differently, forming a circle that moved to the left, with each participant making a low jump with both feet.

The two clubs are so closely allied in native thought that one informant gave a single origin account for both. A Crow, he said, returning from a buffalo hunt, saw a vision in which were revealed two hooked and two straight pine sticks wrapped with otterskin, the latter emblems tipped with eagle feathers. On getting back to camp, he cut his hair short, leaving a central roach, and plastered the shorn part of his head with white clay. He also made a headdress of bear guts painted with red stripes. Then he organized the Foxes and the Lumpwoods, but the latter cut their hair short only in front.

If this report is taken at its face value, it further illustrates the tendency of Crow clubs to take over one another's features. For among the Hidatsa the bear-gut headgear was distinctive of the Lumpwoods only, and among the Crow it is described as an actual characteristic in recent times only of the Muddy Hand society (p. 197). The hair-roaching naturally suggests the Half-shaved Head society, which the Crow consider a precursor of the Lumpwoods, but here the Hidatsa parallel bears out the story, since the Hidatsa Foxes are said to have once roached their hair.

Other origin accounts envisage only the Fox club. A Crow traveler who fell asleep in the course of his journey saw many foxes approaching, lying down, and singing Fox songs. He organized the society on his return. At first it was composed exclusively of young men, but later older people also joined. According to another statement, an old man, having had a revelation to that effect, would hold up a fox skin while performing the dance that became typical of the club, therefore the members were called Foxes. Finally, Gray-bull offered the remark that *all* the clubs were inaugurated by Old Man Coyote.

These several reports well illustrate the Crow tendency to assign cultural origins either to a vision or to the culture hero.

Informants occasionally referred to belts of kit-fox skin or fox-skin capes. These latter were made by bisecting the skin and uniting the halves so as to leave a slit for the head, the tail hanging down the wearer's back. Such capes figure in the Kit-fox organization of the Oglala Dakota, hence similar insignia were probably at one time typical of the Crow equivalent. One informant alleged a distinctive kind of paint: the Foxes painted one side of the face red and the other yellow, using black and yellow body paint, while the Lumpwoods substituted pink.

The majority of my witnesses denied any distinction in dress between Foxes and Lumpwoods. I conclude that this holds true for 1870, but that in an earlier period these clubs had different insignia.

In organization the two societies were doubtless strikingly parallel in the latter half of the last century. Thus, there were Fox subdivisions corresponding to those of the Lumpwoods, though perhaps more definitely on a basis of age-grouping. The youngest members formed the bākawi'a, Naughty ones, possibly 18 or 20 years of age; intermediate were the Little Foxes, i'axuxk-i'ate; and last came the i'axuxke proper, described as quiet, good-humored men of mature age. Bell-rock started in the Naughty group and automatically passed into the two others.

In addition there were several lesser groups. A body of intimates might be collectively designated by some sobriquet. Thus, if from five to ten comrades had never abducted a Lumpwood woman, they were labeled "Foxes without Sweethearts" (see p. 175); several corpulent members were dubbed "Fat Foxes" (i'axuxk īra'pe); and those who first bought the large black hats sold by traders were set off as Big Hats (ikyu'p isā'te). The last-named, according to Sitting-elk, united all the members except the Naughty Ones. Child-in-the-mouth declared that he entered as a bākawi'a, next became a Big Hat, and finally a Fox without Sweethearts. He gave as an additional group the Foxes with Many Sweethearts (i'axuxke dās ahō').

As to dress, emblems, and eligibility to office, there were absolutely no differences between any two of the subdivisions, but the bākawi'a had a special function. If at the annual kidnapping a Lumpwood's wife refused to go with a Fox on the plea of never having been his mistress, the Fox was obliged to prove his former relationship with her. If he succeeded, the bākawi'a then took her by force.

The bākawi'a all sat in a separate section of the club lodge, but with two older men they had chosen to think for them. The bākawi'a were considered children and acted accordingly, playing about the lodge and taking meat before it was cooked. As soon as a song was sung, they rose and danced. Though they were forever joking, their older fellow-members never resented their behavior, but were glad to see the boys enjoying themselves.

Precisely as among the Lumpwoods, the officers were regarded as men "made to die." Their attitude is reflected in the following song, which, however, may be taken as embodying the ideals of all the members:

| i'axuxkekatū'we, | bacbi'awak, | cē'wak. |
| You dear foxes, | I want to die, | thus say I. |

Another feature shared with the Lumpwoods and other clubs was the limitation of tenure to one season. An officer was chosen in the spring and relieved from his obligation with the first snowfall. However, he might be reëlected in the following spring.

The Foxes, like their rivals, had two leaders, two hooked-staff bearers, two straight-staff bearers, and two rear men. In addition there were one or two akdū'cire,—functionaries some witnesses, however, credit to every club. These were to be the bravest of all, whence their privilege to select whatever food they wished at a feast and eat it before the rest had begun their meal. As to the other officers, a standard-bearer would plant his staff into the ground when in view of the enemy and then had to remain there irrespective of danger. He might not tear out the standard himself, but was allowed to flee if a friend plucked it out for him. According to Gray-bull, the carrier of a hooked pole might run a short distance before making a stand, while a man with a straight staff was not supposed to retreat at all; that, correspondingly, it was more ignominious for the latter officer to shirk his duty. Child-in-the-mouth suggested differentiation along other lines: the leaders were to strike the first coup in an encounter. "If they were not afraid and struck the enemy, people liked it very much." On the other hand, the owners of hooked staffs had to dismount, plant their emblems, and make a stand if all the other members were fleeing. In a similar predicament the function of the rear man was to face about, put the enemy to flight and make a killing. Other authorities failed to note, or even denied, any specific differences of this sort, but any officer who ran away was held in contempt and compared to a menstruating woman.

Child-in-the-mouth said that the sticks symbolized trees too heavy to be lifted. No special value was set on the shafts, which all the former owners I visited had discarded. On the other hand, the otter-skin wrapping was highly prized (see p. 177), and several of the men had kept theirs; thus, they were able to make models of their emblems for me with the very skins once used on their real standards. As in the case of the Lumpwoods, a newly chosen officer's parents paid as much as a horse for such an otter-skin, and Muskrat bought one for an elk-tooth dress at the time of her son's election. Unlike the equivalent standards of some other tribes, the shafts of the Crow officers, which were of pine wood stripped of the bark, did not have a stone or iron spear-head attached to the lower end but merely tapered to a point. Most of the shaft was wrapped with otter-skin and at two or three spots on the staff hung a pair of little strips of otter-skin. This applied to either variety of standard, but the straight form was in addition topped by an erect eagle feather. On the other hand, the hooked standard was made by lashing an arched stick of red willow to the pine shaft and holding the end in position. The loop thus formed was also covered with otter-skin, and strips of this material were attached to the tip of the hooked part.

The election of officers paralleled that of the Lumpwoods. Old men debated outside who should be chosen, and approached their candidates with a pipe, but members often declined to serve, saying, "I am afraid I am not strong enough." Sometimes an elector surreptitiously touched the lips of his candidate with the mouthpiece of the pipe, thus compelling acquiescence. Exactly as in the rival society there was resort to strong-arm methods. When Gray-bull was chosen to bear a hooked staff the pipe had been vainly offered to every one; then his comrade seized him by the bang of his hair, pulled him up, and forced his lips against the pipe. As in the other club, peeled willow-sticks with their bark simulating otter-skins served as dummies until the proper wrapping could be secured.

After all the officers had been selected the membership ranged themselves in fixed order. The leaders stood beside each other, behind them the first pair of standard-bearers, then the rank and file, including the musicians, who held one-headed skin drums and drumsticks. There followed the second pair of staff-bearers, and the two hā'ke brought up the rear. In this order they marched through camp, singing their songs. The parents of the new standard-bearers cast about for otter-skins, for before the end of the procession one entire skin had to be obtained for each. Then the club broke up into four parties, each helping one of the officers to cut up the otter-skin and wrap the strips around the shafts. Predecessors of the newly chosen men recounted their feats while in office and concluded with some such words as: "I should like you to do the same and to strike the enemy. We know you are brave, we wish you to fight for your people." The knife used by the man who cut the skin was painted black to symbolize a coup. In general, black betokened victory. The trimmer of the skin kept the knife and the awl used in stitching the strips. After some singing the members all went home.

Between this time and the first snowfall some person occasionally asked the Foxes to give an open-air performance, indeed, Bull-chief declared that each of the clubs danced four times during such a season. On such an occasion the Foxes formed an unclosed ring. The staff-bearers would turn their backs on the rest of the members, being the only ones privileged to act in this way.

In the 'sixties and 'seventies the grouping of most men into either the Lumpwood or the Fox club provided a natural line of cleavage; accordingly, we learn that in certain games the men of one of these societies and their wives were pitted against the members of the other society and *their* wives. But alignment in two opposite camps revolved essentially about two activities: mutual wife-kidnaping (batsu'ara.u; bats, one another; u'a, wife; ara'.u, taking), and competition for the honor of striking the first coup of the season.

After the spring election of the officers the members of either club would begin calling out, "Hu'hu!" This was a challenge: it meant that they were ready to start with the abduction of women. During the period in question this practice was limited to these two societies. It would be a disgrace to run off with a fellow-member's wife. When Charges-camp had joined the Lumpwoods, the wife of one of his brethren asked him to change his allegiance so that he might elope with her, but he refused to do so.

Theoretically a man had the right to abduct a woman only if he had previously been her lover. If he mendaciously claimed a wife on this ground, she would call him a liar and refuse to accompany him. But if she untruthfully denied former relations, his comrades seized her by force. As noted, among the Foxes it was the youngest group of members that would tear her away. In practice, various accounts suggest, there was an element of luck about this. Some men alleged an intimacy that had never existed and wrongfully carried off women by sheer force, which was all the easier because of the masculine code that forbade any display of jealousy on the husband's part. Such a woman's point of view is clearly brought out in the following narrative by Strikes-at-night, a River Crow woman and the mother of Bull-weasel. I cannot, of course, guarantee that she ought to have enjoyed the immunity she claimed.

"My husband was a great warrior. He was a Fox. The Lumpwoods and the Foxes were stealing each other's wives one season while my husband was on the warpath. Before I got married, another man had courted me with gifts of beef and horses, but

I married Bull-weasel's father. Now this suitor came with other Lumpwoods to get me. I was afraid they were going to take me by force, so I sneaked away to the hills, where a woman was mourning her dead son. Another woman came with me for the same reason; she was the mourner's sister-in-law. It was she who planned the way to escape. 'My sister-in-law,' she said, 'goes out every morning to fast; let us go with her.' We all got mourning blankets and early every day we went out together up the hills, where no one could find us. We were not so far but that we could hear the Lumpwoods hallooing and see them searching for women to steal. When the 'showing-off' ceremony was ended, we saw the abductor take the stolen woman to his home. We fasted and watched up there all day. We had no water. In the course of the day the mourner's relatives came to bring her food and water. Then we two others hid, begging her not to tell about us. When the relatives had gone, we all feasted on what they had brought. At night we returned to camp with the mourner. Mourners then slept in very small tents without any decoration. We slept in such tents and sneaked out with the mourner early next day.

"My husband returned with Big-ox's war party, and I saw him looking for me. The people told him I had fled in order not to be taken away. He did not come near me because he did not wish to be present if I should be kidnaped. One night I stealthily approached him. He told me that if the Lumpwoods came for me while he was present he would let me go, but if I hid it would be well. I thought that if the camp moved during the wife-kidnaping period I should have no way of escape. The people really did move. My husband painted me up, and I rode his horse. Now the Lumpwoods planned to catch me, but my husband's sister warned me and told me to go with her, saying that then they would not take me. The Lumpwoods were riding abreast in the rear of the line of march, making a show of six Fox women captured by them. I was riding with my sister-in-law when they approached. My sister-in-law would not let me run away, but they were coming fast and I got scared and broke away. Some tents had already been pitched by the Crow in the van, and I ran into the lodge of a Fox's wife. She helped me unsaddle my horse, turned him loose, and covered me up with rawhide bags. There I lay. I heard the Lumpwoods outside.

They had taken the wife of a man who had been living peacefully with her for several years. He got furious and was going to kill her with an arrow as she was being shown off. He let fly and barely missed her. The Lumpwoods all scattered. They took revenge on the Foxes by cutting up their robes into strips and pounding their horses' feet.

"Towards evening we heard a shot. We saw a man running back and forth, raising a blanket and throwing it off several times to indicate how many Crow had been killed. He did this three times, then we could not count any more. We thought the Main Body had been wiped out. We learned that they had had war parties out in two directions and that all the warriors had been killed. The woman shot at by her husband had lost two brothers. Our whole camp mourned. Thus, the wife-kidnaping stopped, and I escaped."

This story demonstrates much more than merely a wife's reluctance to be parted from her husband: other women are seen coming to the harassed woman's rescue, while her husband, eager as he is to keep her, yet remains mindful of the gentlemen's code that prohibited any show of resistance if she were seized in his presence. His desire to be away if that should happen is typical. No man wanted to see his wife kidnaped before his eyes (see p. 53), though if surprised in the lodge he was bound to assume an air of bravado and might himself order his wife to go with her former lover. Yet not all men were paragons of manly conduct; witness the husband in Strikes-at-night's story who would rather kill his wife than be humiliated by her public exposure.

Muskrat, a very alert-minded woman of the old school, also commented on the institution. She disapproved of it though personally she had not been molested, her husband being a Fox while all her brothers were Lumpwoods. Her husband kidnaped not less than nine Lumpwood wives, but all of them left him or were sent away. They did not give her any trouble except the eighth, who once jerked a blanket from her and her husband. Muskrat told her she was crazy and recovered the blanket.

Being a mother did not insure against abduction. A Lumpwood once kidnaped a Fox woman nursing an infant. The baby was put on a papooseboard and carried about by a Lumpwood, who would dance with it. When it cried, the dancer ran to the mother, who then gave it suck. A woman might throw herself on the former lover's generosity, possibly saying, "Yes, I was once your sweetheart, but I beg you to let me alone." Then she was generally spared. Sharp-horn was about to claim a woman once, but her parents asked him to desist and he consented.

Some men dreamt songs for use in wife-abduction. Presumably they are supposed to render a woman readier to elope without hesitation. Immediately before the period of kidnaping began a Fox once dreamt a song, the words of which are supposed to be uttered by a woman:

> bakī'a bara'cde kōm, bā'wiky; bara'cde kōm barē'wiky. (My sweetheart is the one I love, I'll go.)

A similar song of this type is the following:

> i'axuxke i'tum, bakī'wake. (The Foxes are good-looking, I'll make them my sweethearts.)

The actual procedure followed by a kidnaper varied somewhat. After the election the young women were eager to find out whether their sweethearts had received hooked or straight staffs. During the public parade of either club the drummers would stand within the ring of the other members and the standard-bearers pointed their emblems at the onlookers as if to shoot them. On that occasion a Lumpwood woman would tell her one-time lover in the Fox club to call for her, or *vice versa*. After the dance, the Fox would peep into her lodge and announce, "I am coming for you." Then she followed her lover. Or, the man might take the initiative, send a messenger to the woman, and have her set the place and time of the elopement.

As explained (p. 56), nothing was more disgraceful than to take back a stolen woman. Such a man was dubbed the "holder of a crazy (lewd) woman," lost caste, and was derided in song for the rest of his life. After a kidnaping the boys were on the lookout lest the bereaved husband clandestinely visit or remarry his lost wife. If caught in the act, he was tied up and they smeared dog or other excrement all over him. Moreover, his fellow-members were held collectively responsible and their opponents had the right to cut up their blankets. Hence, in such a case, the club members would run away with their blankets, pursued by the other society.

One Lumpwood who had remarried his stolen wife was mocked with these words:

> maraxi'cekatū'we dāk akē'ret bā'wiky; dū'o awa'xpewiky. (Dear Lumpwoods, I'll make their children parentless; I'll marry your wives.)

A similar song ran as follows:

> ā're-tatse'we u'a kurutsi'm, kanda'kure kō'otem, du'a hu'‘kawe. (Straight-arm took back his wife; it was well for you to take her back, let your wife come.)

In fact, any display of emotion in these circumstances aroused pitiless mirth. When a husband had gone out of the camp crying over the loss of his wife, the other club made up this song:

> ī'itsic bāraskawī'a ri'awawiky, ī'we wā'wiky, karā'-wa‘tsēwiky. (Pole-crotch,—I'll make him grieve, I'll make him cry, I'll make him flee.)

After an abduction there was a ceremonial display of the captive women. The successful club would announce: "One of the Lumpwood (Fox) girls has married one of us Foxes (Lumpwoods) of her own accord!" They took her to the club lodge, where they kept up drumming, singing, and dancing most of the night. She was the only woman present. Her kidnaper's family treated her as a true bride, bringing her an elk-tooth dress and other garments. Early the following morning an old member went through camp, shouting, "We are going to have a good time today, get your horses and prepare for today's big dance!" The stolen woman dressed up in her new clothes, her face painted with red stripes, while the members painted as though for war. She was to ride behind a member who had once saved a Crow from a pursuing enemy, taking him up on horseback behind himself and thus earning the title of akbāpī'cere (one who takes some one behind). Any other man presuming to ride with the woman was jeered and at once thrown off by the rival club. There were, in fact, further restrictions. The feat must have been achieved on the warpath,—not while defending the camp against a hostile attack, in which case the danger was not reckoned so great. Further, the horse mounted by the pair must be one cut loose from its picket in the enemy's camp; otherwise the riders were thrown off, the bridle was torn, and the horse turned loose.

The entire club paraded in regular formation, two abreast, with leaders and rear-men in the van and rear, respectively; only the akbāpī′ cere and the woman remained outside the line. Similarly, they kept outside the circle formed by the society in the center of the camp, where the dancing commenced and continued until evening. The society losing the woman ostentatiously looked on during the performance with feigned indifference. At last the members of the triumphant club returned to the lodge, leaving the woman in her lover's custody. As noted (p. 56), she was generally dismissed by him after a brief period of co-residence.

This season of licensed kidnaping was brief,—possibly not longer than a fortnight. When all wives amenable to capture had changed husbands, the two clubs went on the warpath, each striving to score a coup before the rival organization. Whether any other club got ahead of both, did not matter. This competition made men fearless. Ordinarily a Fox was not allowed to sing a Lumpwood song and *vice versa;* it would be an affront. But the society that struck the first coup was said to "take away the Foxes' (Lumpwoods') songs," that is, it might use the losers' tunes and adapt to them words composed for the occasion. This meant, of course, mockery at the expense of the vanquished, who did not recover the songs until *they* had struck the first coup in a subsequent encounter.

The spirit engendered by this rivalry is illustrated by the following incident. At one time the enemy was entrenched on a high butte. A Fox officer bearing the hooked-staff went up some distance but then lay down with his emblem. A brave Lumpwood of the rank and file asked, "Has any one struck the enemy yet?" "No, it is difficult." Then this man snatched away the Fox officer's pole, ascended the hill and struck an enemy with it. Leaving the standard over a hole on the hill, he ran back, reached his people in safety, and challenged the Foxes to retrieve their standard. None of them dared go for it. On returning to the camp, the Lumpwoods took away songs of the Foxes, who were obliged to borrow the songs of other societies.

On another occasion a Fox officer carrying the same kind of standard fled from the enemy. The Lumpwoods composed the following derisive song:

i′axuxkakatū′we daka′re watsā′tsk. batsē′t cē′wiaruk. (You dear Foxes, you run fast. Men are wont to die.)

Once Young Jackrabbit charged the enemy and struck the first coup and was going to take away the Foxes' songs. However, his younger brother, a Fox, claimed the first coup for himself. The Lumpwoods protested, saying the Fox had earned first honors, but Young Jackrabbit yielded because it was his brother, —family loyalty carrying the day against club solidarity.

According to Gray-bull's recollection, two Lumpwood officers with hooked-staffs were killed in successive years, and in the third year one of their straight-staff bearers was killed. Then the Lumpwoods mocked the Foxes for their cowardice, seeing that they had not lost any of *their* officers. It certainly appears from the accounts that towards the close of their heyday the Lumpwoods excelled their rivals in derring-do.

With the first snowfall the spirit of competition disappeared, and the two clubs lived together in perfect amity until the next spring. The psychology of their mutual relations resembled that of rival colleges, say, the University of California and Stanford, whose hostility is likewise restricted to special occasions.

THE BIG DOGS

The Big Dogs (micgy-isā'ate) ceased to be active so long ago that in 1910 I found only a single man, Fire-weasel, reputed to be over ninety years old, who had been a member and indeed one of the sash-wearing officers. His account was not wholly consistent with itself and that of outsiders, but the combined statements give a fairly clear picture.

As shown by the history of the Lumpwoods, Crow clubs were not in stable equilibrium. Apart from changes in numbers and influence, old features were sloughed off and new ones adopted. The Lumpwoods once carried knobbed sticks that were completely superseded by replicas of the Fox standards, and batbā'tua practice was transferred from the Big Dogs to the Lumpwoods (p. 179). Again, Beckwourth mentions a feud— presumably about 1830—between "Dog Soldiers" and "Foxes" over "the prowess of the respective parties." In the first half of the nineteenth century, then, the Dogs rather than the Lumpwoods figured as competitors of the Foxes,—which tallies with the picture of one of my Crow informants, though an uncorroborated one. Of course, Beckwourth may describe a purely ephemeral misunderstanding between the two societies. On the other hand, where martial achievement loomed so large, disputes could easily arise between different groups; and the intense rivalry of Foxes and Lumpwoods in the known period may well have been merely a pattern that at different periods affected different clubs. Indeed, it was applied to recently borrowed societies (p. 214). Certainly the alignment could easily be modified by a chance constellation of circumstances. At one time, I was positively informed, the Big Dogs united with the Lumpwoods against the Foxes and Muddy Hands for purposes of joint wife-kidnaping; but on reconsideration the Big Dogs decided to refrain.

Certain statements by Fire-weasel open up an interesting historical perspective. On the one hand, he derives the club from the Hidatsa,—a view supported by others. He also recognizes no such subdivisions as occurred in the Lumpwood and Fox societies, but describes the members as generally old but choosing some young men to succeed relatives who had fallen in battle. The term here translated "old" simply indicates maturity, as is borne out by other facts. In 1910 I interviewed the survivor of the Hidatsa society; he had become a Dog in the prime of life, which is consistent with Maximilian's data of several decades earlier. Indeed, the Crow accounts of Big Dog behavior bar senility. They are pictured going up a knoll to sing and dance, with their sweethearts in attendance to fetch water. Again, in the spring or summer, after many buffalo hides had been tanned, young women would invite the Big Dogs, just as they might any other club, to a large tipi, where each member in turn sang club songs with one of the hostesses for a partner. When every pair had sung, they all received food and feasted; any couple so desiring might sleep there overnight. Equally conclusive are Fire-weasel's data on Big Dog police activities, which conformed to the general Crow norm. That is, the organization took turns with the rest in policing the camp for one season,— especially during the communal hunt. If any one moved prematurely so that he might frighten off the game, the Big Dogs, led by their officers, advanced upon him and addressed him as if he were a dog: "Stop, go back!" When he halted, they asked, "Why are you moving away?" If he replied gently, showing his willingness to obey orders, all was well; otherwise they whipped him sometimes so vigorously that he was unable to move. Obviously this was not a job for dotards.

But, even so, why should this club, in contrast to the Foxes and Lumpwoods, be associated with *any* age-class? Because, I think, of Hidatsa influence. The Mandan and Hidatsa, unlike the Crow, ranged all their clubs in a definite sequence, each being at a particular date formed by approximate coevals. For instance, in 1833 Maximilian set the age of the Mandan Crazy Dogs at from 10 to 15, of the "Crow" society of this tribe at 20 to 25, of the Blacktail Deer at over 50. But by the Crow scheme, allowing a man to cling to one club all his life, all ages might be represented in each club. However, if the Big Dog society came from the Hidatsa, or was influenced by its namesake there, its association with a particular age in Fire-weasel's mind is intelligible. Either the idea survived from a time when the parent tribe of both the Hidatsa and Crow had a Big Dog society for mature men; or the Crow society was more recently patterned on the Hidatsa model. Nevertheless, any vital connection with a definite age was doomed as soon as the Crow assimilated the society to their own system. Of such adaptation there is little doubt. Among the Hidatsa, not the Big Dogs, but invariably the Black Mouths guarded the camp and directed the communal hunt; the *Crow* Big Dogs took turns at such duties with other clubs. Their mourning observances closely resembled the Lumpwood ritual and their reorganization in the spring was equally true to type; old men offered a pipe to various young men, and those who smoked it were pledged to special bravery. The customary parade followed the election, and the parallel even extended to a division into four groups, each accompanying one of the sash-wearers (see below). When the emblems had been completed and donned by their owners, all the members reunited outdoors and performed a dance, started by a belt-wearer seizing one of the sashes and pulling it forward. The dance consisted in a forward jump, performers, unlike the Foxes, leaping individually instead of lining up in a row or circle; also they leaned their bodies further forward. At the last song they jumped more vigorously than before. There were no initiation fees. Vacancies were filled as in other Crow clubs: even an infant might be chosen to succeed a slain kinsman, though naturally he was not taken in until old enough. Finally, the scheme of officers varied only in detail. They were paired off, pledged to bravery, served normally from early in the spring until the first snowfall, but could be reëlected.

In contrast to other clubs, *all* members had a common badge,—a stick about two feet long in a cover of tanned buckskin with pendent deer hoofs or dewclaws, later superseded by tin cones and little bells. This rattle, called māxaxorē', took the place of the single-headed drum of other societies. Every novice first secured this instrument, either making it for himself or gratuitously getting a former member's. Gray-bull adds as a general emblem an owl-feather head-dress; Fire-weasel restricts this to part of the membership but credits them all with a whistle worn round the neck to be blown at will during a dance.

The officers numbered either nine or ten. Two leaders and two rear men were equivalent to the same functionaries of other clubs. Four men (i'axtsewice, sash-owners) wore rawhide—later cloth—emblems slipped over the head by a slit. Of this quartette, one pair wore only one sash each, the other two sashes apiece that crossed each other in front. In a parade an officer with one sash walked abreast of another with two sashes. Corresponding to the Fox akdū'cire were two men (naxpitse'-ihē'rupte, bear around the waist) wearing a belt of bear-skin with the legs and claws; they painted their bodies with mud and bunched up their hair to resemble a bear's ears.

In one interview Fire-weasel listed a single naxpitse' ihē'rupte. Though agreeing with this reduction, Gray-bull paired this officer off with a "whipper" (itsi'ratsek-ake, quirt-owner) or "urger" (akbiretsirixī'a). He also mentioned a single pair of sash-wearers (with two sashes each). The line of parading Big Dogs, according to him, would thus comprise the two leaders, two sash-wearers, the rank and file, the single naxpitse' ihē'rupte with the whipper beside him, two akdū'cire, and two rear officers.

A Big Dog offered the bear-skin belt hesitated a long time, for he was expected to excel in bravery. It was his part to walk straight up to the enemy regardless of danger; under no condition to retreat; and to rescue imperiled tribesmen. These duties entitled the belt-wearers to precedence at a feast, said Fire-weasel, for to eat before one of them meant being killed even before him. At a feast the belt-wearers were followed by the leaders, the sash-wearers, rear-officers, and finally by the rank and file. At a Big Dog assembly a belt-wearer would seize one of the sashes and begin to dance, leading its owner behind him, then the other members also began to take part. At the close of the singing, all stood still, some blowing whistles while the rest clapped their mouths. Then the belt-wearer, carrying a quirt, touched each member with it, thereby allowing him to be seated. If any one continued dancing, it was a symbol of bravery; such men the belt-wearer then lashed more vigorously. During a public parade a belt-wearer remained among the singers. While the rest danced he might sit down wherever he pleased, and in general act as he wished. At a club meeting a seat was reserved for him near the door. Such a session might take place at any time, but was particularly common when a Tobacco or Sun Dance was in progress, i.e. presumably when most of the people were gathered together. The Big Dog who owned the finest lodge then offered it for the use of his fellows, all of whom were summoned to dress up and assemble there. They put on their club emblems together with the customary symbols of exploits (see p. 217), and went to the lodge to dance.

Sometimes they met at night and, joined by women, went through camp singing. Forming a circle outside a chief's tipi, they sang, and the chief was likely to have food cooked for their entertainment. According to Sharp-horn, the Big Dogs set out on such jaunts with a rawhide having a rope passed through perforations along the edge. When standing in a circle, they beat this hide with their dewclaw rattles. Thus they proceeded from lodge to lodge, expecting food or tobacco from each host.

To return to the officers, the leaders, One-horn said, wore no specific emblem and were chosen for their "strong hearts," that is their coolness at times of excitement. The sash-wearers, though brave, were permitted to move about in battle, while the belt-wearers must not budge.

Gray-bull, partly because of his individual scheme, outlined the functions of officers somewhat differently from others. The leaders, he explained, took the initiative in any emergency. If the enemy were entrenched, it was their duty to charge against them. However, they were not pledged to make a stand if the Crow were routed; they often did so voluntarily, but not as a matter of obligation. The sashwearers also might flee, but as soon as they heard a Crow crying for help they must face about and rush to his rescue, whether by offering him their mounts, taking him behind themselves, or fighting in his defense. The belt-wearer had no special duties if all went well; but if the Crow were fleeing, he immediately dismounted to arrest the pursuers, otherwise some one was sure to bid him to do so. If he failed to make a stand, he was henceforth treated as a coward and outcast, irrespective of his former standing. At a dance he remained seated to indicate that he would not run away in a fight. But his mate, the "urger" or "whipper" of Gray-bull's tale, would rush up and whip him into rising. In a battle, if the belt-wearer was defying the enemy, the whipper also whipped him, thereby absolving him from his duty; otherwise he had to face the enemy beside him. The akdū'cire, Gray-bull added, were expected to die in any event: to return alive was to become a laughing-stock. This witness recalled several of these officers who had been slain in battle, but not one who had acted the craven. On account of their risks they feasted before other members, tasting a little of each kind of food and taking as much as they pleased of their choice. When through, they spread their blankets on the ground and sat down; only after this signal did any other members receive provisions. As for the rear officers, they stayed behind the rest in battle and held back the pursuing enemy.

Since Gray-bull was not a Big Dog himself, Fire-weasel's account may be more trustworthy. However, Gray-bull's exposition is interesting as that of an intelligent outsider.

THE MUDDY HANDS

Like the Big Dogs, the Muddy Hands conformed to the general Crow pattern; like them, too, they had become obsolete very early, so that I was able to find very few one-time members, of whom Bear-ghost proved the best witness.

This club had three subdivisions, composed of boys, middle-aged, and old men, respectively. Their names were: Those-who-put-on-guts for head gear (cī'p aktɔicc); the Muddy Hands (i'ctse cipī' a) proper; and the Bags-for-necklaces (ic-apī'a). Any one entering from another society joined the group suitable for his age. The bear-gut cap, according to one informant, belong to certain officers (see p. 198).

There were two leaders, two or four sash-wearers, two rear officers, and two akdū'cire. The leaders performed feats of bravery at the beginning of an action, while the rear men were the last to flee. The akdū'cire never retreated but helped any dismounted tribesman to escape, hence had the right to eat before their fellows. The sash-wearers practiced no distinctive form of bravery; each wore two red flannel sashes (Fig. 13*b*) that trailed along when he was afoot and touched the ground when he was mounted. At a dance these officers were led around by their trains. A model sash made for me was over twelve feet in length.

Child-in-the-mouth described as part of the sash-wearer's regalia a cap of dried bear-guts painted red. The guts of this species were used because of the strength and ferocity of these animals. Any officer derelict in his duty was derided and lost standing; he could redeem his prestige only by bravery in the next battle.

This club, too, reorganized in the spring, recognizing the same period of office. On this occasion four old men stayed outside the lodge to discuss candidates, then entered the assembly to offer the pipe. Some members brought willow bark from which to make the sash surrogates, with a loop so they could be slipped over the heads of the officers-elect. After the election, the Muddy Hands paraded, sang, and danced through camp, finally dividing into four groups, one to accompany each sash-wearer. In the tipi of every one of these new officers a piece of cloth as large as a blanket had been prepared. A one-time incumbent who had distinguished himself in office told about his deeds, then cut up the cloth into strips about 5 inches wide, and sewed them together to make a proper length. Finally he made the slit and put the novice's head through it. Then all went to dance outdoors to let the people know who had been chosen. Apart from this, Gray-bull thought, they did not dance very often,—mainly at the period of the Tobacco ceremony. Charges-camp regarded all the Muddy Hands as old people, who were expected to be brave, since old people cannot run fast. He was possibly thinking of the Muddy Hands proper, who were at least mature men. His statement certainly cannot rule out the definite testimony of Bear-ghost, himself a member. Senility is barred by the undoubted police services of this club; in fact, the dauntlessness

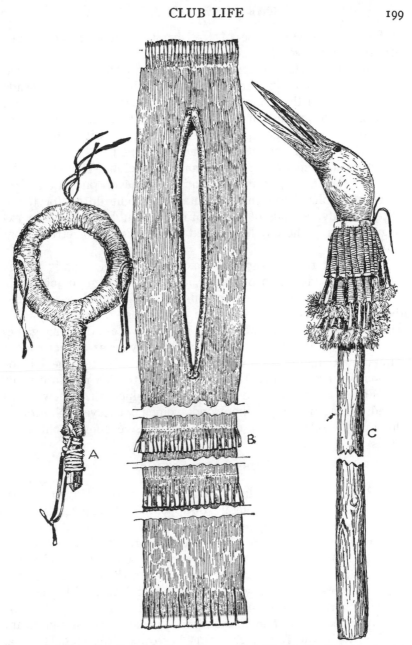

FIG. 13.—Society Regalia; (a) Crazy Dog rattle; (b) Muddy Hand sash; (c) Hot Dance stick.

of His-horse-is-white, one of the members, led to their reappointment for several successive seasons.

At Muddy Hand performances, Charges-camp reported, two men dressed in their war suits, with medicine on their heads and weapons in their hands. A pole representing the enemy was stuck into the ground, and a buffalo robe, hair side out, tied to it. The two men rode up and struck the pole with coup-sticks or acted out other exploits they had performed.

A curious custom was peculiar to this club. Whether on the prairie or in camp, members practically never put out a fire, which symbolized the enemy; outsiders might do so for them. Exceptionally, a man of great bravery would dismount to extinguish a fire, whereby he pledged himself never to retreat from an enemy.

In about 1865 or 1870 the Foxes came to the Muddy Hands with a pipe, offered them smoke, and asked them to join their ranks. The Muddy Hands, possibly fifty in number, accepted the proposal, and in consequence Bear-ghost promptly lost his wife, who was now fair prey in the wife-kidnaping game. According to Sharp-horn, the Foxes' motive was to get aid in wife-abduction, for the Lumpwoods had just beaten them ignominiously at that game. However, even with this reenforcement the Foxes remained at a disadvantage, since their new allies failed to capture any Lumpwood women whatever. Naturally, the Lumpwoods at once made up a derisive song about their rivals.

Clubs Long Extinct

Prince Maximilian lists a Little Dog and a Raven society (p. 173), but both completely disappeared so long ago that in 1907 I found not a single survivor of either. Sitting-elk, however, had witnessed a dance of the Ravens, or rather Raven Owners (pē'ritsake) in his childhood,—presumably about 1845. The performers, all elderly men, he recollected, had their bodies painted red and wore stuffed raven skins for necklaces, with the tail-feathers spread out on their shoulders. The namesake of this society ranks highest in Maximilian's Hidatsa list, a significant fact if the Crow Raven club was borrowed from the Hidatsa, as another informant believed, for then the relatively advanced age of members would be accounted for. Strangely enough, Fire-weasel, though still older than Sitting-elk, declared that the society had become obsolete long before his time. Indeed, it was only from her grandmother that his wife had heard some details about regalia. One Raven, she had learnt, carried a long pole, topped with a single eagle feather, while to the center was fastened a string of raven feathers perforated at the butt for stringing and trimmed at the upper end. Other members bore poles feathered from top to bottom, still others had raven-feather fans decorated with quill-work. Bull-all-the-time ascribed to the Ravens a herald, sash-wearers "made to die," and functionaries charged with preparing food.

The discrepancy between Fire-weasel's and Sitting-elk's chronology is perhaps due to Sitting-elk's having been a River Crow, so that in his band the club may well have survived an extra generation or two after disappearing in the Main Body.

The Little Dogs (micgyi'ate) in their earlier phase are credited with either two or four wearers of red-flannel sashes and two officers carrying each a board of arm's length, notched on one side and trimmed with raven feathers. Child-in-the-mouth derives the society from the Hidatsa, who certainly had such an organization. Subsequently,—during Sitting-elk's youth—the Hidatsa Black (= Muddy) Mouth society visited the River Crow and taught their dance to the Little Dogs of that band, who thereupon assumed the name of Black (= Muddy) Mouths (i'i cipi' a). The Black Mouths—noted by Maximilian as "Soldiers" among both Mandan and Hidatsa—were middle-aged men who alone exercised police control among these Village Indians. Such monopoly being contrary to the Crow scheme, this club like the other societies took turns at police duties. On the other hand, it evidently imitated its Hidatsa model in restricting membership to middle-aged and distinguished men.

Before a Muddy Mouth dance, dogs were tied up, for if any of them pursued the performers, these shot them or struck them down. Child-in-the-mouth witnessed a single performance, which he considered similar to the Hot Dance. After a dance one officer wearing a bearskin belt touched performers with a quirt, for until then they had to remain standing. The rank and file wore no distinctive costume but daubed black mud or a mixture of pounded charcoal and ashes over their mouths or in streaks across their eyes. Some members carried tomahawks in token of having struck enemies with them, others had warclubs with skunk skins around the grips.

All members were expected to be brave, but Sharp-horn denied that there were any emblem-bearers pledged to special dauntlessness. The only officers were two rattlers,—according to Black Bull, the headmen of the society. In dancing, the membership divided into two lines facing each other, with these rattlers standing between them. They would begin to sing, shaking their rattle, and danced, crossing each other's paths. At the very moment when they did so, every one shouted, and the rank and file also began to dance.

My Crow informants make no mention of the lances that certainly figured as officers' insignia in the Hidatsa club; but the intersection of each other's paths by the rattlers was common to both tribes.

When the Crow Muddy Mouths had dwindled in number, they joined the Crazy Dogs (see p. 213).

THE HAMMERS AND THE BULLS

The Hammer Owners (bū'ptsake) included practically all the boys about sixteen years old; a pair of older ones instructed them and made four wands for as many officers. As the members grew up, each entered one of the regular clubs whose activities they had hitherto closely imitated. Thus, there was an outdoor assembly in the spring, to which all brought pieces of dried meat for a feast, deciding to hold an election the following day. When they gathered in some lodge the next day, four willow poles were laid outside against the tipi. The two older boys went outdoors to discuss potential officers, reentered with a pipe and chose successively the leaders, rear officers, four staff-bearers (bū'ptsake proper), and four akdū'cire. On leaving, each member was asked to which staff-bearer's lodge he wished to go, the society thus breaking up into the usual four companies. When the sticks were finished, each group feasted, sang, and danced, finally reuniting outdoors for a common dance, kept up until dark. Then they proceeded in a body to the home of each staff-bearer, formed a circle outside, and began to drum and sing. The boy's father would then come out and either hand them a pipe or invite them to a feast.

The staff-bearers were to be especially brave in sham fights, and the akdū'cire in encountering wild animals, such as wolves or buffalo, on which they counted coup as though they were enemies. The emblem of the organization was a bū'ptsa, i.e. a "hammer", more or less egg-shaped or of diamond-like cross-section and perforated so it could be stuck on a tall staff (Fig. 12a, b, c). The models I bought were of wood and decorated with yellow and red, or yellow and blue paint, these colors corresponding to the members' body paint. A Hidatsa model representative of the equivalent society was of stone, and Maximilian lists the Crow bū'ptsake as the Stone Casse-tête society, but according to Gray-bull, the Crow used nothing but wood. The shaft of a model was over 8 feet in length, painted with white clay, and decorated with a long erect feather at the top; at three distinct points along the pole were two other long feathers and a bunch of shorter ones (Fig. 12a).

The boys were not restricted to mock-fighting; during some seasons they took part in real battles, struck coups, and were more reckless than their elders. The following song reflects their spirit as idealized:

batsē' tsirī'kātuac   bā'wiky
The men are afraid,   I'll meet him [the enemy].

Thus members came to be killed. Gray-bull recalled one mourning ceremony. The corpse had been laid on the ground, propped up against a buffalo-skin backrest, with the emblem planted near-by, and picked members were singing and lamenting their loss. A young spectator named Rides-the-spotted-horse, known for his intrepidity and good luck in battle, approached and was stopped by the dead Hammer's father, who put his hand on the young man's head in token of pleading and offered him gifts. Then he said, "You know how the Dakota have treated me, I depend on you to repay them." For a while the young man said not a word. At length he answered, "You have appointed me to die, I will die to revenge your boy's death." Then they plucked out the dead boy's standard and gave it to Rides-the-spotted-horse. All cheered. The old man cried again, pressed Gray-bull's head, gave him a shield, and asked him, too, for revenge. Gray-bull thought it over for a while, then he, too, consented. Though quite sincere in his determination to die, he struck a coup and escaped with his life. Rides-the-spotted-horse ran into the thickest part of the Dakota ranks, struck a coup, and got back safe, though his horse was killed under him. One of the other bū'ptsake officers was killed. The bereaved father offered Gray-bull all kinds of property to make him risk his life again, but Gray-bull's brothers watched closely and prevented him from venturing another dash.

If a member failed to attend a club meeting, the bū'ptsake all went to his lodge and stood there until his father came out and mollified them with a pipe or a gift of food.

Uniting practically all boys old enough to imitate the adults' clubs, the bū'ptsake formed a true age-society even within the framework of the Crow system, since by necessity the upper and lower age limits were narrowly drawn. It is not so easy to understand how the Bull Owners (tsī'rukape, by metathesis from tsī'rupake) could have preserved their alleged status of old or elderly men in the Crow system. On the other hand, if the society came from the Hidatsa, as most informants declare, it could easily have started as an old men's group, since in Maximilian's day, at all events, the Bulls formed one of the highest of the Hidatsa age-societies. Actually, there was some divergence among the Crow as to the age of the Bulls, though of course Indians were not accustomed to reckon age by years: Gray-bull set it at about 65, Bell-rock at 50 years. I incline to the lower estimate for several reasons. The Bulls acted as police and took part in warfare, always acquitting themselves well until one fight when they were driven down a cliff, whence they were dubbed "Bulls-chased-over-the-cliff." The mockery thus incurred put a stop to the society—in about 1875 according to my narrators. If this is approximately true, Leforge must have been about 25 when, after leaving the Foxes, he joined the Bulls. The club was therefore then not *exclusively* an old man's organization. However, mature men may well have predominated, since Leforge takes pains to contrast their conservatism and dignified behavior, their "quiet, meditative, prayerful" meetings with the conduct of the Foxes. Incidentally, he also mentions the unique feature of having given a non-relative a horse as an initiation fee. If so, the Bulls were quite anomalous in this respect, since none of the other clubs exacted payment.

The members whose foolhardiness made them roughly

equivalent to those "made to die" in the other societies wore buffalo head masks; their number, probably two, is also given as one and four. Bull-chief identified them with the leaders, but this is denied by Gray-bull. There is equal discrepancy as to the scheme in general. Child-in-the-mouth listed two leaders, two rear officers, and two mask-wearers impersonating blind bulls, reputed to be very fierce. Sitting-elk added two men wearing bearskin belts who whipped tardy members into rising to dance and also touched performers with their whips, thus allowing them to sit down when the dance was over. Bear-gets-up thinks there were four officers,—two mask-wearers and two merely wearing skin caps topped with horns, but some witnesses ascribe the latter headgear to all the rank and file. According to others, these wore red-flannel aprons with bells and blackened their bodies with charcoal. Lone-tree mentioned only one leader and one rear officer. Probably some variation was allowable at different times. According to Gray-bull, election to office followed the usual pattern, and those became mask-wearers who kept still while others put the masks on them.

About sunset a herald summoned the Bulls for a gathering in one lodge, a drum being beaten to hurry them along. In the center a large kettle with mud enabled the members, all of whom pretended to be bulls, to paint their faces and bodies in imitation of wallowing buffalo. They decorated their legs with anklets of buffalo skin and put on other finery. The mask-wearers plastered their hair and the horns of their headgear with white clay. When the musicians beat their drums, the parade started, with the leaders in front, followed by the rank and file, while about six, or even as many as ten, drummers brought up the rear. One man carried water in a large vessel and held it out for the members, who simulated shyness, sticking out their tails, and ran away prancing and snorting. Those who had dismounted in battle were privileged to wear buffalo tails, made to stand up erect; these men snorted at their fellows and made them retreat. The mask-wearers imitated wild bulls, snorting and charging the crowd so as to frighten women and children. Boys looking on sometimes prodded the Bulls with sharpened sticks to make them jump and snort like real bulls. Sometimes the dancers jumped up with both feet, sometimes with each foot in turn. Those who wished to die approached the vessel, bellowed like bulls, and drank, lapping up the water and shaking it off like bulls. The women, some of whom took part in the singing, clacked their tongues in praise of these braves, who walked off pawing the ground. Pounded-meat once drank and would not go away; though others also came to drink, he kicked and beat them back till one of the officers hooked him, when he finally trotted off. After the performance Pounded-meat mounted his horse and said, "Whenever you are afraid of going against the enemy or hesitate, I'll go straight toward them. If you retreat, I will dismount and fight afoot." All agreed that drinking symbolized a pledge not to flee. Some said that the water was carried by a woman selected for the purpose,—according to Sitting-elk, a *virtuous* woman.

The Bulls carried shields, lances, and guns on such occasions, and some of them wore war-bonnets. Brave men told about their feats and enacted them; a coup-striker would count coup on some spectator, while those wounded in battle pretended being shot. Many discharged their guns. Fire-weasel, though not a member, was allowed to recount some of his exploits on such an occasion. One-horn even contended that any one was free to join the Bulls in addition to being a Fox or Lumpwood, but this seems improbable. Possibly brave men were privileged to take part in the public show.

The Hot Dancers and the Crazy Dogs

In about 1875, the Crow adopted two features from the Hidatsa,—the Hot Dance (bātawe' disu'a) and the Crazy Dog (mi'cgye warā'axe) society, also called Long Crazy Dogs (mi'cgye warā'axe ha'tskite) to distinguish it from another institution of the same name (p. 331).

The Hot Dance corresponds to the Omaha or Grass dance of other Plains tribes, but the organizations performing it among the Crow remain obscure as to their origin and mutual relations. In 1910 practically all the men except the very oldest belonged to one of the four clubs associated with the performance. A dance house with log walls roughly resembling the earth-lodge of the Village tribes but surmounted by a short pointed tower with windows was common to all four, and in it the men sat quartered off according to their affiliations. This suggests that they may have been equivalents of the *subdivisions* of such ancient clubs as the Lumpwoods. On the other hand, the Big Earholes (a'panō'pise) and Night Hot Dancers (ō'tsiac bātawe') of the Lodge Grass district—though not at Pryor—regarded themselves as rivals in somewhat the same way as the Lumpwoods and the Foxes. These two companies furthermore had straight and hooked staffs wrapped with otter-skin, while there was nothing distinctive about the regalia of the two other groups,—the Last Hot Dancers (bātawe' hā'ake), also called Hot-dancers-with-plenty-of-money, and the Dakota (nakō'ta). The Crow claim to have created the last of these themselves, the rest being of Hidatsa origin. At first there was also a group of Day Hot Dancers, but it was superseded by the two last-named companies. The nickname of the Last Hot Dancers came from their once making the largest contribution to a common fund; also on one occasion they put up an enclosure of red flannel at the dance house and distributed the cloth among the women.

The Hidatsa used to *buy* the privileges connected with their clubs, hence when they brought the necessary regalia to the Crow they naturally received ample pay,—about 600 horses and property to boot. The idea came to the Crow from one of their own number who had visited the sister tribe and learnt the songs of the Hot Dance, which found favor with the other Crow. Following his instructions, they got up a performance one winter, but without the proper paraphernalia. In the spring, however, they sent messengers to the Hidatsa, asking them to bring the regalia, and in the fall the Hidatsa came.

The Crow suggestively combined the Hidatsa notion of purchase with their own idea of free admission. The former, indeed, was familiar to them in regard to *religious* prerogatives (see p. 248); in such cases the seller became the buyer's "father." This concept was applied to special emblems in the Hot Dance: an officer might "adopt" his successor by giving him his insignia, in return for gifts possibly aggregating $100 in value. On the other hand, mere admission as a commoner did not involve formal adoption or payment. Desirable members—persons of known munificence, hence likely to feast their fellows—were invited to join and even bribed to leave one Hot Dance group for another by a substantial gift. Even more typical of the old Fox and Lumpwood pattern is the following instance. Wolf-lies-down was a Last Dancer. When he died, his company induced his brother, Bird-far-away, then a Big Ear-hole, to take his place.

The four modern clubs were largely mutual benefit organizations. If any one had to do a certain amount of work on his farm land, all his associates came to help him. When a man sought admission to one of the Tobacco societies, his fellow-members aided him in making the heavy adoption payment. In July 1910 a member of the Night Hot group was being initiated into the Tobacco society. All his fellows in the club lined up outside the Tobacco lodge, in turn approached a woman who acted as receiver, and handed her a quarter or some such coin. The following year a little boy was admitted into the Tobacco organization. His father was a Last Dancer, accordingly Gray-bull and others belonging to that club contributed toward the fee. From time to time there were club feasts. I attended one of them in 1910, during an intermission of the above-mentioned Tobacco adoption ceremony. All the Night Hot Dancers gathered in the tent of one of the members, and two distributors equitably disposed of the contents of a large case of fruit, handing all the guests exactly equal shares. The only woman present was the host's wife.

Child-in-the-mouth listed the following officers: two leaders, two drummers; four crane-stick bearers (Fig. 13c), eight officers wearing the feather bustles called "crow-belts" by writers on the Grass Dance of Plains tribes; two heralds; two pipe-fillers; one man privileged to sing the closing song; four women singers; two whippers; two war-bonnet wearers; two men with long sticks feathered from top to bottom; one man carrying a stick representing a fork wrapped with beads and with a scalp at one end; one officer with a flag, which was hoisted on a pole; and one man wearing a red-fox skin necklace. The officer with the forked stick danced before the food was distributed and dipped his emblem into the bucket containing the dog meat, then four brave men licked off the stick, whereupon he ordered all the others to eat. At the close of the performance one Crow-belt officer who had been wounded in battle went out before the rest. The bearers of crane-sticks were to strike enemies with them.

According to Gray-bull, there were at first only four feather-bustle officers, but later their number was doubled, at least in Lodge Grass. He gives two war-bonnet wearers (possibly the headmen); one man with a pointed ceremonial wand; one herald; one whipper; one pipe-bearer; one drummer; and one officer with an American flag. The headmen decided when to hold a dance and gave away a horse each. During a parade through camp any member so disposed might give away his mount. After this procession they would enter the dance lodge. Every one was expected to eat a little dog meat. After a certain time the door was shut, and only one who had at some time been shot by the enemy was allowed to leave. If such a one led, the rest might follow, otherwise they would be fined. In case of physical necessity the headmen gave permission to leave.

One late afternoon in July, 1910, I saw a procession of men dressed up who were passing from lodge to lodge, planting a stick in front of each one. They were requisitioning food for a Hot Dance feast,—a custom called tsī'rukape and copied from the Dakota. It had nothing to do with the similarly named Bull society (p. 204).

On another occasion all members of the four clubs were summoned to take part in a dance. Four marshals, one for each group, were appointed to punish laggards, who either paid a fine or were thrown into the creek. This actually happened to one man. My then interpreter was a delinquent, but I succeeded in pacifying the officers by means of a small gift.

What impressed me particularly in the Hot Dance performance was the lavish generosity with which members gave away property of all kinds to aged and destitute tribesmen, or to alien visitors. I saw women staggering away under loads of blankets presented to them and their husbands. Some men rode horses directly into the dance house and there finally gave them away. I once saw a man strip himself to his gee-string before a large crowd, giving away all his clothing. This was formerly also the occasion of "throwing away" wives (see p. 57).

The ceremony, as performed at the time of introduction, was described by Scolds-the-bear. His scheme of officers differs from that of the informants already quoted. The evening before a dance, one member beat a drum three or four times in succession, the rest merely singing. Then the first drummer would rise and say, "Let us have a dance tomorrow." The two headmen, always seated in the middle of the rear, ordered the herald to select two men who were to kill and cook two dogs for the ceremony. Likewise he was to summon ten officers to cook food for all the people, while ten men—not regular officers—were to form a ring of cloth goods and to lend for the occasion what property they could. The herald made this proclamation: "I am going to announce the dance four times tomorrow. If anyone enters after me, I'll make him prepare the dog the next time" (as a punishment).

The next morning the herald arose at daybreak and summoned the ten men to put up cloth and prepare the lodge. They did so, planting in the center a long lodge pole with a flag. The second time the herald shouted: "Take a bath and comb your hair!" The third time he cried: "Paint yourselves and put on your best clothes!" The fourth time he said: "Go to the ring where the dance is to be held!" After this last proclamation he remained outdoors for a long time, then entered.

The drum used had a deer or horsehide head. It was held sacred and at first only two special officers were allowed to touch it. One of these held as an emblem a drumstick decorated with feathers and ribbons. The herald had the right to punish the rank and file, but not the two drummers. When these had beaten the drum four times, the singers seated themselves round the drum and were then allowed to beat it. The dancers entered and suspended their regalia from the lodge poles,—two whips, eight "crow-belts" (feather bustles), and two buffalo-horn headdresses topped with eagle feathers and in front decorated with weasel skins.

The first song sung by the musicians was a signal for the officers to take down their insignia, but first they danced round the pole three times, whereupon they gave presents to any one they pleased. The second song was for the headmen, who followed the example of the other officers. The third song was for the herald alone, the fourth for the drummer, the fifth for the drumstick-owner. Each of these got up and danced. Four women had been appointed to take part in the singing, and for them, too, a song was sung; however, they did not dance, merely giving away presents. The next song was for all the officers, who rose, danced, and gave away property. Next the headmen told the herald to announce that the rank and file were to dance. The two whippers now took up positions at opposite ends of the dance ground and lashed any one who failed to dance; however, if they caused anyone to bleed they indemnified him with a horse.

The dog-killers put the kettle containing the meat near the entrance, and the bustle-wearers sat down, one of them in front of the rest. A song was sung four times, the bustle-wearers merely swaying their bodies in accompaniment. At the last song they got up, danced backwards and finally approached their belts with hands extended. When close, they made an upward motion. They danced four times to the same song, then girded on their bustles and danced to the side, where the dog-meat was. Three times they danced toward it, the last time they passed by it. The rear men picked up the kettle, and lifting it circled it round four times before setting it down. The man in front of the crow-belt wearers was holding a plate; another, the "dancer toward the meat," danced and put the meat into the plate. Then this dancer and the plate-holder each took one of the dog heads and put them in two different places. Each of them ranked as the chief of one of the two quartettes of bustle-wearers, and each selected four renowned warriors, who were not to eat but merely sat there.

The food-distributors now served first the selected men and officers, next the other people. They started from the drums. Every one got a share, but as yet all refrained from eating. One man, "the feeder," carried a pointed stick trimmed with beadwork, with eagle tail-feathers hanging from the end of the handle. After completing his task, the plate-holder returned to his seat with the plate and was the first to eat, followed by the feeder, who swayed his body three times in accompaniment to his song, rising to dance at the fourth intonation. Towards the end he suddenly stopped with the drum beats and pointed his stick north. When the drumming was resumed, he began to dance again as before. At the end of this dance he pointed his stick west. The third time he danced toward the north, and at the end approached the center and pointed his stick east. Thus he moved around in a circle, covering one quadrant during each song. He came straight to the dog flesh, made a motion over it with his stick, broke off a morsel, impaled it on his emblem, pointed it toward the four quarters, and gave it to the plate-holder to eat. Next he broke off a morsel for another dancer. Then he gave further morsels to the two headmen and thus went on serving all the officers. If any one of them had had sexual intercourse on the previous night, he would not take the food into his mouth. The feeder took him into the middle of the ring, and the people clapped hands and jeered at him. When the Hot Dance was introduced, such men would not even wear the bustles but merely carried them in their hands. The plate-holder rose, walked up to the eight selectmen, and said, "I have put these men here because they are renowned for such and such a deed. That is why I have given them dog to eat. Now you may all eat." Then the members all ate.

After the feast the eight braves had the dogs' skull bones laid down and danced toward them, enacting the exact part they had played in battle. Then they all stood in a row, each in turn recounting his deeds. When the headmen wished to stop the dance, they thanked the crowd, the people responded, and at this the ceremony came to a close. One of the bustle-wearers had the privilege of leading out of the dance lodge. This man put a blanket by the door. Four times he danced toward it, picking up the blanket, and passed out the fourth time.

The chief dancers held office for about a year, but occasionally for a longer period. A meeting of all officers was called. Then some one would say, "Now we'll give up our regalia, do you others do likewise." At the next dance two crow-belt wearers were appointed to choose new incumbents. The rank and file did not know anything about it beforehand. Then all the officers resigned their insignia and whatever else pertained to their offices.

The eating of dog flesh was an essential part of the Hot Dance among the people who passed the ceremony on to the Crow and Hidatsa. Thus the Crow sometimes came to eat dog in this context nothwithstanding their general aversion to its flesh. Even so, Hot Dancers, I learnt, sometimes substituted other flesh, such as chicken.

The ceremony is not yet wholly obsolete. In the summer of 1931, shortly after my departure from the Reservation, it was celebrated in the town of Hardin in honor of the (white) attorney of the Crow. Jim Carpenter wrote me: "They were going to adopt him (bici"tse-wiak; literally, they were going to cause him to be born); according to the Hot Dance fashion of adoption they adopted him. I saw it, it was fine. They went through the meat ritual (iru'ke i'axtak), they did the adopting in the old way. There were eight who ate the dog heads, I was one. There were over a hundred, probably two hundred people. They sang the ritual song for making people eat, they impaled meat and took it to his lips, they gave our attorney the emblem used in the dance. 'Now you are one of us, do not forget us' (kan dī bare' hawa'k, bare' karā'xtasa), they said. . . . They made Iron-necklace give him a name. Iron-necklace took this white man out to the inner space and named him 'Star-chief.' Several times they performed the dance, then they stopped. Then we feasted incomparably well."

* * * * *

The Crazy Dog society, introduced about the same time as the Hot Dance and from the same source, naturally got to the River Crow first; some informants even incorrectly limited it to that band. Actually the society came to differ in the two bands because the Main Body injected the wife-kidnaping procedure of the Lumpwoods and Foxes.

The Crazy Dogs were young men but often served as police and are even credited with special strictness in that capacity. The officers were elected in the spring according to the usual fashion. Their number may have varied locally, for in contrast to others, Lone-tree, a River Crow, who set the rank and file at about twenty-five men, mentioned only a single leader and a single rear officer. The former, he said, wore a buckskin cap with furbished deer horns and trimmed with weasel skins in the back; he was obliged to advance against the enemy and must never retreat. The rear officer wore a red-flannel sash with bead-work and had to dismount for a stand against the enemy if the Crow were fleeing. Bear-gets-up credits all the members with spherical or ring-shaped skin rattles (Fig. 13a) and distinguishes a dance director, four sash-wearers and four officers with horned caps. According to Old-dog, there were either two *or* four sash-wearers, while another informant gave a pair of leaders and of rear men in addition to four sash-wearers. Finally, Sitting-elk, over and above all these, enumerated two whippers and two akdū'-cire. The rank and file used paint of dark and light shades of red, as well as white clay. Distinguished warriors wore weasel-skin shirts, the rest dressed alike.

The modification of the Crazy Dog club by the Main Body is well brought out in Gray-bull's lively report:

"All the men of the Main Body who had not joined the Hot Dancers went to Plenty-coups' lodge and formed the Crazy Dog society. I also joined. The Foxes and Lumpwoods had given up wife-stealing. We met in the spring and made long sashes with slits, one for each of two officers. Punching holes in baking-powder cans and putting beads inside, we made rattles. The dance was similar to the Hot Dance. At the end of a song all members raised and shook their rattles, the eagle feathers on them producing a fine effect. Those who in battle wished to aid the two officers 'made to die' seized the trains of their sashes. After the dance we all assembled in the evening and went around the camp, where we were sometimes invited to partake of a feast indoors.

"One night we were parading in this way, and the Hot Dancers likewise. The cry of challenge was sounded, 'Hu, hu, hu!' The next day the wife-stealing was to begin. Plenty-coups said, 'We'll strike the first blow, I'll capture some women directly.' He talked it over and we proceeded on horseback, riding double. At Bear-claw's lodge he got off, peeped in, and saw the owner's wife there alone. He said, 'Come on, I want to marry you.' She took her blanket and came out; Plenty-coups bade her ride behind his comrade. The Crazy Dogs cheered: 'Here is one coming already!' They began to sing and rejoice so much that the tipi began to shake. The captive was considered her abductor's wife, so Plenty-coups' sisters brought her an elk-tooth dress. Her face was painted yellow, with red stripes across to symbolize his coups. The men said, 'It is all over, let us go out and dance.' Because of my war record I was asked to ride, while others remained afoot. I was told I might take my comrade behind me if I so wished. Having put on my ermine-skin shirt, I did so, and took the lead. Granulated-eyelids had once dismounted in battle and taken another Crow behind him, so he was chosen to take the kidnaped woman on his horse. He rode, not in the line of march, but alongside, so as to be conspicuous. I also had that privilege, and the spectators uttered shouts of praise.

"The wife of one of the Crazy Dogs was captured by the Hot Dancers while looking on at the performance. Then the Crazy Dogs did not want to go home lest their wives be abducted before their eyes. We could hear the Hot Dancers rejoicing."

X. War

SOCIAL standing and chieftainship, we have seen, were dependent on military prowess; and that was the only road to distinction. Value was set on other qualities, such as liberality, aptness at story-telling, success as a doctor. But the property a man distributed was largely the booty he had gained in raids; and any accomplishments, prized as they might be, were merely decorative frills, not substitutes for the substance of a reputation, a man's record as a warrior. I know of at least one Crow of the old school whose intelligence would have made him a shining light wherever store was set by sheer capacity of the legal type, but who enjoyed no prestige whatsoever among his people. In fact, I was repeatedly warned against his mendacity, though his accounts of tribal life tallied perfectly with those of generally accredited informants. The point was simply that he had gained no honors in war and had tried to doctor this deficiency when publicly reciting his achievements.

War was not the concern of a class nor even of the male sex, but of the whole population, from cradle to grave. Girls as well as boys derived their names from a famous man's exploit. Women danced wearing scalps, derived honor from their husbands' deeds, publicly exhibited the men's shields or weapons; and a woman's lamentations over a slain son was the most effective goad to a punitive expedition. There are memories of a woman who went to war; indeed, Muskrat, one of my women informants, claimed to have struck a coup and scalped a Piegan, thus earning songs of praise.

Most characteristic was the intertwining of war and religion. The Sun Dance, being a prayer for revenge, was naturally saturated with military episodes; but these were almost as prominent in the Tobacco ritual, whose avowed purpose was merely the general welfare. More significant still, every single military undertaking was theoretically inspired by a revelation in dream or vision; and since success in life was so largely a matter of martial glory, war exploits became the chief content of prayer.

Glory, however, was rigorously defined. There were the four standard deeds of valor grouped under the head of the probably synonymous terms ackya'pe or araxtsi', a man with claims to any one of them being an araxtsi'wice, honor-owner. The touching of an enemy—whether he was hurt or not—counted as the "coup" proper, dā'kce. Four men might count coup on the same enemy, but the honor diminished with each successive blow. Also, in any one engagement only one man ranked as the striker of a first-coup; in other words, the first striking of other foemen was not so rated. Snatching away a bow or gun in a hand-to-hand encounter was a second honor; and the theft of a horse picketed in a hostile camp so that it had to be cut loose, bāpa'ckyua (cutting-something) was still another. Being the pipe-owner (ī'ptse-ake') or raid-planner (akdu'xigyutsgye) was the fourth deed that counted toward the chieftainship; and a "chief" (see p. 5) was simply a man who had achieved at least one of each of these four feats.

In 1910 only two residents of Lodge Grass were regarded as such,—Medicine-crow and Gray-bull; in Pryor there were several, including Bell-rock and Plenty-coups. Though the latter doubtless had an enviable record and was recognized as *the* Crow chief by the U. S. Government, most informants considered Bell-rock supreme among then living men. In Gray-bull's words, Bell-rock was the very first, kambasā'kāce, excelling all others on every count; he had captured five guns, cut loose at least two tethered horses, struck six undisputed coups, and led more than eleven war parties. Gray-bull himself, universally esteemed for bravery, claimed no more than three feats of each category. Hillside fell short of chieftainship only because the enemy retrieved a horse he had cut loose; and Flat-head-woman lacked merely a coup.

Whether all four exploits were on a par remains an open question. Blue-bead gave precedence to captaincy and the coup proper, Gray-bull, speaking in general terms, considered all honors approximately on one plane; yet he put Plenty-coups below Bell-rock notwithstanding Plenty-coups' having seven coups (against six) and four horses (against a possible three). Unconsciously, then, he gave special weight to Bell-rock's two extra war parties.

Irrespective of titular recognition, each new feat added to

one's kudos. Even if a man fell short of being a chief, leadership of a successful raid or scalp hunt qualified him as herald and put him next to the chiefs.

Each exploit was symbolically represented on the performer's dress, but the devices varied somewhat. A coup-striker, said Yellow-brow, wore wolf tails at the heels of his moccasins; a gun-snatcher decorated his shirt with ermine skins; and the leader of a party that brought spoils fringed his leggings with ermine or scalps. According to Gray-bull, a captain had the right to put hair on his moccasins as well as his shirt, while a gun-taker or coup-striker might decorate only his shirt in this way.

In the thick of battle disagreement might arise as to which of two combatants had dealt the first blow. This sometimes led to an ordeal or oath-taking called ackya'p-bats-ā'pasū'a (war-honor-mutually-disputing). Each contestant took a knife, put it into his mouth, pointed it toward the Sun, and uttered such a formula as, "It was I that struck the enemy. Sun, as you looked down, you saw me strike him. Hereafter when I meet an enemy, may I again overcome him without difficulty." Another wording would be: "I struck the coup, you [Sun] saw me. May the one who lies die before winter." In one form of the procedure the people impaled some lean meat on an arrow which they placed on an old dry buffalo skull with its tips painted red. Each rival in turn raised the arrow, pointed his right index-finger at its head, touched the meat with his lips, and pronounced the oath. If both took the test, the people could not at once determine the merits of the case. But if some misfortune befell one of them after the ordeal, he was considered the perjurer and his opponent then justly claimed the contested honor.

Other deeds than the "big four" ranked as meritorious, hence were recited on public occasions and pictured on a man's robe, on the draft screen in his lodge and, rarely, on his tipi cover. In 1910 Shows-a-fish had such decorations on the canvas lining inside his log cabin. On a robe I bought from Charges-strong, pipes near the top symbolize the wearer's captaincy; outlines of heads with upturned lock represent Shoshone, simple outlines standing for Dakota; and horse tracks suggest the capture of horses. In another section of this robe a scout is shown going to the hostile camp and returning to a pile of buffalo chips (see p. 220). Still other parts of the robe depict such details

as coups counted on two enemies by the mounted hero, his over-
taking and striking a foeman, his driving off Shoshone horses.

At large gatherings the men always formally enumerated
their deeds. In 1907 No-shinbone gave me the following list of
his own, drawing a line on the ground for each item:

> I captured a gun.
> I captured a bow.
> I led a war party that killed an enemy.
> I was shot.
> I killed a horse.
> I shot a man.
> I brought home ten horses.
> I went to war about fifty times.
> The Dakota were harrying me, I shot one of them.

After each item at a public recital of this type the musicians
present would beat the drum once.

The taking of a scalp was evidence of a killing, but did not
rank as a deed deserving special notice. "You will never hear a
Crow boast of his scalps when he recites his deeds," an informant told me. Some men stretched the trophy in a hoop, scraping off the flesh with a knife and blackening the dried scalp with
charcoal. It was subsequently held aloft at the end of a long
stick.

*   *   *   *   *

Training for war began in childhood. Apart from athletic
games, boys counted coups on game animals, made the girls dance
with the hair of a wolf or coyote in lieu of a scalp; and in the
Hammer Society specifically imitated the adults' military societies (see pp. 38, 202).

An ambitious lad, however, would not be content with sham
activities, but cast about for a chance to go with a raiding party.
On the subject of warfare the older generation, otherwise little
inclined to interfere with youth turned didactic. "Old age is a
thing of evil, it is well for a young man to die in battle," summed
up the burden of their pedagogy. The prompting of young men
by precept and example to gain renown recurs again and again
in native tradition. In one story a handsome youth idles at home
while his contemporaries go out against the enemy. At length
his father, incensed beyond endurance by his son's inactivity,
flings himself into the fire, injuring himself, and thus goads the

laggard into setting out on a raid. When a youngster did come back from such an experience, he lorded it over his mates, twitting the stay-at-homes with being like a woman. "You are not a boy," Gray-bull used to say to Bird-tail-rattles, "your vulva is blue."

On his maiden trip a boy did not have an easy time of it, for he became the butt of practical jokes. The men were likely to send him to one of their number for shavings from a buffalo hide; on hearing the message, the man told him he had eaten them up and made him go to another member of the party, and so the novice was sent from pillar to post. Moreover, youngsters had to do menial tasks; they were sent for water without instructions where to find it and had to carry the meat. In order to lighten their load, it is said they would encourage their elders to gorge themselves.

Sometimes, of course, a whole band found itself facing a large hostile force, but by far the most typical form of military enterprise was the raid (du'xia) organized by the leader of a small party, the so-called raid-planner or pipe-owner. His venture was a purely personal one, in no way directed by the chief or council; in fact, when the chief considered raids impolitic, he ordered the police to prevent any parties from leaving the camp. Sanction was necessary for a party, but was strictly supernatural. The organizer had dreamt about his enterprise or seen in a vision full particulars about the place to go to, the tribe to be raided, even the kind of loot—to the color of a horse's skin—or the manner of man to be killed, say a thumbless Cheyenne. Failing such inspiration, a would-be leader would apply to a man of note owning a war-medicine and follow this mentor's directions,—likewise based on dreams. An untried captain might not succeed in mustering a large company, for there were always skeptics doubting the potency of his revelation. Even if his medicines were strong, strict rules went with them. In some cases, for instance, no one might pass on his right (or left) side the bearer of the captain's sacred bundle; and however inadvertently the law was broken, dire mishap would befall the entire party.

Lust for fame was axiomatically an end in all warfare. In addition there were two dominant motives,—the desire for booty, which in the main meant horses; and the craving for revenge.

Though these drives, varying with individual temperaments and situations, could be combined, we may distinguish horse raids from expeditions for coups and slaughter,—a classification suggested by Flat-back. He set off the former as typically directed against the Piegan from the latter, having the Dakota as an objective.

Raiders characteristically started afoot, hence the need for plenty of footgear. "I had moccasins made for myself" is a formula that denotes preparation for a war party. Often each participant led a dog to carry his moccasins and a small bucket, and afterwards the rope used served to secure the horses purloined. Next to the captain the scouts (ak'tsī'te), varying in number with the size of the party, were the most important members; each carried a wolf skin as an emblem and imitated the howling of that animal, so that they were sometimes referred to as "wolves." At a preliminary gathering they sang scout songs, such as these: "I am going to bring horses, I'll bring some back." After the singing a shout went up. A party frequently set out after sunset or even in the dark. For shelter they put up simple windbreaks (acta'tse') of sticks, bark, and foliage. At the proper time the captain sent out his scouts to sight the enemy. While the others were still asleep they were up climbing hill after hill, fasting all the time till they saw the camp. Then they returned, giving the wolf howl, to make their report, a sort of homecoming called batsī'kya-raku'a. When close to their party, they brandished their guns to signal that they had really seen something. Now followed a characteristic rite. Their associates had prepared a pile of buffalo chips and sang, forming a semicircle around it. Then the leader of the scouts approached and kicked over the heap of chips. The captain asked for the report, and the scout answered, "The enemy is yonder." Now at last they were allowed to eat meat.

The time having come for final preparations, each brave tied sacred objects to his body and painted his face according to the rules associated with them. The captain spread something to rest *his* medicine on and whistled or sang towards the enemy's camp, possibly saying, "So many horses have been given to me." One man was chosen to lead, and they approached the camp. The captain told his men to gather, went round them, and thus prayed to the Sun: "If all my party get home safe with plenty of horses, I'll make you a sweat-lodge." Then he sent one or two men to camp to drive off all the horses possible. If satisfied with the spoils, he decided to start homeward. The length of their journey naturally varied. Typically, they would run at top-speed all night, the next day, and the second night. On the following day they relaxed, tried to kill a buffalo, and feasted on it. When near their own camp they shot off their guns and rode the captured horses round camp.

In strict theory the captain could claim all the booty; in practice he liberally shared it with his men to avoid the charge of avarice. During the parade the scouts carried wolf hides on their backs and sang tsū'ra songs. At night all the party assembled in the captain's lodge, where the young women came to sit behind them. They sang scout songs, and after that the women got some of the pudding prepared for the occasion and took it home.

No-shinbone thus described one of his raids, atypical only in that it started on horseback. "Where the fortifications were, there we camped. There I ordered moccasins to be made for me. The morning after they were ready I brought my good sorrel horse and saddled him. I went out and took my medicine,—that over there [pointing] is it. I rode away and reached my comrade, the two of us went. Young men kept catching up with us till there were twelve of us. We went and lay down in a little wooded river bed and slept in the night. The next morning we ate; the young men brought the horses, we tied on the saddles and went. It must have been this season of the year. We climbed a hill and saw some buffalo; the young men gave chase and killed a very fat buffalo. We got there, all of us, dismounted, and butchered. When through butchering, we kept the meat, then we rode off. We camped in a wooded coulée. We dismounted, they made camp, we built a fire, they cooked the meat and we ate. Then we had our fill, drank water and smoked tobacco. When through, we slept. The following morning we ate, the young men brought horses, we tied the saddles on and rode off. Then in a wooded coulée we camped. We made camp, they cooked the meat, we ate.[1] When done, we smoked; when done, we slept. The next morning they built a fire and we ate. When through,

---

[1] No-shinbone as captain of course did not have to cook,—even though he shared in the eating.

they brought the horses, we tied on the saddles and rode off. We climbed a hill, there were a great many buffalo. The young men chased them and killed three fat ones. We got there, dismounted, took out our knives, and butchered. When done butchering, we packed the horses and rode away. In a coulée we stopped, young men went as scouts, they reported a sighting. They came, they reached us. 'How is it?' I asked. 'Yonder is the Head-cutters' [Dakota] camp,' they said. 'All right, we'll start against them,' I said. Then I climbed a hill and looked. The camp had killed buffalo, they were carrying huge loads home on their backs. I saw, I came, I reached my party. I lighted buffalo chips and took out my medicine. Then I sang toward the camp. At night we rode, we galloped all the way and approached the camp. At the edge of the camp we sat down. I sent two young men to camp; they brought many horses. Afterwards I again sent two, again they brought many horses. I took a good buckskin, then I said, 'Let us flee.' With many horses we took to flight. At night we continued running, until daylight. We got to a river, mightily we swam it. We were so cold we almost died. We crossed, then it was daylight. That day we ran till night, at night we kept on. Many horses we had brought when we swam the river, plenty of them turned back, but with thirty head I reached camp. The camp was by a creek. There was plenty of meat. Thus I returned."

Such parties were no pleasure jaunts. From the continuous riding fugitives' "buttocks were worn out," as they quaintly complain. If they started afoot in the normal way, they were sometimes unable to catch enough of the enemy's horses to provide mounts for every one, so that some had to return afoot, liable to be overtaken and slain by the pursuers. Again, one Crow party succeeded in capturing Piegan horses but was overtaken by a heavy snowstorn, in which most of them perished.

Gray-bull once went to the Shoshone country and for five days his party had nothing to eat. When at last they saw buffalo, almost all of the members were so weak that they had to support themselves with canes. While one man was sent to kill a buffalo, another prayed to the Sun, "If he kills it, we shall all give you a piece of our skin." He succeeded, cut open the buffalo's belly, and drank of its blood, which he dipped up in his hands. "We washed the manifolds in the blood and ate that first.

The rest we took to a creek near-by and ate till we were full. We lay down and slept on the meat for our pillows. We had stomach ache that night and vomited all we had eaten. One of the old men told us it was because we lay on the meat, so thereafter we placed it beside us and did not vomit then."

In such raids a man might gain glory by cutting loose a tethered horse, and a windfall might bring him one of the other formally recognized deeds; but normally the only exploit in the narrower sense would be the captain's, though informally every new raid redounded to a man's credit. If a leader set out to capture horses but decided to do more than that, the less adventurous spirits of his following might object. Thus, in the story of Twined-tail the hero after a successful raid proposes to destroy a hostile lodge, but his brother argues, "Now that we are bringing horses, it is enough, I think. You are going too far."

However,—usually when tribesmen had been slain,—parties *were* specially organized for the gaining of honors and the killing of enemies. Gray-bull's report of one of these expeditions is characteristic. He got his war medicine from a medicine-man who had also instructed Hillside and Flat-head-woman. However, unlike these others, who obtained arrows from their adviser, Gray-bull received a tooth extracted from the corpse of a famous Crow warrior killed by the enemy; all three men got similar accessories. Because the original purchaser of the tooth had been notably successful, Gray-bull bought it for ten horses. He, too, enjoyed good luck and got together a herd of from 70 to 90 horses.

One day Gray-bull was seated by his mentor, when a woman mourning her son put a pipe in front of him. The medicine-man told him to light and smoke it. "I obeyed and then handed the pipe to him. There was a crowd of people in the lodge and the pipe was passed round the circle. I did not yet know that the woman had a horse loaded with gifts outside. She unloaded the presents; my 'father' gave me a striped blanket and had his wife distribute the remainder of the property. She gave me the reins of the horse. My 'father' thus spoke to her: 'Well, you have given my son the pipe; I am angry' [at the enemy]. He then spoke to me for a while, and I called out to her, word for word, what he had told me: 'Grandmother, to-morrow I shall make a sweat-lodge, the next night I shall start.' The following day I made a sweat-lodge. Before starting I called on the old woman and again told her I would be on my journey the next morning, that eight days hence she was to pulverize charcoal, mix it with fat, and be on the lookout for me.

"Six days later a body of Piegan saw us and stole our unpicketed horses. We followed in pursuit, found four Piegan, killed them and recovered all but two horses. We then turned homeward. Sarting out we had traveled very slowly, but coming home we went as fast as possible. The eighth night was drawing near and I left my party so as to be home in time. The old woman was waiting for me on the outskirts of the camp. She began to cry and asked whether I was coming back with spoils. I told her I had killed four of the enemy, that she should stop crying and prepare charcoal because the rest of the party were coming. She continued to cry and wished to get further details, but I loped away to report to my 'father,' who was with the expedition.

"In the center of the camp they formed a circle and the Long Dance (bāha'tsgye disu'a) was begun by the men on the expedition. Then each warrior individually invited the people to his lodge to tell them the story of the war party. On this occasion it was a coup-striker's a'sa'ke, i.e. a clansman of his father's, who sang his praises and as compensation received presents, largely contributed by the brave's own clan.

"They waited for a favorable day, then a herald proclaimed a big tsū'ra celebration. The best singers were reassembled for this occasion. Each coup-striker put his medicine on his wife's head and had her carry his weapons. The captain would tie his medicine to his wife's back or to a long stick which she was to raise. All the camp turned out to watch. If a man had duplicate medicines, he and his wife took one apiece. The wives of the captain and the coup-strikers stood in the center and danced till evening, then stopped; but the mourners, with blackened faces, kept on till the next morning. Old men again led the coup-strikers around.

"The next morning, before sunrise, people sneaked into the lodges of the warriors and threw off their blankets, even though they might be lying with their wives. Then the men dressed up and danced with the mourners. The captain called to the coup-strikers to prepare food for these men jostled out of bed. There was bustle in camp and people went to watch the performance. The coup-strikers were again praised in song; and the mourners danced until noon."

Warriors always blackened their faces to symbolize the killing of an enemy, so that "with black face" is a stereotyped phrase for a victorious return. This is the meaning of the charcoal paint on Gray-bull's companions when he got back to them. They had evidently also conformed to another usage, that is, had killed a buffalo and put its blood into a paunch as the material for decorating their garments. The blood was mixed and stirred in warm water with two kinds of charcoal. First the men rubbed their robes with wetted clay, then several eminent men, having enumerated their own deeds, painted each robe with the symbol of the first coup struck. Though four men counted coup on one enemy, the honor decreased in ordinal succession and the painting of the robes varied accordingly. The first man to capture a gun and the first coup-striker had their robe or shirt blackened all over, the second and third men had only half of their garment so decorated, and the fourth men had only the arms of their shirts painted. The distinguished men also instructed the members as to other decorations; thus, there would be horse-tracks, parallel stripes, and, irrespective of the number of enemies struck, from four to six roughly sketched human figures. Thus attired, the party approached the camp, spending the last night very close to it. The following morning, as soon as within shooting distance, they fired off their guns and made a characteristic noise. When at the edge of the camp, they sent the coup-strikers to fetch one drum for every warrior. In the meantime the women, who carried the scalp sticks, got ready and danced into camp ahead of the warriors.

A victorious homecoming was called ara'tsiwe,—apparently whether the Crow had struck coups or stolen horses; however, a successful raid was probably not considered sufficient to "make the women dance." Supposing the warriors had killed an enemy, they painted their faces one or two nights after their return and marched through camp, with the captain in the rear and a herald behind him. The herald cried out, "You women, all of you put on your finery and go to the Pipe-owner's lodge, we shall feast there tonight." So all the people went there after the parade, the women streaming in and sitting down behind the warriors of their choice. They sang scout and scalp songs; each took her favorite's robe and tomahawk, stood up in a conspicuous place by the door, and began to dance. The herald, seated by the door, named the first coup-striker, and after his response told him to fill a pail with cherry dessert brought by the women and give it to his wife. The first scout to sight the enemy was allowed to choose whatever food he preferred, turned it over to his wife, and then waited on the other women present. Both scouts helped themselves first, then waited on the other men. After every one had feasted on stewed berries and other food, the older men ordered the women to take the residue home and return for the performance of "lodge-striking" (ac-ditu′a).

For this act the boys cut willow poles and leaned them against the tipi, then lined up to wait for the women's return. A herald shouted, "Untie your horses and take them further away, these young men are going to strike the lodge!" Those of the party who were singers beat drums, the rest took willow sticks, as did the young women, for each man had a girl with him. Amidst victory songs and beating of drums, all rushed towards the captain's tipi and struck it, some men shooting off their guns. The noise was such that horses got frightened and ran away. Hitherto the songs had been without words, but after the striking of the tipi they sang this sentence, "Recently 1 went away, I have returned, kiss me." Then they proceeded to the center of the camp, where they danced, the men with blankets wrapped about their women partners, and all circling about with a step of the Owl dance type (p. 93), moving both right and left. Usually five or six tents were struck. The celebration after a killing would last a day and a night.

Praise songs (mā′tsikarū′a) in honor of the returning braves were a distinctive feature of the celebration. It was above all a man's a′sa'kua and isbāxi′u, i.e., his father's clansmen and clanswomen, who led him about camp as his public panegyrists, calling out his name and singing these chants, which originated in dreams. The words bear no obvious relation to any meritorious deed, Gray-bull and Medicine-crow independently furnishing the following sample: "I'll adopt you as my grandmother" (dī′wasa'kā′m bā′wiky). In return the singer received presents. Such songs were sometimes sung on the expedition itself by the leader or old members of the party. In 1910 aged Crow men still sang mā'tsikarū'a in honor of younger people who had presented them with other valuable gifts. Gray-bull sold his praise songs for a horse.

But not all war parties had an auspicious ending. There is a tradition in which the best sorts of captains are mentioned, and "those who never signaled a loss" (ak'-tsicē'rēte) take precedence of "those who regularly bring horses" and "those who regularly kill." If a member of the party was killed, his associates did not at once enter camp, but dispatched a messenger, who fired off a gun from some high eminence. When people looked thither, he waved his blanket to show from what direction he had come. Every one then knew what had happened and who was the unlucky captain. For each man killed, the messenger lowered the blanket or threw it to one side. He did not approach the camp but sat down, and men were sent to interview him about the details of the disaster. The camp went into mourning while the party stayed in the hills, mourning for ten days; during this period they did not drink from a cup, being served with drink by others. They then set off again without having entered the camp. If they lifted horses on this second trip, their grieving was over; but the bereaved family kept up their mourning until the death of an enemy.

The notion was deep-rooted among Plains Indians that no tribesman's life should be lost if by any possibility it could be avoided, hence the sacrifice of men on behalf of strategic gains was utterly foreign to Crow conceptions. Of course, there were daredevils who risked their necks for sheer bravado, and others who ignored danger from a sublime faith in their supernaturally guaranteed invulnerability. But though long life was theoretically contemptible and a glorious death in battle was held up as ideal (p. 218), in practice more prosaic counsels prevailed with the average man. Hence the amazing phenomenon that recurs in Plains Indian traditions of a single desperado holding back and even routing a dozen foemen; hence the oft-repeated Crow prayer that the supplicant may kill his enemy easily, safely, without injury to himself (i'tsikyāta).

Why did the Crow fight? Certainly not from an uncontrollable instinct of pugnacity. It was disgraceful to fall to fisticuffs within the tribe, and I have heard unfavorable comments on the brawls of white men. Enemies, of course, were fair game, but in spite of high-flown phrases about "wiping them out," I know of no concerted effort to oust the Dakota or Cheyenne from their territory, and tradition tells of relatively few ancient enterprises on a really large scale. Minor operations, sufficing to gratify both the sportive urge and even the craving for revenge, could be more readily harmonized with the repugnance to any loss of tribesmen.

Doubtless the stimuli for military enterprise were not uniform, varying with different men and different situations. Utilitarian urges appear but were certainly not dominant. The desire for horses was the most "economical" motive of Plains Indian warfare, yet a Crow rated higher for cutting loose one picketed horse than for lifting a dozen freely roaming about. And what was the use of horses after one got them? Gray-bull acquired 70 to 90 head, but a few fleet animals for the buffalo chase, several mounts, and a few pack-horses would have been more than ample for his needs. The Crow, unlike the Central Asiatic Turks, never dreamt of milking mares or eating horse flesh. A large herd had sheer ostentation value; the owner could offer twenty horses for a wife instead of five; and he could give frequent presents to his father's clansfolk if he liked to hear himself eulogized.

Again, it was meritorious to kill an enemy, but the lightest tap with a coup-stick was reckoned higher. Obviously the idea was not primarily to reduce a hostile force but to execute a "stunt," to play a game according to whimsical rules. Intrepidity was, it is true, cordially admired,—as when a Crow turned back to save a disabled tribesman (see p. 190). But, like chastity, such daring was praised rather than emulated. Here, too, concessions were made to original sin: in the clubs even the officers "doomed to die" were held to their pledge only for a single season. What is more, the very Crazy Dogs (p. 331) who volunteered deliberately to court death were scot-free of their obligation if they happened to escape by the close of the season.

Counting the capture of a picketed horse toward the chieftaincy was assuredly to reward boldness; yet Hillside who achieved the deed failed to score because the enemy recovered his prize. On the other hand, when the first man to *touch* a foe ranked above the one who had laid him low, it was fleetness, not skill or valor, that carried the day. Similarly, the Crow who struck the first enemy in an engagement need not have been a whit braver than another who struck the fifth or tenth; yet it was the former who gained preeminence. In a possibly historical tale, Plays-with-his-face, a picked champion, together with an inexperienced boy, surprises a Cheyenne easing himself at the edge of the hostile camp. They pursue him, the ingenuous youth boldly dashing into the midst of the camp, where he thinks he is counting coup. But his wily companion has already struck a conveniently close enemy and tauntingly establishes his claim to the highest honor.

The coup was indeed interpreted in so conventional a way that often it bore no relation to true bravery whatsoever. When Bull-tongue was once sent to a Dakota camp as scout, he found a woman urinating and killed her,—which was sufficient. On another occasion a Crow party were patiently but vainly lying in ambush for some one to leave the Dakota camp. At length one of them possessed of power sang his chant, made a motion with his pipe, drew the picture of a man on the ground, and put his pipe on it. Soon an unarmed Dakota sallied forth, riding toward the mountains. "We chased the man toward camp and killed him"—the first one to touch the body naturally claiming first honors. It was enough to warrant a big celebration: "We danced mightily," Grandmother's-knife told me. Again, Flat-back piqued himself not a little on having killed four squaws near a hostile camp. "Medicine-crow is a chief," he said, "yet he does not equal me." This was mere pleasantry, for Medicine-crow was a "brother-in-law," hence fair butt for raillery about war though never about sexual matters (p. 29); but the jocularity did not disguise the speaker's conviction that he had achieved a real exploit.

The treatment of prisoners differed according to circumstances, but was often in sharp contrast to our notions of chivalry. The lot of captured women was, it is true, generally an easy one; that is, they were married to Crow men and merely performed the usual feminine tasks. Male captives, especially young boys, might also be spared, though their foreign origin was remembered, and for certain tasks in the Sun Dance such "dä'tse" were deemed essential (p. 312). But when inflamed with rage over their own losses or the stubborn resistance put up by their opponents the Crow did not refrain from torture. Leonard, the old trader, tells of a fight with the Blackfoot, who had constructed a breastwork of logs, brush and stone on the brow of a hill, where they heroically defended themselves for a long time. The Crow finally gained the victory, cruelly tormented their helplessly wounded enemies before massacring them, and after two days beat and mangled the corpses. Subsequently, Leonard observed the slaying of a single marauder from the same people, who was hung from a tree by the neck, whereupon the men shot at him, and the women pierced him with sharp sticks. More recently Leforge noted the mutilation of dead enemies and corpses dragged about by a rope round the neck.

Crow war psychology is a queer blend of cruelty, vanity, greed, foolhardiness, literalism, and magnificent courage.

Though not usual, major encounters were sometimes thrust upon the Crow. One such is described at length in a quasi-historical text. The account stresses preparatory measures, so that while doubtless partly fictitious and touched up for literary effect, it serves as an invaluable document for the military psychology of the people, the speeches cited being particularly illuminating.

Prior to the hostilities in question, a small company under Dangling-foot had separated from the Main Body and was largely wiped out by the Cheyenne. The Crow mourned grievously, especially the slain leader's kin, and the chief Sore-belly (=Rottenbelly) was moved by their wailing. The main camp of the Cheyenne happened to be near by, and Sore-belly hinted at being willing to direct a punitive attack. The mourners then brought him a sacred pipe; having accepted it, he mounted his horse and harangued the camp: "When I went fasting [for a vision] I would lie down in diverse places. I thought to myself: 'If I get a vision and my Crow, my people, are ever in distress, no matter where I may be *I* shall protect them.' That is why I lay down in diverse places. I fasted, I thirsted, on behalf of my Crow I shed my tears. . . . Now the Man with Stench in his Hair [2] is afflicting our people, he is making some of them cry, he is causing them grief. I have had enough of that Man. It is not yet time to go against him, but I'll go soon. . . . The Cheyenne Man yonder thinks that he alone is brave; he causes my poor [captive] people to sit where the water drips on them [from the paunches hung up near the door]. He strikes them, he kills them at his pleasure. Well, now there's an end of it. My young men,

[2] Unflattering reference to the Cheyenne chief.

drink your fill, thin out your blood. We will challenge the Man.
When men meet, they kill each other. Whether he kills us,
whether we'll kill him, we'll have a decision. . . ."

When he had finished his speech, he went to his lodge and
summoned Good-herald, a very brave man, whose body was
scarred all over, to act as his crier. After smoking together,
Sore-belly said, "Well, a day has come such as I have never
experienced so long as I can remember. My manhood, my visions,
my wailings—I have them all now. Well, I am ready. Go out,
your Crow want to hear something; well, let them hear something." That was at night. The next morning, with the dawn,
Good-herald rose and went heralding:

"Crow in distress, get up, drink your fill, thin out your
blood. Get up, women, cook, feed your young men. Foxes, breakfast is ready in the lodge over there; get up, take a swim, go
thither. Lumpwoods, in yonder lodge breakfast is ready, they
are waiting for you; get up, swim, all of you go there and eat! Big
Dogs, in that lodge breakfast is ready, go thither, eat there!
Poor Crow, whatever you do, hasten! A man is ever enslaving
you. Your captive kin have surely been looking hither. 'Would
that they helped us!' they keep thinking to themselves. The end
has come. Nothing lasts forever. Even the trees, rooted as they
are, fall down. You are not like them, you have no roots, your
soles barely skim the ground. He [the enemy] acts as if he
alone were brave. He strikes your distressed kin at his pleasure,
he kills them at his pleasure. This is the end. We'll challenge
him. When men meet, they kill each other. Whether he kills us,
whether *we* kill *him*, it will be settled."

Next Good-herald gave directions to the three military clubs,
specifying a few picked men who were to be mounted while the
majority of the members remained afoot. In the middle of the
camp a pile of stones was heaped up. The crier now introduced
the horsemen to the people at large as their chief champions.
To quote the narrative:

"Then the Foxes came out and advanced; with drums thundering they approached. Near the pile they came to a halt. The
mourners came. Good-herald shouted: 'Hē, hē, hē!' He took the
horse of Young-white-buffalo [of the Fox club] by the reins,
led him away from the crowd, and brought him to the middle
[of the camp]. . . . He tapped him on the chest. 'Miserable

Crow, your protector is here, look at him well! When we were little and strange children came to strike us and ran away, our elder brother would chase them and avenge us. Thus Young-white-buffalo. Crow, wheresoever the enemy may abuse you, this Young-white-buffalo is the avenger, he is your protector. Look at him, miserable Crow, even now he will on your behalf inflict some harm upon them [the Cheyenne]. That is what I wanted you to hear.' He dismissed him. Next he took Small-back's horse by the reins, took him to the center, and said: 'Here is the one named Small-back, look at him!' He tapped his chest. 'Tomorrow, when you meet the Cheyenne and one of them dismounts, fully bent on slaughter, Small-back will not possibly be afraid of him. At once bumping against his side, he will snatch his gun away and bring it with him. This Cheyenne who considered himself dangerous will have no way of being dangerous. The one who makes what is dangerous *not* dangerous is Small-back. . . .' He dismissed him and took Passes-women next. 'Tomorrow he is bound to do something. Crow, of all your possessions, he is the most precious. Look at him.'

"Now came the Big Dogs, their drums a-thundering. They came to this pile [of stones]. The mourners came. Good-herald came. He led Wants-to-die's horse and brought him to the center. 'This is the one called Wants-to-die. Look at him! Distressed Crow, he is your protector. Tomorrow, when you meet the enemy, he will run among them. They, too, are but human; what will they be tarrying for? They will flee.' Then Wants-to-die spoke [to the crier]: 'My elder brother, please be silent for a while, I will sing for you.' Good-herald cried out: 'Distressed Crow, this Wants-to-die has just spoken. I'll tell you what he said. Keep still, be silent. He says he is going to sing for us, that's what he said.' He rode about singing. At once the old men began to chant songs of praise. 'That's the way, Wants-to-die,' they said. At the same time the women gave their call. There was a confusion of songs. He [Wants-to-die] stopped singing. 'I'll say a few words, I'll tell you something. Even were I the bullet-plug, they could not hit me. There is no one like this [invulnerable] on the other side of the hill, of all the people on the earth I am the only one. That is what I wanted you to hear.' . . . Then Double-face came; Good-herald was leading his horse, he led him to the center of the circle. 'Distressed Crow, your protector is here, look at him!' He tapped his chest. 'This is he. Take a tree with big branches standing by very swift water, the roots facing upstream, the branches downstream. Because it is very heavy, it does not float away. Because of the swift water, small driftwood and flotsam circles around on the sheltered side; it does not float away but gets entangled. This Double-face is the sheltered side you run to. Tomorrow wherever they chase us, he will dismount, he'll be our sheltered side. There we shall be entangled, *he* will shield you. . . .' Double-face spoke: 'Well, do not speak! I'll make them hear my words. Women in labor hold on to a digging-stick; when they scream we think they are delivered of the child, yet for a long time the child remains unborn. [I am not delaying like that.] I want to take part in your battle, I am eager. Now, somehow I might die before the fight, for persons may die from guns by accident, and I might die by some other accident. For my sake, by the love you bear your children, Sore-belly, go out to battle on this very day. I want to see that Man. He thinks he is the only man. I want to pierce the bellies of some of his followers. . . .' When he had spoken, Good-herald answered: 'Double-face, I will tell you Sore-belly's opinion about this speech of yours to him and about your question. When our mourning is over, we'll ponder it and I'll tell you our opinion, he said; that is what Sore-belly said.'

"Then the Lumpwoods came, drums a-thundering. . . . Good-herald went out and spoke. He led the horse of Plays-with-his-face to the middle of the circle. 'Dear Crow, here is the one named Plays-with-his-face, look at him. What is called death he is not at all afraid of, he knows nothing about it [such fear]. It is a marvel we own. Tomorrow or thereabouts he will not be among us. When the madcap goes into battle, he will be killed. Your own will be torn to pieces, the strewn fragments will be lying there.' "

At this point in the tradition Plays-with-his-face addresses the women in the audience and in extravagant verbiage boasts of his virility, which he contrasts with the meager capacities of all other men. Then, turning to the chief, he, too, begs Sore-belly to attack the enemy at once. Good-herald, answering for the chief, bids every one go home and enjoy life until the morrow:

"In speaking I am not speaking for myself; when I tell you

something, the words are Sore-belly's. Today go home, prepare food, cook what you like best and serve your young men. Hallo, all you young men, all you young women! I want you to listen. First I'll talk to you, young women. Tomorrow or thereabouts you will no longer see some half of your young men. Tonight keep not watch on your husbands, turn them loose. Don't reproach them, pay no attention to them whatever they do. Now, young men, it is your turn. After tomorrow I shall not see half of you again. If you are any decent sort of men, let your wife use her best clothing today. All of you Crow, wear your best clothing, eat your best food, in your speech with one another be as amiable as possible. Young women, you want to see your sweethearts; young men, you want to do likewise. Meet one another openly. Let none of us Crow do anything to hurt one another. This is all now, these are Sore-belly's words. . . .' "

The people then followed the crier's directions. After a while he issued new orders: some young men were to level a plot of ground, others to take sweet-smelling sage there. Sore-belly himself heaped up buffalo chips to more than a man's height. He was going to resort to augury. He dressed up in a calf-skin robe, had his entire body blackened, as well as most of his face, and carried a very large shield on his back. He approached the pile of chips gradually, sitting down four times on the way and singing a song each time. The last time he sat down at the foot of the pile and called Good-herald, who stood behind him. "Now," said Sore-belly, "I'll sing four times, then I'll ascend these buffalo chips. . . . When I sing this last time, you men shall clap your lips [sign of applause], you women give a call. Do it again and again, all of you men! If I fail to get up on these chips, we shall not go; if I get up, we'll go," he said. At his fourth song, the men clapped their lips and the women gave a loud cheer. Then he climbed the chips, holding a bird wing in each hand and imitating flight. He was tired out before he reached the top. When he had got quite to the top, he laid down his wings and took his shield. "Now then, when I sing the fourth time, I'll send my shield rolling. Then, men, keep clapping your mouths; old men, sing praise songs; women, give your call and make plenty of noise. If, when I throw the shield, the side with the drawing touches the ground, we shall not go [to attack the Cheyenne]; if the drawing remains on top, we'll go." He sang and sent his shield rolling. The men clapped their lips, there were praise songs, and the women gave their call with a loud noise. This shield went wobbling from side to side. Then the drawing was lying on the upper side.

Sore-belly rose and began to sing a praise song: "ā hahé! My dear Crow, hahé! Do you not see them? As I threw my shield, the people on the opposite side were lying dismembered everywhere. As far as my eyes could see, not a single one of you was killed." The Crow remained silent, they did not believe him. They were thinking, "We are about to meet a host of enemies, how is it possible that none of us should be killed?" They went away, Sore-belly in the lead. He warned them not to shoot at little birds. As they were moving along, a meadow lark came flying close to the face of a woman named Likes-the-old-women. She was angered and struck it dead. "Sore-belly, I have just killed a little bird," she said. Sore-belly said, "I ordered you not to do it, yet you have killed it, I can do nothing about it."

Sore-belly now unfolded his plan. He was going to send a few active young men to lure the Cheyenne into an ambush. There were two river-beds, and he filled both with men for a great distance. At the junction there was a big hill. The decoys were to keep clear of the coulées and to draw the enemy on through the intervening territory. The main body saw the Cheyenne coming. Sore-belly urged them to hide till they got near the hill, then they were suddenly to cut off the rear of the Cheyenne from the van. The Crow hidden in the riverbeds then suddenly rushed up and attacked the enemy, who tried to retreat. "It was just like a whirlwind, there was dust and fog everywhere, and the report of guns was heard till the dust settled." Double-face, Eager-to-die, Plays-with-his-face, Passes-women all attacked the enemy. The Crow pursued the Cheyenne, killing them as they went along.

The chief of the Cheyenne was named Striped-elk. He scolded his followers because they had not obeyed his warning against giving chase to the small Crow party. The Crow saw him from a distance and recognized him. They hated him because of the way he had abused Crow captives. Thus, a story was current that a Crow woman had been made to climb a tall cottonwood tree, which was then chopped down. One Crow, Sits-in-the-middle-of-the-ground, struck his side, produced a magical bullet and powder, then shot at the Cheyenne chief. Though beyond the range of an old-fashioned gun, Sitting-elk was hit. He tottered on his horse amidst the mouth-clapping of the Crow and fell to the ground. His companions fled. The Crow ran towards him, took his scalp, and captured his horse. They riddled Sitting-elk with shots and crushed his skull into fragments.

Sore-belly said, "It is enough, let us stop." Others wanted to pursue the fleeing Cheyenne: "This is the first chance we have had, let us go right away, take their children, their wives, their horses, their property." But Sore-belly insisted, and they stopped. "How many have we killed?" they asked. They turned back and began to count up to a hundred. Then some one said, "Well, stop, it is dangerous [to go on]." They had not counted half of the slain. Then all met. "Well, it seems none of us has been killed." The younger brother of the old woman who had killed the meadow lark was missing; they did not know whether he had been killed or not. No one else was killed, only some men were wounded, and some horses. "They reached camp, they were happy, they had had their revenge. They sang, they danced."

XI. Religion

IN a crisis an African Negro calls a diviner, who casts his sacred dice and by occult lore interprets the throw: such and such a one of his client's ancestors is angry and so many head of cattle must be slaughtered to appease his wrath. The Crow had no system of divination, never worshiped their ancestors, and made no bloody sacrifices. When hard put to it, the Indian tried to meet divinity face to face. A direct revelation without priestly go-between was the obvious panacea for human ills, the one secure basis of earthly goods. It might come as an unsought blessing, but only by a lucky fluke; hence a Crow strove for it by courting the pity of the supernaturals in the traditional way. To any major catastrophe, to any overwhelming urge, there was an automatic response: you sought a revelation. Every Crow, battered by fortune, writhing under humiliation, or consumed with ambition set forth on the quest of a vision. To take a few random samples: A legendary hero who has been spurned by a supercilious beauty at once goes to a solitary rock, is blessed by a spirit, and becomes a great man. Another lover meets an elk, who teaches him to charm all women, so that the haughty maiden is now seized with an uncontrollable passion for her erstwhile victim. When a cruel chief steps on an orphan's neck, the poor boy at once gives notice to his kin: "My elder brothers, give me moccasins, give me arrows, I am going for a vision. Don't worry about me, some time I'll return." A bear takes pity on him, and enables him to turn the tables on his enemy. Again, when a Crow is killed in a clan feud, his brother forthwith departs; successively blessed by a bear, a jackrabbit, and a hawk, he returns to slay the murderer. A mythological gambler who has lost at play not only his property but his wife, seeks supernatural power, and by the grace of a white-headed eagle retrieves his losses. Finally, an orphan taunted for his poverty by a wealthy bully seeks redress in the mountains, gains the favor of several spirits, returns triumphant from the war-path, and confounds his enemy.

237

As success results from revelations, so conversely failure is due to their lack. "All who had visions," Little-rump told me, "were well-to-do; I was to be poor, so I had no visions." Yet all men want some measure of security in life, so Little-rump had at least substitutes in the form of dreams. As a member of the Tobacco society (see p. 274), he used to dream about his chapter's eponym, heard the Tobacco sing, and learned the songs. "Some of them," said he, "I consider sacred. When I hear a song and have good luck immediately after that, then I consider the song sacred." This statement is doubly significant. In native speech the same word—bacī'ri—applies to visions and dreams, but the Indians did not confuse an everyday dream with a revelation. It was only those dreams which were intrinsically stirring or proved harbingers of good fortune that stood as more or less equivalent to visions. Quite as typical is Little-rump's pragmatic attitude toward such experiences. The supreme test for both the dreamer and his tribe was whether a revelation "worked." Hardheaded empiricists, the Crow knew that not every one who claimed supernatural blessings could be signally successful. There were several explanations: either the visitant was not strong enough, or his protégé flouted his commands, or a being might maliciously deceive the god-seeker. "Sometimes everything told in a vision is false; perhaps some animal plays the part of another." There was no way of detecting such trickery beforehand: "They only find out from what happens later."

This attitude leads to a sturdy eclecticism. In 1887 Wraps-up-his-tail led an abortive uprising against the Government. He had gained a small following by demonstrations of miraculous power. Gros-ventre saw him paint his face by merely pointing his finger at the sun; Muskrat was present when he cut down pines by moving his sword, as he intended to do in mowing down the soldiers. Why, then, did he fail? "Half of his vision was true; in part he was fooled." And there was a second reason: "His vision was to come true in the spring when it thundered, but he waited until the fall."

In every generation, then, there were men with outstanding powers,—the medicine-men or batse' maxpe' (maxpe' = sacred, mysterious); but their fame rested on *proofs* of their worth. Dap'i'c was a great doctor because he had cured patients on the brink of death. Plenty-fingers, a contemporary of Medicine-crow's father, loomed in memory not because he claimed a bear revelation, but because he worked miracles by it. In midwinter he would produce turnips and sarvis-berries; he could transform bark into dry meat; bullet-proof, he merely spat on his hands when shot, and immediately recovered. Again, Gray-bull believed in Wants-to-live because of ocular demonstration. One night the two wanted to smoke but lacked the wherewithal, but Wants-to-live asked for some bark, shook it in the air, and produced some tobacco, which Gray-bull smoked. On another occasion, the same wonder-worker rolled mud into four balls, which turned into beads for Gray-bull to wear in his necklace.

Sometimes the shamans gave a public exhibition of their powers. Gray-bull saw a contest with the two sides laying wagers against each other. One medicine-man rose and said he would knock all his opponents over on one side with his hand. They began to sing against him and defied him, but he danced by the door and the fire, made a motion with one arm as if to push them, and all fell toward one side. The spectators cheered. Then one man from the other group got up, ran round the fire four times, hooted like an owl, and disappeared. "We did not know how he went up but heard him hooting from the top of the lodge." Whether such scenes are due to sleight-of-hand, hypnotism, collusion, or what not, thoroughly intelligent Indians accepted them at their face value and as proof of supernatural blessing.

Growing up with a firm belief in the all-sufficiency of personal revelations, youths sought them without any prompting by their elders. From the stories of renowned contemporaries and of mythical heroes they had learned that this was the way to make their mark. In later life it was usually some special reason, say, the desire for vengeance, or worry over a sick child, that drove a man to look for supernatural aid. In any case a Crow followed a well-established norm.

Most probably he would set out for a lonely mountain peak, fast, thirst, and wail there. The Crow word for the enterprise is birici'sam, which means, "not drinking water." Almost naked, the god-seeker covered himself with a buffalo robe at night as he lay on his back facing the east, his resting-place being framed by rocks. Rising at daybreak, he sat down towards the east. As soon as the sun rose, he laid his left forefinger on a stick and chopped off a joint. This he put on a buffalo chip and held it out towards the Sun, whom he addressed as follows: "Uncle (i.e. Father's clansman), you see me. I am pitiable. Here is a part of my body, I give it you, eat it. Give me something good. Let me live to old age, may I own a horse, may I capture a gun, may I strike a coup. Make me a chief. Let me get good fortune without trouble." Then, to quote from a legend: "The blood from his forefinger came in sprays. When the sun was further up, he fainted. The blood oozed out of him. That day he lay unconscious till evening. When it got cool, he rose. That night he was so cold he could not sleep. For all of three nights he had no vision whatsoever. On the fourth night he was so cold he could not sleep till midnight had passed; then he slept." And in his sleep he is taken into a tipi to receive his blessing.

Cutting off a finger-joint was so popular a form of self-mortification that in 1907 most of the old people I met were disfigured in this way, some of them, to be sure, because of the mourning ritual (p. 68). However, a man might prefer other austerities. On the eve of his trial he might plant a forked stick on a hill and go there the following morning with an old man who was to pray on his behalf. This mentor painted the faster with white clay, invoked the Sun, and pierced his ward's breast or back. By this perforation he fastened the visionary to the crotched pole and went home, while the younger man began to run round his post. When tired, he was allowed to sit down, then he would resume his running. Some tore through the flesh, others failed to do so. Then, in the evening, the old man returned, cut at the edge of the dry flesh, showed it to the Sun with another prayer, and once more withdrew. The visionary slept there for the night, and might then receive a revelation. Again, a faster sometimes cut off a piece of his flesh, possibly in the shape of a horseshoe, so that he might own horses.

When Flat-dog had his back pierced, a horse was tied to one side of it and a war-bonnet on the other. Towards evening the horse, getting thirsty and restive, jerked Flat-dog's skin. He pulled out the skewer to set it free. Worn out from his exertions, he fell asleep as one dead, then a man came to him, saying, "Now you will remain alive for a long time. You are poor now, but you are going to be a man of consequence. I'll cause you to live for a long time." In true experimental spirit Flat-dog added: "Today people speak of me as old, then I think of this statement."

Still different was Hillside's way: his brother pierced his back in two places and tied a buffalo skull to it. This he dragged all day outside the camp, though in sight of the people. "I started early in the morning and traveled all day with the skull; when the sun was low I was too weak to drag it any longer. I went to the mountain with it, my brother cut it off, and I slept on the skull for a pillow. It was raining hard. In my sleep I heard a man say: "Wait, poor fellow, you will eat now!" He had the foot of a buffalo on him. On the Pryor side I saw a large crowd of people with this person in the lead. When I was asleep, a buffalo came up and licked me. His hair was gray; this showed that I was to live to be an old man. His being leader showed that I was to be a leader of my people. The buffalo snorted while licking me. . . . I made a buffalo skin to represent my dream. While dragging the skull I was fasting. The buffalo was my real visitant; he had transformed himself into a person. On another occasion I dragged a skull."

In the Sun Dance (p. 298) both the pledger of the ceremony and a goodly number of volunteers fasted in public; and the former tried to work himself into a trance condition not essential for the ordinary vision. At the other end of the scale, both in shunning strenuous methods and in the modesty of the results, stood the custom of lying by the Tobacco garden after a planting (p. 238), a practice that might yield new Tobacco songs or dreams promising an abundant harvest.

Although the revelation was normally sought, Crow folktales bristle with unsolicited apparitions that opportunely rescue a hero from the brink of disaster. Nooks of the universe seem to harbor kindly beings who keep on the lookout for distressed mortals and extricate them from perilous situations. When a cruel stepfather throws a boy down a cliff, the victim's fall is broken by a ledge, where he clings to a pine tree till a being called Big-iron pities him, sends four mountain sheep to bring him down, gives him his own name, and grants him extraordinary powers. In another story a young wife is unjustly blinded, maimed, and cast out by her husband but befriended by his younger brother. When death seems imminent for both of them, a deer and an owl treat her while a mysterious stranger feeds the compassionate brother-in-law and shows him how to kill buffalo: "That's what you'll do too. I pitied you long ago, but never reached you. I am a snake." In a third tradition a fugitive about to freeze to death in a snowstorm crawls inside a buffalo carcass still warm; the buffalo snorts and promises that he shall live to be a toothless old man. In still another instance a pair of lovers are driven from camp by a tyrannous chief. On the point of starving they are befriended by a benevolent dwarf. When he takes the man to his home, a woman reproves him for the tardiness of the rescue: " 'Bring my son soon,' I said, you have done it late, they almost died."

Not all supernaturals are equally considerate and genial. Some complain of being disturbed by having to take cognizance of human woes. When a supernatural girl brings her protégé home, her father is a bit nettled at the break in his routine. "You have done wrong," he chides, "here we have been living in peace and now you have brought some one!" But his wife at once counters: "It is well, it is a good thing that she is bringing him."

Such experiences in critical situations are not wholly legendary. When a young boy, Lone-tree told me, he went on a war party. All his elders having been slain, the rest fled, himself being overtaken by a heavy thunderstorm. As he looked for shelter, a large white bird came from the clouds, the lightning flashing from his eyes. Hailstones were falling as big as a man's fist, but they left a circle clear around Lone-tree and the eagle. The bird said: "I live up in the heavens, I am going to adopt you." He came to him a second time and said, "Whatever you ask, we shall do it for you. I am the High Thunder." To symbolize the hail, Lone-tree thereafter wore a necklace of large white beads, and he also carried on his person the head of a bald-headed eagle. It was part of his power to make rain or hail and to stop a storm. When Short-bull offended him, Lone-tree declared, "You will nearly die this summer"; and his enemy was struck by lightning, but escaped with his life.

Full-fledged visions *may* come not only unsought, but without hardship or self-mortification. These, however, are windfalls capriciously granted, hence beyond normal expectation. One-blue-bead rather pharisaically gloated over his good luck: "Other people have to torture themselves; I never cut myself. My only

marks were those of arrows in battle." As a boy he had dreamt
of a Crow on a buckskin horse; the rider's face was painted red,
he wore a buckskin shirt, and a chicken-hawk feather was tied
to one of his shoulders. A voice said, "Chief Chicken-hawk is
coming from there now." One-blue-bead was warned against
eating meat with blood on it and has never touched it since.
When he went to battle he would tie a hawk feather to his back
and sing the song the bird-man had taught him. Hitherto he had
been poor and of no account. After the vision he struck three
enemies and became a distinguished man.

Buffalo and snakes, the chicken-hawk and the Thunderbird, a dwarf or a mysterious old man, may thus bestow favors
on mortals they pity. Often a visitant appears first as a man,
but later introduces himself as what he is, or actually assumes
his animal shape. Or, the song he teaches will define his nature,
which may likewise be announced by a voice. Besides his unsought Thunder vision, Lone-tree also came to see the Seven
Stars through deliberately fasting. First a man sat beside him,
offering food, but a voice warned him it was human flesh. Something at the back of Lone-tree's head whispered that the visitant
was the constellation, and when the mysterious person rose my
informant saw the Seven Stars hanging down the back of his
long braided hair.

Some sixty reports of such encounters, traditional or historical, bring out some significant facts and problems. Is there
one ultimate source of power? God-seekers invariably address
the Sun, and offer their flesh to him; and in one narrative the
Sun announces the advent of his servant, the Eagle or Thunderbird. Are, then, the Thunderbird and other visitants mere messengers and deputies of a great Sun god? Given our monothe-
istic bias, the inference seems natural, yet evidence for it is
almost wholly lacking. Always invoked, the Sun hardly ever
appears; and several dozen reports of apparitions by birds, buffalo, bears and less popular mammals contain no suggestion that
the visitants were sent by higher authority. In the overwhelming
majority of cases animals, dwarfs, and nondescripts confer boun-
ties in their own right, their independence being at times explicitly asserted. Scratches-face was the only informant who tried
to bring all mystic experiences under a common head: "Old
Woman's Grandchild told all the animals to help the people of

the earth, and that is why they appeared in these dreams. The animals gave power to these Indians." Since Grandchild is the son of the Sun, this view would ultimately trace all blessings to a solar deity, but it is clearly an anomalous position.

Yet the Sun was certainly the most dominant single figure of Crow belief. He was the first to be invoked for aid and had a monopoly of such offerings as albino buffalo and sweat-lodges. Anticipating what I have to say about Crow gods generally (see p. 251), I suggest that the Sun is an old tribal deity who looms preeminent in an individual's consciousness *except* when ousted from that position by a guardian spirit. Such a one assumed the position of a special providence, was regarded as the visionary's "father" and sometimes formally adopted him as a "son,"—a pattern for all ceremonial transfers (p. 249). To this familiar a Crow looked for protection and guidance,—above all, in the situations indicated by his revelation. How this "father" compared in strength with the Sun or the patrons of other Indians, was a problem that did not spontaneously arise. It became significant only when and if there was a clash of interests; and then the assurance with which a Crow relied on his individual patron against the rest of the universe, conceivably including the Sun himself (see p. 253), was amazing.

Supernaturals may come to loggerheads on behalf of their mortal sons as Ares and Pallas contended over Trojan and Greek heroes. At a trial of strength referred to about the middle of the last century one shaman began to cough, spitting out supernatural worms that rapidly grew in numbers and advanced against his opponent. But his rival merely struck his side, whence issued a little woodpecker that devoured the worms. If a man only had confidence in his "father" he might snap his fingers at the most dangerous of other powers. Big-iron (p. 241), whom tradition puts ten generations before the coming of the whites, received a club from his supernatural old man. Once it was thundering, but Big-iron sallied forth and defied the Thunder, who vainly tried again and again to throw lightning at him. "The fourth time Big-iron took out his club and pretended to throw it at the lightning. Then the clouds all burst up and nothing but the blue sky was to be seen."

Yet frequently the supernaturals cooperate, as in the doctoring of the maimed and blinded woman (p. 241). Sometimes distinct beings of one species jointly bless a person,—seven cranes or seven bulls, four men, or a human couple. In mythology a veritable relay of birds and beasts may succor a hero in distress; and in the Twined-tail story appears the principle of *noblesse oblige;* the hero's patron wants to get for his child some extra power, so he summons an old man: "Yonder is a man; *he* has a child and has invoked me [on his child's behalf], now *I* will invoke *him.*"

Nothing prevents a man from gaining power from several independent supernaturals. Lone-tree had the Seven Stars as well as the Thunderbird for his patrons; and the legendary Raven-face was blessed successively by a bear, a rabbit, and a deer. One version of the story has its amusing side. As the hero walks along, the rabbit, pursued by the bird of prey, leaps inside his blanket. The hawk offers to adopt Raven-face if he will surrender the fugitive. But the rabbit says, "Don't do it. *I* am the more powerful. Take some snow from that drift and give it to him, let him eat *that.*" The hero throws the snow at the hawk, and as he watches it, it turns into a rabbit, which the pursuer eats. Thus, Raven-face gets the power of both animals.

The nature of a blessing often corresponds to the "father's" natural gifts. Lone-tree became a weather magician because the Thunder had adopted him. A deer says to Raven-face: "Of all things on this earth that step on the ground there is nothing that beats me in running. By that save yourself in time of trouble." Similarly, Humped-wolf, having met a buffalo, becomes heavy and slow in battle, so that no matter what happens he shall not run away.

This type of revelation merges into another, in which the patron confers not merely the gifts of his species but his individual status or capacity. Humped-wolf's buffalo sees him worrying over a wound and opens its mouth, which proves to be toothless. "You shall be the same as myself. . . . You cannot die until then (when you have no more teeth). That is the first thing I will give you." So the buffalo-man who blessed Hillside had gray hair and was leading a large crowd of people: ". . . this showed that I was to live to be an old man. His being leader showed that I was to be a leader of my people." Again, Full-mouth-buffalo, returning to camp, is caught by a bear. "He lifted me up so that I could see all the earth. He made me touch his teeth;

he had none at all. 'You may jump among high cliffs or do what you please,' said he, 'you cannot die. When you have no more teeth and all your hair is white, you shall fall asleep without awaking.' " Medicine-crow's stepfather almost duplicated this legendary experience. "A bear jumped up and caught him. He thought he was being killed, but the bear held him up and asked whether he could see all the world. 'Yes.' Then the bear said, 'Put your fingers into my mouth.' The bear had no teeth." On the same principle, the benevolent Dwarf of a myth, whose body is "of stone," transfers his own invulnerability to the poor man he befriends: "Now *your* body is of stone."

But whether the visitant transmits his individual powers or not, he commonly employs a transparent symbolism to indicate the nature of his gift. Bull-all-the-time gained a doctor's powers while asleep in his tipi. He saw a horse fastened to a rope, which was lengthened up to him, and simultaneously heard a person sing. He was told to treat the sick; an old man with a pipestem was standing over a recumbent patient and blew over him through the pipe; the sick man rose and my informant saw all the sickness come out of the patient's blood. He showed me the pipestem thus revealed to him. The horse stood for the horses he was to get as fees. Arm-round-the-neck had a similar promise of wealth: "I dreamt someone was kicking my foot and there were horses all round me with ropes to their necks and fastened to my body. I heard someone say, 'Wherever you go, you shall have horses.' Ever since then I have had horses. I think this dream was given me by dogs. I was walking, followed by several dogs. I lay down under a tree, and fell asleep, with the dogs lying round me about the tent. So I thought they took pity on me and gave me horses."

Sometimes the circumstances of an apparition are set forth in simple terms involving a mere vision or audition, the adoption formula, and a few instructions and taboos by the supernaturals. Gray-bull had inherited his grandfather's sacred bundle and went out to fast with it. "I saw a bird flying over me in a circle. It descended and went down into a canyon whistling. On both sides there were rocks. The rocks began to shoot at the bird but failed to hit it, so that it came out unhurt. . . . I did not know that I could not be shot until long afterwards. I was never shot. I kept my dreams secret, for I was afraid if I told them I might get shot. Once many Piegan were lying under a pine tree. One was some distance in front of us. . . . He shot at me when I was just above him but he did not hit me. . . . That night I dreamt and someone said to me, 'Don't you know that you cannot be shot?' "

Gray-bull's contemporary, Scratches-face, after much hemming and hawing, divulged the following experience. After chopping off the customary finger-joint, offering it to Old Woman's Grandson, and swooning from loss of blood, he had heard a person clearing his throat, the snorting of a horse, then a human voice. "I saw men riding on horses . . . I heard little bells. They were not men or horses but shadows of these. One man was riding a bobtailed horse and had painted his horse with a lightning mark on all four legs. . . . His rear braid reached the ground, the rest of his hair was clipped short. 'I will show you what you want to see. You have been poor, so I'll give you what you want.' . . . All the trees and everything growing around there then turned into men and began shooting at them. . . . The dust flew up to the sky. It flew up again on the east side of the horizon, where the riders had gone, and there I heard a lot of talking. . . . They came and passed behind me. I heard them yelling and whistling. They came and stood in front of me. The rider of the bobtail said to me, 'If you want to fight all the people of the earth, do as I do and you will . . . not be shot.' All the six horsemen started eastward. The rider of the bobtail held a spear; it was like fire. They were shooting as before. This rider knocked the people down with his spear. . . . Then followed a hailstorm. The hailstones were as big as my fist and knocked down those shooting at the horsemen. I saw them riding around in the storm. This storm was the Thunder and helped the six riders; it was caused by a man with wings. When I went out . . . against an Indian tribe up north and fought in battle, I did just what I had seen in my dream. . . . I was not shot. They killed an enemy; I struck him first. I fasted in the spring when I was eighteen years old. Ever since then I have owned good and fast horses. . . . I prayed for a good-natured and hard-working woman; my present wife . . . is like that."

A suggestive variation of this experience is attributed to Andicicopc. The spokesman of his visitants urges several of them successively to give his "child" their power, they turn into birds, and the trees, transformed into enemies, shoot off some of their feathers. The last one transforms himself into a screech-owl, remains unscathed, and henceforth the visionary was bullet-proof.

Visions, then, were the basic means of controlling life, and virtually every man tried to secure one. Yet there were men like Little-rump who failed even after repeated self-mortification. They were, we may guess, folk unsuggestible even in fasting and solitude or in other ways disqualified for the part of seers. More numerous, I take it, were those who gained supernatural experience of a sort but not of the kind backed by outstanding success; reliance on their revelation might thus be tempered by a measure of hard-headed skepticism. Yet all men crave the life values, so the Crow fell back upon the notion that supernatural power could be transferred: the vision still remained its fountain-head, but its benefits could be transferred by purchase or inheritance. These practices were tied up with a number of significant conceptions.

In the first place, the feather, rock, or bundle that symbolized the power granted to a visionary had a potency in its own right. By teaching the relevant rules the owner could therefore bequeath or transfer it to a close relative, who thus became a beneficiary without himself enjoying direct spiritual contacts. For instance, Strikes-at-night had escaped poverty by obtaining a Horse medicine. When she showed it to me, its virtue, she explained, was still there, for her son Bull-weasel, over whose bed she kept the bundle, owned plenty of horses.

The idea of transmission appears again and again. The outsider who wished to buy especially valuable medicines was at first treated as an undesirable intruder. When Flat-head-woman wanted to gain part ownership of the Sacred Arrow the chief holder demurred: "Why do you want this so badly? You are not related to us, you are a different person altogether." Then Hillside, the speaker's brother and thus himself joint-owner, interceded, "He was the comrade of my dead younger brother. They loved each other, that's why I wish to give it to him. Don't say any more against it." Sometimes a person coveting a particular medicine slily got into the owner's good graces until native etiquette made refusal impossible. Thus, Strikes-at-night, when still destitute, found out that the owner of the

Horse bundle needed a new tent cover. Being a good tanner, she offered to assist in the preparation of the hides, which she tanned whenever the owner brought back hides from the chase. Thus, she tanned fifteen hides, sewed them together, and put up the tipi. Now the owner's wife asked what pay she would like to get. Then Strikes-at-night explained that she was poor because her husband was blind and that she wanted to acquire the Horse medicine. The other woman got angry: "If you had told me before, I should never have let you finish the hides. Now I can hardly refuse you." For a long time she remained silent, at last she asked my informant to bring her husband. She told the couple that she had hitherto refused to adopt any one. However, "Now you have worked hard on this tent and finished it. I have thought it over and I will give it to you." Strikes-at-night added: "The other people were telling me I was very cunning because of the way I got the medicine. I had merely followed my husband's directions, but they all laid it to me."

In other words, power with its symbols could be transferred in whole or in part. That compensation should be paid for the benefit of a vision was, indeed, so firmly rooted an idea that some ceremonial privileges had to be paid for even if a son got them from his own parent. However this be, the Crow could indefinitely extend the range of beneficiaries from a vision. In such cases the visionary (or transferror) was conceived to stand to the purchaser in the same ceremonial relationship as the supernatural being to the visionary: as the supernatural adopts the visionary as his "child" so the owner of a medicine becomes the buyer's "father."

Every sacred object was revealed in a vision, but it could also stimulate a vision, as in Gray-bull's case (p. 246). Child-in-the-mouth told me of a corresponding experience. He was once so poor that he had to travel afoot. He was not yet a member of the Tobacco order, but his mother-in-law had inherited a Tobacco necklace and through her daughter she sent my informant out fasting with it. He was blessed by an aged couple, who promised him wealth and good luck generally. He subsequently went to war, struck coups, captured guns, and was never poor thereafter. Flat-head-woman's case was similar. He had received a sacred arrow from the owners of the Arrow bundle. When they felt that he knew the associated rules, they sent him out on his own. To quote him: "I was now to have visions of my own. I did not see an arrow as they did, but a long species of grass. I would see the stalk flying like an arrow and follow it with my eyes till it alighted somewhere, then I would go thither. From now on everything depended on myself. I had visions of different things. I made a little notched stick about four inches long myself, because I had a vision to that effect. If the enemy had stolen our horses and I put this on their tracks, they would sleep too long or be otherwise delayed, so we would catch up if I led the party."

The sacred objects revealed either singly or in combination as "bundles" may be regarded as essentially fetiches. Even when not actually manufactured, they are generally dressed up, as in the case of sacred rocks (see p. 261) or arranged; and they unquestionably are regarded with awe and are often invoked. In other words, the Crow personify inanimate objects and invest them with supernatural power. This is not pantheism, for I do not believe for a moment that they consistently elevate all objects of the external world. It is rather that *potentially* anything whatsoever can be brought within the sphere of the mysteriously potent. Because a chickenhawk feather appeared at the back of a visitant's head, the visionary looks for a feather of the same type, wears it in battle, and prays to it, as did One-blue-bead. But he would not pray to any other kind of feather, though he certainly recognized that others, on the basis of *their* revelations, might venerate whatever *they* had seen. Thus, the owners of a sacred Arrow bundle took it on their war parties. To quote one of them: "When we saw the enemy, we took it out and prayed to it. . . . This spring, when Flat-head-woman seemed to be dying, they opened it for him and prayed on his behalf." According to Hillside, the Seven Stars had given this bundle to his brother with an appropriate song. But it was the arrows themselves that were invoked, received offerings, spoke to Flat-head-woman and laid down rules for his conduct; and through their power, he believed, the Dakota had failed to destroy the Crow. A similar shift appears in the very instructive sweat-lodge prayer already quoted for its literary interest (p. 115). Generically, a sweat-lodge is considered an offering to the Sun, but in this particular case the sweat-lodge itself is supplicated, and so

are the willows composing it, nay, even the charcoal and fat in it.
I interpret this to mean that inanimate things can become per-
sonified, holy, and for the time being divine through their contact with a mystic or awe-inspiring context. Whether any other
worshiper would make a similar extension, whether even the
same man would subsequently deify charcoal and fat in similar
situations, is doubtful. We are, I think, dealing with nonce-gods
created by a momentary impulse but one none the less real at the
time and none the less illuminating as to the potential range
of Crow worship.

What holds for inanimate things is equally applicable to the
animal kingdom. No Crow worshiped on principle the entire
fauna of his country. But accounts of recent and legendary
visions prove that no species can be ruled out as a possible
source of power. Not only such impressive species as the bear,
buffalo, and eagle, but prairie-chickens and blackbirds, lizards
and weasels, even ants and bees, figure as helpers in particular
situations. The Crow world-view, in other words, precludes nothing from the range of the mystically potent, but the individual
consciousness ascribed power to a relatively narrow selection
of beings, their identity being determined by chance experience.

To discuss Crow religion in terms of a definite pantheon
would therefore be preposterous. Crow "gods" are not clear-cut
beings with sharply defined cosmic or social functions. Divine
power is not concentrated in a few major personalities, let alone
a single supreme ruler, but diffused over the universe and likely
to crop up in unexpected places. A Crow does not first envisage
a god and then worship him; he starts with the thrill, with the
sense of a supernatural agency, and objectifies his emotional
stirrings. To us the indifference as to the precise source of power
is almost incredible. Thus, as already noted, Hillside derived the
Arrow bundle from the Seven Stars, who had given it to his
brother. But Flat-head-woman, who became a part owner
through Hillside's intercession, traced its origin to a black-haired
but white-faced female visitant. There *had* been a primary vision,
the boon conferred—the Arrow bundle—had proved its potency,
and that was the really important thing.

This statement, roughly accurate though it is, requires some
qualification. There are certain supernaturals that appear with
tolerable frequency both in ritual and visionary experiences,—

notably the Morning Star (usually identified with Old Woman's Grandson), the Thunder (usually in eagle shape), buffalo, bears, various birds, and above all the Sun, who comes as near as any being to the dignity of a supreme god. Yet though the Sun (a'xace) is invoked in oaths and in the vision quest, though albino buffalo and sweat-lodges are regularly dedicated to him, though he sporadically figures as superior even to such obviously strong powers as the Thunder, the picture formed of him is singularly puzzling. Is he, or is he not, equated with The One Above (bā'kukure') whom the Indians sometimes addressed in prayer? Probably so, but it is impossible to tell with assurance. Is he the originator of the Indians and the shaper of the earth? That, too, remains a problem. There is no question whatsoever that these functions are assigned to Old Man Coyote; and if the Sun and Old Man Coyote are one and the same, then obviously the Sun is the creator. Now, Medicine-crow, one of the most devout and conservative of my informants, constantly wavered as to this crucial point in his version of cosmogony. Others took sharp issue with such identification. The Sun, said White-arm, was regularly supplicated, Old Man Coyote never; according to One-blue-bead, Old Man Coyote was the creator of everything— the equivalent of the white man's God (akbā'tat-di'a, The Maker of Everything), while the Sun was distinct.

There is a real dilemma here. To treat "Sun" and "Old Man Coyote" as synonyms does indeed reserve for the single most eminent figure of ritual the rôle of creator. But it also saddles the Sun with all the grossness, the low cunning, the lechery of the Trickster, who constantly defies the most sacred native institutions, such as the incest taboos. Further, it would degrade the Sun in point of sheer power, for Old Man Coyote is repeatedly himself duped, exposed, humiliated. I accept the majority verdict—confirmed in myth—that the Sun is distinct from the Trickster, but that leaves him an extremely vague personality. Generally the suggestion is certainly that of a benignant and powerful supernatural, the father of Old Woman's Grandson (Morning Star), a being more likely to be invoked than others *in the absence of a specific tutelary.* When such a patron appears, the Sun recedes into the background of the religious consciousness. To quote One-blue-bead: "The only thing I prayed to specially was my feather. I might pray to the Sun any time." That is to say, in a particular crisis, a Crow was likely to rely on his *providentia specialissima,* the visitant of his revelation, the "medicine" then conferred upon him. Lacking a condition of peculiar stringency or if no specific medicine was his, he would fall back upon the most commonly revered tribal deity. The Crow were not philosophers but opportunists. They were rarely bothered by the question how a sacred feather might be metaphysically linked with the Sun. As already noted, supernaturals often appear as though belonging to different universes, as wholly incommensurable quantities when not brought into direct collision. Indeed, comparatively well-defined gods are sporadically impotent in the face of obscure agencies. The legendary medicine man Big-iron mocks the Thunder with impunity. Whence his assurance and strength? From an otherwise unmentioned supernatural old man who had given him the blessing of four successive lives. Old Woman's Grandson, the child of the Sun, conquers all the monsters infesting this earth, but flees in horror from the foetus of a calf. The explicit explanation is that everyone is afraid of something! So the Sun himself is described in one tale as petulantly starving the Crow because his mistress is enamored of an orphan boy; and what is more, he is *worsted* because the human hero magically lures game to the camp. In short, there is no absolute ascendancy in the Crow universe; supernaturals represent shifting values, determined empirically, case by case, via a pragmatic test.

From the foregoing it is clear that religion and ethics are largely divorced. The really vital social canons, such as the incest taboos, the laws of chivalry, and the ideals of chastity, have no supernatural sanctions. It does not shock the Crow sense of congruity to have old Man Coyote lust for his daughter, or the Sun eat human flesh. When a prospective visionary calls upon the supernaturals to favor him, he hardly ever stresses his moral worth but his pitiable plight. What he begs for is not moral elevation but some material benefit; and it is compassion that animates his patron in granting it. Often, to be sure, the visitant lays down rules of conduct, but they have no bearing on social considerations, they are capricious taboos of a dietary or ritualistic character. Flat-head-woman's arrow forbade him to throw anything in the lodge harboring it lest he lose his property; and on pain of blindness he was never to cook fat above a paunch or to throw ashes from his tipi. Consistently with this point of view, good intentions were no safeguard against the consequences of transgression. A man who unwittingly ate forbidden food or whose visitors broke rules imposed upon him in the conduct of his lodge had to bear the brunt of the threatened catastrophe.

The individual Crow seems absolutely free in his religious life. He may believe what he will as to creation, cosmology, and the hereafter; he is not coerced to worship this or that deity; he is apparently guided only by his own specific vision, personally or vicariously experienced. Yet in reality he cannot escape the subtle influences of social tradition. For when this subjective experience of the vision is scrutinized, what do we find? Men covet it for the social eminence it brings, seek it by techniques traditionally handed down, sell its benefits according to established usage. What is more, the very details of the mystic experience are not spontaneous growths, but in large measure recombinations of the same old motifs. If the visions were really independent psychic manifestations, how came it that visitants always adopted their favorites as their "children," that they usually came after four nights of waiting, imposed generically similar taboos on different visionaries? Wraps-up-his-tail, killed in 1887, could paint his face by merely pointing his finger at the Sun, but the very same power is granted to Twined-tail in a folkstory. Gray-bull, fasting with his grandfather's medicine, saw a bird flying; the rocks turned into enemies shooting at the bird, but failed to hit it. Thus he gained invulnerability. But that is virtually the very thing that befell Scratches-face: in his experience equestrian visitants are shot at by trees but remain unscotched. What is more, the essentials are told circumstantially of an anonymous hero. In short, the visionary does not receive an individual vision. The way he gets his revelation and its very content as well are determined by the ideas current in Crow society, though of course remodeled by his individual fancy and the needs of the moment.

Compared with beliefs and practices of other natives the whole world over, Crow religion exhibits most of the features found elsewhere but with a difference of emphasis. Of the attitude toward the Sun I have already written at length. Ancestorworship is indisputably lacking, but few of the other major religious manifestations are wholly absent. Thus, nothing has been said of local genii, yet Pryor creek was conceived as the special haunt of a benevolent dwarf. The native name for this watercourse is "Arrow creek," the vicinity being called "They shoot at rocks" because Indians passing by would make an offering of arrows to the dwarf, shooting them into the crevices. My informant Bear-crane had himself done so in his younger days. Again, while the rôle of ghosts has been discussed, I have not referred to the deification of a definite person after death,—not of course as the ancestor of an individual or group, but as a supernatural for the tribe at large. Yet there is one clear instance. When the great medicine-man Big-iron died, he declared that the Crow were to lay down presents at his tree-burial—specifically beads—and he would fulfill their prayers; and the people obeyed his commands. This same character illustrates another unique conception. His supernatural patron had granted him fourfold life and shown him how to rejuvenate himself. Accordingly, when he grew old, he had himself thrown into the water, became young again, and lived until the end of his fourth period. Divination is rightly considered atypical for American Indians, but forms of augury do occur (p. 234). Fetichism flourishes in the form defined (p. 250). Finally, imitative magic is a common if unobtrusive element. A game-charmer puts a buffalo skull with its nose toward the camp and reverses it when buffalo are no longer needed. Tobacco dance celebrants raise their drumsticks to further the growth of their weed. Sun-dancers blacken their paraphernalia to suggest the blackening of the face that betokens a slain enemy.

My conjectures are these. The Crow world-view is consistent with a great many of the beliefs typical of primitive tribes generally, hence sporadically similar notions arose among them. Some of these conceptions, such as imitative magic, are presumably of hoary antiquity, and they have persisted among the Crow irrespective of subsequent notions. However, they have not retained their ascendancy as in other areas. The hypertrophy of the individual vision represents an overlay that has pushed other beliefs into the background, encroaching even on the widespread American worship of the Sun. Visions themselves are doubtless very old, but the one-sided stressing of individual visions as the source of power is a comparatively late development that largely remolded the rationale of Crow religion.

XII. Rites and Festivals

Acts that are purely matter-of-fact with us are often matters of ceremony with the Indian, who may insist on tedious sequences prescribed by ritualistic etiquette, as in the routine for important events on a war party, in doctoring the sick, or even in smoking. It was proper, Gray-bull told me, to point a pipe first upward, then to the ground, next to the four quarters of the globe; and in so doing he himself would pray to the winds of the cardinal directions. I once asked Medicine-crow to show me his sacred shield. He consented, but did not at once unwrap it. First he got some live embers and burnt wild-carrot root for incense, allowing the smoke to play on the shield. Then he raised the shield a little, again lowering it. Once more he raised it, a little higher than before; and he thus continued until the fourth time, when he raised the shield high above his head. Only after these preparations he was ready to remove the buckskin coverings.

The use of incense is typical. In 1910 I bought a weasel-skin stuffed with buffalo hair; its original owner, a noted brave, had taken it with him on trips against the enemy, unwrapped it, smoked it with incense, and held it toward the hostile camp. So with all manner of sacred objects. The Crow cherished curiously shaped rocks called bacõ′ritsi′tse and ascribed to each its characteristic incense,—either of sweet grass or wild-carrot. In 1914 Flat-head-woman showed me his sacred Arrow bundle, but not before preparing incense and smoking each end of the package.

Equally characteristic is Medicine-crow's repeated lifting of the shield. Four is the mystic number. In one creation story three birds fail to bring up mud from the depths, finally the hell-diver succeeds. Old Man Coyote commends him, saying, "To every undertaking there are always four trials; you have achieved it." In harmony with this principle many rituals are prolonged by a fourfold performance of significant acts; and there are often deliberately three feints or mistrials before execution.

When Strikes-at-night was adopted into the Horse Dance, she did not at once accept the proffered eagle head and tail. Ostensibly she was too nervous to take them, as though restrained by a magic spell. "I was shaking, afraid I should fail the second time. The . . . woman made an eagle come out of her own mouth [see p. 264], which excited me still more. It was like some one seizing me by the neck and choking me. I failed the second time. They started the third song. Every one was scolding me: 'You've been working to get the medicine, now you have a chance, why don't you get it?' The third time incense was burnt over the woman to make the eagle recede [see p. 265], which gave me time to brace up. The fourth time the man sat down by the door, and his wife was standing alone. At the fourth song she whistled and made the eagle wobble. I could hardly move. I stopped dancing when she got close, seized her by the armpits and gently rubbed down her arm. Every one was glad and I heard expressions such as, 'The poor woman got it after all'." After this four songs were sung.

To take another example of ritualization, the Crow do not treat a vapor bath as a form of ablution but as an offering to the Sun. The dome-shaped willow sweat-lodge (awu'sua) was thus put up only as a serious undertaking; people would not sweat themselves except ceremonially, when prompted by a dream or under the guidance of a properly sanctioned tribesman. In the old days it was largely reserved for the aged and for votive performances. A sick man would say, "If I get well by fall, I'll make a sweat-lodge"; or a warrior, on setting out, would thus address the Sun: "My Uncle, if I bring back good booty, I'll make a sweat-lodge." The sweating, accordingly, was linked with much solemnity.

In the center of the dome-shaped structure there was a pit for the rocks, which were heated outside for hours and then put in with a forked stick. Their very presence was enough to produce a terrific heat. The celebrants stripped to their gee-strings, then an attendant covered the willow frame with robes or blankets so that it was pitch dark inside. From a vessel with water the headman sprinkled four cupfuls on the rocks. Steam at once began to rise so that the atmosphere became almost unbearable. In 1910 I sweated with Medicine-crow, One-star, and Plenty-hawk and found it so stifling that I clandestinely raised the flap of one blanket under cover of the darkness and thrust my nose into the air. After a while an attendant would remove the blankets, so that the inmates, now streaming with perspiration, could cool off. Now one of them prayed: "Sun, we are doing this for you! May we live until the next winter!" Every one, inside and outdoors, cried, "Thanks! May we live until then!" Once more the covers were put on, and seven cupfuls thrown on the rocks, followed by more sweating, and another prayer. There came again a brief respite, and when the frame was covered ten cupfuls were poured on the rocks. Then followed a final intermission, whereupon "uncounted" cupfuls were thrown, another man uttered his wish, and the blankets were flung aside. The sweaters, who had been scourging themselves with buffalo tails to perspire still more, dashed into a near-by creek, or, in the winter, rolled about in the snow.

Sweating, tobacco-smoking, the use of incense, and the fourfold repetition of acts or songs all enter conspicuously into Crow ceremonialism, which is best approached by some of its simpler manifestations.

Meat Festival

In the winter a person so prompted in a dream played the part of host at a Cooked Meat Singing (irū′k-ōce waraxu′a), a medley of social and ritualistic customs, in which sacred rocks (bacō′ritsi‛tse) and a bear image played an important, though obscure, part.

Once Sitting-elk's wife dreamt about the ceremony and told her husband, who the next day notified the guests. Each was to bring mashed bones and cooked meat. The hostess boiled the bones in a large kettle to extract the grease and thoroughly soaked the meat with it, which was then carefully stowed away. After dark Sitting-elk went to the lodge of each guest and from the outside said, "I sing for you." The guests came with their wives, bringing whatever sacred rocks they owned. A buffalo-calf skin was spread between the door and the fire. Beginning at the left of the door, the visitors passed their stones from hand to hand. Sitting-elk took the first one, laid it on the skin, and smoked it with wild-carrot root incense. He treated all the stones in the same way, putting one beside the other. He also smoked a round rattle with incense, gave it to his neighbor, and told him to sing. This man also received a pipe of tobacco to be smoked. Before singing he gave Sitting-elk a present. Each man in turn sang,—songs connected with war or the clubs or of sacred character. Thus the rattle passed from hand to hand. Whenever a captain got the rattle, the fire was put out and he received a special pipe; this honor was conferred on only four men. After smoking, one of these leaders would hold the pipe in both hands and rise. Sitting-elk walked over to him and seized the pipe. The captain said, "I dreamt that you and your family would reach another year in good luck!" The host replied, "Thanks!" (ahŏ!), and sat down. When the last man had sung, the rattle was returned to the host, who passed it to his neighbor, a man with bear-medicine. It was now time to distribute the meat loaves, which were of four grades in size. The man now holding the rattle sang a bear song, faced the meat and holding out one hand towards it, palm down, he divided the food among the guests, giving every one a sample of each grade of loaf. The bacō'ritsi'tse were returned to their owners, then all went home.

Before singing, each guest gave away property to a paternal uncle (a'sa'ke) or aunt (isbāxi'a), which of course may mean merely a member of the father's clan. This has already been described as a basic Crow usage. At one of these feasts arranged by Muskrat a man whose wife had brought her baby got up and announced, "This baby has given a horse to its father's brother." Similarly, a war leader whose son was present declared, "This boy has given six dollars to his father's clansmen." When the lights were put out he also gave a gun and a powder sack to one of his own a'sa'ke, saying, "I give these away because I want to sing." The next captain said, "Look outside whether any horse has been brought." They found a horse there, and he said, "I give it to my a'sa'ke. I want every one to keep still, so I can sing." Other guests gave their father's kin war-bonnets, money, blankets, leggings, and food. In return the clan nephew might get his paternal kinsman's share of pemmican.

Since the wives as well as the husbands gave away presents, and host or hostess likewise received gifts from all guests, this meat festival occasioned a considerable transfer of property.

Highly typical is the conception of married couples as units. Sitting-elk issued invitations because his *wife* had had a dream; and the guests brought their wives, each sitting behind her husband and in duty bound to join him in singing. If she failed him, her joking relatives at once asked, "What is the matter? Is she dumb (irī'se)?" The bear-medicine rattler was also accompanied by his wife in singing.

The mystic number is conspicuous. There are four captains and four kinds of meat-loaf, the hostess sometimes had four assistants, four buffalo-chips were put between the incense and the hide, the rattle was shaken over the incense four times, and the man who used it last sang four songs to the meat.

The invitation etiquette is interesting. The dreamer first issued a red stick to each guest. When the meat was prepared, he or she went to every one again, and repeated the formula, "I sing for you." It was proper to utter thanks and the stereotyped prayer that guest and host might jointly see such and such a season of the year. On this round all the sticks were collected and carried to the lodge. As soon as each guest arrived, one stick was removed from the batch. They waited for late-comers, but a person prevented from attending might send the host gifts and receive pemmican in return.

Even the office of tobacco-lighting, usually filled by a captain's son, was ritualized. When the pipe had been emptied, the Lighter held it out, saying, "Take your pipe." Both men then held it, the owner with his left hand first brushing down the Lighter's shoulder to his hand before he took the pipe away, while the Lighter prayed that they might live until such a season. The distribution of food, part of the Lighter's duties, was likewise conventionalized: the distributor crossed his arms so that the recipient at his right received a portion from the giver's left, and vice versa.

War psychology intruded even more than Sitting-elk's summary account suggests. The songs sung by a captain had a predominantly military setting: they belonged to his club or to a war party making a display of booty or a killing, or they might have been revealed to him in an audition as scout songs. Either he or the host—especially when stimulated by the gift of a horse —was likely to celebrate the deeds of those present. Again, when the host had laid the rocks down, he might indulge in a favorite Crow gesture: taking a pronged stick, he would point it toward some hostile tribe and say, "I poke it into their eyes" (ictu'a wapaxa'xiky). In the Sun Dance a virtuous woman pointing her prong at the main pole expresses a similar thought, but there it is relevant to the general purpose of the ceremony as a prayer for vengeance. However, such worthy sentiments are never out of place in a Crow performance.

But what about the sacred rocks? Their shape usually suggests some part of an animal's body, perhaps most frequently the head; probably they are ammonites. They are found accidentally, sometimes by the odor they emit, which at once indicates whether wild-carrot or sweetgrass incense is requisite. In a legend a boy who goes out fasting sees a light in the night and with some difficulty discovers the black bacō′ritsi‘tse as its source. He takes it home, hangs it up above his pillow, gets sweetgrass for incense, and puts it into a container.

In historical times Medicine-crow's mother had a similar vision. She had had trouble with her husband and went around wailing at night, when she suddenly saw something shining. She reached the spot, and it was a bacō′ritsi‘tse. Taking it up, she said: "Thanks! I am poor; this is fine." The rock spoke: "Go home, you will not be poor any more." She put it inside her dress. When she slept that night the rock sang: "Buffalo are plentiful, here are plenty. What are you worrying about? Of marriage with Looks-at-a-bull's-phallus you shall have your fill. Whenever one of you dies, that alone will divorce you." "Thanks!" she said. "The next night he will come in, bringing the child by the arm, he will take you back." "Thanks!" Her husband actually returned with their son. She showed him the rock and made him dream about all sorts of things. The rock spoke to him, telling him how to lead a war party and to lure game. At one time all the people were starving. Looks-at-a-bull's-phallus made buffalo tracks, sang his chant, and shook his rattle. The next morning wherever the Crow looked, there were buffalo. The medicine was thus proved genuine.

A little stone owned by Gray-bull and originally found by a child had grown to twice its earlier size, and by general agreement bacō′ritsi‘tse multiplied like living beings. When Medicine-crow's mother showed her husband the medicine, she had four stones, one suggesting a bird, another a buffalo, the third a horse, the fourth a person. They were light in weight early in the spring, but grew heavier by the summer; in the coldest winter there would be frost on them, for they breathed. These rocks told Medicine-crow's stepfather where the Crow should spend the winter so as to avoid a famine; and he would have a crier announce such instructions. Thus hard times were avoided. The medicine was good for warfare: the owner sent Medicine-crow and two others to get horses for him and they brought back a great many, all black. Once he sent out Takes-it-back-twice, giving him the bacō'ritsi'tse to take along. Unfortunately one of its horns was broken off, so he failed; the next time, however, he captured a white horse and gave it to the medicine-owner.

There was one peculiarity about this rock: it was never taken to a Meat Festival, because it tabooed Medicine-crow's parents and himself from eating tongues. At one of these feasts each bacō'ritsi'tse was passed around, each guest pressing it to his body or kissing it. Hence the danger of contaminating this particular rock could be avoided only by not bringing it to the Cooked Meat gathering.

Gray-bull showed me several of his bacō'ritsi'tse. One of them he, too, never took to a Meat Festival except when he himself played the host. It was shaped like a mule's hoof, and soon after finding it Gray-bull obtained three mules and got together a herd of one hundred and twenty horses. Another stone resembled a buffalo head, still another had horns and the semblance of eyes. His principal bacō'ritsi'tse, inherited from his stepfather, was kept in several cloth wrappers, the whole being stored in a rawhide bag of envelope shape. This stone was completely covered with buckskin, decorated with rows of beads. On one side, I was told, it bore natural horsetrack markings, on the other it suggested a human head; and a deer was also indicated. It always faced upward. As usual, there were trimmings of weasel skin, elk-teeth and similar offerings; also some sweetgrass. In the same container, but ranking as a distinct medicine, was the little stone that grew to twice its size. Gray-bull would pray to it as follows: "May I have horses and property, live till the next year, and prosper!" While wearing it round his neck, he had experienced all kinds of good luck; for instance, he had captured a rifle, two horses, and an eagle feasting on a buffalo.

Naturally, objects of such practical utility were treated with the utmost care and highly prized. Offerings of beads, decorative strips of skin, elk teeth and the like were wrapped up with these medicines and they were greased with castoreum. As in the case of Medicine-crow's and Gray-bull's principal rocks, they were usually inherited rather than bought from the discoverer. Looks-at-a-bull's-phallus refused to sell his bacō'ritsi'tse for ten horses. He sometimes opened the bundle to show it to close kin, but would not allow any handling. One informant described it as customary to unwrap the sacred rocks at the first thunder in the spring.

I bought several of the bacō'ritsi'tse, one for ten dollars, and declined another valued at thirty. Obviously even that price was in no way commensurate with its power in native belief. The sellers were young Indians who had inherited the stones but lost faith in their utility.

Clearly, the bacō'ritsi'tse are conceived not only as growing and multiplying organisms, but as powerful personal beings, that reveal themselves in experiences equivalent to visions. In Medicine-crow's version of the Creation myth their prototype is described as the oldest part of the earth, as a being that with several others existed independently of any creative act from without.

To combine this conception with a series of irrelevant religious and social usages, such as the bear effigy and the giving of presents to paternal kindred, is wholly congruous with Crow ceremonialism.

XIII. The Bear Song Dance

As the sacred rocks are the religious core of the Meat Festival, so the belief in bātsira'pe is the outstanding feature of the Bear Song Dance (naxpitse' icū'o disùa). The bātsira'pe is a mysterious animal or part of an animal or inanimate object that dwells within a person's body, emerges on some definite stimulus, and in most cases must be made to go back unless its host, who at once goes into a trance, is to come to grief. Generally he is restored by smoking him with incense. There were exceptional variations: Otter-chief, for instance, could not eat a cherry without going into an ecstatic condition and acting like a bear, yet he did this without exhibiting any part of a bear's body; and I heard of an old woman who on occasion would produce pieces of shell and give them away to the Crow for ear ornaments, without reabsorbing them. But the typical phenomenon was that defined above. It was noted by Maximilian among the Missouri tribes a hundred years ago. He learnt that many Mandan and Hidatsa harbored live animals, that one Indian sometimes felt a buffalo calf kicking around inside of him; and he actually saw a Hidatsa woman "dance a corncob out of herself," which proper treatment caused to go back again.

Precisely how the Crow conceived the phenomenon, I do not know. According to one informant, they did not believe that an entire animal dwelt inside a person's body, but only the part displayed,—also that in making a tail reenter his body the performer reduced it to a very small size. This sounds like a rationalization and hardly agrees with either Maximilian's Mandan information or other Crow data. Belden, writing in 1875, bases the whole Crow theory of disease on the bātsira'pe concept: all persons, he gathered, have tails in their bodies, and when these "get out of order" their owners get sick; vice versa, any cold, fever, or other affliction comes from an injury to the tail. This is certainly inaccurate (see p. 61), and we shall see that by no means all bātsira'pe are tails. However, Belden's description of what he *saw* is worth quoting:

"Several romping Crow girls being present at my quarters one day, one of them, for sport commenced tickling another, who could not bear to have any one touch her under the arms. The poor girl screamed frantically, and rolled over and over, but the other kept poking her in the ribs until she fainted outright. Basache, then, in great alarm, raised her up and called to me to bring the scented grass quickly; for the girl's tail was coming up in her throat and choking her to death. I brought the grass, of which Basache kept a good supply on hand, and lighting some of it, one held the fainting girl over it while the other threw a shawl about her head. She soon revived. . . ."

How does a person acquire a bātsira'pe? According to Graybull it entered his body if he kept medicine in his hair or might grow internally if he tortured himself by dragging buffalo skulls. Most Crows simply regarded a bātsira'pe as the result of a special form of vision. Of such visionaries I found Muskrat the most articulate, though not a wholly consistent informant in her several reports. An old couple had initiated her into the Weasel chapter of the Tobacco order and given her an emblem, which they later took away from her. She grieved over this and went to the mountains to fast. A cloud came up, so she sought a rock-shelter, where she lay down to sleep. A weasel appeared, stepped on her neck, and entered her stomach; she heard him whistling with all his might. He said, "This is what we want to give you." He gave her a whistle and sang this song: "The weasels are coming out; I'll make Tobacco come out." The weasel warned her not to allow any one to strike her kidneys, for whenever this happened she would go into a trance. This is why other people respected her and avoided bumping into her. Ever since then Muskrat had control over weasels, and she claimed that it was through her the Weasel chapter gained its renown.

Such experiences figure in other chapters of the organization. For example, Mosquito, adopted into the order by Muskrat's father, founded or remodeled a chapter because the Yellow-tobacco entered his body during a dream. At times it would temporarily come out of him. Two other Indians manifested the same power at Bear Song performances. Again, Fire-weasel was initiated by a man who had once wandered about mourning over a brother's death. He discovered a nest of eggs, one of which differed from the rest. He carried it off and dreamt about it. It entered his body through his mouth and thereafter always emerged at a certain song sung in the Tobacco dance. The feature was so conspicuous that the chapter, previously called Wolverene, was renamed after the Egg. Unlike most bātsira'pe owners, this man did not go into a trance during his exhibition.

A person was not limited to a single bātsira'pe. Muskrat claimed to have a horse as well as a weasel inside of her. She had been fasting once, when a gray horse went into her stomach. That is apparently why she was able to cure horses that had difficulty in urinating. She would chew tobacco and put it into a horse's mouth. "Whenever the Bear Song Dance is performed, I am forced over to the site. Once I was doing some beadwork while the Bear Song Dance was going on in another part of the camp. I sat down, paying no attention, but it was just as if some power forced me to go there. I threw off my blanket. I heard voices, 'There's one going already.' Before I arrived, I was out of my senses, and the tail of a horse came out of my mouth. I was married to Bad-man's father at this time. People were astonished to see this. They took warts from a horse's leg, made incense from it, smoked me with it, and this brought the horse-tail back into my body again. Even when children bump against me, this tail will come out, so I always keep some horse wart about me. If people with a bātsira'pe do not get proper incense in time, they die."

Arm-around-the-neck told of a remarkable case of multiple bātsira'pe: the man in question produced elk chips, white clay, black dirt, owl feathers, and "ground moss" leaves; in fact, some added a horse-tail, but *that* Arm-round-the-neck had not seen himself. The performer would not permit any one to touch him; if they did, elk chips came out of his mouth and he became ecstatic. The spectators would then light some powder and make him inhale the smoke, which made him come to.

Those who displayed horse tails owned many horses, while the exhibitors of buffalo tails were wound doctors (see p. 65).

Big-snake had seen bātsira'pe owners pull out of their mouths parts of a jack-rabbit, snake, horse tail, bull tail, eggs, eagle tail feathers, two owl species, a sparrowhawk, a crow, the performer's own teeth, and most commonly parts of a bear's body. One Plenty-bear was in the habit of showing bear's teeth, terrifying the onlookers, who would retreat till some one came with incense to burn over him. Big-snake's own wife sometimes had a swelling of the abdomen, whereupon blood would come gushing from her mouth. He treated this as an equivalent phenomenon, though not accompanied by any display.

In 1910 Cut-ear had the reputation of being able to make flannel come out of his mouth and of rolling it back again. He promised to give me a private show, but failed to appear at the time set.

To sum up. Bātsira'pe were shown at the Bear Song dance, but also at some Tobacco ceremonies, on the breach of special taboos, and perhaps not seldom merely in sleight-of-hand performances. Though Belden surely errs in crediting every Crow with a tail, evidently a fair number in every recent generation believed themselves to be hosts to some bātsira'pe. This may have rested on some mental idiosyncrasy. On the other hand, even Belden's report shows the individual under the spell of a traditional pattern: she faints when the conventional taboo is broken and she responds to the conventional treatment. Let us now see how this concept was fitted into the Bear Song dance.

This ceremony was held in the fall, for it is when the berries are ripe that the bears dance in the mountains. The Crow then set up a cottonwood post and fastened to it a tanned bear skin. A considerable quantity of pemmican or larded meat-balls was brought to the site, and the people formed a sizeable circle round the post. The dancers assembled in a tipi to dress up and, led by an old woman, marched toward the skin in single file, the men in the rear. They danced toward the skin, then backward again. The musicians sang a certain song, the Bear song; then all persons with bātsira'pe were irresistibly drawn towards the pole. Cuts-the-picketed-mule gave the following as the words of the song that made the bātsira'pe come out: "Look at Lodge Grass creek! The bear cub is there, its parent is here."

On one occasion a man wearing a robe over his head approached the skin and rubbed his face against it. He blew out red paint from his mouth and stood back; then the people saw a bear's teeth protruding from his mouth. This man was said to have once dragged a bear skin fastened to his back. Several bystanders put blankets over him, threw him on the ground, held him, covered him with a blanket, smoked him with wild-carrot incense, and finally gave him a big lump of pemmican to take home. Next a woman came. She did not rub her face against the skin but displayed a buffalo tail and white clay. She was not so wild as the man who took part. Some women seized her, made her sit down, and restored her with the same incense. The tail receded and she went off. Another old woman rubbed her face against the bear, showed the feathered tip of a stick and said it was a coup-stick. She was treated with sweetgrass. Then the first woman returned but now showed the tail of a gray horse. Another performer struck his side, and blew out three bird's eggs. The people examined them, and they were real eggs. Sweetgrass incense was made, the performer smoked the eggs with it, put them back into his mouth, and swallowed them. He got three pieces of pemmican. Sometimes more than ten persons performed in this way. Whatever pemmican remained fell to the share of the dancers and singers.

In this performance we note again a union of irrelevancies. The bear is a fairly frequent but by no means overshadowing figure among supernaturals who bless the Crow. A celebration in his honor is intelligible enough, but why it should be coupled with the bātsira'pe motive is far from clear. The marching to the site of the dance resembles—in simple form—the Tobacco procession: there is a preparatory tipi, a woman leads out of it, the men are in the rear, and all walk in single file to the dance ground.

XIV. The Sacred Pipe Dance

A LL Crow agree that the Sacred Pipe (ī'ptse waxpe') came from the Hidatsa in relatively recent times; and Mr. Curtis sets the date in 1825. In a way it remained an alien medicine in tribal consciousness, and many were afraid to own it for fear of breaking some of the taboos. In 1910 there were probably twenty-six owners in the whole tribe. Nevertheless, the ritual has played its part among the Crow and lingers on, so that in July 1931 I still saw a performance, though an indifferent one held in a circular shade instead of a large lodge.

While adoption is at least implicit in connection with any Crow medicine, it forms the very essence of the Pipe ceremony. Each owner had the right to become a "father" four times, but many prized the privilege so much that they declined to adopt more than three couples. The Pipe-owners, unlike the Tobacco owners, did not consider themselves a society, but they did sometimes meet informally at the invitation of one of their number in order to hold a feast in honor of the Pipe. At such gatherings there was singing but no drumming; the host planted his Pipe in the ground, but the rest were not obliged to open their bundles.

The initiative might be taken by the prospective "father," who without at first revealing his purpose would bring food to the person he wished to adopt. If the gift was accepted, it would have been unlucky to reject the offer. This form of procedure, that is, inducing a man to be adopted, occurs also in the modern history of the Tobacco ceremony, but it probably does not represent a transfer from that source since it has been noted for the Pipe dance of the Upper Missouri tribes, from whom the Crow derived their Pipe bundles. In both instances the situation is somewhat anomalous: the medicine-owner instead of being besieged by an eager suppliant inaugurates the negotiations. I suspect the point is that certain individuals piqued themselves not only on the possession of bundle rights but on the number of their "children," their ceremonial flock.

However, the probably earlier method was for the "child" to seek initiation on the basis of a vow. A man who was himself sick or had a sick relative would vow to be adopted in case of recovery. Thus, Pretty-horse made the pledge when his father seemed to be on the point of death. Similarly, Bird-above made a like declaration on behalf of his son. When no one volunteered to initiate the boy after this vow and he was again threatened with an attack, Bird-above directly approached a Pipe-owner, explained the circumstances, and had his son adopted that very day. A declaration of the same type also issued from warriors when sighting an enemy's camp. Such a one might announce, "If I capture a good gelding, I shall become a Pipe-owner."

A bundle includes two pipestems decorated among other things with a fan of eagle feathers. It also encloses corncobs and sweetgrass. Wrapped in flannel or a buffalo-calf hide, it was generally hung outside over the door, but taken inside in rainy weather and hung from the rear lodge poles. Corncobs and stems are painted blue; the former are considered female, the latter male. This is corroborated by what a Mandan woman once told me, viz., that at a corresponding adoption she received a cob and her husband a pipestem. A redstone bowl belongs with the outfit but is taken off during the dance lest it drop. It is put on when the novice receives tobacco for smoking. A "father" gives his "child" his own Pipe and makes a new one for himself.

Bear-gets-up said the Sacred Pipe belonged to the Sun, hence people were afraid of it. It served as a peace-pipe, e.g. if a Dakota approached the Crow with one in a battle no one would dare molest him. Within the tribe it was used by the police to pacify a murdered man's kin, but I doubt whether it was the only type that could be used on such occasions.

Evidently holding a Sacred Pipe conferred distinction and, according to Crow theory, good luck. Outsiders came into connection with the Pipe in several ways. A sick man, without seeking initiation, might promise to feed the Pipe if he got well. On recovering he would visit a man with a Pipe, who would call the other bundle owners, and there followed singing and jollification. Also, a war captain sometimes took a Pipe on his expeditions and would tie an enemy's lock to it. At an adoption itself the dancers, too, were not owners but men chosen for their skill as performers.

Unquestionably the outstanding feature of Pipe ritualism was the adoption ceremony. According to Scolds-the-bear this might take place at any season of the year, but another witness assigned the preliminaries to the winter and the consummation to the summer. After the vow had become a matter of public knowledge the novice and his wife were certainly instructed for four nights. At the first meeting there was a feast of buffalo tongues, and the bundle was laid on a spread every night. A special officer lit sweetgrass for incense and smoked four drums, which were then beaten to the accompaniment of four different songs, each sung four times. During this chanting the "parents" sat by the adopted couple and gently swayed their bodies. On the last night the Pipe was taken out, a bowl put into the stem, and all present smoked from a single filling.

At the actual initiation the tyro and his wife, dressed in ragged clothing, were supposed to hide in some tent. There was a preparatory tipi in which the bundle was spread, and from this the Pipe-owners proceeded in search of the "children" amidst beating of drums and singing. In front of them a man holding a Pipe led the procession, dancing. The rest all walked abreast, with one participant on the extreme right carrying a buffalo skull slung on his back by a cord of sweetgrass. The party raised the door flap of one tipi after another in search of the novices, the dancer performing whenever the musicians sang. At last they discovered the "children's" tent.

Now followed a characteristic feature of Northern Plains psychology. Whatever the motive of the adoption, the fixation on military affairs was too strong not to make itself felt. So it was four warriors who claimed coups in a hostile tipi that alone were allowed to lead out the novice. After four songs had been sung, these men entered, the first crying "hahe'" as though actually striking a coup and lightly tapping the "child's" shoulder. He gently raised him and announced that on a certain expedition he had entered an enemy's tipi whose inmates were asleep and had scored a coup. The second man now seized the tyro's arm. He explained, possibly, that he had once struck a second-coup against a fleeing enemy and captured his gun. The third brave in turn grasped the "child's" arm and recited a first-coup scored in a charge; and the last man told of killing some enemy and taking his gun. After his recital each speaker voiced his hope for the tyro's future prosperity, and the last warrior [1] took him by the hand, leading him out, with another brave supporting the other arm. Without further singing the parade now approached the adoption lodge near-by, made by joining together two large tents. In this lodge the Skull-bearer stood in the center, where his burden was removed to be laid on some blankets. All manner of presents were brought in and placed under or before the skull; they were appropriated by the Skull-bearer,—usually a close kinsman of the adopter's.

Now the time for the dance had arrived. Gray-bull spoke as if there was a single performer, but in 1931 there were two, both clad in tight-fitting suits, the one of yellow, the other of black color. Both wore bustles and deertail headdresses, and each held a rattle in one hand and a pipestem in the other, crossing the two objects at certain points in the performance. One dancer knelt down once or twice and a low stoop was evidently characteristic of the movements. On this occasion the stems rested on a kind of altar and at the beginning of each act White-arm, the adopter, who incidentally received four horses as his fee, gave them to the dancers.

Probably the usual thing was a dance by two men, each holding the stem in his left hand and the rattle in his right, which conforms with Mandan and Hidatsa reports. The crossing of the dancers' regalia was evidently a distinctive feature of this ceremony. During the performance the spectators encouraged the dancers by cries of acclamation, i.e. sounds accompanied by lip-clapping. The dancers performed to each of four songs, then laid their stems on a new quilt. They were entitled to a choice of four articles from the gifts offered to the adopter. Those present then smoked from an ordinary pipe.

One of the four warriors next rose, stood by the novice, and publicly recited a deed, whereupon he touched the novice's ear with an awl, with which he pretended to perforate it. This symbolized the piercing of an infant's ears a few days after birth (see p. 34). When Bird-above was initiated, he was asked to furnish not only an awl but also a butchering knife, with which a second warrior simulated cutting his navel-string. There was

---

[1] According to another account, the "father" leads the "child" by the little finger of his right hand, and the "mother" by the corresponding finger of the left hand.

also a kind of baptism to represent the cleansing of a newborn child. That is, the "father" poured a little water on his head, wiping it off with new cloth, which was thrown towards the door, where any one present might take it. Before this ablution the novice's face was painted on both sides with a representation of the Pipe and a corn stalk was rubbed down his face. His immediate family sat behind him and were also painted. Finally, the "child" received fine new clothing and the best of food from his "father," which still further suggested the parental-filial bond between them.

At last the adopter formally handed over the bundle to the novice, saying, "It is yours, it is not mine any longer." This was, however, preceded by further solemnities, such as smoking the Pipe and its future coverings with incense. The bundle was attached to the wife's back and henceforth she would thus carry it whenever the camp moved. Here, too, husband and wife are treated as a ceremonial unit. Exactly the same idea appears with the Horse bundle. When Lone-tree was adopted he and his wife were each requested to choose three objects from a sacred bag and jointly learnt the ritualistic songs. Similarly, when Strikes-at-night acquired the same medicine, her husband, as well as herself, was ceremonially painted, though because of his blindness the older of his sons was substituted for parts of the transfer ritual.

XV. The Tobacco Society

TOBACCO is the most distinctive of Crow medicines, but the species ceremonially planted, Nicotiana multivalvis, or "Short Tobacco," ōp pu'mite, (also i"tsi'tsi'a), is not the species anciently smoked. This latter, derived from the Hidatsa, is in Crow called "Tall Tobacco," ōp ha'tskite, and botanically Nicotiana quadrivalvis. Only Nicotiana multivalvis was considered holy, being mystically identified with the stars. In Medicine-crow's version of the Creation story, the Creator, or rather Transformer, walks about the newly-shaped earth with his companions and catches sight of a person. "Look, yonder is a human being. . . . That one is one of the Stars above. He is down here now and standing on the ground. Come on, let us look at him." As they approach, the being has transformed himself into a plant, the Tobacco; "no other plant was growing yet." The Transformer decrees that the Crow shall plant it in the spring and dance with it; it shall be their "means of living," their mainstay. The Sun himself adopts a poor fasting boy and thus starts the Tobacco order. For sowing the sacred seed is a prerogative that can be secured only by due initiation into the bacu'-sua (= "Soaking" = Tobacco) organization.

The theory of its further development, borne out by recent history, is simple. The founder adopted novices, precisely as any visionary became ceremonial "father" to those who craved a share in his supernatural blessings. But newcomers might have independent visions supplementing the primary revelations, whence sanctions for adopting further novices. Thus, branches sprang up,—each little group under its own leadership, with distinctive songs and emblems as defined in the visions. Though these divisions are called by the same term—araxu'a'tse—as the independent military clubs, I prefer designating them as chapters of one order, for a strong bond unites together all bacu'sua initiates.

With Crow of both sexes constantly yearning for revelations, an indefinite number of chapters could arise, and actually

I secured the names of about thirty subdivisions. However, these certainly did not all function at the same time as separate units. Sometimes a distinct name merely suggests a potential new group that has not yet fully segregated itself from the parent body. For instance, some of the Weasel members wore otter-skin belts with little hoofs that made a rattling noise; and there was a special song for the belt-wearers to get up and dance. Members of other chapters said, "They are just like Crazy Dogs" (see p. 331). The name stuck, but the belt-wearers remained part of the Weasels. The case recalls the subdivisions of the Foxes and Lumpwoods (pp. 175, 183). In other instances separation was attained; and again, some chapters dwindled in numbers and allied themselves with larger groups. My oldest informant, Strikes-both-ways, reported to be about a hundred years of age, listed only five chapters as belonging to the early days,—the Weasel, Otter, Elk, White Bird, and Tobacco chapters. The last of these may reasonably be conceived as the parent body; of the rest, the Weasels and Otters were doubtless also old, for they appear in all reports and their medicines figure conspicuously. Fortunately there are several origins that fall within the historical period.

In Medicine-crow's youth, he told me, he once went out to pray to the Sun, offered him a finger-joint, then fell unconscious from the loss of blood. A young man and a young woman came toward him, saying, "We have seen that you are poor and have come to see what we can do for you." Each was holding a feathered hoop in one hand and a hoop with strawberries in the other; to the back of the head was fastened a Tobacco "cherry," a strawberry, and the entire body of a red-headed woodpecker. The woman spoke: "We have come to let him hear something." The man went to the other side of the ridge and reappeared with a herd of horses, which he drove up to Medicine-crow. Next the woman went off and came back with horses. They showed him twenty head. These apparitions were the Tobacco plant (i"tsi-'tsia) himself. One of them said, "I have shown you all these horses. I am the Tobacco. I want you to join the Tobacco with these crowns." The man said, "Look at this young woman, she is Walks-with-her-dress." She had half of her face painted red. She forbade Medicine-crow ever to bring guns to the planting of Tobacco. After a while he came to. He got himself adopted

by a member of the Otter chapter, but by stressing his own revelation remodeled the branch into the Strawberry chapter. All his
"children" wore crowns of the kind revealed to him.

Another recent chapter was founded by Big-shoulderblade.
He was fasting four days as a mourner because of his brother's
death and met four men wearing horned buffalo-skin caps. They
offered him their several blessings and promised him revenge.
When Big-shoulderblade returned, the Indians were skeptical
about his report, but he went on a war party and killed a young
enemy of his brother's age, became a leader himself, and organized a Buffalo dance. Later Leads-the-wolf adopted him into the
Tobacco branch of the order. When Big-shoulderblade in turn
took in new members, he made buffalo caps for them and thus
started the Buffalo chapter.

A third report is of the same general tenor. Breath was already a member of the bacu′sua when his father gave him his
medicine, a stuffed blackbird. Breath dreamt a song about this
species and thenceforth made replicas of the medicine for his
novices, thus founding a new branch. When the Blackbirds
danced, they wore blankets in imitation of their eponym and
tied skins of the birds to the backs of their blankets. In the
Lodge Grass district there was no headman for the chapter, so
my informant, Gros Ventre Horse, joined in the activities of the
Weasels.

Anciently there were far fewer members of the order than,
say, in 1910. By that time the social factor had become prominent, many were willing to spend exorbitant amounts of property
to be taken in, and they were allowed to do so. But even in its
earlier exclusive stage, the Tobacco order was conceived as pro-
moting the welfare of the entire people. There was no trace of
any antagonism between the initiates of a secret society and the
outside world. While only those duly adopted might plant the
weed, or indeed had any means of getting the seed, outsiders
were not barred from all contact with the Tobacco. In the garden
they were allowed to put up a miniature sweat-lodge as an offering to the Sun. On the warpath men sometimes achieved success
by singing as prayers the songs heard at the public Tobacco
ceremonies. Each member of the company would announce that
he was imitating such and such a member of the order and
promise to give him horses in case of good luck. Once a man

imitated Three-wolves in this way and succeeded in striking a coup. On returning he gave Three-wolves a blanket and prepared a feast for him as well as for Tobacco members. Ordinarily people were afraid of thus mimicking others, but on the warpath it was reckoned a form of prayer. After the harvest outsiders sometimes gave the Mixers (p. 287) a horse for a Tobacco medicine, such as a necklace. Indeed, they themselves might have visions of the Tobacco; Bull-chief had such a one and attributes his longevity to it, though for some reason he never joined the society. To others such an experience was doubtless a stimulus to seeking admission.

Tobacco ritualism includes the adoption solemnities and the ceremonial of planting and harvesting.

Adoption. Here, as in the transfer of the Sacred Pipe privileges, the novice is the child (dā'ke) of the adopters, his "parents" (akse'), and the entire proceeding is sometimes called "having children," dā'kbisu'a. "He adopted me" is mī rā'kĕky, i.e. literally, He made me his child; and to indicate that his wife was adopted simultaneously, a man says, "In my company they caused her to be born," mī ā'pa wici' 'kyūk. This bond held for occasions other than a Tobacco ceremony and was logically extended to other persons. For instance, Gray-bull, having been adopted by White-stripe-across-his-face, a "son" of Bell-rock's, called Bell-rock his "grandfather" and his wife his "grandmother." The terms of address were, however, somewhat affected by the relative age of the persons concerned. The sentimental ties created by adoption found expression in gifts: Gray-bull used to bring a whole buffalo—later, a beef—to Bell-rock and his "father," receiving return presents; and to an adopted "daughter" he gave money whenever he had any.

As in the Sacred Pipe and Horse ritual, husband and wife were normally initiated together and coöperated in the planting. Individual circumstances might affect this rule, for example, divorce and remarriage. Thus, Little-rump and his former wife were properly adopted into the same chapter, but a subsequent wife declined adoption on the ground of being blind.

As a rule a member remained in the chapter through which he had entered the bacu'sua, but there were exceptions. Survivors of a dwindling branch might attach themselves to another subdivision. Again, by a substantial gift, a chapter eager to increase its numbers would induce individuals to join its ranks. This seems contrary to the old basic ideas but is in harmony with the recent practice of inducing a first initiation into the order (see below). Finally, a man might leave his chapter because of a misunderstanding with his adopter. I know of two instances but because of the sentimental bond deemed proper between "father" and "child," this was not a common occurrence.

Anciently the quest of admission was probably as a rule linked with some emergency or difficult enterprise that led to a vow. A man with a sick child would pledge his or its adoption on its recovery; or a man setting out against the enemy might say, "If I strike some enemy, I'll join the bācu'sua." When Old-woman was seriously ill, her father promised to have her adopted by any one who cured her; Pretty-enemy's father succeeded and became her "father." However, in recent times members often took the initiative, offering presents to outsiders in order to induce them to seek adoption. This suggests a relatively recent innovation, perhaps influenced by the military club pattern (p. 172). The development, I think, went hand in hand with increased stress on the social side of the organization. That is, kudos was gained by having many "children." Incidentally, the fee they paid would vastly outweigh the value of the bait. Thus, Bear-gets-up received buckskin leggings and moccasins from his prospective adopters; he ultimately paid four horses, many quilts, and other property to boot.

Two concrete instances illustrate the motives that entered into admission in the latter half of the last century. When Cuts-the-picketed-mule gave birth to a daughter, the name-giver promised that she would live beyond childhood; in return the parents pledged themselves to let him adopt her into the Tobacco society. However, the man was killed, whereupon his "father" offered Cuts-the-picketed-mule food, clothing, and blankets in order to be allowed to adopt her. Gray-bull joined a war party under the captaincy of White-stripe-across-the-face and captured a horse for him. The leader, however, refused to accept it, saying, "I want to adopt you." On their return he invited my friend to a feast and reiterated his wish. Gray-bull was craving the Captain's war medicine, so he asked whether he would be permitted to obtain it if he consented to the proposal. White-stripe-across-the-face answered in the affirmative and adopted Gray-bull with his wife that summer. The novices, aided by their kin, paid thirty-three horses, of which ten were contributed by Gray-bull himself.

In both instances the adopter's attitude is significant. The name-giver is to be rewarded for his well-wishing,—if proved efficacious; and his substitute is willing to confer further benefits, which of course, are sure to be ultimately more than repaid by the admission fees. In the second case the initiative lies wholly with the captain, whose eagerness to gain an additional "child" is shrewdly exploited by Gray-bull for getting the medicine he really covets.

This modern zeal for adding to one's ceremonial-following contrasts sharply with early practice, as indicated in legend and the explicit statements of informants. According to general consensus of opinion, Tobacco was originally restricted to a few people, and preponderantly old ones at that. More than one informant pointed out the change of usage by which even young children had been deemed eligible in recent times. On such occasions the Indians would cite the prophetic warning of an ancient Crow,—also ascribed to a prairie-dog blessing a visionary: "When all of you have joined the Tobacco Society, you will be poorly off!" Nevertheless, between the eagerness of outsiders to join and that of members to enhance their standing by large numbers of "children," a great many Crows were in the bācu'sua in 1910. Not long after, however, partly owing to new conditions, partly to direct discouragement by the Agency, the organization came virtually to die out.

Originally a candidate was instructed during the winter and formally initiated in the spring, immediately after the Tobacco planting. In recent times the initiation proper was deferred so as to fit into the week of Fourth of July festivities authorized by Government officials. Adoption, then, involved a preliminary stage in which the novice was privately taught by his sponsors; and, several months later, a partly public ceremony in which initiation was consummated. This latter consisted of several divisions, all of which, however, hardly required more than twenty-four hours. Essentially, there was a gathering of the adopting chapter in a preparatory tipi; its formal march to an adoption lodge; a sweat-lodge ritual; and the selection of medicines by the tyros.

The preparation of a candidate consumed four consecutive winter nights. On the first three, he and his wife were feasted by the initiating chapter and allowed to watch the dances. On the last night the "father" gave property to four different members, who gave one song each to the couple adopted. Husband and wife received two apiece and now for the first time danced with the song-givers.

The semi-public initiation several months later presupposed an Adoption Lodge (actsitu'a). Putting it up was a highly prized privilege; some chapters lacked a "copyright-holder" and had to appeal to other branches for help. This illustrates the sense of solidarity in the order as a whole, which also appears in other ways. Thus, both the musicians and other participants at an adoption might belong to *any* chapter of the bācu'sua, though naturally the fees went only to the "parents" and their associates.

The Lodge consisted of ten large pine trunks, tied together at the top and spread out in the shape of a huge tipi. The Lodges I saw were imperfectly covered so that sunlight could stream in from one side. Most conspicuous in the unoccupied structure was a cleared oblong space about five by two and one-half feet, the arā'ca, which for convenience sake I will call the "altar." Subsequently the members laid down their bags at its head and planted slender leafy sprigs of willow there, one for each novice.

The long sides of the altar were bounded by a row of willow arches, outside of which lay a parallel log of equal length. Within the space there were four rows of juniper sprigs. Cow chips on the altar served for fuel in pipe-lighting and the smoking of incense. Sometimes the whole altar was strewn with juniper. The altar represented the Tobacco garden, forming part of its original revelation. It remained intact after the ceremony; the logs, for instance, were not removed for firewood. The arā'ca was generally in the very center of the Lodge, and the medicine bags were put down on its short west side. However, details varied according to the Owner's dreams.

When the public performance was celebrated the candidates first met their chapter in a preparatory tipi, with musicians in one part, women and spectators in the remainder of the space. Here the members were painted with designs depending on individual visions, hence treated as transferable prerogatives. In 1911, at a Strawberry adoption, Medicine-crow's wife painted the women with four blue dots on each cheek and herself with one much larger blue dot. Gray-bull had once paid his own mother a horse, an ermine-skin skirt, and some money for her painting "patent" and later sold it to Plenty-coups for four horses. There was a distinct style for the two sexes, Gray-bull's wife actually putting the designs on the women. This division of labor is characteristic; in the Strawberry chapter, e.g., Old-dog and Medicine-crow painted the men, and their wives took care of the women. Medicine-crow had himself dreamt the decorative pattern.

In 1911 there were about a dozen drummers ranged in an arc in the rear of the preparatory tipi, with three rattlers, including Medicine-crow, at one side. Originally, according to general agreement, the rattle was the distinctive instrument for the ceremony, but later drums were introduced. The drummers belonged to the order, but not necessarily to the initiating chapter; they were chosen for their skill as musicians and paid for their services. The drumming is taken to imitate thunder. In front of the musicians the Tobacco bags were laid out in a row, and as only one novice was to be adopted that time a single willow stick with a kerchief and a small Tobacco bag was set at the extreme right of this line. It was supposed to invoke the protection of the powers above on behalf of the candidate; it symbolized his safety until the willow would again bear green leaves. The small bag contained very rare and valuable Tobacco seeds, on which the figure of the morning-star could be seen. The women present were ranged in two arcs on either side of the door and extending towards the row of bags. Before leaving the tent, all of them received eagle-feather fans hitherto kept in a bundle.

After the painting of the performers, the musicians beat their drums; and the women, holding unwrapped medicines, such as stuffed duck skins, gently swayed their bodies without moving from the spot. After several of these dances the Lodge Owner's wife took up a position by the exit, holding a catlinite pipe. She wore a crown of juniper leaves and a skin in the back of her head, while the other women wore a feather in the back and a strip of weasel-skin in the front of the hair. Her exit always conformed to the same pattern. The musicians would drum and sing a song, at the close of which she made one step forward, but only to draw her foot back again. With two further songs she acted in the same way, but at the end of the fourth she passed out of the preparatory tent, followed by the women in single file. After an interval of about six feet came the drummers, all of them men. In 1910 there were about twenty-five women and fifteen men. In the old days the candidate always walked, holding his willow stick, for which he paid a horse. In 1911 the novice, a girl of twelve, rode horseback at the tail of the procession, her mount being led by Medicine-crow. It was a rule that no person must get in front of the leader during the procession to the Lodge. But before reaching it four stops were necessary, and at each a different man sang four songs to the accompaniment of the drummers, while the women danced in position. Singing at these stations was considered a ceremonial privilege. The performers now all entered the Lodge, the drummers sitting down on the west side in a small enclosed ellipse west of the altar, with the rattlers south of them. The women of the two groups in the preparatory tipi sat, respectively, to the north and south of the foot of the altar.

Almost immediately after the entrance of the procession two famous warriors played their respective parts. One of them built a fire, over which tongues were anciently cooked in a kettle. This man, who was selected by the Owner, must have killed enemies as they were seated round a fire, and he now recited his deed. The other brave would formerly run to a creek and return with water, but more recently a large vessel with water was placed near the actsitu'a; the warrior took a small bucket, ran to the large vessel, filled his container, and came dashing back to report to the Owner.

What I actually witnessed in 1911 was the following. Medicine-crow got up and told about seven Dakota Indians seated in a canvas tipi by a fire; the Crow swooped down upon them and exterminated them, with Medicine-crow playing an active part. After this recital he broke up some little sticks and threw them on the bare part of the oblong to represent the fire. For the part of the Water-carrier (ak ĩ'cde) had been chosen Packs-the-hat, eligible by virtue of two coups to his credit. He stood on some leaves, which symbolized the wish safely to see the next year when everything would be green. Banks (the Lodge Owner), and his wife, stood behind Packs-the-hat, and swayed him four times, while Banks shook a rattle and sang a song. The songs customarily at this stage resemble praise songs rather than Tobacco songs. The fourth time the couple pushed Packs-the-hat out of the Lodge, he made his dash for water, returned, and in a very low tone of voice made his report to Banks. This represented the report of a returning war party. The Owner dismissed the runner, saying, "It is finished, go!" Then he heralded aloud the Water-carrier's news, and the crowd shouted, "Thanks!" (ahō'!) The water was passed around the Lodge and drunk by the old people and the musicians.

The Water-carrier's speech was identical in sentiment, though not wholly in wording, in three different versions I secured. One of them follows: "There was a war party, and I went along. We ran towards the enemy and made a killing; I captured a gun. I returned. When I reached the place where you had planted Tobacco, it was growing most plentifully. Round about the chokecherries were most abundant. Then I came hither. When I reached the camp, of sick people there were none; in peace you were harvesting the Tobacco."

After the fire-building and water-fetching episodes came another act prior to the actual dancing within the Lodge, viz. smoking by the male members present. The tobacco used was not the Sacred Tobacco (see p. 274), which would have caused a rash on the face, but ordinary trade tobacco in recent decades and, I presume, the Hidatsa variety before that. On entering the Lodge the leader of the procession handed her redstone pipe to her husband, the Owner. Opinion differs as to whether he need be identical with the Tobacco-Lighter (ak'ō'para'xia), who now lit the pipe and handed it around. At all events this office was important, for in the Strawberry chapter it was filled by Medicine-crow, the founder himself. The Tobacco-Lighter sat by the door and no one must pass in front of him. He received food even before the singers, whose turn came next. He and his wife sang the first song, a cue to the musicians, who were supposed to catch the tune at once. According to Lone-tree, the Tobacco-Lighter set a precedent for the whole ceremony: if he sang three songs, all the subsequent singers did likewise; if he sang only two, they followed suit, etc. Similarly, if he started with an eagle song, the women danced with eagle-feather fans; if he substituted a weasel song, they took up weasel skins.

At all events, the musicians began to sing and beat their drums and the members rose to dance, women being by far the more frequent performers. There was never any movement from position, but the hands, with or without medicine skins or eagle-feather fans or willow sprigs, were alternately advanced and drawn back, or raised and lowered, in a peculiar convulsive manner. Sets of dancers took turns, each corresponding to a set of four songs. Moving the clenched hands, with thumb up and little finger down, was considered the proper way for the Tobacco dance. To hold thumb and little fingers of the clenched fists in one horizontal plane is really distinctive of the Bear Song Dance (p. 267), though this movement is permissible in the Tobacco ceremony.

Theoretically, at least, each person sang one or two songs, thus protracting the ceremony until the late afternoon or evening. The really essential thing was to have each novice dance with the persons who had taught him his ceremonial songs. Graybull recalled that at his adoption his two song-instructors danced with him, one at a time; and similarly his wife danced with her instructors. I once saw a male candidate dancing *between* two men, presumably his teachers, at the foot of the altar. At the first dance all three held up willow sprigs; the next time, feather fans; the third time, rattles; and finally they merely moved their hands. The novice then resumed his seat and left the Lodge soon after. A girl initiate I saw dance simultaneously with a number of women, one at her right and all the rest at her left.

Besides these indispensable dances there were a great many by other members. At noon there was an intermission partly for feasting, partly for the piling up of property for the "parents" as part of the admission payment. At the Weasel ceremony I witnessed the "son's" kin brought in quantities of quilts and other presents, which a young woman took in charge. Since the novice belonged to the Nighthawk club (p. 207), his fellow-members all lined up outside the Lodge and contributed a quarter apiece toward the initiation fee. Having a Nighthawk interpreter, I also contributed this modest sum, and in return we received a case of fruit, which was equitably distributed. In the old days brave young men would at this juncture thrust their sticks into the Lodge and receive tongues impaled on their points. It was one way of advertising one's achievements since only really brave men were entitled to get tongues. The idea of assistance from one's club antedates the Nighthawk organization: at Medicinecrow's adoption his fellow-Lumpwoods similarly gave away property in his behalf.

Of the entire performance the procession to the Lodge and the dramatic scenes immediately following entrance into it were the most impressive features of the ceremony. In the subsequent dancing the impression of high seriousness was often wanting. In fact the performers and spectators indulged in occasional joking.

In 1910 another chapter held its adoption on the same day as the Weasels, but its ceremony ended earlier in the afternoon, possibly because there were fewer members. Accordingly, they came to the Weasels, some of them even taking part in the dances and thus again demonstrating the solidarity of all bācu'sua devotees. At about four o'clock an old Weasel woman called out a song to the drummers, then she and a middle-aged man knelt at the foot of the altar, each with a rattle in one hand and a fan in the other. At first they beat the ground with their rattles, simultaneously shaking the fans, later they raised the rattles and, still kneeling, shook them in the air. The kneeling was in imitation of Tobacco growers working in their garden, the striking of the ground referred to the Tobacco that had not yet sprouted, and raising the rattles symbolized its growth. At about five o'clock an old woman wearing a headband and holding a fan in one hand, stood up alone for the final song. Toward the end all members present took little willow sprigs, shook them, and raised them aloft with a sudden movement to make the Tobacco grow, while the musicians similarly lifted their drumsticks. In such unobtrusive manner the Crow display their faith in imitative magic. This closed the public part of the adoption ceremony, which was followed by a distribution of victuals.

Sweat-lodge Ritual and Selection of Medicines. By this time the novice had mastered his dancing and singing technique, but he was still without any Tobacco. Before receiving his medicine, however, he had to undergo sweating.

When Young-crane joined the Otters, her husband Crazyhead and his second wife also entered the sweat-lodge, along with several other members of older standing; altogether there were about eight people and the lodge was somewhat larger than usual. It was covered with buffalo skins, on which rested tobacco-filled bags owned by the chapter. After the usual sweating ritual (p. 257) the bags were laid out on a spread by the side of the sweat-lodge. Then all the sweaters came out, bathed in the river, and went home. The next day Crazy-head and his wives met the members in a tent, the medicines having been placed in the rear. Hunts-the-enemy, the son of the chapter's founder, had been Lodge Owner until then, but now he turned over the privilege to Crazy-head's second wife because of the horses and presents the initiates had offered. Thereafter any one who required an Adoption Lodge had to apply to both wives. Having with the aid of their kin paid for their adoption, these two women were entitled to choose medicines for themselves. Young-crane, being ignorant in such matters, had Wolf select for her. He chose an otter skin, a medicine blanket, an otter-skin belt, a certain plant, and some buckskin bags with Tobacco seed. Subsequently, in Tobacco dancing she would hold the otter skin by the neck; I bought it in 1910.

The bags mentioned in these accounts are of two quite different categories as to size. There are little pouches, often tied in pairs, which directly enclose the seeds; and there are large rawhide or tanned skin bags with straps so as to be carried on the back in processions. The larger bags are often decorated with stripes, circles, and dots, designs usually interpreted as representing the seeds or the garden.

According to Gray-bull, the people who sweated with the novice were song-instructors, and theirs were the medicines he was allowed to choose from, while his "father" and "grandfather" selected from the bundles of other members for him.

Medicine-crow brought out some further points: The sweat-lodge, he said, might be constructed of 14, 24, etc., up to 94 willows, or the number might be 100. At his own adoption, before the second pouring of water on the rocks, his "grandfather" washed him with a mixture of wild-carrot root and water, and thus prayed on his behalf: "I want him to be an old man. All you above, let him live to be an old man." (Child-in-the-mouth similarly recalled being "washed," i.e. having sagebrush rubbed over his body, from head downward.) On removal from the lodge cover, the bags were made to face the mountains. When the sweaters learnt that they were taken away, they would scourge themselves and recited each a prayer. When the cover was thrown aside and the sweaters betook themselves to the river, any sickness on them would be washed away. In his own case his wife had been preparing a feast, which a herald announced. Then the adopting chapter came to his tipi with their medicine bags, which were first smoked with incense, then the contents were exposed. For each medicine chosen he paid a horse; he also picked out one bag. They sang three songs and three times he pretended to put the objects chosen into the bag, which he actually did at the fourth song. Thus he became an Otter member (see p. 275) and was henceforth treated by the members like one of their own family.

The total amounts paid in connection with initiation were simply staggering. When Bear-wolf adopted Old-dog into the Strawberry chapter, Old-dog with the help of his kin paid fifty horses. Bear-wolf gave one to each of the song-instructors, whom he had selected, and distributed the others among his fellow-members. A horse for one medicine object seems to have been a standard price.

Planting. In order to plant effectively, members had to have their seeds properly mixed with water and other ingredients. This was the duty of a qualified officer of their chapter, the Mixer, who was entitled to a fee for his services. The native name of the order, bācu'sua, Soaking, is derived from this procedure; and altogether the Mixers were probably the most important functionaries of the organization. Usually there was probably a single Mixer couple for each chapter, but the Weasels at one time had several of these Mixers; in 1911 the Strawberries and the Ducks had a mixing ritual in common.

It was the Mixer who determined the site of the Tobacco garden each year. If one of them had dreamt of the plant during the winter, he invited the other Mixers, of both sexes, for a feast in the beginning of spring. After the meal the host inquired of each guest whether he had dreamt about the planting. Then some reported dreams of the weed growing to such a height, others had seen the leaves, the plant just appearing above ground, the maturing crop, the enclosure, or the site. When all had said their say, the host described his own dream. If several Mixers had seen the same site, it was chosen for that year. If no one had a definite dream, they used their judgment as to the location. According to Lone-tree, any member of the order might attend this gathering, and a dance was held there.

Between this occasion and the planting, the members gathered fresh bones, pounded them up, and got together as much fat as possible. The Mixers generally supplied meat for hash, which later served to pay outsiders for various services.

The proper time for mixing is "when the chokecherries are in bloom," that is, in May. The Mixers all prepared the seeds of the members on the same day, though in different tipis. The details of the process varied according to different visions, and modern conditions made further modifications necessary. Formerly, elk or deer or buffalo dung was mixed with the Tobacco, also several species of flowers and roots. More recently, cow dung was substituted and, according to Pretty-tail, eight different roots and flowers served as ingredients. The Mixer used a wooden bowl, with a red ring painted inside; in former times he dipped water with a buffalo-horn, later replaced by a cow-horn ladle. Pretty-tail described his procedure as follows. Shaking his rattle, he would begin to sing, while his wife sat beside him. At the close of each song she made a motion as if to dip her ladle into a bucket, and after the fourth song she actually put it in and poured water into the bowl up to the red ring. Laying down her dipper, she opened several small Tobacco bags, while her husband sang four songs. At the fourth she emptied all the contents of one bag into the bowl, then she added other ingredients, and finally when they were all mixed, the cow dung. By this time cow paunches were ready to receive the contents of the bowl, which were poured into one paunch. Smoke from a big pipe was now blown into the container, which was quickly tied with sinew so as to retain the smoke. They had a cherry-stick, sharpened at one end and hooked at the other; this they painted red and then tied the paunch, now full, to the hooked end. They fixed other paunches in the same way, then stretched a rope between two lodge poles and tied the cherry-sticks to it. These labors took up a whole day. In the evening the members began to dance in the Mixer's lodge and kept it up all night. Finally they went home.

On the following day the members, sometimes accompanied by the whole camp, set out towards the site of the garden. But first each chapter met separately, and their Mixers painted the members, all of whom were dressed in their best clothing. The women carried blankets on their arms and large Tobacco sacks on their backs. Every one got up and the musicians intoned a certain song. By this time one woman, carrying a special medicine, had taken up a position far in advance, possibly fifty or even three hundred yards away from the rest of the society. She is termed akbasā'nde, The one who goes first, but to distinguish her from the actual leader out of the preparatory tipi, I will call her the Medicine-bearer. Many considered hers the greatest office in the order; as usual, it was conceived as belonging to a couple, but it was normally the wife who went ahead of the procession.

Owing to the distances on the Reservation, each district naturally had a distinct ceremony and Medicine-bearer, so that differences developed even as to the medicine itself. In early times it consisted of an otter-skin with some associated emblems, and at Pryor this tradition persisted. But at Lodge Grass Medicine-crow had a vision of a crane, and about 1895 he succeeded in substituting a crane for the otter-skin at the Tobacco procession of his district. In the Bighorn district a pipe was substituted for the otter about the same time because the woman owning the relevant privilege had died; in this part of the Reservation a male Mixer had twice served in this capacity. The medicine carried in advance was usually multiple, the several components being apportioned among certain members. Thus, in early times the skin itself was carried by the Medicine-bearer; while an old Otter man wore a crown of white feathers; and another old man a Tobacco sack with meadowlarks, his head being likewise decorated with these birds. The skin, the crown, and the birds were reckoned a single medicine. Similarly, at Pryor the Medicine-bearer's husband wore an elk-skin headband, feathered at the back, and carried an eagle-feather fan. No one was allowed to walk in front of the Medicine-bearer. There were watchers to prevent a breach of this rule. Also one of the police societies followed the procession on horseback, armed with long sticks, to prevent outsiders from approaching the paraders.

The musicians in the preparatory tipi of the Medicine-bearer's chapter sang four songs. Then the Leader, who was at least sometimes also Owner of an Adoption Lodge, after walking round the inside of the tent, led her group outdoors, the women coming

first. All of them formed a horizontal line, joined by the men of
the chapter with their drums, who stood to the right of the
women. To the right of them, in turn, followed the women of the
second chapter, and so on until all the members of the order
stood abreast of one another. According to another account, however, the women were all in one body, with the men in another
to their right, but both groups segregated by chapters.

The procession set out towards the site of the garden, but
only walked a short distance. There every one sat down, the
women laying their bags before them and the men sitting in a
row behind. The Medicine-bearer at this juncture walked about
40 yards ahead of her position in order to plant a stick into the
ground and put her medicine between its forks. She then walked
backwards. Here she sang a song, taken up by the musicians,
and all the members danced in position, including the Medicine-
bearer. Pretty-tail, as her husband, would now fill a pipe and
offer it to each man in turn. At first every one declined it, for,
as Mr. Simms learnt, to take it was possibly sacrificing one's life
on behalf of the growth of the Tobacco: some catastrophe was
sure to befall the smoker if the crop failed. However, finally one
man accepted the pipe, smoked it, and passed it on to the other
men. The women now shouldered their bags and the men took
up their drums. The smoker and his wife stood up before the
women, facing the Leader, whom Pretty-tail approached, inform-
ing her that a man had taken the pipe and was ready to sing.
The smoker first sang in a low voice, to teach his tune to the
musicians, who then sang it aloud to the beating of their drums,
while the women danced. After four songs the procession resumed
its march. There were the usual four stops with a similar performance at each. According to Gray-bull, the pipe was each time
offered to a different Mixer, who would smoke it, pass it to his
fellow-members, and announce his dreams—what he had seen
of the next season or of the growth of the Tobacco—, and sing
four songs.

At the fourth station the procession was possibly a hundred
—some say, three hundred—yards from the garden, and the
Medicine-bearer within fifty feet of it. Without looking back,
she would call to one of her "children" to remove the medicine
from her back. There was now to be a race to the site: before
the last Mixer's final song each member selected a fleet runner

to take her Tobacco bag and run with it. The Medicine-bearer decorated the sides of a horse's body with red paint and allowed a prominent man to mount it. At the close of the last song this horseman and the runners all dashed toward the garden. The Mixers had previously set up their sticks there and told the run- ners which ones to take for their goal. According to Crow belief, whoever won the race would enjoy good luck that season; in the old days he would be fairly sure of striking the first coup that year. A racer would sometimes pluck out a stick and an- nounce that he had captured a gun. Every runner placed his bag on a blanket and covered it with another blanket. The members of the order next advanced to the site, on one side of which the Mixers spread a blanket as a resting-place for all the medicines.

Twenty years ago the site was prepared by plowing, but the old way was to burn over its surface. Members and outsiders got axes, hoes, or other implements, removed all the grass so as to smooth and lay bare the ground, and spread dry grass and twigs over it. A man with an eagle medicine—not necessarily a member—had to sing to the ground. After his four songs, the people set fire to the grass. The singer, holding a feather fan in either hand, fanned the fire. When the grass was consumed, the people took leafy branches and brushed the site with them. The Mixers gave pemmican to all helpers in this work. Outside the garden plot the people began to cook and eat, then sods were removed and laid as a sort of enclosure at the edge of the burnt surface. On opposite sides of the site two sticks were planted and a rope was stretched between them, thus marking one per- son's allotment. Every Mixer counted the members of his chapter and divided up his plot accordingly. Some people dreamt of spe- cial sections in which they were to plant so as to achieve a maximum crop.

The gardens I saw conformed pretty well to a single type. In 1910 I rather closely examined the one at Lodge Grass. It was situated at the foot of a hill and consisted of two enclosures, one serving for seeds left over after the main planting and smaller than the space allotted to a single chapter in the main area. This larger enclosure was an oblong about six yards wide and sixty yards in length. There were half a dozen subdivisions for the several chapters, adjoining plots being sometimes separated by parallel rows of little willow wickets extending across the width of the garden. The fence enclosing the garden as a whole was very crude, branches and tree trunks being thrown together helter-skelter. Within this fence each plot was further subdivided, with two rows for every couple in the chapter. These rows were sometimes marked by little stones extending across the width of the field. Each couple used their digging-stick as a property mark, set near either end of the appropriate row, though generally on the east side of the oblong. These sticks were of cherry wood and differed in various ways: one was longer than the rest, another had a crooked handle, to the top of the third was tied a little willow branch, and while most of the sticks were painted red one had remained unpainted but was stripped of its bark. Again, there were different ways of peeling the bark: one stick was unstripped at the top, another had kept its bark down to the middle. Further, some people had tied seed-bags to their sticks; others, wreaths of grass or juniper leaves. Such tokens, Gray-bull suggested, were more than mere markers: based on visions, they promoted the growth of the Tobacco.

In the plot of the fourth chapter, outside the line of cherry sticks and quite close to the fence, I saw a miniature sweat-lodge frame formed of two willow arches crossed at right angles by five others; its diameter was from 18 to 21 inches, its height about 8 or 9 inches. Remnants of a fire were visible. A similar structure was found on the opposite side. These tiny sudatoria were conceived as sweat-lodges for the Tobacco, i.e. to make it grow; and wild-carrot incense was burnt in them. Each chapter properly erected its own miniature sweat-lodge, differences in detail being again due to specific visions.

When the garden had been parceled out, there was a close parallel to the Water-carrier episode of the adoption ritual. Each Mixer selected a renowned warrior to stand before him on the site. The Mixer held this man by the back, sang four songs, and after each pushed him a little. The fourth time the warrior ran across the garden in a line parallel to the short sides of the garden and back again. In a low voice he reported that he had gone on a war party, struck a coup, then got to the garden on his return, where he had seen plenty of Tobacco, berries, and buffalo. The Mixer repeated the statements aloud, and every one then prayed for an abundance of Tobacco and food.

The Mixer next took a sharp stick, sang four songs, and at the close of each pretended to pierce the ground, which he actually did after the fourth song, making a hole two inches deep. This inaugurated the planting. The women danced, pointing their sticks at the ground; after four songs they punched a hole, each then walking backward along her allotted space. Their husbands followed in their wake, walking forward and dropping the seeds into the holes. When done, the women lined up across the far end of the garden. Each Mixer sat opposite his own plot and chapter, and sang four songs, to which the women danced. Then the rank and file went home, but the Mixer couples remained to make more medicine, shook their rattles, and sang. At last, they also went home. That night there was a dance. In the old days the adoption ritual followed the next morning or at least in the immediate future.

After the planting it was customary to lie at the garden in order to get a vision. Tobacco songs were especially likely to be revealed in this way. Gray-bull once lay thus for three days and nights. He finally saw a man, whose hand was clenched, though not tightly, as he moved it gently forward, singing the first sentence of a song. At the second he touched his body. These were the words: "I am Tobacco. My entire body is Tobacco." Gray-bull found his Tobacco growing very well and attributed his success to his song. Others asked him whether he had seen anything and he told them his vision. Then all said, "Thanks! We shall surely have a good crop." In 1911 he was still using this song to dance with.

In 1914 Flat-dog and the wife of Not-mixed, both in mourning, fasted while others were planting, but entered the garden to seek a vision when the rest had gone away. Flat-dog was blessed with the promise of a fine crop of Tobacco.

Between the time of planting and the harvest a number of rules were observed. Members of the order would motion outward and upward with their pipes when smoking, a practice discontinued after the seeds were gathered. They burnt no grass, and neither the fire-fanner nor his chapter associates permitted any one to move firewood in their respective tipis. Members of the order abstained from various kinds of food, such as a bull's testes and wild celery, lest the Tobacco crop be injured. When the plants had come out, shinny games were taboo for the same reason. On the other hand, to be the first to eat young deer meat after the planting augured harvesting a big crop. During the period in question members danced rather frequently in order to make the weed grow faster, but the songs sung referred to the Tobacco itself—not to the Weasel, Otter, etc.—otherwise there would be a poor crop.

Four formal trips of inspection were made to the garden. Four days after the planting the Medicine-bearer's husband returned, sometimes accompanied by his wife, always by a chief or great warrior, who first looked at the Tobacco. According to Arm-around-the-neck, experienced scouts were sent ahead when the party got close to the garden. They looked, returned hallooing as though actually on a war raid, and told the rest that the Tobacco was growing well. On returning to camp, the inspector reported to the Mixers, who then sang songs of jubilation. Several days later the man who sang at the second stop in the procession to the garden inspected it and made a similar report, followed by the same procedure. Twelve or fourteen days later a third inspector made the trip, probably finding the weeds about two inches high. The fourth man went from twenty to forty days later and gave his report that the Tobacco was growing well. After the return of each inspector a Tobacco dance was held.

This procedure was evidently not rigidly fixed. Perhaps the most commonly given time intervals between the planting and the several inspections are four, seven, ten and fourteen days, but Bear-crane said he went seventeen days after the garden ceremony and returned with a uniform interval of seventeen days between successive visits. At the fourth inspection, Bear-gets-up explained, a Mixer went to the garden with all his associates. After a meal he built a fire in the garden and made wild-carrot incense. Then the people came to pull up the weeds growing in their plot. Somewhat later the Mixer again viewed the ground and notified the members, who would come to remove the weeds.

Originally harvesting one's crop was a ceremonial prerogative to be bought from the Mixer for four presents, and those who had failed to acquire the privilege would get their "parents" to harvest for them. In recent times virtually all members had the right to "take back" their Tobacco.

The season for the harvest is "when the cherries are ripe." On July 12, 1910, I attended the first harvesting of the year, with only half a dozen persons, all of the Duck chapter, in the garden. They removed the seed cases not with their thumb nails but with a small piece of wood. Another rule, which I observed on August 25, 1913, was against pointing at the Tobacco with one's fingers, for which a stick was substituted. The same taboo applied to the stars, which are identified with the Tobacco. The harvesters rubbed wild-carrot root on their hands and feet before plucking the Tobacco seeds (see below).

Bear-crane plausibly spoke of four harvesting visits to the garden. However that be, there were several such, for not all the Tobacco matured at the same time. Each time before picking the seeds the members sang at the plot and danced by separate chapters on returning to camp. If any members failed to go along, the Mixer tied up their seed in separate bags and handed these to the respective owners of the Tobacco, who repaid him with gifts. After the final crop of the season, an Adoptive Lodge was put up and a dance held there. The performers rubbed their hands on the ground, otherwise their faces, if touched by their hands, were liable to itch and break out in sores and pimples. At the close of the dancing they sang a special song, then the dancers ran home and the one who got there first would enjoy good luck, they said. The Tobacco stems and leaves were plucked out, cut up fine, mixed with meat and ordinary tobacco, and thrown into a creek. Gray-bull did not know the reason, but suggested it was a natural thing to do since the Tobacco had been mixed with water before the planting.

Summary. What is the meaning of all this apparent rigmarole? The Crow firmly believed that it was necessary to plant Tobacco in order to ensure the continued welfare of the people; and they were completely unanimous in identifying the Tobacco with the Stars. According to different versions, it either represents them generically, or is the morning-star specifically, or the second body—the *alter ego*—of a particular star, or was at least given to a visionary by the stars. Are we, then, dealing with an astral cult? Nothing seems further from the facts. There is no portrayal of any celestial phenomena; no consistent supplication of the stars as such; and though references to them occur, as in the pointing taboo, they are incidental, almost deliberate attempts to bring in an association which the origin legends all affirm. The lack of anything more significant is all the more striking because the most popular of Crow hero tales is precisely that of Old Woman's Grandson, the child of the Sun, who is ultimately transformed into a star after overcoming the monsters of this world. Nothing would seem more obvious than to dramatize his exploits in a ceremony explicitly coupled with stars, but the idea never occurred to the Crows.

What, then, is the essence of the bācu'sua ceremonial? Essentially it is nothing but a combination and elaboration of the generic Crow ideas of "medicine" and associated ritualistic technique. The Tobacco is a specific "medicine," that is, a particular supernatural gift with its own distinctive laws, positive and negative. As sacred rocks must be wrapped up and placated with decorative trimmings, so the Tobacco must be planted. Like other sacred possessions, it confers benefits on its votaries that may be extended by adoption. Adoption and elaboration play the same part as in the case of other holy objects. When Medicine-crow combined his Strawberry vision with the older Otter chapter of the Tobacco order, he was following a thoroughly orthodox pattern. With the same sort of sanction, for instance, Flathead-woman added a little notched stick to the sacred Arrow bundle. The founder of a chapter was like a war-bundle owner outfitting a number of braves, like a Sacred Pipe owner adopting three "children"; the difference was one of degree and not of kind. Tobacco for some reason came to appeal to Crow imagination so that an indefinite number of special revelations merged with its cult; and the ban on restricting one's ceremonial dependents to four was lifted. These were the only factors required to create a large society with distinctive subdivisions,—the order and its chapters. Everything else is duplicated in other rituals; the fourfold repetition of acts, the coöperation of husband and wife, the sweat-lodge, the recital of coups are ritualistic clichés that enter with equal prominence in the Meat Festival, the Pipe ceremony, the Sun Dance. With the Bear Song Festival some of the chapters share the emergence and regurgitation of the bātsirā'pe and a formal procession, which we shall find still more definitely in the Sun Dance. Less conspicuous than in the Sun Dance, yet sporadically clear enough, we find acts of imitative magic, intended in the present case to further the growth of Tobacco. In short, the Tobacco ceremony resembles not a unified plot but rather a chain of casually coupled episodes from the tribal repertory.

XVI. The Sun Dance

IN outward activities the Crow Sun Dance (acki'cirua) resembles its equivalent among other Plains tribes, but it has highly distinctive features. The native name of the ceremony gives no clew to its significance: it refers to a miniature lodge such as children put up in play. Some, to be sure, interpret it to designate a miniature of the Sun's lodge, but this explanation does not shed much additional light. The Sun is the great Crow deity and therefore enters significantly into many religious situations; but the acki'cirua cannot, as a whole, be regarded as a ritual of Sun-worship.

Essentially, the Crow Sun Dance was a prayer for vengeance. A man overcome with sorrow at the killing of a kinsman resorted to this as the most effective, if most arduous, means of getting a vision by which he might revenge himself upon the offending tribe. The difficulties were such that only an exceptional mourner would shoulder the burden, hence the performance was not periodical—in contrast to that of other tribes—and might lapse for years. Between 1830 and 1874 the average interval between successive performances was probably not less than three or four years. Indeed, Young-crane, a River Crow about eighty years old, recollected only six dances, and a still older woman not more than five. Obviously, the ceremony was bound to pass out of existence with the establishment of peace in the West. Further, because the primary object was the killing of an enemy, the Crow ceremony had no fixed duration. No sooner had the pledger announced that he had gained his end than the performance automatically stopped. Indeed, in one exceptional case even the vision proved unnecessary: on the first night of the festival an enemy was found and killed in camp, which was felt to fulfill all requirements, so that the dance at once ended. This was interpreted as an unusual stroke of good fortune for the mourner, whose suffering was forestalled by this initial happening.

Normally the Whistler (akō'oce)—as the pledger was called

—required the services of a medicine-man called akbā.e'axtsia, the owner of one of a number of sacred dolls (marē'wiraxbā'ke). Through his doll the owner was to put the Whistler into a state of ecstasy in which he would behold a slain enemy. This medicine-man was thus the master of ceremonies; he and his ward, the Whistler, were the only indispensable actors; and their ritual formed the core of the entire festival. Rationalistically, we might go so far as to say that the rest was mere decoration, but that would miss an essential aspect of the *native* attitude. To the Crow the Sun Dance was precisely *not* an occasion for righting a private wrong but a public spectacle in which the whole tribe took part, as performer or spectator; and there were at least half a dozen distinct mental states in connection with it, as shall be shown presently.

A mourner who was planning a Sun Dance did not announce his intentions at once or in direct fashion. Instead he would say to the man who cut his hair, "Leave a little hair on my head so that I can tie a feather to it." This was how Holds-the-tail vowed to put up one of the last of the Crow Sun Dance lodges. The clipper spread the news, and thus the people learnt there was going to be a Sun Dance. Again, the herald would some time announce a big buffalo hunt. Then the Whistler asked the first person he met to send for the chief. By this time the mourner would already be haggard and lean from eating very little food. Without looking at the chief, he would say, "On this hunt I want you to have all the tongues kept, do not let the children have any, I want them all." This was another way of declaring his intention. The chief at once issued an appropriate order through the herald: "Save all tongues, he is going to cut ankles!" The pledger's name was not mentioned. After the chief's visit, the Whistler no longer absented himself but returned to camp that very night.

Collection of Tongues and Choice of Master of Ceremonies. Buffalo tongues were required as fees for tribesmen who performed special services and also in order to entertain the people at large every noon during the course of the ceremony. Big-shade, as Whistler, failed to get a vision until the sixth day, hence the supply of tongues had been completely exhausted and he was obliged toward the end to feast his guests with dried meat. A single hunt was not always sufficient to secure the desired number of tongues, which some set as high as a thousand, and there were informants who, evidently under the influence of the mystic number, considered four hunts proper. In each case the tongues were collected on pack-horses by two or more functionaries and unloaded in a special tipi while two old men sang songs of joy. The Whistler's kin there strung the tongues together in sets of ten, and they were thus carried out and away on the horses that brought them. The collectors unloaded the sets at the lodges of preëminent warriors, whose wives spread them on their best blankets. Some say the party included the comrades of the Whistler's lamented kinsman on his fatal journey. According to Bear-crane, the Doll Owner and the Whistler took part in the collecting trip, the former with blackened face shaking a rattle and singing songs of jubilation. Other data suggest that he was not chosen until after the collection of tongues, though before the redistribution to distinguished men.

However this may have been, at an early stage the Whistler had to approach one of the Doll bundle owners with a filled straight-pipe and ask him to smoke it. By taking the pipe the owner accepted charge of the ceremony and became the Whistler's "father." The "son" might try to buy the bundle outright, but the holder very rarely consented, and then only for a high price.

Bear-crane recollected six such bundles, Young-crane only four, viz. those owned by Wrinkled-face, Twined-tail, Iā'kac, and Wandering-old-man. Several Crow spoke of one doll manufactured on a pretended revelation with dire results vouched for by Gray-bull as an eye-witness. At a performance in which this was used all the guns taken from the enemy were placed in a ring. Though all of them were supposed to be uncharged, one gun suddenly went off, the bullet first grazing the buffalo skull (p. 308), then killing the Whistler's wife. From this the Indians inferred that the doll was not genuine. But even apart from such spurious medicines, the several bundles were not of equal potency. According to all Lodge Grass informants and most others, the doll owned by Wrinkled-face took precedence not only of other dolls but of all other Crow medicines whatsoever. It had been revealed to one Little-son while mourning a brother's death; he passed it on to his brother, who bequeathed it to Ake'kuc. Thence it descended to Ake'kuc's brother, Wrinkled-face, and by his death his widow, Pretty-enemy, gained possession of it, a duplicate of lesser value having been buried with her husband. This particular doll was not supposed to be handled by a woman, hence Pretty-enemy served merely as custodian. Old men sometimes came to her house, requested to see the medicine, themselves opened it, and presumably addressed it in prayer. When an elderly Crow heard that Pretty-enemy had unwrapped it for me, he at once prophesied that she or some relative of hers would die for this breach of taboo. It was doubtless this rule that had made Pretty-enemy restive to the point of offering to sell me this to her useless possession, which until that day she had never dared open. She at first offered to let me have it for $400, a price not at all unreasonable from the native point of view, but far beyond my means. After several weeks she sold it for $80. In bringing the bundle to my shack, she was visibly disturbed for fear the other Indians might discover the transaction in the near future and herself sought out the most inaccessible part of my room as a hiding-place for it.

Owing to the taboo in this case and Pretty-enemy's insistence on secrecy, which barred questioning other Indians, very little information could be obtained about this bundle. Apart from its service in the Sun Dance it had only been used by warriors setting out on a war party, who would have it unwrapped and then pray to it. The entire medicine set is enclosed in a rawhide envelope painted with triangular figures. It is now in the Museum of Natural History. The lower part of the doll itself is covered by a piece of buffalo skin with the hair inside. Eyes and mouth are crudely indicated in black; the head is topped with a profusion of plumes; and several rectangular crosses—partly faded in 1910—were interpreted as morning-star designs. Pretty-enemy did not know the kind of stuffing, but according to another Crow such a doll was generally stuffed with sweetgrass and white pine needles and its hair was parted like a woman's. Besides the doll itself, the envelope contains a number of supplementary objects. There are three strips of skunk skin, almost certainly representing the anklets worn by the Whistler and the necklace put on him to induce a trance (see p. 325). There are two rawhide effigies, one of which was said to have been attached to the Whistler's hair. In both the head, with crudely indicated eyes and mouth, is sharply set off from a triangular legless body, and a rectangular cross (see below) stands out in the upper half of one of the tapering bits of rawhide. The bundle also includes two little beaded plaques with pendant feathers, an owl mounted in a wrapped handle, bunches of feathers, and hair.

I had a chance to see one other doll, that owned by Sharphorn, who had inherited it from his brother, the original visionary. After four days' mourning over another brother, slain by the enemy, this man heard the beating of drums inside a mountain. Some one was shouting, "Everybody, come in! There is going to be a Sun Dance here!" Some one came out, took the mourner inside, and showed him the dance. Thus he became a medicine-man and afterwards made his doll according to his instructions. If there had been enemies in 1910, Sharp-horn felt he would still be entitled to conduct a Sun Dance. His doll was rather smaller than Wrinkled-face's, hardly over five inches in length. Small circles were painted for eyes, and the mouth and nose were indicated. The body was triangular, with a belt round the waist and a rectangular cross of greenish-blue beads on the chest to represent the Morning star. The neck was wholly covered with a strip of weasel skin, and attached to the back were shells and strips of skin. Owl feathers almost completely concealed the entire figure, which was meant to be suspended by a twisted string, near which was fastened a little bag filled with tobacco. The doll was stuffed with parts of herbs and roots, also with tobacco seeds. This bundle, too, contained ancillary objects, such as a large spherical rattle of buffalo hide, and the rectangular bag for the bundle was painted with a large central circle connected by symmetrical slanting lines with two smaller circles, one on either side. These lateral circles symbolized persons, but for the central one Sharp-horn had no explanation. Plenty-coups thought it might stand for a lodge.

Apparently all the dolls could be supplicated on behalf of men wishing good luck on the warpath. Such a brave would, according to Birds-all-over-the-ground, pay the owner, who then unwrapped his bundle, made a smaller copy of his doll to be tied to a little willow hoop, smoked it with sweetgrass incense, and hung it round the brave's neck. If the warrior was successful, he would give the medicine-man a horse and return the doll. But after doing this four times he merely gave the owner a horse and kept the doll. This procedure tallies exactly with that followed by a young man in getting the blessing of *any* war medicine (see p. 223).

Each bundle had its own history and distinctive rules. One was said to have been revealed to a woman; in fact, the doll entered her body and she took it out only directly before her death. However, being a woman, she was not qualified to put up a Sun Dance lodge. She made four dolls, which her son inherited; after him a brother of his passed one of them on to his son, Bear-from-above. Though his two predecessors had directed Sun Dances, Bear-from-above never exercised his right to do so, and when his wife died he buried the doll with her corpse. Before that he used to place it outside his tipi, where it remained untouched by any one as long as the Crow camped in the same locality. When he had dreamt to that effect, he would take it down the next morning, smoke it with cedar-leaf incense, lay the bundle on a blanket, and unwrap it so as to expose only the head and shoulders. The face was painted yellowish and red. The same procedure was followed if some one else requested to see the medicine.

According to Sharp-horn the Sun Dance was started by Iā′kac. Once he was fasting for five or six days, then he saw the Sun Dance lodge, which was very large, and in it the doll. Returning lean and sore-lipped, he told the people that any enemy coming to the lodge at night must be killed. Once an enemy was found sitting in the lodge unarmed, and the Crow killed him, took his scalp, and rejoiced over his death. Whenever any one wished to celebrate a Sun Dance because of a relative's death, he would come to Iā′kac. Iā′kac's ordinary tipi was painted to represent the Sun Dance lodge, as he had seen it in his vision: the upper half was painted black, and four streaks ran down to the ground, one on either side of the door, the others to the east and west, respectively.

Finally, Birds-all-over-the-ground ascribed the original discovery of medicine dolls to one Andicicō′pc (Dances-four-times?), famous in legend for his exploits in war and his invulnerability. Fasting on a high peak he was addressed by a little bird, which told him to look westward toward a mountain named I′axuxpec (Hide-flesher). There he beheld seven men and in front of them a woman wearing an elk-hide robe and holding a doll before her face. Several of her companions were beating drums painted with the figure of a skunk. Andicicō'pc could plainly hear their songs and learnt them. For an instant he looked around and when he had turned back, his visitants were standing nearer to him, on the top of a high hill. After a while he again looked away and when he turned back they were moving on the top of a bluff between the sites of Park City and Absaroka. When he looked away again, he did not see them again until he heard a noise at the foot of his resting-place, where they all then appeared.

The woman, who was the Moon, was standing in front with the doll in its buckskin wrapper in both her hands. One of the men said to the rest, "We live so far away and have come so far to see this boy [the hero]; we are tired." They again began to sing, and at the close of the first song the doll's head suddenly popped out of its own accord. When the second song was sung, the Moon shook the bundle at the boy and stepped back, then the doll emerged far enough to expose its arms. At the end of the third song, it showed its waist; after the fourth, the woman stepped first forward, then back, then the doll came out completely in the form of a screech-owl and perched on the Moon's head. The visionary was lying straight on his back and the screech-owl sat down on his breast. Suddenly one of the men loaded and cocked a breech-loader, stepped toward the boy and sang a song. Moon said to the bird, "Now, little screech-owl, this man is going to shoot you, you must make your medicine." It stood up and flapped its wings. He drew closer and shot at the bird, which entered his breast and began to hoot inside. Andicicō'pc looked towards the northeast and in the valley he saw a Sun Dance lodge. The eight visitants got up, singing and beating their drums. They moved towards the lodge, halting four times and singing at each stop. After the fourth song they entered. Andicicō'pc looked into the lodge and saw the doll tied to a cedar on the north side with a Whistler flat on his back at the foot of the tree. The seven men again sang four songs. Moon went to the Whistler, seized him by both hands, and at each song raised him slightly, but put him back to his former position until at the fourth song she pulled him up completely. Moon then stepped up to the doll and gave it to the Whistler, who held it in both hands. After a short time he put it back in its place.

They sang and danced, facing the medicine doll. Thus the doll was discovered, and whoever wished to start a Sun Dance asked Andicicō'pc to direct it. The doll represents the Moon, and the lodge in the vision is the Sun's lodge.[1]

The owner of one of these traditional Doll bundles, then, was chosen by the Whistler to become his "father" and thus automatically came to control all subsequent proceedings. These were fairly numerous. The site of the ceremony had to be selected; the entire band moved towards it in four stages; preparatory rituals occurred in the Whistler's lodge; the Sun Dance lodge had to be erected, but with ritualistically selected and felled trees as lodge poles and with ceremonially secured bull hides for tying the poles. Informants differ as to the relative sequence of events: I will follow Bear-crane's narrative.

The Preparatory Lodge. After the tongue collection the Whistler's tipi was carpeted with juniper leaves, and in the rear a bed of small-leaved sagebrush was prepared. As soon as the lodge was ready, the Whistler entered from the left side and approached the bed, followed by the Doll-owner, who sat down at his right, while on the mourner's left, but without coming close to him, old men sat down uninvited. They asked the Whistler how many days he intended to dance, and he would tell them what period he hoped for, though this actually hinged on the time of his trance. Then the Whistler said to his "father," "Sing for me tonight, and I will dance for you." The Doll Owner pondered this for a while, then promised to do so and went to his own tipi, where he asked his wife for any tanned deerskin. She went out, got one, and following her husband's instructions, took it to a virtuous woman, who was to be the garment-maker. This woman accepted it and brought it to the Doll Owner's tipi, where he smoked with incense first the skin, then himself, then the chaste woman's body and hands. He also smoked a knife with incense, and after three sham attempts actually cut the skin, of which the virtuous seamstress made a kilt with lateral seams. Takes-the-dead, when young, had filled this office; she used not sinew but buckskin thread and made four mock attempts before beginning to sew. The "father" smoked the completed garment, wrapped it up and stowed it away. Then he sent

[1] It is likely that the seven men symbolize the Pleiades or the Dipper, but the narrator did not expressly state this.

his wife for an unworn robe, which he also smoked with incense and put away.

The Doll Owner now said, "I will see my 'son' and find out whether he has any medicine and can get some." He went to the Whistler and seated himself in his customary place, smoking a pipe and remaining silent till the Whistler asked him what was the matter. The "father" told him to get eagle tail-feathers and at once returned to his home, while his "son" got feathers from relatives who were willing to give them gratis because they were full of pity for the Whistler. They sent a man to give the tail to the Doll Owner, who sent the bringer to summon a certain man, for during the ceremony the Whistler's "father" had the powers of a dictator. When the man sent for appeared, the Doll Owner told him to order five or six women famous as good workers to cut branches and foliage for the Tóngue lodge. When this was ready, a crier announced that the tongues distributed among distinguished warriors after the hunt were to be brought to this structure.

Among the articles made for the Whistler was a pair of plain moccasins sewed by the wife of a man who had killed and scalped an enemy. The moccasins were blackened with charcoal to represent the killing of an enemy, and buffalo hair was sewed on them to represent an enemy's scalp.

With everything ready for the first preliminary performance, the best singers were summoned, including two women. The Doll Owner, bringing a cup of white clay, and his wife came in and sat down beside each other. Approaching his "son," he brought within easy reach other essential paraphernalia, viz., juniper leaves, a whistle, a rattle, two plumes, a necklace of skunk hide, the kilt, and the robe. No one went near the Whistler and the Doll Owner couple. Since the beginning of the preparations the Whistler had been obliged to keep away from any other woman. The Doll Owner took some of the clay, shook his rattle, and sang the first song of the ceremony. No sooner had they heard this than all the people ran over to watch the performance at the Whistler's lodge, of which the door was flung wide open.

In front of the Doll Owner's seat there was a pit with burning buffalo chips. His wife put some juniper leaves over the fire, smoking them for incense after each of four songs she sang with her husband. After the last of these the medicine-man slowly lifted the kilt as if it were some delicate object, smoked it, and put it down. The same songs and actions were repeated, then the Doll Owner gently raised his "son" by his thumbs; and the Whistler, wearing only a clout, put his left foot over the chips to smoke it, then stepped into the kilt with it. A crier inside the lodge called upon the people to be silent and listen. The Doll Owner's wife gently raised the kilt into position, tied it with a leather cord, and tucked in the upper part of the garment, while her husband viewed his "son's" emaciated form. The musicians put down their pipes and prepared to sing. The Owner called for the best drum, and the drummer in handing it to him took pains not to pass the Whistler, going round by the door instead. The Owner's wife cast more juniper leaves on the chips and turned the drum back and forth over the fire, while her husband sang. At last the drum was returned to the musician, who resumed his seat after retracing his steps. The Owner smoked his rattle and sang in a low voice until he got to the fourth song, when he sang aloud and was joined by all the singers.

Now he was ready to paint the pledger. At the first song he smoked his own hands, held them close to his "son's" head, and slowly lowered them till at the end of the song they reached the ground. He acted in the same way during the second and third songs, but after that he dipped his hand into the white clay, which at the fourth song he put on the Whistler from head to foot. He then painted his "son's" back, then his left and right sides. Or rather, he went through the *motions,* and it was the woman who actually spread the white clay all over the Whistler's body. The same song was repeated again and again. When his wife was finished, the medicine-man made a cross on the Whistler's chest and another on his back, both symbolizing the Morning Star. With his fingers he marked lightning designs from the "son's" eyes downward to represent the mourner's tears and put the same mark on his forehead to indicate the Sun's way of painting. Making a slit in the middle of the skunk hide, he smoked it and painted it with white clay, then put it round the Whistler's right side, round his neck, and at last round his left side. Since no one was to pass in front of the Whistler, even the Doll Owner went behind him in putting the skunk skin on him. Then he tied a plume to the top of his "son's" head, repainting with white clay wherever the paint might have been rubbed off in the process of tying. He stood back and looked squarely at the Whistler. Having painted a plume with clay, he fastened it to the little finger of the Whistler's right hand, stepped back, and again looked at him for a long time. Next he tied a plume to the corresponding finger of the left hand. During all this ritual the drummers kept up their chant.

The woman now threw juniper leaves into the fire and smoked the moccasins already prepared. The Whistler being passive at this stage, she put on first the left and then the right moccasin. Her husband smoked the robe and three times pretended laying it down at the end of as many songs; at the fourth, he actually did so. Taking his "son" by the arm, he made him sit down and put the flaps of the robe round him, for the Whistler did not so much as touch it, so that the woman adjusted the garment for him. The Owner next smoked the whistle with incense, put clay on it, knelt before his "son," and during the space of four songs put the whistle into his own mouth, blew it while facing the Whistler, and danced in kneeling posture. The Whistler opened his mouth to receive the instrument and his "father" took it out of his own, but three times he merely pretended to give it to his "son." The fourth time the Whistler took it and began to dance in imitation of his mentor and in accompaniment of four songs by the drummer. Taking the whistle out of his mouth, he shook it; then his "father" took it and placed it round the stooping Whistler's neck.

The musicians stopped singing and emptied their pipe in four smokes. Four eminent warriors now entered,—from either side, all equipped for a raid afoot, and remained standing. Each had a rope and a bundle of moccasins tied to his belt; wolfskins served as scout badges, but guns were barred. The musicians waited until the two women among them sang this song:

"Woman comrade, sing my song; my home is here."

All the other drummers took up this chant, while the warriors gave a cry, clapping their mouths and flirting with the women. After four recitals of the song, the two warriors closest to the Whistler on either side said: "Well, to begin, just like this I did when I went to war." Hereupon each told about his captured horses or other undisputed honors, the drum being beaten for each feat. When all eight men had told their deeds, they left. The musicians smoked once more, then resumed singing. The Owner, after three sham attempts, removed the plume from his "son's" head and laid it down, and after his wife had thrown juniper leaves on the fire, he smoked the plume and laid it down. He similarly took off the skunk-skin, the plumes on the little fingers, the whistle, and last of all the moccasins, the kilt not being removed. The musicians kept on singing. The Owner said, "Bring in his quilts," and then sagebrush and cedar were brought in two bundles, of which the Owner made a bed and a pillow, respectively. Taking hold of the Whistler, he made him sit down, gently threw him on his back, and put his arms down, palms up. Three times he pretended to cover the mourner with the robe, then he actually did so. The Whistler had to remain thus on his back all night, with his feet toward the fireplace. The Owner now ordered a buffalo bull to be brought in, meaning a skull with the horns, which he put close to the Whistler's head and facing the same way.

All the singers went out, leaving the Owner couple to discuss the best site for the Sun Dance lodge,—possibly three miles away. When they had come to a decision, the man had his wife summon the herald, who received orders to notify the camp. The two next decided whether the Big Dogs, Muddy Hands, or some other club was to serve as police. The herald made this announcement also and told the society chosen to put up a wood pile as a marker of the site. This was about fifteen feet in height. The police waited there, and the whole band came and camped round the pile under the direction of the society. The Whistler's and the tongue lodge—the latter shaped like a summer shade—were moved together and placed not at the circumference but a little ways in toward the center. The Whistler's lodge faced the pile.

Now the performance of the preparatory lodge was repeated on three nights.

Getting the Essentials For a Lodge. Before erecting the Lodge, the Crow had to obtain suitable poles and two bull hides for tying together their tops. The relative order of these expeditions is differently reported; I follow Bear-crane in giving precedence to the bull hunt.

After the fourth preparatory performance the Owner pondered as to the location of buffalo. When he had got an inspiration from some supernatural source, he also thought of the best Crow sharpshooter and the best butcher. To the hunter he said, "Look here! Tomorrow get up at dawn, choose a fast mount to carry you out there and a fast buffalo-horse. Take two arrows from your quiver, with each you must kill a bull. Kill one six, seven, eight, nine or ten years old, but not one less than six years." This was a difficult task, for the bull had to be shot before sunrise and killed by the first shot; further, since a single hole in the hide was imperative, the arrow must not pass clear through the body. One of these marksmen, Sharp-horn, told me that if his arrow went through the beast he at once discarded it and cast about for another victim. To the butcher the Owner said: "Sharpen your knife as much as you can. Ride one horse, use another for packing. Do not eat any part of the bull, not the smallest piece. Do not taste of it, for it belongs to the Sun, who will watch, looking down at you all the time." Both men received two plumes and a string. To the sharpshooter the Owner said: "When you shoot the first buffalo, let him die. When you shoot the second, you must tie one plume to his tail and the other between his horns before he falls to the ground." The butcher was to treat the first bull in the same way. This part of the task was extremely dangerous, and one informant spoke of having been repeatedly put to flight by a wounded bull on these expeditions.

The party set out according to directions, and the butcher carefully but with the utmost dispatch cut up each bull as soon as he had expired. Except for the tongue and nasal cartilage, the head was discarded, as were the feet and the backbone; the remaining parts of the body were taken to camp, the hide being thrown over the marksman's horse, the meat on the pack-horse. On the way home the sharpshooter, who rode ahead, gave his knives and weapons to the butcher so as not to carry anything sharp. According to one informant there were *two* rival parties in search of a bull, each trying to return before the other.

The Owner appointed the best scouts to go out after preparing the usual wolf-hide badges and white clay. As soon as they sighted the returning party, they painted themselves, returned to camp, howling like wolves as though actually scouting, and went straight to a four-post shade in the center, where the hunters' meat was to be put down. There was a great stir, the people came out, sang songs, and inquired what they had seen. The scouts reported a killing or at least the sighting of a defenseless enemy, then all rejoiced and shouted. When the scouts appeared at the edge of the camp, the people were likely to dash up and treat them as enemies, i.e., count coup and capture their weapons, at the same time defining their deed, for example, saying, "Here I strike an enemy."

When Sharp-horn came back as marksman, a medicine-man with blackened face, wearing a juniper headband, and holding a rawhide rattle lay in wait for him and immediately began to sing when he saw him. As my witness rode nearer, the medicine-man seized his bridle and led him to the lodge of the Whistler, who was now wearing his bone whistle round his neck and had his whole body painted with white clay. Sharp-horn only dismounted when one of his own paternal clansmen came to aid him get off and this uncle told him to enter the tipi, where he found the Whistler and Doll Owner—in this case, Iā'kac (see p. 302). The Owner asked what had been done, and Sharp-horn answered: "I saw two enemies moving away. They did not see me. I ran up and killed one, the other escaped." Then he was asked to smoke from a pipe and went home.

According to other accounts the Doll Owner himself approached the hunters with a rattle and blackened face. All guns, arrows, and knives had to be removed from the place where the Owner met the returning party. The Whistler faced the hunters in his tipi, the door of which was flung open, and the whole camp was lined up to watch, but left a free passageway. After the hunter's report, the Owner sang a song of jubilation and led the hunter and butcher to the Whistler. No dog was allowed to get in front of him. Juniper leaves had been spread on the ground on two plots outside the entrance, and several lucky warriors lifted the riders from their horses so that they stepped on this carpet. They were made to sit on robes, and the meat and hide were unloaded and spread out on the foliage indoors. Some men examined the buffalo parts brought. If they found nothing wanting and there was a single hole in the hide, a herald told the old men and women to come and sit in a ring outside. Two lucky chiefs were chosen to cut up the inside, while two others sliced the meat. The entrails and marrow bones were given to the old

men, the meat to the old women. Now one man seized the first
bull-hide by the neck end, another by the tail, the hairy side
below, and thus they carried it to the Whistler's tipi. The other
hide was put on top with its hairy side up. Water was poured
on each hide, then it was folded and stowed away with as much
water retained as possible. A large lump of pounded charcoal
was laid with it. During the day old men would come in to smoke
with the Whistler and his "father."

The Owner now declared, "Tomorrow we shall cut lodge
poles." A crier accordingly ordered the people to rise as early
as possible on the next day, and a lucky warrior or one of the
policemen was sent out to scout for the most suitable trees. The
first of these was generally a cottonwood, the rest were either
the same or pine trees according to the Owner's revelations. Early
the next morning the herald roused the camp, ordering the young
men to fetch their horses, using their best saddlecloths, and the
young women to paint and put on their best clothes.

The Doll Owner bent a willow stick into a hoop with a
network of twelve willows, each topped with an eagle feather
painted black. In the center of the hoop he fastened his Doll,
which symbolized the Sun's face. Standing beside the Whistler,
who was facing the Owner's wife, he held up the Doll in the
hoop and said to the woman, "I am holding this Doll. Sing your
song of joy, then put the tongues into a kettle. When you return,
we shall start." She sang the song four times and went to put
the tongues into a kettle. A real scalp was tied to the forked
stick she used in cooking, and she sent for fresh willows, which
were sharpened and painted black.

When the Owner's wife returned, the procession for lodge
poles set out, the Whistler far ahead with the Doll, behind him
the Owner couple, then the singers and the police, finally four
women carrying all the freshly cooked tongues they could. One
policeman went in advance, pointing out the site of the trees.
There the Whistler halted, facing eastward. The tongue-bearers
put down their load and made a small shade for the Doll, which
was also made to face east; the Whistler sat down under it. The
police, half of whom remained in the rear, allowed no one to
come too close to the tree; on the other hand, they made all but
the sick and decrepit go toward the site. At last the rear guard

notified the police in front, and a herald then announced that all were present and that everybody was to keep still.

It was essential to select an absolutely virtuous woman to serve as Tree-notcher (akī'tsia-ō'waxe), one who had been purchased in marriage and had been scrupulously chaste. Even eligible women might decline, however, because by accepting the position they forfeited the right to remarry if widowed. For this reason my informant Takes-the-dead seems to have declined at first, though she remained virtuous in the face of frequent temptation. But when her son No-horse was almost dead, she vowed to serve as Tree-notcher provided he recovered. He got well and she carried out her pledge, praying at the same time that her husband might live for a long time. Hereafter she was highly respected and received the first share in food distribution.

Takes-the-dead told me the Whistler himself, leading the Owner and volunteer fasters, chose the Tree-notcher. According to Bear-crane, however, the Owner ordered the police to bring her, but first they obtained the best of the tongues. One of the policemen, followed by the rest, took it to a woman reputed to be irreproachable and offered her the delicacy. If, notwithstanding her reputation, she was not immaculately pure, she would openly confess her fault. For to accept was equivalent to an oath, and perjury would bring bad luck to all the camp. The formula of refusal because of unchastity was: "My moccasin has a hole in it" (masa'pe' hupi'ky). Mr. Curtis heard that a woman who accepted was led through camp and that any young man who had evidence against her was bound to challenge her. In one case the claimant to virtue was ignominiously dismissed and ever after taunted by her joking-relatives. A test of this sort is also indicated by Beckwourth's old account. The Tree-notcher handed the tongue to her husband, who felt proud of his wife. She was taken to the Whistler, who had remained under the shade with the Owner couple.

Two other officers had to be chosen; one was a berdache, the other a captive from the tribe that had caused the Whistler's mourning, and each received a tongue as fee. The berdaches were in hiding at this stage, but finally the police would discover and bring one. Amidst general merriment he would cover his face from bashfulness. A crier now announced that everything was ready and that everybody should approach.

The three special officers stood by the tree, the Tree-notcher holding a stone maul and the prong of an elk antler blackened at the top and chipped into a fine point at the other end. She faced west, the captive east, and the berdache north. The Owner couple stood behind the chaste woman, the man holding her by the shoulders, singing and shaking a rattle. At the close of his song he pushed the Tree-notcher a little, and she touched the tree with the prong, pretending to drive it in with the maul. In so doing she would think to herself, "I'll stick it in his eye,"— meaning the enemy (see p. 260). The captive and the berdache made similar sham motions, while the spectators shouted. Amidst growing excitement on their part the Owner sang his second song, the men preparing to fire their guns at the tree. Again the Notcher pretended to drive in her wedge. After the fourth song she tapped the tree with her prong—but without driving it in—; the berdache touched the tree with an axe, and the captive painted a black ring round the tree, having previously greased his or her hands and blackened them with charcoal. Then both the captive and the Notcher stepped back, and the berdache fell to chopping down the tree. It represented the enemy to be killed as a result of the Sun Dance, and all the people accordingly shouted and shot at it, young men striking it with their coup-sticks. When his job was done, the berdache slunk away.

According to Bear-crane, this first tree was not used in the structure to be put up but allowed to rest where it fell. However that be, the other poles were cut down without ceremony by young women, and they with their sweethearts, riding double, dragged twenty logs to camp, where they were set in a row. The police were closely watching the crowd, for the young braves now to be chosen for sitting on the logs tried to run away, since the first four—or, according to others, all twenty—thereby assumed the duty of never retreating from an enemy. So the young men would take to their heels, but were pursued by the police or the Whistler's kin, who rode fast horses. When seized, the fugitives cried out four times and sometimes resisted, but if necessary were dragged in by the hair. The Whistler, painted white all over and wearing a robe, was waiting for the fugitives. When the horsemen brought them in, he approached them and touched the captives with his hoop, which at once broke their resistance. Each merely uttered a cry of distress and sat down on the edge of a log. They also received tongues. The first four had their faces painted by the Whistler, who brushed them from head to foot with the Doll, a fact at once announced by a herald. The others were not so treated and, according to my best accounts, were selected for wealth rather than bravery.

In any event, the kin of all the log-straddlers put down before the young men such property as robes or beadwork, and little sticks to symbolize horses as gifts. All went to the Doll Owner, but after appropriating what he pleased he distributed the rest among the people who helped in the performance.

Young men and women, riding double, now dragged the poles to the site of the Lodge. The first man to untie his log had the right to lead in an expedition for willow branches to shade the Lodge. Again young women, who did the actual cutting of the twigs, rode double with the men. There were two of these trips, then the military clubs went about on opposite sides and wherever they met they laid the willows in a ring round the poles. By this time it was evening and every one went home, the members of clubs going round with a few young women at night and singing in front of various lodges.

The tongues were returned to the tongue lodge, and the Whistler went back to his tipi. People took pains not to pass him from the side whence the wind blew, and menstruating women avoided him. He had not eaten or drunk anything for days now, and was in a weakened condition. The Owner had abstained largely but not wholly from food, and was also emaciated. Visitors came in and out of the tipi, but dropped out till only the Whistler and the Owner couple remained. The Owner gave instructions to his "son," but in so low a tone that no one else could hear him. Only these two were permitted to smoke a straight pipe; indeed, the Whistler must not touch any other, and the Owner only when outside. The woman had her husband announce that the Lodge would be erected on the next day. The Owner planted a cedar tree behind the buffalo skull, tied the Doll hoop to it, and obtained a second skull,—the two together representing the two bulls killed by the sharpshooters. Finally, the Owner took off his son's ceremonial raiment, smoked him with incense, and retired with his wife.

Erection of the Lodge. At dawn the crier woke up the people because the Lodge was to be erected. The young men saddled their horses and invited young women to ride behind them to get firewood. When they had gathered it, the police chose for leader of the returning party a virtuous woman, though not necessarily a purchased wife. If she accepted, she took the tongue offered her, gave it to her husband, and joined the assembled party of both sexes, where she was put on a horse, and took the brushwood in front of her saddle. Thus she became akbiri't basā'ndc, the one who goes first for firewood. She was led by a renowned young man selected by the police and also receiving a tongue for his service. In single file they went round the inside of the camp, then straight to the Lodge site, where they set down the brushwood in a big pile.

Variations in detail were allowable, for according to Redeye the leader was afoot, leading the bravest warrior's horse. The chastity of this woman, however, was essential, and if one who had failed to be perfectly virtuous took the office, some man would shout, "She has a hole in her moccasin!" or "You are crazy! You have done so-and-so!"

Next the men were ordered to get outer tipi poles, i.e., those corresponding to smoke-regulators. They tied them together in pairs, then joined three of the main Lodge poles and made them rest on the pile marking the site, while the other poles and the willows were laid down.

The Owner smoked the two hides and after singing four songs painted them black with charcoal, with which he also decorated the Whistler, who was now made to sit on the juniper leaves in front of his tipi. A female relative of the Whistler's brought a sharp knife, a whetstone, and a hoe; the Doll owner took them and sharpened the knife, which was blackened. He had his own chin, forehead, and cheeks blackened; and he wore a cedar crown and moccasins like the Whistler's. The black color, as usual, meant vengeance. The people looked on while the police tied together the first three (or four) poles with a bundle of willows.

A famous horse-raider was sent to cut willow sticks about two feet long, and two other men of similar distinction were chosen to tell their deeds and to sharpen the points of the sticks, while the woman painted the willows with charcoal. After she had sung four times, she began to cut the hide. For the Doll Owner juniper foliage had already been placed wherever he had to step. He motioned toward the four quarters, then made a cut at one foreleg, repeated his motions and cut the hind leg, then proceeded to the other side of the first hide and to a similar ritual with the second. He found out how many pins were required for fastening the hides, then made the necessary perforations along the edge of both. A company of valorous men took each of the hides and rubbed it under one of the Lodge poles, but so it did not touch the ground. They made both heads face east, and the pins were run through the peripheral holes so as to fasten the two hides together. Other hides were soaked in water and cut into strips now; these were to be tied to the Lodge poles for voluntary self-torturers to swing from.

The three—some say, four—main poles were raised at one end so as to rest on the woodpile marker, and their point of intersection was wrapped with willows. Then the ends of the poles were pushed through the holes, the hides being twisted so the poles could be run through several times; and the sharpened pegs were run through the hides to hold them together. Those hides, with a wrapping of willow sticks and juniper leaves, symbolized an eyrie, and the next step was for the police to make a man with bird medicine sit in the nest. This man, wrapped in a robe pinned with a wing-feather, painted his face according to his vision, tied his sacred objects to the back of his head, and taking an eagle-feather fan in each hand began to whistle in his own lodge like a bird. Then with four stops and singing at each he approached the site. The police allowed no one, not even a dog to pass in front of him. If he heard a dog bark, he would at once return to his tipi. He imitated a bird's actions, walked toward the poles against which the hides had been rubbed, and again began to sing. After the fourth song he walked up the pole, flapping his "wings," and sat or knelt down in the nest. Everybody shouted, and with the aid of coupled tipi-poles the main Lodge poles were raised a short distance, then lowered again. The bird-man whistled. Three times the poles were raised and lowered, finally they were raised to the proper height. Then the man stood up and faced first west, then north, east, and south. Holes were dug and the butts of the poles put into them. The bird-man continued to impersonate a big bird in flight and to raise the main poles as they were hoisted into place. The rest of the Lodge poles were lifted by the same device of coupled tipi poles as if to push the nestling down, but he managed to get out of the way. The people threw him a rope, and he tied the main and supplementary poles together. Below the people now used the willows and brush brought in by the special parties of young folk to construct the covering; that is, they tied the willows between the poles from the ground to the level of a person's chest, where a space was left so that outsiders could look in. Thence the covering was resumed to the top. On a windy day the lower part of this screen was superseded by cloth, and at times rawhide was used in the upper space.

The woodpile was taken away, and the bird-man slid to the ground as fast as possible and ran home. He was entitled to four choice articles from the lot set down by the log-straddlers' kin. Before leaving, he announced a consolatory vision, such as: "I have seen a person killed, a little ways off on the prairie I saw a person lying dead already."

Unlike the structure of their neighbors, the Crow Sun Dance Lodge has the shape of a very large tipi on the style of a Tobacco Adoption Lodge, but still larger (Fig. 14).

The police now notified people that the time had come for the Fireless Dance (birā'retarisu'a), and every one came scurrying to the screen. According to Bear-crane, the Morning Star founded this performance with the Sun's sanction. Its essence was the entrance of several war parties for the purpose of possibly seeing a vision in the not yet quite completed structure. Each company came by itself, headed by a scout, while the captain with a scalp tied to his pipe brought up the rear. These performers had got ready towards the close of the pole-lifting and now came out of the captains' tipis, to the singing and drumming of musicians seated in the Lodge. The young women clapped their mouths, and others shouted, "The captains are ready to come now!"

The warriors ran to the Lodge, halting four times. Some were dragging ropes, others carried whips, and all acted as if in a fight. The first group came in, swung about to the right, circled round looking at the nest for a vision, then faced the door, i.e., east. The captain might then declare that he had not seen anything, or that he had seen a dead Dakota, etc. Then he and his followers passed out on the side to avoid collision with the next company. They would dash home to redress and rushed

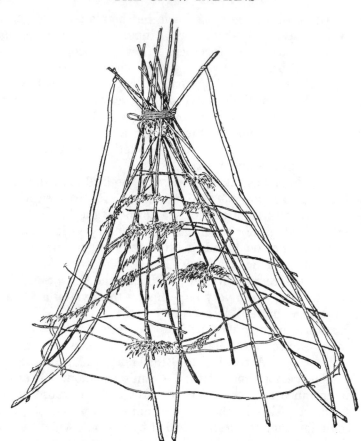

FIG. 14.—Model of Sun Dance Lodge.

back to watch the next group. Possibly as many as ten parties
succeeded one another, thus consuming several hours' time. At
last everybody went away, the musicians adjourning to the
Whistler's tipi, where they sang all evening. No one was allowed
to enter the Lodge. A herald went through camp ordering all the
people to get up early the next day since one more thing had to
be done. That night the Whistler was almost exhausted, though
he had as yet suffered but a small part of what was to fall to
his lot.

The final preparatory act was to get white clay for the
Whistler's bed. The police made all the young women dress up

and assemble once more, and the men selected partners among them. Now the police took a tongue and offered it to a virtuous *man*, i.e., one who had never taken liberties with a woman not his wife,—specifically, one who had not played with his sisters-in-law or tried to touch a woman's genitalia (see p. 28). Whoever had broken these rules would excuse himself with the formula, "I have made a hole in my moccasin." If a pretender accepted, the women would give public testimony against him, such as, "You touched my breasts! His moccasin is soleless, cast him aside."

At last a suitable man was found to lead the procession. He picked up some white clay at the proper spot, but first he said, "Because I never did such and such things, I wish to kill an enemy and have a good time." Then he put the clay into a cloth, the others following suit. Returning, he led the horse of the best-looking woman so all could see them. He and the woman got a tongue each. He laid the clay down in a big pile by the Whistler's bed in the rear of the Lodge. The police came in and a man who had accompanied a party that captured an enemy told of the deed. The police then smoothed the oblong site of the Whistler's bed, where the clay was put on in form of a little ridge.

The Consummation. While the police were arranging the clay, good singers had been called to the Whistler's tipi. The Whistler for the present remained there, having been painted with the same ceremony as on the first preparatory day and wearing his skunk-skin regalia, as well as the plumes tied to his solitary lock and to his little fingers. The several sacred objects, however, were taken from his tipi to the Lodge,—two men carrying the cedar, two others the buffalo skulls, with the Owner couple following in the rear. The husband adjusted the pole and the skulls behind the bed and sprinkled charcoal on the fireplace, while his wife brought in some fat from a buffalo's neck and put greased charcoal on the bottom of the cedar. As soon as the couple came back, they joined the singers in a song to which the Whistler danced, blowing an eagle-bone whistle round his neck and holding the hoop with the Doll. The people at large were lined up in two rows to watch his exit but left a passage for the procession. The Whistler stepped towards the door and after the first song thrust out his hoop, but then stepped back.

At the close of the second song he put the hoop outside so as
to expose a little more of its feathers, but also his head and
chest. After the fourth song he went out and walked a little
ways, followed by the singers. There he halted and danced,
looking at the Doll. He went on, making four stops before he
reached the entrance. Going in, he put the feathers in front of
him and walked up to the cedar, followed by the Owners. The
husband took the hoop and tied it to the cedar, fixing the Doll
so it was on a level with the Whistler's face as he stood up. The
musicians entered on the right side and formed a circle. No
sooner had the Whistler entered than the onlookers ran to the
Lodge to watch the ceremony, the men allowing the women to
lean against the railing and hugging them from behind.

The fire was built and kept up in an oblong space in the
center, the tenders being members of the slain Crow's war party.
Over the fire the kettles were suspended from a crosspiece connecting two poles on either side. The cooks, wearing juniper-leaf
headbands and carrying blackened forked sticks decorated with
scalps, brought in tongues and cooked them; this was their daily
task henceforth. Either that evening or on the next day eminent
young men would thrust sharpened poles into the Lodge by way
of demanding a tongue. If their record was really good, those
inside stuck a tongue—in case of special distinction, two tongues
—on the point. The warrior took his prize outside and gave it
to his sweetheart.

While the first night's cooking was going on, some informants report, a pantomime was staged. Renowned men painted
themselves according to their medicines, while their wives,
painted red, carried bundles of spoils captured, laying down bows
and guns in front of the warriors. These men had the privilege of
entering from either side, but the first one came in on the right
side. Each captain chose several men to play the part of his
followers and some others to impersonate the enemy, and thus
they gave a series of performances of their respective exploits.
Bear-crane puts these sham fights at a later stage in the ceremony, and Red-eye substitutes a mere recital of deeds. According to him, the braves were obliged to walk toward the left when
in the Lodge and he recalled a case where an offender was
rebuked and had his face slapped with the foliage on a branch.

It was about this time, too, that one of the most spectacular auxiliary performances began. Men eager to obtain visions would have their bodies daubed white all over and suspended themselves by the chest or shoulders from the twenty Lodge poles. For an excess of would-be visionaries two ropes were tied to a pole, or the self-torturers erected forked posts outside from which they would hang. There was a variation: sometimes a man had his back pierced with a skewer, to which as many as seven buffalo skulls were attached, and these he would drag through camp until they were torn loose. All these sufferers were aided by medicine-men and other notables. Thus, a famous man would first tell of his deeds, adding, "This man wishes to do likewise," and then pierce his protégé's chest. The self-torturers began in the morning and were released at night, when each retired to a little four-pole structure covered with brush and leaves. According to one authority, they finally announced the nature of the blessing granted them.

The Whistler did not undergo such austerities. Until his entrance his fast had not been complete, but thenceforth he neither ate any food nor drank any water. This abstention held also for the self-torturers and the fire-tenders.

After the famous men had come in and the tongues were ready, the musicians sang their first song: "Water weeds are your lodge poles, beat ye the drums!" Then the Doll Owner took a whistle, began to dance, and at the end of the song put the whistle into the mouth of the Whistler, who now began to dance himself on his clay bed, making the dirt fly and continually gazing at the Doll. At the first drum-beat the self-torturers, whether inside the Lodge or outdoors, began to run around their poles. The first song was sung four times. Then one renowned man after another would mimic his exploits, return to his place, and there recount them orally. The song was then sung eight times for a second man, and for his successors, making probably not more than six actors in all on the first night, certainly not so many as ten.

When the deeds had all been told, the Owner beat his rattle and sang a song, which the musicians took up. Standing behind the Whistler, he slowly and ceremoniously removed his dress and regalia, tying the whistle, necklace and head-plume to the Doll and his own rattle to the cedar. In the meantime the Whistler continued standing with his face toward the Doll. The Owner took the plumes from his little fingers, seized him by the thumbs and made him lie down on his bed, where he covered him up to his neck with a robe. At the foot of the bed a pit was dug to hold charcoal, and juniper needles were smoked there. The Whistler went to sleep and the spectators went away. Except for the fasters, no one was allowed near the Lodge. The self-torturers' kin made beds of juniper and scented sagebrush for them. The Doll Owner couple also went home, ordering a crier to rouse the camp before dawn.

Early the next morning the herald shouted, "Our friend has been lying on his back for a long time! Get up and eat!" Then the young people of both sexes dressed in their best clothes and painted up, while the musicians, after breakfast, went directly to the Lodge and began to sing. The Doll Owner was still at home, bathing, resting, or combing his wife. When ready, he slowly walked toward the Lodge, stopping to look about, and at last slowly sat down with his wife amid the beating of drums. The people all rushed towards the Lodge when they saw him start so as not to miss any part of the performance.

White clay, scented sagebrush, and juniper leaves had been prepared. The clay was soaked in water, then the Owner's wife laid it before her husband, who smoked a straight-pipe laid by the Whistler's side. Scooping up buffalo chips with a buffalo shoulderblade, she put them into the pit at the foot of the bed and built a fire there, throwing in juniper needles for incense. The large central fire had gone out, but was renewed by the tenders before the Owner's coming. The Owner put some juniper branches below the Whistler's feet, smoked his hand with the incense while a song was being sung, and after three sham attempts removed his ward's robe, smoked it, and laid it down as on the day before. He, then, removed the right and left moccasins, and laid them also down as before. Holding the Whistler by his thumbs, he raised him. The Whistler, trying to limber his legs, nearly fell down from weakness, but was supported by the Owner. He stepped on the juniper needles and was turned around to face the white clay prepared in a cup. The Owner now, with customary attention to the fourfold repetition of acts, put his hand into the container, painted the Whistler's body from head to foot, making a cross in front and back, tied the plumes, danced with the whistle in his own mouth beside the Whistler, who was standing still at this time, and then put the whistle into his ward's mouth. The drumming ceased and excited cries came from the crowd: "He is going to dance!"

An indefinite number of prominent men now came in, properly painted; and those on the right side staged a sham battle against those of the left, one party representing the Crow, the other the enemy. The Doll Owner was sitting down and smoking. The musicians, joined by the women, were singing a song, repeating the first one sung in the preparatory tipi, while the Whistler was moving only his hands and the upper part of his body. Two women in charge of the tongues began to cook them. They wore juniper crowns and a spring-calf skin kilt with the hairy side out.

At first the Whistler danced slowly, at the second song a little faster, at the third words were sung and his heels began to move. These were the words,—past in form but prophetic in intent: "What you are dancing for has come!" With the beginning of the fourth song the Whistler danced as vigorously as he could. Without purposely blowing his whistle, he produced sounds from it automatically by his panting. The singers continued until tired out, when they stopped drumming. The sham fight likewise ceased then, three or four warriors telling about their deeds, the musicians beating their drums for every exploit. The fighters resumed their play, discharging shots without paying any attention to the Whistler. After their performance, their father's clansmen sang songs of jubilation and received horses for their efforts.

The drumming stopped only four times all day. During the second or third intermission the Whistler's kin piled up gifts for the Owner and left horses for him outside. After the third song there was smoking. The Whistler had to dance as long as there was any singing. When he got very tired at the fourth song the musicians would try to give him a rest, but the women wanted to utterly exhaust him and began the first song over again; thus forcing him to go on dancing. The song was repeated twenty times. Then the Whistler, quite worn out, would go into a trance: he was like one demented (warā'axe) according to one informant, like an intoxicated (kā'xutsēky) person according to another. The Doll seemed to him to be directly between his eyes and he fell back panting, while the people cried: "Leave him alone! Don't touch him!" The Owner waited to see on which side the Whistler would fall, then whirled his rattle over him till the panting subsided, and dragged him to his bed.

This was the acme of the whole Sun Dance and was by no means always reached the day after the entrance to the Lodge. Big-shadow, as Whistler, is reported to have had a six days' wait before his revelation, though One-horse gave three days and two nights as the longest period he could remember. On the other hand, a Whistler tutored by Iā'kac (p. 302) was fortunate in having a Piegan killed on the first night of the ceremony proper. This was considered the most miraculous sort of occurrence, and Iā'kac accordingly took rank as the foremost of Owners. In the absence of such windfalls the Whistler had to continue to suffer till his revelation came. White-spot-on-his-neck, starved and worn out by the excessive heat, arbitrarily tore off his paraphernalia and dashed for water after a single night in the Lodge. He should have patiently waited for a vision, for the Doll he used was the famous one I bought from Pretty-enemy, which had never failed. Hence every Crow had foreboding of evil. As they were moving towards the Bighorn, the Dakota came upon them and killed eleven young men and one woman. This loss was generally imputed to White-spot-on-his-neck's pusillanimity at the Sun Dance. Misfortune came also if a Doll was used without the sanction of a real vision (p. 299).

There was some variation as to the final stage. Some Whistlers had their vision while falling, others apparently the very night after going home, in which case it is difficult to see what made them terminate the Dance. One man had a revelation first in the Lodge, and afterwards at home. The Whistler did not describe his vision immediately, but contented himself with saying, "I think it will be well, I shall have revenge." Most Whistlers made their announcement just before setting out on the punitive trip; more rarely the statement came after the enemy had been killed.

No Whistler was living at the time of my field work, but the power exerted by the Doll was attested by various eye-witnesses. All the spectators would watch both the Whistler and the Doll. Whenever a warrior lied about his deeds, the Doll winked its eyes. "We looked at it," said Bear-gets-up, "and as we looked at it, it changed." It was the Doll that showed the

Whistler slain enemies as he was dancing back and forth before it. Some saw the entire scalped body of an enemy in front of the Doll. The Whistler, one informant stated, directly prayed to the Doll, saying, "I am miserable, I put up the Lodge so I might kill an enemy soon."

In the above account the assumption is that a trance came automatically. But sometimes the Whistler's kin paid the Owner to bring it on, though occasionally they considered it better to prolong the period of fasting and would defer taking this step. When inducing a trance, the Owner took a rattle, made incense of cedar needles and made the Whistler smoke himself with it. Seating himself at the foot of the pole from which the Doll was suspended, the Owner ordered the Whistler to look at the image, shook the post and looked at the Whistler, who began to dance to his instructor's chanting and riveted his eyes on the Doll. After a while he would see it blackening its face and promising that he would kill an enemy at a certain season and under certain circumstances. Suddenly, the Whistler would stop dancing and fall down in a swoon, his eyes still fixed on the Doll.

When the vision was obtained, each person within the Lodge got a tongue, and every one, including the self-torturers, went home. The Owner smoked until all had gone, then put down his pipe, removed the Whistler's regalia, and smoked each article in turn with incense. After smoking the robe, he put it on the Whistler, who went home, sometimes aided by relatives because of his weakness. The gifts offered to the Owner were taken to his tipi and distributed there. He removed the Doll from its hoop and carried it to his tipi. Later a kinsman of the Whistler's came, to take the hoop and offer it to the Sun in some exposed spot, possibly the top of the Lodge poles. The Lodge was left standing to fall a prey to the elements.

The self-torturers who had broken loose before the Whistler's vision waited till the close of the ceremony before touching their ropes. The rest were released by their several spiritual sponsors, each of whom would first recount one of his exploits. Little boys took down the ropes, whose owners then took them home.

With the close of the ceremony ended the Doll Owner's dictatorship. The camp chief resumed control and the people moved toward the enemy to see the vision fulfilled.

Summary. The Sun Dance looms as the grandest of Crow ceremonies, and it is also the one best integrated. The unification does not, however, consist in the adoration of a particular supernatural being. The Sun, to be sure, is recurrently mentioned, yet most of the ritualistic performances are not connected with him. The factor that binds together otherwise uncoördinated elements is the overshadowing idea of revenge. This, from first to last, dominates the action. The primary means for gaining the end is the Doll, with its assumed power of stimulating the proper type of revelation. But virtually every one is trying to help by bringing the universe into accord with this object. Hence the interminable blackening of faces and even of material articles, hence the mention of successful war enterprises, the attempt of the war captains to secure auxiliary visions, the counting of coup not only on the Lodge pole but on the returning scouts as well. Every one seems imbued with the craving for condign punishment of the offending tribe, and the incessant suggestion or memory of events similar to the coveted aim of the ceremony constitutes a subtle form of imitative magic and imparts a sort of unity to the Dance.

XVII. World-View

THE Crow universe was narrowly bounded. To the north and east flowed the "Great River" on which their kin, the Hidatsa, lived with their fellow-agriculturists, the Mandan and Arikara. But that far to the south there were Indians planting corn to the practical exclusion of hunting, people who dwelt in stone houses, made painted pottery, wove cotton fabrics, and, among many strange calendric festivals, also danced with snakes in their mouths,—that was something wholly beyond the Crow ken. In 1916 I once sketched to a few elderly Lodge Grass men what I had seen among the Hopi; they listened with interest but without the slightest sense of kinship with these weird folk: I might have been telling of a trip to the moon. Nor did any Crow divine that on the coast of British Columbia there were members of their race who traveled in forty-foot canoes, built solid wooden houses, and recognized sharply separated social castes. Crow geography was of the Northern Plains, sweeping within their ethnographic horizon only a few marginal parasites like the "Pierced Noses" (Nez Percé) and "Bad Lodges" (Shoshone).

Within the radius, then, of a few hundred miles the gunless, horseless Crow of pre-Caucasian days sought to preserve his existence. It was a sorry kind of life. "Savages," says Dr. Marett, "live at but one remove from death." The ancient tales are charged with that theme: "In the early days the Crow were moving camp, they were roaming about seeking food." And Old Man Coyote is forever pictured going about, racked with hunger, "looking for food." But to seek and to find were not the same. Again and again a band was reduced to rabbit fare and threatened with starvation when big game capriciously stayed away. But even at best foraging was no light task. Individual hunters were gored by buffalo; the tribal hunt failed unless there was perfect coöperation; women on a berrying-bee were surprised by bears or abducted by enemies; even a fair-sized party of men were liable to find themselves surrounded by a superior force of Cheyenne or Dakota.

Sorry, indeed, was the plight of the disabled or orphaned. We hear of a man with failing sight; his wife goes digging up roots and follows in the wake of the camp, picking up what food others have scorned. More circumstantial is the legend of two kinless boys: "Whenever the camp moved, they followed behind; when the camp was pitched they made a shelter for themselves, that is where *they* stayed. Whenever meat was plentiful, they picked up what had been left and dried it. When the camp moved, they [the boys] took the discarded moccasins; the best part of these they would sew together and put on." Twined-tail and his brothers eked out their existence in similar fashion (see p. 158).

Emergencies at times presented a grim alternative. Should a crippled tribesman be shielded at the risk of peril to his mates or abandoned to his fate? On-top-of-the-bull goes on a war party and a shot fractures his shinbone. His friends drag him into a wood and discuss what ought to be done. But the hero grasps the situation with relentless objectivity: "You had better leave me, you can't help me, you had better go home." So they put up a shelter, fill a paunch with water, bring him firewood, and leave what provisions they can spare. This legendary episode was almost duplicated in the life of my informant Yellow-brow's maternal uncle, Young-cottontail. As a youth of eighteen he went on a raid organized by Twitching-eyes. An arrow pierced his knee-pan and would not come out; his knee swelled up— "There was nothing like it." His fellows were helpless, and he himself urged them to abandon him. So they made him a shelter, stocked it with buffalo flesh and water paunches, and went away.

Yet in both cases the human spirit rises superior to the urge of self-preservation. Among On-top-of-the-bull's comrades is his own younger brother. When this lad has gone a little ways, he bursts out crying: "If I leave my brother while he is still alive, I'll never forget that. I will not go, I'll stay with him." So he goes back to tend his brother and hunt game for him. Nor is this all. When the party gets home, On-top-of-the-bull's sweetheart learns of his plight and decides to rescue him. One of the warriors tells her the route, but with scant encouragement: "If you don't freeze and are not killed, you can get to him." She steals away with provisions, crosses river after river on the ice, finds her lover, and brings him her food. Yet another trial awaits her. The brother sights a hostile party advancing toward them, and the older man bids his mistress conceal herself. She answers: "I have come a long way to see you and shall die with you now." By a lucky chance the enemy turns in another direction, and the rescue is consummated. The historical parallel holds similar acts of devotion. When Young-cottontail's mates have gone a certain distance, they turn back crying and offer to take him along. A second time he bids them leave him and save themselves. When they return, the youth's father finds out all about his whereabouts and at once starts out with a rescuing party. " 'How is he getting on, I wonder? Is he still alive?' he said and went off crying." They reach the hero and bring him back in safety.

Tales like these explain what social bonds mean where there is no paternalistic State to guard its wards. The single human being is a mere worm at the mercy of the elements. A man may be a champion marksman, but when there is no game to shoot he falls back on the pemmican his wife has stored against that very emergency; and even in the chase he is most efficient when he hunts in company. His robes and leggings are the work of his wives or kinswomen; his very arrows are not of his own making but the handiwork of skilled craftsmen. If he seeks renown, what are his chances as a lonely raider? Even a well-organized party was likely to be cut to pieces or be hard put to it when fleeing from superior numbers. Crisis lowered on every side, and it meant everything to be able to face life not alone but with a comrade, shielded by one's family and clan, in the bosom of one's club. That is why the kinless man was an outcast and byword of shame, the target for the brutality of sadistic tribesmen, forced to throw himself on the mercy of benign supernaturals.

Yet here is a curious fact. Battered by natural forces and surrounded by enemies, the Crow managed to wrest from existence his portion of happiness. Ask an Indian of the old school whether he prefers modern security to the days of his youth: he will brush aside all recent advantages for a whiff of the buffalo-hunting days. If there was starvation then, there were buffalo tongues, too,—supreme among earthly dishes; if you were likely to be killed, you had a chance to gain glory. What is a Crow to look forward to nowadays? Shall he enter unequal

competition with white farmers? And his sister aspire to wash
the laundry of frontier towns? Under the old régime, harassed
as he might be, the Crow was owner of his soul. He had somehow hammered out for himself standards that lifted him above
the sordid animal-like fray for survival. So with all the grossness
of his sex life there evolved awe-inspired reverence for immaculate virtue; the callous egotism of the daily struggle for existence
could be transmuted into purest self-sacrifice; above the formal-
ized and sometimes tricky competition for honor emerged the
loftiest defiance of relentless destiny.

We have found the Indians a mass of contradictions; and
nowhere more so than in the matter of bravery. On the one side,
old age is decried and youthful death alone looms as a man's
proper lot in life. Yet more often than not discretion seems the
better part of valor. More than one character in the tales lives
to be "so old that his flesh cracked whenever he moved." The
visions that mirror so faithfully the hidden longings of the soul
again and again bring out the same urge for longevity. Hillside's
protector appears with gray hair in earnest of the visionary's
old age; a buffalo opens his toothless mouth to show Humped-
wolf that he need not fear death until he has lost his teeth; and
so forth. So the commonest form of prayer asks for life to be
continued until such and such a season. Again, a warrior *could*
scry before setting out on a raid: if he saw his image with
wrinkled face in a mixture of buffalo and badger blood, all was
well; if he saw himself scalped or bloodstained, evil awaited
him. But, Gray-bull admitted, people in his heyday were afraid
to use this kind of divination; and his grandfather had become
very brave *after* seeing his reflection with white hair and wrinkled face.

But as in every generation there were women who would
not yield to the temptations of the flesh and fulfilled the qualifications of a Tree-notcher in the Sun Dance, so there were men
to whom the traditional ideals were more than empty words to
be sung at a dance to impress the young women. "I do not want
to be old . . . I don't want to be afraid of anything . . . I'll do
something to die," said one Rides-a-white-horse-down-a-bank.
He went on four parties and dug himself a hole. When the enemy
surrounded it, he leapt out and drove them back. Once there
was a Lumpwood dance, and he allowed himself to be led about

camp by a man who declared: "If any young women want this man for a sweetheart, let them do it forthwith, he does not want to live long." The young man painted himself white, mounted his white horse, covered its eyes, and made it jump down a steep and rocky bank, so that both of them were crushed.

Such aversion from life was sufficiently common to be pressed into a fixed pattern. A man no longer interested in living became a "Crazy-Dog-wishing-to-die" (micgye-warā'axe-akcēwī'a); he wore sashes and other trappings for regalia, carried a rattle, danced and sang distinctive songs as he rode about camp. He "talked crosswise" (irī'-watbakarā'), i.e., he said the opposite of what he meant and expected to be addressed correspondingly. Above all, he was pledged to foolhardiness. In this as in other features he conformed to the pattern of the military clubs. But while the officers in these societies were in the main obliged merely to hold their ground, a Crazy Dog deliberately courted death, recklessly dashing up to the enemy so as to be killed within the space of one season. Whenever one of them rode through camp, the old women cheered him lustily and younger ones came to comfort him at night. But his own kin naturally tried to dissuade him and grieved over his resolve to die. "Why have you done that?" Spotted-rabbit's mother asked: "you are one of the best-situated young men . . . you are one of the most fortunate men who ever lived . . . and were always happy." But Spotted-rabbit was bored with life because he could not get over his father's death. Similarly, Cottontail's sister tried to dissuade him: "This is a bad thing for you to do. Even if you want to die without good cause, there are plenty of enemies and if you are not afraid you can get killed without special effort. If men become Crazy Dogs and are not killed, they become a laughingstock, . . . they are said to be worthless." The account continues: "He did not say 'Yes,' he said nothing at all, but one night some time after this when the people had gone to bed he came out, shouting, and sang the Crazy Dog songs. His sisters fell a-crying, but there was nothing they could do." Cottontail, too, had a motive: he had never wholly recovered from the injury to his knee (p. 328). "Whenever young men went afoot on a raid or hunting, whenever they undertook anything, he was handicapped and felt envious."

Such men grew restive if the days passed and their longing

remained unfulfilled. When Spotted-rabbit received a gift of plums, he said, "I began to be a Crazy Dog early in the spring and did not think I should live so long; yet here am I today eating plums." And Cottontail would complain, "Methinks, we'll *never* meet the enemy." But he, like Spotted-rabbit before him, had his wish. Once the Crow made the enemy fortify himself in a trench. Cottontail said, "Already I was thinking I was not to see the enemy . . .; yonder I see some. This is what I am looking for." He advanced, shot down at the Dakota, and was instantly killed. That night it rained violently, and the corpse lay in the water until daybreak. Then the Crow hung it over Cottontail's horse. "Then they brought him home, grieving they took him to the camp, all the Crow, the entire camp cried. They laid him on a scaffold, they stuck a tipi pole into the ground and tied his sashes to it, his drum and rattle they tied to it. Above they were blowing in the breeze. Then without him they moved."

The respect paid to a Crazy Dog was probably not altogether due to admiration for egotistical recklessness. It was a foregone conclusion that a man who had renounced life would do the utmost damage possible to the enemy. More than a mere paragon of valor, he was thus at least potentially a source of power to the tribe. But the altruistic value of intrepidity appears in more explicit fashion. There were men willing to make a stand to rescue a fleeing fellow-Crow and honored accordingly (p. 190). A bereaved mother would go about wailing and implore brave men to avenge her wrongs: "The Dakota have killed my . . . child, who is going to kill one of them for me?" And the warrior's mentor would encourage him with such words as: "A child has been killed, a woman has asked you for help, that is why I want you to help." In the herald's speeches already quoted (p. 231) the appeal is constantly to human sympathy with the pitiable captives subjected to humiliation by a cruel chief and casting wistful glances toward their possible liberators.

The same narrative contains an extraordinary human document exposing at once human frailty and grandeur in the same individual and culminating in a magnificent blending of patriotic fervor on behalf of the oppressed tribesfolk and the spirit of the Crazy Dog who has faced reality and turns his back upon this vale of tears. Double-face has been one of the young braves publicly presented to the tribe by the herald as their champions in the impending battle. But when the crowd has dispersed, Double-face is racked with doubts. To quote Yellow-brow:

"Then this day Double-face was lying around; he stripped, he was nervous, he was uncomfortable. Whatever he undertook turned out ill. The reason he was upset was that there was to be a battle and he was nervous: whether because of eagerness or fear, whatever the cause, that is why he was upset. He would smoke, he would sit up, he lay down, he got up and bathed, he would return and stroll about, then he sat down. Now he had an elder brother, Deer-necklace, and him he sent for. He came and entered. 'Sit there.' This man who had just entered said, 'Well, why are you calling me?' 'Well, I am upset now, that is why I am calling you. There are three things I am now eager to do: I want to sing a sacred song; I want to sing a Big Dog song; I want to cry. Why is it thus?' Double-faced asked. This man answered: 'You are about to go to battle, your medicines are anxious, that is why. Wait!' He boiled wild-carrot root . . . and mixed it with a little white clay. He [Double-face] took it . . . and swallowed it. 'That is all, I'll go now.' This man went out and away.

"Double-face got very hot, he began to perspire. His horse had been standing. 'I have been upset, but I shall accomplish my purpose,' he said and went out. He took his horse, marked it, fitted on his medicines, painted himself, and went out mounted to wail within the camp-circle:

" 'I used to think that since my birth I had had many sorrows. It turns out that there was something in store for me. I was grieving, but I did not know that today all manner of sorrow would be coming to a head. The women at my home are miserable, I daresay. 'How are the captive Crow faring?' they are ever thinking to themselves. My poor dear housemates, my distressed kin, the enemy makes them sit under the dripping water, he is ever abusing them, he thinks his men are the only ones to be brave. What can I do to distress him, I wonder?

" 'You Above, if there be one who knows what is going on, repay me today for the distress I have suffered. Inside the Earth, if there be any one there who knows what is going on, repay me for the distress I have suffered. The One Who causes things, Whoever he be, I have now had my fill of life. Grant me death, my sorrows are overabundant. Though children are timid, they die harsh deaths, it is said. Though women are timid, You make them die harsh deaths. *I* do not want to live long; were I to live long, my sorrows would be overabundant, I do not want it!'

"He went crying," the tale continues, "and those who heard him all cried."

We have here reached the peak of the Crow spirit. With a splendid gesture the hero turns away from the earthly goods that figure so largely in Crow prayer; he has no thought even of glory, he thinks only of his suffering kin in a hostile camp. Bruised by the problem of evil that in retrospect seems to have dogged him from infancy, he asks only for release from his torture. Why linger? Earth and sky are everlasting, but men must die; old age is a scourge and death in battle a blessing.

Appendix I: Sources

The only previous account known to me of Crow life as a whole is that by Mr. Edward S. Curtis in his "The North American Indian," vol. IV, 1909. It is an excellent piece of work and while not written either by or for a professional anthropologist lives up to high standards of accuracy. The account of the Sun Dance is especially noteworthy. Unfortunately the de luxe make-up of the book has precluded wide circulation.

Of other writers the following may be cited with some comments as to their character.

Beckwourth, James P. See Bonner, T. D.

Belden, G. P. See Brisbin, James S.

Boller, Henry A. Among the Indians; Eight Years in the Far West 1858-1866; embracing sketches of Montana and Salt Lake. Philadelphia, 1868.

Bonner, T. D. The Life and Adventures of James P. Beckwourth, Mountaineer, Scout, and Pioneer, and Chief of the Crow Nation of Indians. London, 1856 (republished by Alfred Knopf, New York, 1931).

Whether the mulatto Beckwourth was or was not a chief, he lived among the Crow for many years and while a Münchhausen in the recital of his own deeds, he reproduces with admirable correctness the martial atmosphere of Crow life in the 'twenties and 'thirties of the last century. He refers to such social usages as the parent-in-law taboo, the rivalry of clubs, the restraining power of the police. Rotten-belly is made to figure as head-chief and his divining with a shield is an interesting detail (cf. p. 234 of this volume). Every once in a while the genuineness of the record is forcibly demonstrated, as when a maiden promises to marry Beckwourth "when the pine leaves turn yellow," an expression still in vogue. The book is disappointing on Crow religion. While Beckwourth repeatedly notes the planting of sacred Tobacco and essays a description of the Sun Dance, he evidently does not know clearly what it is all about. Nevertheless, for the latter ceremony the recital of coups, the sham battle, and the part played by a virtuous woman are registered.

Brisbin, James S. Belden, the White Chief; or, Twelve Years among the Wild Indians of the Plains. From the Diaries and Manuscripts of George P. Belden, the Adventurous White Chief, Soldier, Hunter, Trapper, and Guide. Cincinnati and Chicago, 1875.

A superficial account of experiences among various Plains tribes, with a few worth-while details about the Crow. The most important is the explanation by Belden's Crow cook of the batsira'pe phenomenon (see p. 264 above).

Campbell, W. S. The Tipis of the Crow Indians, American Anthropologist, vol. 29, p. 87, 1927.

An excellent and detailed descriptive account.

Catlin, George. Illustrations of the Manners, Customs, and Conditions of the North American Indians. 2 vols. London, 1848 (also later editions).

A few worth-while statements, mostly on material aspects of Crow life, can be gleaned from this work.

Clark, W. P. The Indian Sign Language. Philadelphia, 1885.

This curious work (on pp. 135-136) gives a very brief but essentially correct description of the Sun Dance.

Culin, Stewart. Games of the North American Indians. (24th Annual Report, Bureau of American Ethnology.) Washington, 1907.

This standard monograph gives detailed accounts of Crow games.

Leforge, Thomas H. See Marquis, Thomas H.

Leonard, Zenas. Adventures of Zenas Leonard, Fur Trader and Trapper, 1831-1836. (Edited by W. F. Wagner.) Cleveland, 1904.

This narrative brings out forcibly the spirit of rivalry among Crow warriors and contains interesting, though not wholly convincing, statements about tribal government. Leonard describes as an eye-witness war and burial customs, hunting methods and other parts of the daily routine.

Linderman, Frank. (a) America: the Life Story of a Great Indian. New York, 1930.

The author, an old frontiersman, here records the main incidents of chief Plenty-coups' life. Though Mr. Linderman has not read what others have written, e.g., about the identity of the Crow Tobacco, he gives not only a live account but in many ways an accurate one. He supplements what earlier writers report about war and social customs and in contrast to them duly stresses the religious side of Crow life. Some of his best material relates to visions and the doctoring of wounds.

(b) Old Man Coyote. New York, 1931.

This collection of tales, by no means all about the titular hero, introduces valuable versions of Crow tales, as well as some new stories. Though the renderings are too free to serve for a study of style, they add to our knowledge of plot and individual variation of story-tellers.

(c) Red Mother. New York, 1932.

This supplements (a), being a Crow *woman's* reminiscences. Thus a good many intimate details are brought out that appear neither in the Plenty-coups book nor any other source.

Lowie, Robert H. (a) Social Life of the Crow Indians (Anthropological Papers, American Museum of Natural History, vol. IX, pp. 179-248). New York, 1912.

(b) Notes on the Social Organization and Customs of the Mandan, Hidatsa, and Crow Indians (ibid. vol. XXI, pp. 53-99, 1917).

The later of these papers corrects some serious errors that crept into the earlier account of the kinship system, which is represented anew. There are also some supplementary facts about social usage.

(c) The Material Culture of the Crow Indians (ibid., vol. XXI, pp. 205-268, 1922).

(d) Crow Indian Art (ibid., vol. XXI, pp. 271-322, 1922).

Both of these papers are quite incomplete. However, they give some notion of the topics treated and a fair number of illustrations.

(e) Military Societies of the Crow Indians (ibid., vol. XI, pp. 145-217, 1913).

(f) The Religion of the Crow Indians (ibid., vol. XXV, pp. 311-444, 1922).

(g) The Tobacco Society of the Crow Indians (ibid., vol. XXI, pp. 103-200, 1919).

(h) The Sun Dance of the Crow Indians (ibid., vol. XVI, pp. 1-50, 1915).

(i) Minor Ceremonies of the Crow Indians (ibid., vol. XXI, pp. 325-365, 1924).

(j) Myths and Traditions of the Crow Indians (ibid., vol. XXV, pp. 1-308, 1918).

In (f) religion is dealt with mainly from the subjective angle, the three following papers being rather devoted to ritual, though they, too, contain narratives of visions. The collection of myths (j), while not complete, is representative; some of them were recorded first in the original, the rest unfortunately only in English. In 1931 I obtained additional tales, exclusively by the former technique; the four stories presented in this volume belong to this later crop.

(k) A Crow Text, with Grammatical Notes. (University of California Publications in American Archaeology and Ethnology, vol. 29, pp. 155-175, 1930.)

So far as I know, this is the first published attempt to present some of the grammatical features of the Crow language. Several of the above-mentioned publications, e.g. (e) contain, however, textual material in Crow.

Marquis, Thomas B. Memoirs of a White Crow Indian (Thomas H. Leforge). 1918.

Dr. Marquis, primarily interested in the history of our Northwestern Indians, has recorded reminiscences of a squaw-man relating to the latter half of the last century. Leforge's intimate contacts with the tribe make his account especially valuable as to everyday social customs, such as the mother-in-law taboo, the rule against social relations with a brother-in-law's wife, etc. There is also a good deal about warfare, corroborating and in part supplementing Beckwourth's earlier observations. On religion he, too, is disappointing, though a few details are worth having. There is a reference to the prophet Wraps-up-his-tail (see p. 238 of this volume).

Maximilian, Prinz zu Wied-Neuwied. Reise in das innere Nord-America in den Jahren 1832 bis 1934. Coblenz, 1839-1841. 2 vols. and Atlas. (Translated as: Travels in the Interior of North America, 1843.)

The Prince was an excellent observer and, though his contacts with the Crow were very brief, he has recorded some important facts, even on social institutions and religion (see Introduction to the present volume).

Morgan, Lewis H. (a) Systems of Consanguinity and Affinity of the Human Family (Smithsonian Contributions to Knowledge, vol. XVII). Washington, 1871.

(b) Ancient Society, or Researches in the Lines of Human Progress from Savagery through Barbarism to Civilization. New York, 1878.

The earlier of these works contains a comprehensive, though phonetically poor, record of the Crow kinship terms. It is, in fact, much better than my own first attempt in this direction (see above), for it clearly demonstrates the equation of certain cousins with relatives of higher and lower generation, a fact that originally eluded me. The later of Morgan's books repeats some of these data and correctly credits the Crow with a maternal clan system, a statement at one time doubted by Swanton but fully corroborated by my field work in 1907 and 1910-1912. Morgan's list of clans agrees with mine as well as might be expected. Altogether, considering his brief contacts with the Crow, his work among them seems highly creditable.

Simms, S. C. (a) Cultivation of Medicine Tobacco by the Crows (American Anthropologist, vol. 6, pp. 331-335, 1904).

(b) Traditions of the Crows (Field Museum, Publication 85, vol. II). Chicago, 1903.

About thirty years ago Mr. Simms, now director of the Field Museum, made an unrivalled collection of Crow buffalo-hide shields for that institution. He also made ethnographical observations, among other things, noting the Crow type of oath (American Anthropologist, 1903, p. 733). His account of the Tobacco ceremony is brief—it was designed as a preliminary report—but accurate. The traditions, recorded in English from the lips of a single informant, represent the first publication of Crow mythology. The collection is incomplete but contains versions of some of the most representative tales, including some not otherwise to be found.

Appendix II: Clan Names

The list of clans (p. 9) may be regarded as more or less standard, but some additional names were recorded. For example, several informants made a trio of my first pair of linked clans by adding the ci′pte'tse (or ci″te'tse), which means something like "the sound of a rebounding arrow." It was assuredly a popular name, since Morgan obtained it in the 'sixties, and Lewis and Clark noted it as "Ship-tah-cha" nearly a hundred and thirty years ago. But one of my best authorities regards this as a mere sobriquet of his own clan, the Thick Lodge.

To the Sore-lip group, several Crow add a Bad-legging (isā′tskaw'ia) clan, but this is identified with the Greasy-inside-the-mouth people. Similarly, the name Muddy-water-drinkers (biricī′cie) was given, but only to be explained as a synonym of the Sore-lips by another informant. One Indian also spoke of a Small Pipe (icī′ptsiatse; literally, their pipes are small) clan as falling into this linkage.

The clan trio that forms my third clan combination had several additional designations assigned to it, such as Big-bellies-men (ē′risā′watse) and Their-horses-are-bad (isā′cgye xawī′ky), but they were regarded by trustworthy witnesses as merely synonymous for the ū′sawatsi'a and xu′xkaraxtse, respectively. Again, the name, "Not Mixed" (ī′cirē'te) is clearly interchangeable with ū′sawatsi'a, for Lone-tree and Big-ox who classed themselves as the latter had given Mr. Curtis the other clan as theirs.

To the fourth group Arm-round-the-neck added the name "They-scrape-water" (biripā′xua) as a synonym of the Bad War Honors. Hairy-legs (hurī′wice) was a supplementary designation assigned to this clan linkage by an old couple but never mentioned by any one else.

Under the fifth head some place the Pretty Prairie-dogs (tsi'pa-wāi′itse), Deer-eaters (ū′ux akdū′ce), and Lodge-that-does-not-look (acbatsī′rice), the last of which is also put into class VI.

The last two major groups present a serious problem, viz. whether even the pair of linked names in my "standard" list refers to more than a single clan with two names. Some of my best authorities were mutually contradictory. "Earless Lodge" (aca'parē'te), for example, is sometimes credited to an independent clan, sometimes identified with the Piegan clan. "Merciless Lodge" (acbā'ta'te) is similarly supposed by some to denote a separate clan, while Arm-round-the-neck equates it with the Piegan clan, and both with the acbatcu'a. "They-eat-their-own-nasal-mucus" (i'pi'skurū'ce) was likewise interpreted as the name of a separate clan, and as the ancient appellation of the Piegan clan.

In making up my standard list I have relied partly on the statements of the apparently best qualified witnesses, in part on an independently made census of marriages, in the course of which I noted the clan affiliation of each spouse. This record was found to contain only two names besides my thirteen,—Not Mixed and Pretty Prairie-dogs; and these have been accounted for above. In deciding that two names were not synonymous I was likewise influenced by the census: when, for example, an old and conservative woman of the Sore-lip clan unapologetically noted her marriage to a Greasy-inside-the-mouth, she was clearly speaking of two distinct clans. Probably my list represents with more than fair accuracy the situation in the second half of the last century. I do not doubt that at some previous period there were other clans that subsequently became extinct. In some instances there may have been a merging of two separate clans; the names were perhaps retained in memory without a sense that they ever represented two distinct bodies. Generally, however, the supplementary names seem to be synonyms of those in my roster.

Glossary

Arapaho—a Plains tribe of Algonkian family, living when first encountered in eastern Colorado and southeastern Wyoming

Arikara—a semi-sedentary tribe of Caddoan family, living near the Mandan and Hidatsa on the upper Missouri, and linguistically close relatives of the Pawnee

Assiniboine—politically independent northern offshoot of Dakota, living in intimate contact with the Cree in western Canada and northernmost Montana

beaming tool—two-handled tool for currying hides

Blackfoot—a confederacy of three closely related tribes of Algonkian family, living in southern Alberta and northwestern Montana

bundle—see medicine bundle

Cheyenne—a nomadic Plains tribe of the Algonkian family, found in the Black Hills of South Dakota by Lewis and Clark, but originally sedentary in Minnesota

chips—droppings, especially of the buffalo

clan—a social unit into which a person is born by inheriting the affiliation of *either* parent according to the tribal rule of descent; thus, Crow clans are matrilineal because children belong to their mother's clan, while Omaha clans are patrilineal because all children belong to their father's clan

coulée—the bed of a stream, even if dry, provided the sides are inclined; Western American term of French origin

coup—the war exploit of touching the enemy with the hand or something held in the hand; derived from the French word for "blow"

Dakota—branch of the Siouan family, including the Western Dakota (Teton), who were naturally those in intimate contact with the Crow

exogamy—the rule that one must marry outside of one's group, especially one's clan

Gros Ventre—a Plains tribe of the Algonkian family, a northern offshoot of the Arapaho subsequently closely affiliated with the Blackfoot. The name has sometimes been applied also to the quite distinct Hidatsa, but is no longer so used scientifically

hand-game—gambling game found by Culin among 81 tribes of western North America. It is characterized by the guessing of which hand contains a lot, the lots most frequently being pairs of bone cylinders, and the object generally being to point out the unmarked member of a pair

Hidatsa—a semi-sedentary tribe of Siouan family, living on the upper Missouri, in what is now North Dakota; closest relative of the Crow

levirate—the custom of a man's inheriting a brother's (or equivalent male kinsman's) widow

Mandan—semi-sedentary Siouan tribe of upper Missouri in present North Dakota, culturally very close to neighboring Hidatsa, though linguistically only remotely related

medicine—applied to anything supernatural, hence "medicine-man" = shaman

medicine bundle—an object or set of objects kept in wrappings when not in use; associated with a ritual based on a revelation and usually with definite rules

Nez Percé—tribe of the Sahaptin family, discovered by Lewis and Clark in western Idaho and adjoining regions

parfleche—an oblong rawhide case, generally with painted flaps, originally designed for the storage of dried meat

pemmican—sliced, dried and pounded meat, mixed with melted fat, sometimes with dried fruit

Piegan—one of the three tribes of the Blackfoot Confederacy; not to be confused with the Piegan clan of the Crow. The Piegan habitat is in northwestern Montana and southern Alberta

polygyny—marriage of one man with two or more wives; the opposite of "polyandry," both of which terms are technically comprised under "polygamy"

shaman—a person who has obtained direct contact with the supernatural world through a vision, audition, or possession; a "medicine-man." The word is of Siberian origin

Shoshone—tribe of the Shoshonean or Uto-Aztecan family, occupying in separate bands parts of Idaho, Wyoming, and neighboring regions. Like the Ute they have a fundamentally Basin culture with Plains Indian overlay

Siouan—large linguistic family, including mainly Plains tribes, such as the Dakota, Assiniboine, Crow, Hidatsa, Mandan, Omaha, but also a branch on the Gulf of Mexico (Biloxi and Ofo) and an Atlantic branch (Tutelo, Catawba)

Sioux—popular name for Dakota Indians

Snow-snake—a game in which darts or javelins are competitively hurled along snow or ice or free in the air. Culin recognizes three forms: long polished rods made to glide on the surface; bone gliders, in which a piece of bone or horn, stuck with two feathers, is slid along the ice; and javelins, sometimes feathered and commonly horn-tipped, which are slid or darted through the air after being made to glance by striking the earth or some other obstacle

sweat-lodge—a small dome-shaped structure covered with skins. The inmates sweat themselves by exposure to the vapor from hot rocks on which water has been poured

tipi—also spelled "teepee"; conical skin-covered tent. From Dakota Sioux: ti, to dwell; tipi, dwelling

travois—a Plains Indian device for transporting goods originally on back of dogs, later of horses; the front ends of two poles were attached to the beast, the butt-ends dragged along the ground; in between, the poles were united by a carrying-frame

Ute—tribe of the Shoshonean or Uto-Aztecan family, once occupying central and western Colorado and eastern Utah. Fundamentally a Great Basin people in culture, they adopted superficially features of the Plains

Index